PENGUIN BOOKS

THE NATURAL HISTORY OF THE MIND

Gordon Rattray Taylor is one of the best-known science writers in the English language. He has published many books, the most popular of which have been *The Biological Time Bomb* and *The Doomsday Book*. Mr. Taylor lives in England and is chief science adviser for the B.B.C. His strict fidelity to scientific reasoning combines with the perspective of a humanist to make *The Natural History of the Mind* a uniquely valuable contribution, especially to readers who may be happy to learn that there is something that differentiates a man from a machine.

The Natural History of the Mind

Gordon Rattray Taylor

PENGUIN BOOKS

Penguin Books Ltd, Harmondsworth,
Middlesex, England
Penguin Books, 625 Madison Avenue,
New York, New York 10022, U.S.A.
Penguin Books Australia Ltd, Ringwood,
Victoria, Australia
Penguin Books Canada Limited, 2801 John Street,
Markham, Ontario, Canada L3R 1B4
Penguin Books (N.Z.) Ltd, 182–190 Wairau Road,
Auckland 10, New Zealand

First published in the United States of America by
E. P. Dutton 1979
Published in Penguin Books 1981

LIBRARY OF CONGRESS CATALOGING IN PUBLICATION DATA
Taylor, Gordon Rattray.
The natural history of the mind.
Bibliography: p. 341.
Includes index.
1. Mind and body. 2. Brain—Psychological
aspects. 3. Brain. I. Title.
BF161.T23 128'.2 80-17761
ISBN 0 14 00.5703 X

Printed in the United States of America by
Offset Paperback Mfrs., Inc., Dallas, Pennsylvania
Set in Monotype Plantin

For Christine and Peter

Contents

Acknowledgments

The authors and publishers would like to thank the following for permission to reproduce copyright illustrations: p. 26, Macmillan Publishing Co. Inc. (from *The Correlative Anatomy of the Nervous System*); p. 37, Penguin Books Ltd and the author (from *The Working Brain* by A. R. Luria); p. 125, the American Association for the Advancement of Science and the author (from 'Cerebral Organization and Behavior' by R. W. Sperry, *Science*, Vol. 133, pp. 1749–1757, 2 June 1961, copyright © 1961 by the American Association for the Advancement of Science); p. 195, Weidenfeld & Nicolson Ltd and the Experimental Psychology Society (from *Eye and Brain* by R. L. Gregory); p. 212, the American Association for the Advancement of Science and the author (from 'Binocular Depth Perception without Familiarity Cues' by B. Julesz, *Science*, Vol. 145, pp. 356–362, 24 July 1964, copyright © 1964 by the American Association for the Advancement of Science); p. 290, W. H. Freeman & Co. (from *Neuropharmacology and Behavior* by V. G. Longo, copyright © 1972).

Thanks are also due to Oxford University Press, New York, for permission to reprint the poem on p. xiii ('Mr Jones Addresses a Looking-Glass', from *The Coming Forth by Day Of Osiris Jones* by Conrad Aiken).

Foreword

It is more than ten years since I conceived the idea of this book and began to do the research, but the more I read the less ready I felt to begin to write. Finally, it became clear that if I attempted to read everything the book would never be written at all. I am very aware of the cursory nature of some of the discussion – but the book is already long – and of many things omitted, some by design, others no doubt through ignorance. I made a deliberate decision to omit the subject of mental illness, as the term is normally used – schizophrenia, manic-depression, epilepsy and so on – although I had amassed a good deal of material. The subject is too complex to compress into a chapter or two and fortunately it was not essential to the theme, which is the content of the mind in relation to the hardware of the brain.

I have also made no reference to psychoanalysis. The pendulum of opinion, once over-favourable, has swung to the other extreme. Freud provided a useful language for discussing mental processes at a particular level, and advanced several valid concepts. (Despite assertions that what Freud said was untestable, Paul Kline made an analysis of Freudian concepts and found many of them to be confirmed by the data.) But it is not the level of analysis which is useful for my purpose here.

I must apologise for repeatedly having used dualist expressions, although not taking a dualist stance. So deeply is dualism embedded in our language that it is difficult to avoid doing so without writing almost unreadable sentences. It is hard to avoid writing phrases like 'We compare what we see with what we remember . . .' as if we were somehow sitting inside the skull, like the little man in the Disney film, using our senses to detect what is going on in the brain. Even the great cosmologist Sir Arthur Eddington wrote: 'The only subject presented to me for study is the content of my consciousness.' But of course 'me' and 'the content of my consciousness' are not two things but one.

In a lecture entitled 'The Final Revolution', Aldous Huxley declared that our language 'is not now suitable to describing the continuum of mind and body, a university of complete continuity. Somehow or other we have to invent the means of talking about these problems in an artistically varied way which shall make them accessible to the general public. Ideally, for example, we ought to be able to talk about a mystical experience simultaneously in terms of theology, of psychology and of biochemistry.' He appealed, therefore, for a closer collaboration between writer and scientist, between specialist and generalist. Though I did not come across this appeal until late in the day, it was with the same conviction that I ventured into this difficult field.

I would like to thank Professor Richard Gregory and Christine Restall, who read this book in draft and suggested alterations; they are not of course responsible for errors which remain. I am also grateful to the help I received at the Brain Research Institute in Los Angeles, the Neurosciences Research Program at MIT, and elsewhere. Finally, I must acknowledge the help of the libraries at Bath and London Universities, and at the Society of Psychical Research and, above all, that of the Royal Society of Medicine: without the amazing collection of periodicals held by the last-named this book could never have been written.

G.R.T.

'Mr Jones Addresses a Looking-Glass'

MR JONES: So this is you
THE MIRROR: yes this is me
JONES: but I am more
than what I see
MIRROR: what are you then
if more than that?
a coat a collar
and a hat
JONES: also a heart
also a soul
also a will
that knows its goal
MIRROR: you are a razor
in a claw
and more than that
I never saw
JONES: far more than that
I am a mind
whose wanderings
are unconfined
north, south and east
and west I go
and all things under god
I know
MIRROR: speak if you must
but I distrust
and all that glitters
is but dust
JONES: but I remember
what I see
and that, in mirrors,
cannot be
MIRROR: well, Mr Jones, perhaps it's better
to be, like me, a good forgetter
JONES: how can you know what here goes on
behind this flesh-bright frontal bone?
here are the world and god become
for all their depth a simple *Sum*.

Conrad Aiken: *The Coming Forth by Day of Osiris Jones*

PART ONE

Scene Set

I

Something Funny Is Going On

No Laughing Matter

The crowd stands at the graveside: a funeral is taking place. Suddenly one of the onlookers, a boy, bursts into uncontrollable laughter. The mourners are shocked at first, then realise something strange has happened. He is led away. It turns out that a blood vessel in his brain has burst, flooding the third ventricle – the open space in the centre of the brain. An event known to doctors as a subarachnoid haemorrhage.

Now the scene is a railway train. One of the passengers in the carriage is a girl, returning home after her day's work. She begins to laugh uproariously. The other passengers stare. She becomes intensely embarrassed, but continues to rock with laughter, tears running down her cheeks. As the passengers begin to mutter, the train stops. Although it is not her destination, the girl staggers from the train and clings to the railings, laughing frantically. Two months later she develops a severe paralysis of her left side.

Such fits of uncontrollable laughter are rare, but well attested. The eminent French doctor, Féré, had a patient who used to laugh involuntarily every time his carriage (the year was 1903) rolled over the rough French pavé. There is even a case on record of a woman who really died of laughing. She laughed herself into a coma from which she never recovered. She was found to have a tumour of the third ventricle, and Dr Martin, of Queen's Square Hospital, who assembled this information, considers there must be a motor centre for the physical act of laughter situated nearby. He cites in support the case of a patient whose third ventricle had to be swabbed out after the removal of a cyst had suffused it with blood. Every time the surgeon inserted the instrument, the patient laughed, whistled, joked and uttered obscene remarks. But none of these unhappy individuals reported that things struck them as funny.

I offer you these curious clinical observations right at the start of our exploration because they bring out rather vividly the central question we shall be trying to answer: are our subjective experiences – amusement, grief, joy, pain, love and so forth – simply by-products of the workings of the biological computer-system known as the brain? Or do our thoughts and emotions dictate our behaviour, merely using the brain as a servant to implement our aims?

Common sense says the latter, but the majority of scientists together with many philosophers deny this. Some of them deny that mental events exist at all; others concede that they exist, but simply as by-products. Back in the last century, Darwin's ally T. H. Huxley declared firmly: 'Consciousness . . . would appear to be related to the mechanism of [the] body . . . simply as a [side] product of its working and to be completely without any power of modifying that working as the [sound of a] steam whistle which accompanies the work of a locomotive . . . is without influence upon its machinery.'

Huxley's friend, the philosopher William Kingdom Clifford, put it more tersely a dozen years before: 'All the evidence we have goes to show that the physical world gets along entirely by itself' – a view we may call materialism.

In short, the question is: are we machines? In due course, I shall try to analyse what such a question means, in precise terms, but for the moment let us leave it open. Certainly, the boy who laughs without feeling amusement is hard to fit into a purely mechanical conception. For if amusement is merely a by-product of laughing, he should have felt amused even though he knew not why. But there are more persuasive reasons for doubting the mechanical view of man. Our subjective experience is not just a single meaningless addendum like the whistle of the locomotive. It is enormously rich and varied: it comprises, as we shall see, half a hundred emotions, all the complexities of thought, a dozen different sensations, many levels of consciousness. If all these are to be explained away as by-products, then it is up to the materialists at least to explain why the brain has so many different by-products and why they are interwoven so intricately. But this is by no means the only reason for doubting the accepted material view of man. Let me put forward another piece of evidence of quite a different kind.

How to Keep Abreast of Things

In the United States, several thousand women every year undertake surgical operations to enlarge their breasts. 'Augmentation mammoplasty', as the operation is politely called, is one of the most frequently sought of all cosmetic operations. The results are often as much psychological as physical. Many women report increased interest in sex, an improvement of their marital relations, greater confidence and, in a few cases, that they achieved orgasm for the first time. But the operation is not without risk. Where silicone gel (or similar material) is inserted, it may edge its way into the wrong position; and no one knows whether the long-term effects of foreign material in a sensitive area may not prove harmful. It would be pleasant if similar results could be achieved in a simpler way.

Back in 1948, some experiments in using hypnotism to enlarge the bosom had been reported, and in 1974 one J. E. Williams reported some success. Soon after, R. D. Willard, who was working at the Institute of Behavior and Mind Sciences, decided to test these claims scientifically. He rounded up twenty-two volunteers, of all ages from nineteen to fifty-four. Their breasts were carefully measured by an independent physician: height, diameter and circumference. They were told to imagine warm water flowing over their breasts, the breasts becoming warm; if this did not work, they were to imagine a heat-lamp playing on them. They would begin to feel their breasts pulsating. These suggestions were made under light trance. They were given tape-recorded instructions, with the aid of which they were to repeat this routine daily. There were periodic check-ups. At the end of twelve weeks, twenty-eight per cent of the women had reached the size of breast they aimed at, and ceased to practise. Eighty-five per cent had achieved some enlargement, and forty-six per cent had to buy a bigger bra. The average increase was about two-thirds of an inch vertically, over an inch horizontally, and 1.37 inches in circumference. Some women managed almost twice these gains. A cynic might wonder if they had simply put on weight in general, but in fact forty-two per cent of them *lost* two pounds or more. Moreover, fourteen of the volunteers had had children and wanted firmer breasts. All of these achieved some improvement in that respect. And, as a final bonus, those women whose breasts had been unequal in size ended up with symmetrically equal ones.

Even professional hypnotists were somewhat surprised at the ease with which these results were achieved, and two psychologists at the University of Houston attempted to repeat the results. It occurred to them that, as breasts vary in size with the menstrual cycle, a false impression might have been created by the chance of making initial measurements and final measurements at different points in the cycle. They also wanted to know if the gains in size were retained after the treatment was concluded. They made repeated measurements of their subjects and found that the growth was progressive with time, and thus not a function of the menstrual cycle; and that, while there was some loss of size after the treatment ceased, more than eighty per cent of the gain was still retained three months later.

Moreover, they measured the waistline of their volunteers and, in every case, it grew smaller – in one case by as much as 2.2 inches.

The implications of these experiments are extraordinary. If one can increase the size of one organ, why not that of another? Men are notoriously sensitive on such matters. Perhaps one could enlarge an inadequate spleen, for instance? And what about losing weight?

But it is the philosophical implications, not the commercial ones, which caused me to bring these matters to your attention. For here is raised the whole question of the relationship between mind and body. And it certainly seems in this case that the mind, far from being a by-product, is affecting the body in a very direct way. It is not simply determining its behaviour, but is controlling its very growth. The materialists offer us no plausible explanation of how such things can be.

And this is really the central trouble with the materialist view: it does not look at the complexity of the experience it proposes to explain, or explain away. My first purpose in this book is to bring out in much more detail how intricate the nature of experience is. Strangely enough, no one seems ever to have made a survey of quite this kind before. At least I have found none.

While the word 'mind' is commonly used as a comprehensive label for subjective experience of every kind, at other times it seems to be taken as equivalent to consciousness, which is certainly the precondition for experience as usually conceived. Materialists treat consciousness as if it were a simple, quantitative matter: one is either conscious, unconscious or somewhere between the two. But consciousness is of many qualitatively different kinds. Nowadays, thanks to the psychoactive drugs, this is becoming more widely appreciated. But our state of consciousness is quite capable of altering without such aids, or any deliberate effort on our part – as in meditation. For instance, there is the state of mind known to high-level balloonists and some pilots of high-altitude aircraft as 'break off'. In the 1950s the US airforce flew a number of very high level balloon flights, partly to gather physical data, partly to gather material about the behaviour of human beings in these unusual circumstances. Heights of twelve miles were routine. Airforce pilots who had reached great altitudes in aircraft were embarrassed to discuss the experience they called 'break off', but the balloonists were provided with radios via which they were required to report data continuously, no doubt as a devious way of monitoring their state of mind. Periodically, they forgot these obligations or decided to ignore them and began to talk about their internal state.

Thus Bridgeman, during one such flight, began to speak as follows: '59,000, 60,000, reeling off 61,000 – I have left the world. There is only the ship to identify myself with. Her vibrations are my own. I feel them as intensely as those of my body. Here is a kind of unreality mixed with reality that I cannot explain to myself. I have no awareness that I have never experienced before, but it does not seem to project beyond this moment.' During the Stratolab High II flight of 8 November 1956, Simons reached 100,000 feet (nearly twenty miles) in a twenty-four-hour balloon flight, flying alone. After a while he decided to ignore his instructions and take a break from making observations. He felt 'as if I was literally in another world and had lost all sense of time and distance judged by ordinary standards – I had a feeling of drifting up towards space where I belonged'. He felt annoyed by the interruptions of radio messages from the ground, and at one point decided to abandon his task of making observations and simply enjoy the experience. He felt 'above the trials and tribulations of earthly existence'.

After this, solo trips were regarded as unwise, and a two-man crew was employed. Interestingly enough, no such effects had been reported during preliminary isolation tests, nor was the effect explainable by a change in the atmospheric composition. In exceptional conditions the psyche undergoes strange changes.

John Lilly, the one-time delphinologist, described a rather similar state of mind, which he called 'isolation ecstasy', after being isolated from all sensory input (as far as possible), floating in a tank of water at body temperature. After two hours of sleep one feels as rested as after eight or nine hours of ordinary sleep, he reported. 'One's good feelings increase in strength with time until one feels almost overwhelmingly ecstatic . . . If hallucinations develop at this stage they are intensely pleasurable and sometimes quite humorous. Finally one is forced to leave the tank and seek satisfying real actions and reactions with other persons. If one were forced to continue the exposure beyond six hours, I can only guess what might happen.' Others who have undergone sensory deprivation have had a less amusing time. No doubt if one is restricted to input from within one's mind, a great deal depends on what you have there.

'Sensory deprivation', according to the accepted theory, has the effect of making one attend to internal imagery. But there are numerous accounts of hallucinatory experiences which seem to have resulted from social isolation plus physical and mental strain rather than from sensory isolation. For example, the lone yachtsman Joshua Slocum, whose single-handed voyage round the world in 1895–8 was a 'first', was attacked by sea-sickness in the Atlantic and unable to steer his boat. He describes how a phantom helmsman appeared and took control. Slocum had a long conversation with him – he disclosed that he was the pilot of one of Christopher Columbus' ships.

Mountaineers report similar experiences. Smythe, when climbing

Everest in 1933, had a strong sense of an invisible companion, and even broke off a piece of mint chocolate and offered it to him. Arctic and Antarctic explorers have reported much the same thing, while Noyce, in *South Col*, describes how one half of himself hovered airily above the slope wondering 'why in the name of Heaven it was tied to this grinding, panting creature below'.

And it is not only mountaineers, balloonists or high-flying pilots who have had such experiences. Many people have reported a sense of being 'out of the body' – I have even had this experience myself and found it quite alarming. Augustus Hare, who had an exceptionally harsh and isolated childhood, describes in his reminiscences how, when confined to his room by his sadistic parents, he suddenly had the feeling that he was looking at himself from a point near the transom of the door. We do not really explain such phenomena by talking about imagery 'breaking through'. Hare's mind can hardly have contained an image of the room from such an unusual viewpoint, nor, I feel sure, had Noyce ever seen himself from above.

In the course of this book we shall come across other experiences just as strange. For none of them is any adequate explanation available.

How are experiences like these to be reconciled with a mechanical view of man? The materialists tell us almost nothing about personal identity, so let us look in more detail at the phenomenon of autoscopy, as seeing one's double is called. It raises profound questions about the nature of our minds.

Doubles and Quits

The belief that every one of us has a double goes back to unrecorded history and is widespread among primitive peoples. It was felt that the double was one's soul, and so to meet one's double might indicate one's approaching death. According to Otto Rank, the renowned psychoanalyst, twins were often regarded with awe for this reason. Dostoevsky (in his novel *The Double*) and many other writers have exploited this theme. De Maupassant, who was syphilitic, saw his Doppelgänger in the middle stage of his psychosis. Reliable reports in modern times, however, are harder to come by, and especial interest attaches to three cases reported in 1955 by two doctors working at an Oxford hospital, Kenneth Dewhurst and John Pearson. In December 1952 there was admitted to the hospital a male teacher, aged forty-six, who had a form of stroke (technically, a subarachnoid haemorrhage). He was confused, uncomfortable and nauseated. For the first two days his only other symptom was autoscopy. His double appeared quite solid and accompanied him everywhere. He stood behind his chair at meals, and at night undressed and lay down on a couch in the next room. His double never spoke to him, or made signs, but only imitated his actions. Its facial expression was sad at all times, he reported.

The patient was aware the figure must be an hallucinatory one, but so real did it seem that he could not stop himself from automatically drawing up a chair for it (him?) when he (or they) first visited his private doctor. (The French scientist, Lhermitte, had a patient who even tried to tap his double on the shoulder, so solid did he seem.)

A few days after his admission to hospital, his double appeared one night in pyjamas and climbed into an empty bed nearby. After a few days the double vanished, although the patient's sense of malaise and vomiting continued. Eventually he made a recovery. At the age of fifteen he had had hallucinations, when ill from typhoid, and he reported that a brother had had similar hallucinations.

An interesting feature was that the double appeared full length. It is often reported that doubles are seen only above the waist and reversed left for right, suggesting that they originate in impressions of oneself seen in a mirror. Such was the case of a man admitted to the Radcliffe Infirmary in 1952 with a brain tumour. Seven weeks after admission, he began to see a middle-aged man in the corner of his eye and it was some time before he recognised himself. The figure was seen above the waist only.

Dewhurst and Pearson's third case was a man who had been hit in the head by shrapnel during the war. In 1930 – to quote his own words – 'I was in the doctor's surgery staring into the garden, when I saw the man about four feet away to the left. It suddenly dawned on me who it was. It was me.' However, he had no feeling of affinity with it: it was like a stranger. The figure was a mirror-image but of normal size. It seemed solid and hung around for about ten days. Seven years later the same man was walking in a wood when suddenly he felt he was surrounded by hordes of people. Then, in 1954, one January day, he saw 'crowds of tiny figures all the colours of the rainbow – all myself'. He also hallucinated parts of the interior of houses, sometimes his own, sometimes rooms he could not recognise. These hallucinations became almost continuous, lasting for two or three minutes each time, and leaving him with nausea. Nevertheless, he remained fully rational and made a gradual recovery on phenobarbitone.

But the most extraordinary story of this kind I have come across concerns a twenty-seven-year-old Okinawan woman, Mrs F., who was admitted to a hospital in the US in 'a desperate condition'. Her face was swollen and congested. She was covered with blood from a cut in her tongue, and had evidently narrowly escaped strangling. Her story was that, while shopping, she had seen a woman looking at her with a serious expression, who was 'exactly like me and wore exactly the same clothes, but she had a sharp, unkind expression'. She was carrying two parcels at the time, and put them down. When she came to pick them up, there was only one. But when she got home, she found the missing parcel there! She slept badly, and next day telephoned her husband at work to say he was not to phone her at noon, as he usually did, as she was about to take a nap. She began to feed her six-month-old baby when there was a knock at the door. Before she had time to answer it, there was the same woman as she had seen before. The apparition said to her, in poor Japanese, 'Let us go inside.' Mrs F. (who spoke Japanese well) took her baby to a neighbour to look after and, returning to her apartment, was told by the apparition to wrap up the key of the apartment and put it in the mail-box. She thought she smelt ether, and an eerie light seemed to be streaming from her double's eyes. The woman now put a rope or belt round her neck and proceeded to strangle her, ordering her to hold the belt, which she felt obliged to do. She felt she was about to die; then she passed out. When she came to, the woman was trying to cut her tongue with a pair of scissors. The pain was unbearable and she fainted again. When she finally came to, the woman had disappeared. She crawled to the kitchen for water. Her husband eventually returned to find her lying on the floor and rushed her to hospital.

The police were notified and went to the apartment, where all was in order. There were no signs of a struggle, but in a small cupboard, big enough to hold only one person, they found a black leather belt, a pair of bloody scissors and a bit of cut-off tongue. And in the mail-box was the key. The psychiatrists who examined her, C. B. Bakker and S. E. Murphy of the University of Washington's Department of Psychiatry, described her as a frail, attractive woman. Though anxious and depressed, she was fairly well oriented. Tests showed her personality to be immature and she had dealt with problems by denial before. EEG recordings were made and 'truth drugs' administered. There was no sign of organic disease nor of epilepsy. It emerged that she had been brought up by doting, over-protective parents and had then married a man whose parents were so demanding and critical that she lost weight and had a miscarriage. At this stage husband and wife were living in the same house as his parents. She was, naturally, depressed and anxious. Bakker and Murphy came to the conclusion that she was suffering from a combination, unique in the literature of the subject, of autoscopy and multiple personality.

The anecdotes I have related establish the point, I believe, that, although the mechanism of the brain may provide us with an explanation of behaviour, it is far from explaining subjective experience. Materialism does not clarify for us how mind and brain are related. It throws no light on the nature of the self. What, then, is the alternative? That is the question which, a century after Clifford and Huxley, is beginning once more to receive serious attention.

2

The Quiet Revolution

ON NOT HEARING SOMETHING

After the elevated railway, which ran through New York's Bowery, was dismantled, people often woke at the times when a train should have passed and telephoned the police, saying that something funny had happened. And Russian workers, in the course of an experiment monitoring the brain-waves of a subject listening to a sound, found that the waves indicating attention died down as he got used to the sound, but perked up if it got softer. *So it is not events, but discrepancies, which interest memory.*

Source: K. H. Pribram, 'The Neurophysiology of Remembering', *Sci. Amer.* (1969) *220*(1)73.

Upheaval in Psychology

The past half century has seen, almost unremarked, a slow but very significant change in the standpoint of psychologists, who have come to realise that what goes on inside the skull is very much subtler and harder to explain than they once hoped. Parallel with this, neurobiologists have made extraordinary progress in understanding the working of the brain, revealing it as a mechanism vastly more sophisticated than was once arrogantly supposed.

At the psychological level, the story is in part the story of the rise and fall of 'behaviourism'. But it is more than that: it is the story of a growing conviction that subjective experience cannot be ruled out of the account – that we are not, in any narrow sense, machines. Without making any mystical assumptions, we are nevertheless (as most of us intuitively felt all along) minds as well as bodies. It is a change of standpoint, the importance of which for human values and our personal sense of identity cannot possibly be overrated.

At the same time it will, I believe, free neuroscientists from an intellectual strait-jacket which has constricted them for more than fifty years and open up unimagined vistas of research. Just possibly, within the next few decades, it may become clear what differentiates a man from a machine. If so, it will be a turning-point in human history, with implications at which one can only guess.

Let me summarise, then, the change in the attitude of psychologists.

For over half a century psychologists have been dominated by the idea that one must not ask people to report what is going on in their minds, because there is no way of checking what they say or measuring it reliably. When Professor J. B. Watson launched his doctrine of Behaviourism in 1914, he demanded that the word 'consciousness' be expunged from the vocabulary. The mind, said the behaviourists, is a black box: one must restrict oneself to studying the stimuli going in and the behaviour coming out. (In the jargon of behaviourism, people are said to 'emit a behavioural response' – surely a clumsily inept phrase.) From such observations one might, they hoped, be able to infer a simple model of how the two are linked. Initially, perhaps, this represented no more than a desire to be scientific and objective, but it soon developed into the claim that there was nothing in the black box but some crude machinery, by means of which particular stimuli became associated with particular responses, a process known as 'conditioning'.

While Watson's ideas were being enthusiastically adopted in the West, in Russia, Ivan Pavlov, who had won a Nobel award in 1904, was insisting even more fanatically that all our behaviour could be explained in terms of reflexes. It is related that he used to fine any of his students or aides who used the words 'mind' or 'mental'. Yet mental events exist, and behaviourists find it difficult to shut them out. Professor Burrhus Skinner, doyen of living behaviourists, attempts to get rid of mental events, in his theorising, by referring to them as 'covert behaviour'. But this is only a verbal trick: it does not explain the subjective element.

Naturally, this self-denying ordinance cut psychologists off from all that was most interesting in their subject: moods and emotions; dreams and hallucinations; imagery and the nature of pain. Of course doctors and alienists had to recognise the existence of these subjective factors, which their patients brought to them daily. And, as a matter of fact, even psychologists relaxed their rules from time to time: they could hardly have studied optical illusions, for instance, without accepting what their subjects reported about them. The study of memory, too, would be very restricted if one never accepted a person's word about what he remembered.

But the general effect of this doctrine was deadening. Most of the experimental work done was banal. The one outstanding exception was Freud, who, as everyone knows, defied this trend and concentrated attention as never before on what his patients felt, imagined and reported. Today it is difficult to comprehend the boldness of this defiance of scientific fashion, and the obloquy to which he was subjected has been largely forgotten. However, despite Freud and his followers – perhaps all the more strongly because of them – the behaviouristic tradition continued to dominate psychological laboratories, more especially in America.

Behaviourism was held with the force of a religion – the great American psychologist Karl Lashley actually referred to it as a 'faith' in one public pronouncement – and, as with religion, inconvenient facts were simply ignored. For instance, behaviourists claimed that rats learned their way through a maze by associating muscular movements with what they saw; it was a conditioned response. The fact that a rat whose back legs had been cut off could drag itself through the maze by quite different movements, or even swim through a flooded maze, was regarded as an inconvenient detail to be explained by some modification of the theory. When rats were put in a maze which could be turned upside down, so that all the left turns became right turns and vice versa, the canny creatures found their way through just as easily after reversal as before. Today psychologists concede that rats have 'cognitive maps' in their little heads. In fact they find their way about by very much the same means as psychologists do!

Similarly it was predicted that a rat which had found food down one arm of a maze would inevitably return to that arm in search of a reward. The response was conditioned. Unfortunately for theory, rats, being full of curiosity, frequently explore the rest of the maze, when replaced at the entry, instead of immediately going for the reward. No one was surprised at this except the psychologists. To imagine that the behaviour of a rat, to say nothing of a man, could be explained by such a simple mechanism – the linking of a few circuits – was an extraordinary aberration of the human mind. It is hard to understand how intelligent men could have maintained it. They must have had a masochistic wish to 'debunk' – to abolish a supernal mystery.

In the last twenty years or so the atmosphere has changed decisively. Even in the more orthodox laboratories it has become permissible to study such subjective matters as dreams, meditation or altered states of consciousness. Even parapsychology is no longer quite in the wilderness. The American Society for Psychical Research was admitted to membership of the American Association for the Advancement of Science in 1972, though no other country has yet followed suit. I must add, however, that, despite these signs of grace, psychology remains pretty stick-in-the-mud. Reading the textbooks, one would think that mental activity was confined to the classic fields of sensation, perception, cognition and memory. True, emotion is reluctantly included under the antiseptic label of 'affect', but is not much discussed. Yet when you and I look into our minds we find much more: premonitions, impressions such as 'I have been here before', overwhelming experiences of ecstasy, the rib-tickling sense of the ridiculous, despair, love, joy . . .

A few psychologists are beginning to admit their failure. Thus the eminent social psychologist Hadley Cantril, then President of the International Institute for Social Research at Princeton, ended a 'Transactional Enquiry concerning Mind' with the lament: 'But as I read over what I have written so far, I am sadly aware of my own inability to capture even remotely the wonder that mind is, especially when I think of such products of mind as the Fifth Symphony, the Sermon on the Mount, *The Brothers Karamazov*, or the calculus. Whatever it is that enables mind to create and to appreciate such marvels seems to elude almost completely the crude nets of any psychological jargon.'

Silvan Tomkins, of the School of Cognition and Affect in New York, points out that the change is due less to the psychologists than, paradoxically enough, to the neurologists and the designers of automata. 'The neurologists boldly entered the site of consciousness with electrodes and amplifiers,' he notes. 'They found that the stream of consciousness from the past could be turned on and off by appropriate stimulation. They found that there were amplifier structures which could be turned up and down by means of drugs and electrical stimulation, and that consciousness varied as a function of such manipulation. They found that seizures and loss of consciousness were a consequence of excessive stimulation of cortical and sub-cortical circuitry. They found that there were filter networks which appeared to prevent consciousness by attenuation of sensory input at or near the sensory receptors themselves.' And, after commenting on the influence of the computer designers, he concludes: 'Neither the brain as revealed by contemporary neurophysiology nor the brain as simulated by the modern high speed computer gave any support or comfort to the simplistic conceptions of the nature of the human being which had dominated American psychology for the past thirty years. It now appears that the organism is neither empty nor simple-minded.'

Is Man a Machine?

While the psychologists were making their retreat, the neuroscientists were racing ahead, evolving recondite techniques for exploring the brain and steadily revealing it as a structure of incomparable complexity – 'the most wonderful organised structure in the universe', to use the words of the Australian Nobelist, Sir John Eccles. It had long been recognised to be an electrical device, but recent work shows it to be a far more intricate one than was supposed: no fewer than five distinct kinds of electrical transmission occur, not just one as was thought. But even more radical was the realisation that it was incredibly intricate chemically at the same time. First, there was the discovery that certain brain cells secrete chemical messengers; then it was found that the transmission of impulses is governed by at least five distinct families of chemical regulators; recently, a whole new family of neurohormones – the so-called small peptides or endorphins – has been identified, and may provide the key to schizophrenia and other mental disturbances.

This account would be incomplete, even as a summary, if I did not add that the brain has immunological systems the existence of which was unsuspected until recently, and the purpose of which is only now being revealed.

The extraordinary advances in our understanding of the brain have filled many neurobiologists with optimism. Thus we find Professor Donald Mackay of Keele University writing: 'We seem to be at one of those rare moments of scientific history when a coincidence of technological, scientific and clinical discoveries makes possible an exceptionally fruitful co-operative leap forward, in face of perhaps the greatest scientific challenge to the intellect.' Other scientists (I recall David Rioch, of the Walter Reed Army Medical Center, saying something of the kind to me, for instance) have spoken of solving the problems of the brain by the end of the century.

I am sure that is over-optimistic, for the brain keeps revealing new subtleties, but even less euphoric scientists are mostly convinced that the brain works in the same manner as a machine. That is to say, the behaviour which comes out is logically and inescapably determined by the information which goes in. If they are right, the notion of free will goes out of the window. In their view, man is basically no more than a very elaborate automaton. An automaton graced by what I call creative capacities, but an automaton nevertheless.

What will be the effect on mankind if brain research should show that we are simply robots equipped with a superfluous system of sensibilities, a delusion that we are more than machines, a delightful but inessential icing on the plum-cake of mechanism? It could, I suppose, be catastrophic. People might find the realisation of their insignificance too disturbing to live with.

There are, indeed, scientists who are quite dogmatic that man's behaviour is fully determined, and they seem very little perturbed by the possible consequences of their efforts to prove this. One such is Professor John Taylor of King's College, London, who declares that brain research increasingly favours determinism, saying, 'The mind appears now to be a near-powerless "epiphenomenon" of the physical brain.' Then he adds cheerfully that realisation of this fact 'will cause a complete destruction of people's understanding of their place in the world, as well as undermining the traditional institutions of society'. He urges that we should 'start to prepare people to live in a deterministic world . . . Unless care is taken the shadow of the mind may be strong enough to destroy society when the light of truth is brought to bear upon it.'

I take a certain comfort from the fact that shadows usually vanish when light is shone upon them, so perhaps things will not be disastrous after all.

But if he is right, the consequences could be even worse than he implies. For if people are objects, they are expendable. The person who believes that behaviour is determined is likely to try to seize the controls and to determine the behaviour of others. The notion underwrites the materialist conception of history, and can be claimed to justify the sacrifice of the individual to such abstract ends as national prestige, the triumph of Communism, and so on.

However, not all brain scientists agree. Such eminent neurobiologists as Sir John Eccles and Roger Sperry, professor at the California Institute of Technology, take quite a different view, as we shall see in due course. Even Professor Mackay, whose words I quoted a page or two back, is no materialist, for all his optimism about research.

If man is a machine, he is a machine of a most unusual kind, as we shall see. But is he a machine at all?

The Omega Effect

We start with a mystery. Within our skulls there are complex circuits, in which flow electric currents of a special sort. There are arrays of obscure chemical substances which enter into complex reactions. The equipment analyses input from the world around and then selects and executes some behavioural response. Nothing odd in that; a computer, in its crude way, can do much the same. But in our own case there is a seemingly superfluous miracle: we see a brilliantly coloured scene . . . we have the sensation of falling in love . . . we recall events from the past and even, as some would claim, from the future. The humble electrochemistry has given rise to a vivid personal experience. Scientists and philosophers are equally unhelpful about this almost miraculous effect, which does not even have a recognised name. I propose to call it the Omega Effect, since omega signifies the end-point to which everything leads.

In short, when we treat the brain as a machine we ignore the Omega Effect. It is currently fashionable to compare it with a computer. But there is, I insist, this overwhelming, inescapable difference. We might, I dare say, construct a computer system which would recognise a red traffic light. It would scan the scene for light sources at about the right height. It would eliminate by means of suitable filters all but the appropriate hue. It might check the identification by the proximity of green and amber sources, with a specified time difference in their various appearances. Having identified the light it would be no great trick to arrange that the accelerator be released and the brakes applied. But at the end of all this we still could not say that the computer had enjoyed the unique experience which we call 'seeing a red light'.

It is this unique omega experience which I aim to explore and analyse in this book.

Thanks to the remarkable strides made by brain research in the last half century, we begin to see how the brain achieves what it does. The development of computers, and of information theory and cybernetics, has made it perfectly clear that the brain is precisely the sort of machine which is needed to do what it does. The details need working out, to be sure, but we can clearly see that the brain is well designed to analyse information, to compare it with previous experience, and to select and supervise appropriate trains of action. How it devises plans of behaviour, which in the case of man are rather sophisticated, is a bit more mysterious but does not seem to be inherently beyond the capacities of the system.

So the baffling question arises: if the brain is competent for its tasks, why did the Omega Effect evolve into existence at all? (We must assume, I think, that it evolved: but if it was created from the start, the problem is no less baffling.) To all appearances, the brain seems quite capable of achieving the survival of its owner, or at least of improving his chances, without such fancy trimmings as a sense of identity, a sense of humour or a sense of deity. Why, in short, is the world not peopled by robots?

Conversely, if we ever succeed in making a lifelike robot, we shall have no reason to suppose that it will feel love or curiosity or disgust – or even the far cruder sensation of pain, though it might behave as if it did. It is a curious fact that, despite the millions of hours which have been devoted to psychological research, there is (as far as I have been able to discover) no catalogue, still less any general analysis, of the various experiences which go to make up the Omega Effect.

Let us take a preliminary unscientific view of what goes to make up the Omega Effect. Of course it would include all our sensations. Not merely the red of a traffic light but the whole co-ordinated pattern of shape and colour we call a 'scene'. Not only the sound of a horn, but the complexities of a Bach cantata and the simplicities of birdsong. The subtleties of a great Burgundy and the raw horrors of Dr Gregory's powder. It would include other kinds of imagery: dreams, hallucinations and visions.

It would obviously include all our emotions: fear and anxiety, horror and disgust, anxiety and pleasure, joy and love. (I sometimes wonder whether we are right to lump together such diverse experiences under a single label of emotion.) It would certainly include pain: the sharp bite of incision and the slow crunch of bone pain. It would range from euphoria to despair. It would include our cognitive processes: thoughts and plans and attitudes; also will.

But in addition to these, it would include some subtler experiences. The sense of significance, the sense of familiarity, the sense of anticipation, the sense of clarity and of total confusion. Poets tell us of a sense of unity with all life and saints of the mystic union, contrasted with the Dark Night of the Soul. Theologians speak of the sense of the 'numinous', the idea of the holy. These too are part of the Omega Effect. No robot will ever be assailed by existential despair.

But more central and more baffling than all these are the twin concepts of personal identity and of consciousness itself. What meaning can we assign to consciousness? Where can we locate it? And what do we mean when we say 'I'? The sense of personal identity is one of the most enigmatic of all the phenomena of mind. William James called it 'the most puzzling puzzle with which psychology has to deal'.

What is Mind?

In my vocabulary it is precisely the role of the word 'mind' to comprise these phenomena but I hesitate to use this word because it appears to mean so many different things to different people. Thus for some philosophers, the distinctive feature of mind is purpose of intention. To quote William James again, 'If purpose remains the same when means are different, there is mind.'

'Mind is an activity of the brain,' declares the Canadian psychologist Donald Hebb. No, 'of the entire nervous system', retorts the endocrinologist Ernst Gellhorn. Some try to define it in terms of its functions. 'I take consciousness and mind to be synonymous functions,' said the famous neurologist Hughlings Jackson, adding, rather confusingly, 'There is no such entity as consciousness.' E. Roy John, an expert on memory, says: 'Perhaps the most striking feature of mind is the property of *awareness*, particularly self-awareness.' But Percival Bailey, director of a psychiatric research institute, declares: 'Identification of consciousness with the mind leads to much confusion.' For the hypnotist Milton Kline, 'Mind is a function evolving from brain structure.' To confuse matters still further, the Dean of the American Institute of Psychiatry, Dr Harold Kelman, suggests we should use verbs rather than nouns in talking about mind, and, in a paroxysm of gobbledygook, says we should ask: 'What are the what and how of minding?' or, more accurately, 'What are the whating and howing of minding?' He clarifies this with the gnomic comment: 'Whating is a sequence of whats in duration and space. A sequence of whats is the functioning of that what, in this and all instances, is minding.'

Perhaps we had better start again.

Can we classify or enumerate the functions which we regard as mental and, at least for the moment, simply employ the word 'mind' as a label for them? The formula which you will find in most textbooks of psychology is that mental activity comprises Cognition, Volition and Affect (affect meaning, feeling or emotion). It seems a very jejune approach, allowing no obvious place for memories or for imagery or for conscience and it bundles together many items which are ill-assorted. Is frustration, for instance, really the same sort of thing as love? Would hesitation count as an emotion? Does cognition include imagining as well as simple addition? Surely there is a distinction between creative thought and the performance of routines? Where is the ego?

Volition seems to be an odd-man-out. On the shelves of science libraries you will find rows and rows of books about cognitive processes, and a number about the emotions, but virtually nothing about the will. And what would you say about a predisposition to do something?

In his book *Six Theories of Mind*, the Chicago philosopher Charles Morris discussed such positions as 'Mind as Process', 'Mind as Relation', 'Mind as Substance', and traced these views from such eminent philosophers as Kant, Berkeley and Hegel to their more modern exponents. But why try to cram the richness of mind into such narrow conceptual pigeon-holes? Mind is probably all of these things at one time or another. I see no need to recapitulate these lengthy discussions, largely concerned as they are with the use of words.

Although my aim is to avoid philosophical discussion until after the facts have been presented, it will be useful to remind you here that there are two main philosophical positions about the Mind/Body problem, as it is called. These are known as dualist and monist, terms I shall not be able to avoid using. Dualists maintain that the brain and the mind are two distinct things; monists assert that they are only one thing seen from two different angles, so to speak. Dualists are generally divided into three clans: those who think the body creates mental effects as a by-product but is not affected by mind (a view known as epiphenomenalism); those who think the two interact; and those who claim that the two move in parallel by pure coincidence, a view not many people take seriously. Monists are also split into those who deny that mental events exist at all (which smacks of believing three impossible things before breakfast, like the White Queen in *Alice*) and those who claim that mental events are just physical events described in another language. This last position, known as Identity Theory, has recently been restated in emphatic form by a group of Australian philosophers, under the name of Central State Materialism, and is much admired by connoisseurs. Most scientists, on the other hand, are epiphenomenalists, as those who claim that mind is a by-product of the brain are called. None of these views, I may as well warn you, stands up to inspection. Each side points out the fallacies in the opposing position, without finding a way to validate its own. The whole issue is known as the Mind/Body problem; I shall return to it at the end of the book.

Even though this is a book about the mind rather than the brain, it is with the brain itself that we should start our journey. If, as so many philosophers claim, mind is merely a by-product of the brain, then looking at the brain must tell us something about mind. There must be some similarity of structure or pattern between the two.

It is the habit of philosophers to speak of the brain and mind as if they were each rather clear-cut, homogeneous entities. But, as I have just argued, the word 'mind' embraces a wide variety of phenomena. And, as we shall see, the brain also is no mere lump of jelly, but is exquisitely structured. Between the structured mind and the structured brain there must be a homology.

But the curious fact is that our perceptions seem only loosely related

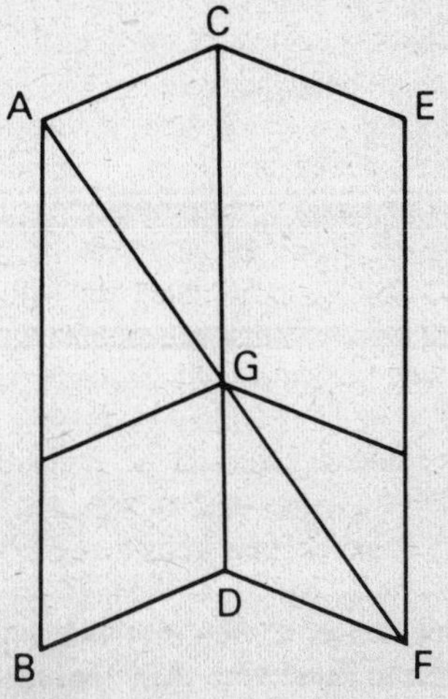

to the input. A simple example of this looseness of fit is provided by various optical illusions. Thus in the figure on page 21, the line AG seems longer than the line GF, although it is not. We are perceiving two lines of equal length, but conceive them to be unequal. A more familiar example is the stick thrust into water which appears to be bent though it is known to be straight. Our impressions overrule our knowledge. And if we rub our finger along a straight rod which is made, by wearing special spectacles, to appear curved, then it will *feel* curved also.

But why should this looseness of fit be confined to visual or tactile illusions? I shall present many examples, in later chapters, of experiences which seem but loosely related to sensory input. This interface between the subjective and objective is where we must look for clues about the nature of mind.

While it is our subjective feelings – often very strange ones – which form the central topic of this book, we need to understand something of the mechanism which underlies them. So the next two chapters are devoted to an account of the brain and its workings, after which we shall return to the mind. And the brain, which has been called the most complex organised structure in the universe, is well worth our attention.

3

Wond'rous Machine

HOT AND COLD BRAINS

Nalorphine is a man-made drug resembling morphine in its analgesic power but, doctors hoped, less likely to produce addiction. However it was soon found to have unpleasant side-effects, including nausea, dizziness and hallucination. At Leeds University a researcher, D. A. Cahal, and sixteen students volunteered to take it – some in a small dose, some in a larger one. Fifteen minutes after administration, the first man to take it began to laugh uncontrollably, to shout and express his views aggressively. He then 'made decidedly improper advances to three girls, having to be dragged off one of them'. After an hour, he was hysterical. Fifteen minutes later, he wanted to rush into the street and expose himself. He explained later – most apologetically – that he was aware that his behaviour was abnormal, but he could not control it. 'I feel I have no soul,' he said.

Other subjects were lethargic, or euphoric; several recalled scenes from their childhood. Four had to be restrained from attacking senior members of the staff. With classic understatement the report concludes that these results 'cast some doubt on the wisdom' of administering nalorphine routinely in analgesia.

Source: D. A. Cahal, 'Effects of Nalorphine on the behaviour of healthy human volunteers', *J. ment. Sci.* (1957) *103*:850.

The Fivefold Brain

'Brain is mind,' cries Professor Arturo Rosenblueth. 'The mind is simply the Brain,' echoes the philosopher, Professor D. M. Armstrong. Leaving aside all the finer doubts about the meaning of such assertions, I simply wish to ask, at this point, whether such a claim is plausible. Is the brain the sort of mechanism of which one could make such a claim with any hope of defending it at all? Does it have the sort of structure which could conceivably support mind?

In the last few decades, the scientific view of the brain has been changing quite rapidly, as more and more new facts come to light. The brain has certainly turned out to be a much fancier piece of equipment than even the most imaginative neurologist had envisaged. And not only is it fancy: it seems to be constructed according to subtler principles than those that we use in constructing our spacecraft, our computers, and our atom bombs.

Therefore, let us take a look at the brain. No, let me rephrase that. Let us look at *our* brains. The reflexive character of this operation makes it unique. When, with our brains, we consider galaxies or microbes we are in a position to feel a certain detachment. We are studying complex objects, no doubt, but the tool with which we study them is more complex than they. But to inspect our own brain we have only our own brains. Some feel, on grounds which are less philosophical than mystical, that the brain can never hope to understand itself. The idea smacks of hoisting oneself by one's own bootstraps. However, we can make a start.

The first person to examine the brain in a modern manner was the Viennese anatomist Dr Gall. Previous investigators had simply sliced it up, as if carving a joint. Gall dissected out the various structures within it and laid the foundations of modern neurology. Poor Dr Gall demonstrates the ironies of human reputation. History remembers only his phrenological theories and dismisses him as a charlatan. In point of fact it was a pupil of Gall's named Spurzheim who exploited phrenology, much to Gall's disapproval: Gall refused even to read Spurzheim's works.

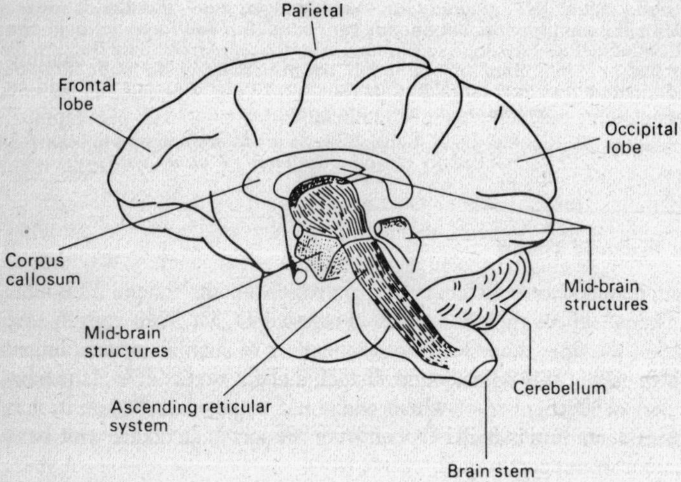

Phantom view of a human brain from the left side. The mid-brain structures are depicted as if seen through a transparent cortex.

What Gall started with was something looking like half a peeled walnut, but bigger of course: two wrinkled hemispheres (actually they are quarter spheres) consisting of a sheet of tissue, a few millimetres thick and about the size of a pocket handkerchief. The sheet is crumpled in the effort to fit a large surface into a small skull. It is officially called the cortex or rind, though the great Sir Charles Sherrington preferred to call it, more appropriately, the roof brain.

Lifting off this roof, Gall found a series of mystifying structures. First, two lobes, closely linked to the cortex, known as thalami, or reeds, in the fanciful nomenclature of neuroanatomy. Below them, the 'almond', the 'olive' and the 'sea horse', and so on. This heterogeneous assortment we call the mid-brain. Stripping it away, Gall found a couple of swellings at the top of the spinal cord, the old brain. Finally, stuck on at the back, another wrinkled, bilobed structure, the little brain or cerebellum. Gall did not of course comprehend the role of these structures. We are each the owner of four brains – or even five, if we count each of the cerebral hemispheres as a separate brain, which we could, seeing that a person can operate quite well with only one.

Like those airlines which operate two computers to record their passenger bookings, just in case one should break down, evolution has blessed us too with spare equipment. All five brains are interconnected.

Two of these brains will not concern us here. The old brain is the body's chief engineer, regulating heart-beat and breathing, deciding whether your blood vessels should dilate or your viscera contract, and so on. It also incorporates the alarm-system, arousing the cortex (the captain) when matters of interest arise, for through it pass all the cables from the sensory organs, and it monitors the information flow in them. The cerebellum is the automatic pilot. When you learn new skills, such as riding a bicycle, you start by using your cortex: you have to think what you are doing. Later, you can ride 'without thinking' or you can think of something else. Your cortex has handed over to the cerebellum. This little brain consists of long banks of similar equipment, fed with data by one set of nerves, and monitored by another, in a manner resembling a computer. The analogy between brains and computers is frequently overdone, but if there is anywhere where it is appropriate to use it, it is here. However, some scientists wonder if the cerebellum may not have other, unobvious functions. Intensive work has been done in recent years on the cerebellum, notably by the great Hungarian neuroanatomist Szent-Agothai. Its relatively simple, repetitive structures may be the first thing in the brain to yield to enquiry. It receives data not only from the cortex but from the mid-brain, which – as we shall shortly see – is concerned with emotions. That is rather odd. Why would an automatic pilot have any truck with emotion? However, I shall say no more about the old brain or the cerebellum.

So I can boil things down for you by saying: We are concerned with two brains merely – the mid-brain which handles our feelings (and smell),

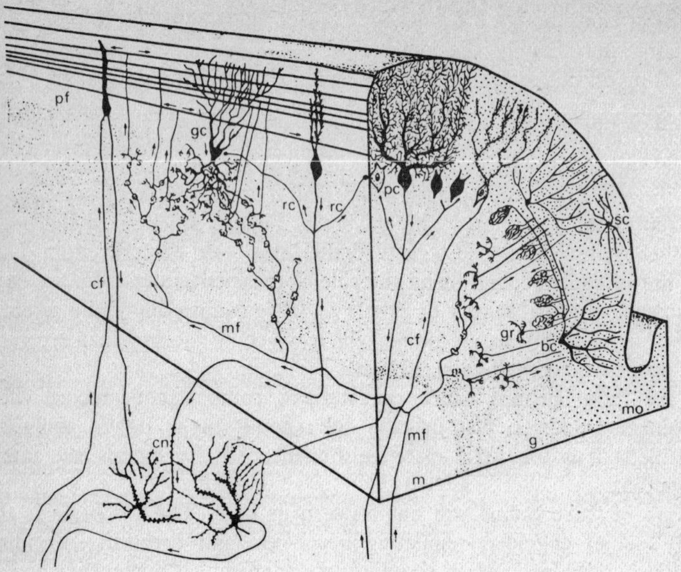

Key to abbreviations:

bc	Basket cells	mf	Mossy fibre
cf	Climbing fibre	mo	Molecular layer
cn	Deep cerebellar nuclei	pc	Purkinje cell
g	Granular layer	pf	Parallel fibre
gc	Golgi cell	rc	Recurrent collateral
gr	Granule cell	sc	Stellate cell
m	Medullary layer		

This schematic drawing of a segment of cerebellum gives an idea of the elaboration of the 'wiring'. The fanlike cell on the front is a Purkinje cell; only one is shown. Countless others lie in planes behind, like the pages of a book. Similarly, only one of the input cells is shown and only a few of the parallel fibres.

and the roof brain which handles all the sensations (except smell), as well as thoughts, the control of movements and perhaps memory.

I find it makes it easier to hold this pattern in one's head if one looks at the brain from an evolutionary and developmental viewpoint. First, the simple nerve net, as in starfish, worms and other creatures. Then the notochord or long nerve running the length of the body, enclosed in due course in a protective sheath which becomes the spine. Then a proliferation of the cells at one end, as the old brain develops to run a more complex body. Now the possessor has a front-end and a back-end: up to this point the two ends were identical. Next the development of the mid-brain, giving a crude awareness of the environment and capable of simple executive actions. A dog from which the cerebral hemispheres have been removed can walk, feed and sleep, thanks to its mid-brain. (Children are sometimes born without hemispheres – they are called anencephalics: they cry, they coo when stroked, they sleep and wake.) Finally, the roof brain begins to develop. At first optic lobes to analyse the input from the eyes, auditory lobes for the ears. (The olfactory lobe had been there from very early on.) Gradually the new brain spreads backwards over the older parts like a cap; and as the sheet of cells continues to grow, it begins to crumple. The cortex of a rabbit is smooth, but that of the more intelligent cat is wrinkled.

When the German physiologist Eduard Hitzig made the first modern studies on the exposed brain, almost a century ago, he tried stimulating portions of the cortex, for this was all he could get at. He found that various sensations and muscular movements ensued. So it came about that the neocortex came to be thought of as *the* brain. Much more recently, scientists have plunged wires and fine tubes through the cortex into the mid-brain, and are beginning to learn about the complex role it plays: it is the seat of feeling and emotion, as well as having taken over some of the automatic control functions from the brain stem.

We shall do better, I think, to regard the mid-brain as *the* brain – the mechanism which really determines what we do – and to think of the cortex as a computer which it calls in for detailed studies. If we remove the cortex from a living animal, it is still vaguely aware of the position of objects, it can move around, it can feed itself, it can withdraw from a painful stimulus. But the universe is blurred. It needs a cortex to identify that dark object as a cat or that attractive smell as a banana. That this is so is shown by the case of a patient (a thirty-six-year-old accountant) with severe right cortical damage who could, for example, feel a pinprick on his left side but could not say where exactly it was. He could describe the shape and feel of an object placed in his left hand but could not identify it. Here was the mid-brain locating the facts, but the cortex was unable to interpret them.

One commentator declares, on the basis of this sort of data, that the cortex cannot see, hear or think. But, as we shall see in more detail later, seeing and hearing are indubitably cortical functions; the fact that a primitive kind of seeing, hearing and feeling is also performed by the mid-brain in no way invalidates the more sophisticated efforts of the new brain. Countless nerve fibres connect every part of the cortex with the several components of the thalamus, and carry impulses both to and fro. The cortex seems to refer its findings about the world (for it is the analyst of vision as well as the executor of behaviour) to the thalamus for an emotional rating. As J-P. Ewert has said: the new brain tells you what it is, the thalamus tells you whether it matters.

In what follows we shall be much concerned with the relations between the new brain and the older mid-brain. The new brain makes plans and looks ahead, it restrains the impulses of the mid-brain.

Hot and Cold Brains

James Olds, whom we shall soon meet as the discoverer of the pleasure centres and the man who punctured 'drive theory', has drawn a happy distinction between the 'hot brain', meaning the mid-brain, and the 'cold brain', meaning the cortex, with its arousal system in the brain-stem. The hot brain is impulsive, wilful, wants everything now. The cold brain looks ahead and evaluates the results of actions. Sometimes it tells the hot brain 'no'. The hot brain tries to impose its pattern on the external world; the cold brain tries to impose the external organisation on the internal one.

You have doubtless noticed that in moments of extreme fear or rage or joy it becomes impossible to think clearly. One is speechless with rage or stunned with amazement. The mid-brain is in such an over-activated state that it swamps or ignores the data coming from the cortex. We may likewise say that the cortex, among other functions, plays the role of super-ego to the mid-brain's ego. The operation of leucotomy, sometimes performed to relieve severe guilt feelings, consists in cutting some of the connections between the front cortex and the mid-brain, so as to reduce its influence. This often relieves the painful feelings but the freeing sometimes goes too far. The patient becomes vulgar in language and behaviour; is sexually uninhibited and also gives way to anger easily. As Freud would say, his super-ego has weakened.

Arthur Koestler has argued that man's troubles arise from the enormous development of the cold brain – from too much rationality, not from too little. He regards the neocortex as developing a good thing to an absurd extreme, like the dinosaurs, and, like the dinosaurs, sealing our fate. He points out that man's problems arise from the pursuit of intellectually imposed aims at the expense of feelings. We are ready to imprison, to torture and kill in order to impose our theories and ideologies. If we gave our feelings more play, he thinks, we should recoil, appalled, at such inhumanities.

I beg to differ completely from this view. The trouble, as I see it, is that our hot brain is too powerful and enslaves our cold brain, which obediently devises plans and weapons to further its ends. Koestler assumes that the hot brain's emotions would be friendly and co-operative if it were free of cortical control. But tigers and sharks are not particularly friendly or co-operative, just self-seeking. The hot brain wants power, position, wealth: it is the source of all the human motives we know so well and see at work in our newspapers every day. The Puritan solution was to clamp down on the old Adam, the Freudian id, the impulsive hot brain. And the results of this battle between super-ego and id are too familiar to need elaboration. The solution, if there is a solution, could only be to modify the demands of the hot brain in a more peaceful and co-operative direction. The fact that destroying the amygdala, a mid-brain structure, causes animals to become unaggressive gives us some reason to suppose that such modification may be possible. Aggression has a chemical basis. The answer may come through a better understanding of brain chemistry.

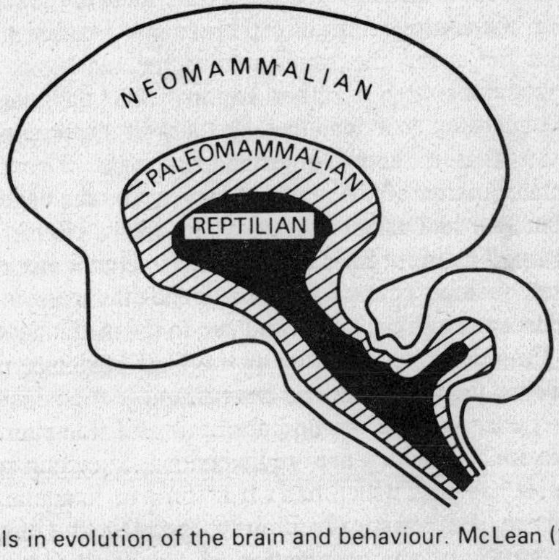

Levels in evolution of the brain and behaviour. McLean (1972)

Though I have presented the brain as having only two levels, the American neuroscientist Paul McLean sees it as having three, which he has picturesquely named Graven Image, Lethe and Guru – the first concerned with the past, the second with the present and the last with the future. He is thinking, however, more in evolutionary than in structural terms. At first there is the reptilian brain, working by instinct, the accumulated wisdom of the past; then the simple mammalian brain, reacting to present situations; finally the human brain, planning far ahead. He has an excellent point. For our cortex is not concerned simply with the finegrain analysis of what is happening, but with expectancies and probabilities.

The point has now been reached at which I should introduce you more closely to this 'hot brain' which is the core of our being. It was an investigator named J. W. Papez who gained a permanent place in the history of neurology when he made the acute suggestion that the various odd-shaped structures which lie below the roof brain constituted a co-ordinated system, which he named the 'limbic system'. Only with the development of techniques of penetrating the cortex with fine needles and recording electrically from these structures was it possible to learn much about them, and they still remain pretty much a mystery, though some broad outlines of their function are beginning to loom through the mist.

Scientists are currently looking closely at some of these structures since they give us some idea how the brain functions, in the sense of 'How does it split up the complex task of captaincy into feasible sub-tasks?'

I shall take for study the hippocampus, or sea horse. A sounder comparison would be with a rather stumpy Bologna sausage. It is a rather large structure; that man has the largest hippocampus of any animal suggests that it serves important functions. The first curious thing is its internal structure. A series of leaves, like the pages of a book. It is as if someone had taken a great many micro-circuit boards and stacked them up. The input lines from the sense organs run through this stack of leaves, making contact with the dendritic trees in each. The output lines descend from the leaves and run to the muscular system. The whole thing reminds one irresistibly of the kind of device made up by electronic experts, much as does the cerebellum.

If you insert electrodes in the hippocampus of a free-running rat you find that there are cells which fire only when it is at certain points in the cage or maze. It has cells which fire when three or four cues are simultaneously present, but erratically if only one. David Olton of Johns Hopkins was struck by the observation of a naturalist that the honey creeper, a tiny bird that feeds on nectar in Hawaii, seemed able to remember which flowers it had already stripped of nectar. He therefore decided to investigate the question of spatial memory. He found that a rat placed in a maze with eight arms could remember which had proved to contain food. It could also do so on a seventeen-arm maze, though it made more mistakes. Varying the conditions showed that it was making

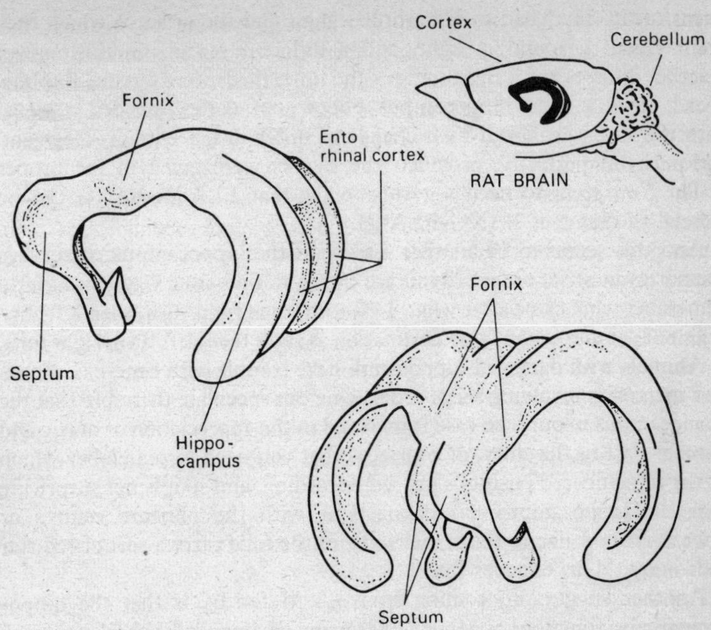

The principal old brain structures as they appear in the rat brain. Two aspects are shown. The inset (top right) *shows how they are related to the brain as a whole.*

a mental map. But if one of the hippocampal connections was cut, the animal's performance after recovery from the operation was profoundly impaired. So it seems that one of the functions of the hippocampus is to compare memories of spatial arrangements in relation to whether they were associated with a reward. The circuitry is just what you need for such a result. This conclusion also conforms with the evolutionary evidence.

Fish, like animals lower than themselves in the evolutionary scale, have no hippocampus. Amphibians have only a primitive one; reptiles do a little better. In the ocean there are few landmarks, and fish are guided only by broad environmental factors like temperature and salinity. But once creatures had climbed on land, to remember where food could be found, or where your nest or lair was, became important. In mice and rats and primitive mammals the fully organised hippocampus appears. Russian scientists tested a range of animals from snakes and turtles through rabbits, hedgehogs and birds to dogs and baboons on the same experiment. They had to note three signals and the order in which they were given: a sound, a light, and a different sound. Goldfish never learned. Turtles got it right some of the time. Birds were terrific. Rabbits, which have a good hippocampus but a poor cortex, needed a lot of tutoring and were foxed by a change of order in the stimuli. Dogs and baboons did perfectly, provided the signals were given in the proper order. You seem to need a cortex to see that FLASH-BANG can be treated the same as BANG-FLASH.

And this seems to be another feature of the hippocampus: it surveys memories in serial order. If you are trying to find your way you have to remember what came after what. Left turn, then right turn, then left turn does not get you to the same destination as right turn, left turn, right turn.

Animals with damaged hippocampi have trouble with time-based tests and memories involving serial order. One can speculate therefore that the hippocampus in our own case is involved in the appreciation of music and speech. Part of the story, of course, is that you need to remember which of the remembered positions proved rewarding, and so it is not surprising that the hippocampus has connections with the pleasure centres or reward areas. I like to think that some of the folia carry a sort of red star indicating, 'This one was fun'.

Another suggestion, coming from T. McLardy, is that the hippocampus also functions as a delay line; many of the cells lie cheek-to-cheek and electric currents permeate through them relatively slowly. This 'seepage' could explain for instance why lights which flicker more than fifteen times a second tend to be seen as a continuous light; and why the successive pictures of a film or TV programme fuse together. He also believes the hippocampus detects intensity gradients. It certainly has further functions and seems to be needed for the unlearning (extinction) of a response. A leading American neurophysiologist, the Vienna-born Karl Pribram, thinks it is concerned with the whole task of organising complex behaviour.

The Hypothalamus

While the functions of the hippocampus are gradually becoming clearer, one cannot say the same for the amygdala or almond. In 1937 the German-born psychologist, Klüver, and Bucy, a neurosurgeon at Chicago, removed both the entire temporal lobes including the amygdalae and hippocampi from monkeys, which profoundly changed their behaviour. They handled snakes (which monkeys normally fear), started eating meat (they're normally vegetarian), repeatedly examined the same objects, became hypersexual (auto-, homo- and hetero- by turns) and showed an almost total inability to learn. Since they also lost all anger and aggressiveness, amygdalectomy has been suggested as an operation to be performed on violent criminals.

More cautious removal of the amygdalae only has done little to clarify the picture. No behaviour is lost when it is removed, but your disposition changes. When it is electrically stimulated, you may feel a bewildering series of mood changes, accompanied by hallucinations or illusions. But he only tried in epileptics. Bilateral removal seems to wreck the power to evaluate the environment, and the animal eventually dies. Every sensory mode feeds into the amygdala. The amygdala is connected both to the cortex and to the hypothalamus, a small lobe at the base of the brain, the function of which is relatively clear.

The hypothalamus regulates the balance between the sympathetic system, which arouses the body to fight or fly, and the parasympathetic system, which damps activity down to relaxation or rest. The forward part calms, the hind part arouses. Damage the forward part and you can't sleep; damage the hinder part and you can't stay awake. Both 'feeling more active' and 'wanting to' may be involved. The physiologist Ernst Gellhorn goes much further, saying that the hypothalamus not only controls motor expression of the emotions but causes the emotions themselves. It once was held that while the brain was the seat of reason, the passions were located in the heart. It would seem that for heart one should read hypothalamus.

I must add that the hypothalamus handles thirst and hunger, and that it releases various hormones or chemical messengers into the bloodstream which affect other organs, notably the organs of sex, and an immense amount of work has been done on this aspect.

The hippocampus is connected to the septum by the fornix (see illustration) – the three form an almost continuous structure, like two bananas fused at one end. But what the septum serves for is almost totally mysterious. It seems to have something to do with learning of active avoidance, but I will not fatigue you with the ill-assorted fragments of information that are the best neurologists can do at present.

I have said enough to impress you with the fact that the mid-brain is, in comparison with the cortex, highly structured. These structures perform specialised functions, but they are not the sort of functions which were originally expected: the brain chops up the task of running things differently – more subtly, you may think – than it would occur to human engineers to do. And although these functions are only now emerging from the mists of obscurity it is obvious that the brain is 'designed' very effectively for the functions it fulfils. (I say 'designed' but who was the designer? Could it have designed itself?)

My chief reason, however, for taking you on this perhaps too detailed and confusing tour of your brain is to bring out how shallow and inadequate it is to say, as the philosophers so often do, 'brain is mind'. The brain is not just an indeterminate, homogeneous mass. So if you are a dualist and conceive the mind as something other than the brain you must tell us more specifically how you think that indeterminate mind is rooted and relates to determinate brain. On the other hand, if you think that consciousness is an epiphenomenon, you must explain how many different structures produce many different sorts and degrees of awareness, and sometimes function without producing awareness at all.

Where is Fancy Bred?

In the days when the mind was conceived as an immaterial gas-bag tethered to the body, the brain was thought to be all of a piece, a sort of sounding-board for the soul. In the Middle Ages naturalists assigned the mental faculties to the three open spaces or ventricles within the brain. The pendulum swung back and forth between the conception of the brain as a 'common sensorium' and the idea of 'localisation of function'. And here is one of the most curious of the brain's features: somehow the cortex manages to be both things at once, specialised, yet generalised. In this paradox is embedded an important truth about the brain and its relation to mind, so allow me to pursue it further.

The first person to put the matter on a scientific footing was the youthful French anatomist Paul Broca; his discovery made modern brain surgery possible. In 1861 he described the brain of a patient who had been kept many years in the Salpetrière, unable to express himself in speech or by writing, a condition Broca christened 'aphasia'. On autopsy, the man was found to have suffered damage to a small area of the brain which has ever since been known to anatomists as Broca's area. Broca claimed, correctly, that the patient's speech problem was directly due to this damage: that this part of the brain was precisely responsible for translating ideas into words. It was the first time a brain function had been localised. Then, in 1873, the German Carl Wernicke identified an area, not very far from Broca's, which he described as the area of understanding speech. His patient could speak and write but not understand what was said to him. The area, naturally, has gone into the textbooks as Wernicke's area. (Fortunately, before the brain became a forest of patronymics, baffling the memory, a man named Brodmann developed a system of numbered areas which, though not very satisfactory, is still widely used. Broca's area corresponds roughly to Brodmann's 44.)

These evidences that the brain actually had some kind of comprehensible structure aroused unprecedented excitement among neurologists, who began to accumulate data with great enthusiasm. The next significant advance was made by Eduard Hitzig, whom I mentioned earlier. It was in 1870 that he published his epoch-making paper in which he demonstrated that, if you stimulated the brain at various points, different groups of muscles were caused to contract. The area across the top of the brain is known as the parietal (paries being the Latin for roof): it is bounded by a deep fold known as the fissure of Rolando, named for the Italian anatomist who drew attention to it. This was the area which Hitzig and his colleague Fritsch stimulated. They found that all the muscles of the body were activated in regular order, from the feet at one side of the brain to the head at the centre, the right side of the body being represented on the left and vice versa. On the other side of Rolando's fissure are the cell groups which connect with the sensory areas of the body, also neatly laid out from top to toe, with large areas assigned to delicately innervated body parts, like fingers and tongue, and small areas for less innervated ones such as the forearm or the sole of the foot.

At the back of the brain (known as the occipital lobe) lies the area responsible for vision: stimulation here produces flashes of light, stars, wheels and other elements of vision. At the side, in the temporal area, stimulation produces sounds, and between the two is an area responsible for linking the two senses. (Another 'association' area links vision with touch.) Just forward of this, as the Canadian surgeon Wilder Penfield discovered much later, stimulation evokes memories – but that is a story I shall postpone telling until we come to the subject of memory.

The only area where stimulation seemed to have no specific result was the frontal lobes – stimulation here only stopped the animal from doing whatever it was doing. They were accordingly dubbed 'the silent areas' and for long were accused of being functionless. Now we know that they are the plan-making apparatus – the executive of the brain. All the rest is simply information processing for the benefit of the frontal lobes. Karl Pribram declares, 'I feel reasonably sure that the dorsolateral frontal cortex, like the limbic, are [*sic*] concerned in the inhibition of interference among brain events.'

Animals in which the frontal lobes have been removed seem to have great trouble in deciding between two alternatives. They fail to learn when tempted by rewards, as if they failed to see the consequences of their actions. The results in the few human cases of cortical ablation are even more bewildering. On the one hand irritability, on the other indifference. Impetuousness combined with lack of initiative. Euphoria and boastfulness. Failure to spot details and poor behaviour on sorting tests – these one might well expect, since the role of the cortex is to make fine discriminations. The frontal lobes seem to exert a restraining role on the impulsiveness of the mid-brain. The operation of leucotomy (replacing the earlier operation of lobotomy, in which parts of the lobes were removed), severs some of the connections between the frontal and the limbic lobes, and is helpful in cases of overwhelming anxiety and depression. After such operations, the patient may go towards the other extreme, become abusive or given to violence and sexually active as well.

One of the classic cases of neurology concerns Phineas Gage, a workman who was tamping explosives into a hole. The charge exploded prematurely, driving the tamper clean through his skull. Afterwards, his friends commented on his changed disposition.

But I have not quite brought the story of localisation of function up to date. The Second World War provided neurologists with a large crop of cases of penetrating brain injury, from which much could be learned. The man who, beyond all others, has devoted himself to the study of such cases is Aleksandr Luria, doyen of Russian neuropsychologists, who has made it almost a life's work.

Luria found men who had lost mental functions of a very specific kind. For instance, soldiers with an injury to a certain spot on the left side of the brain towards the back showed a curious disturbance of their ability to judge space, both when moving and when simply perceiving. Such patients typically 'cannot interpret the position of the hands on a clock or find their bearings on a map; they cannot find their way around the ward where they are staying; they cannot solve even relatively simple arithmetical problems, and they are confused when faced with the problem of subtracting from a number of two digits carrying over from the tens column: when subtracting seven from thirty-one, for example, they do the first stage of this operation (30 – 7 equals 23) but then they do not know whether the odd one should be added or subtracted, or whether their final result should be twenty-two or twenty-four. Finally they begin to have great difficulty in understanding grammatical structures incorporating logical relationships, such as "the father's brother" and "the brother's father"; "spring after summer" "summer after spring", whereas the understanding of simpler grammatical structures remains unimpaired.'

Nevertheless, such a lesion causes no disturbance of processes such as fluent speech, the understanding or playing of musical melodies, the smooth succession of the elements of movement. All the former processes mentioned include a spatial factor, whereas the latter group do not.

Luria observed many other highly specific defects. For instance, there was the man who could start operations but not stop them. One day,

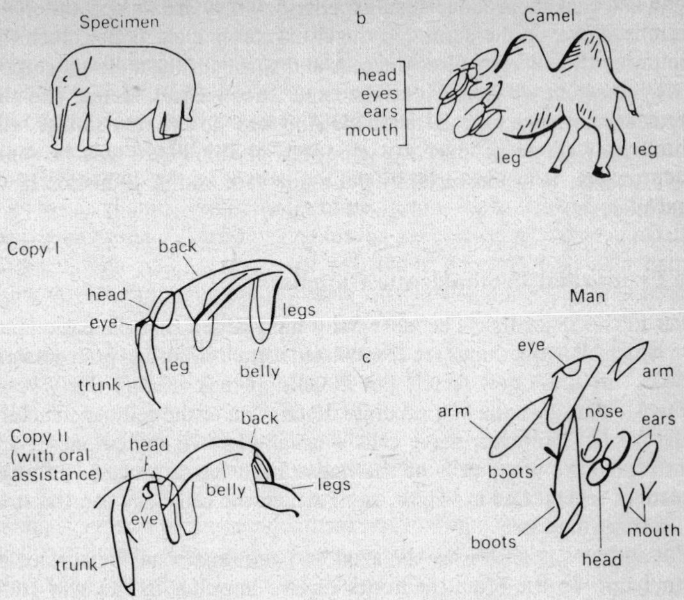

These are the attempts made by a man with localised brain damage to copy the drawings of an elephant, a camel and a man, given to him. Notice how he not only fails to copy the parts accurately, but cannot integrate them into a whole.

when he was planing wood in the workshop, he planed it all away to nothing and started planing through the bench. Then there were patients who would light a cigarette and wonder what to do with it; or place the lighted end in their mouth; or place the match in their mouth and throw the cigarette away.

It would be interesting to pursue this subject further, but it would take us away from our theme and the interested reader should invest a pound or so on Luria's popular introduction *The Working Brain*, even if he shies off Luria's great *The Higher Cortical Functions in Man*, or *The Restoration of Functions After Brain Injury*.

The cortex emerges, then, as a many-faceted computer adapted to handle many different tasks, and to integrate them harmoniously. What the 'brain is mind' party fail to explain is, first, why only some of these functions – all carried out by much the same kind of equipment – produce sensations and experiences of the kind we identify as 'mind'; and second, why, when they *do* produce such experiences, they are so very different. The cells, and even the wiring, in the visual cortex looks pretty much the same under the microscope as the cells and wiring in the auditory cortex. So why does one of them evoke the experience we call 'seeing' and the other the experience we call 'hearing'? And why do the very similar cells in the motor cortex produce no sensations at all? There may be some simple answer. It would certainly put a new face on the discussion if we found it.

The Primordial Protoplasmic Globules

It was in the 1830s that Theodore Schwann realised that the basic units from which all living things are constructed were 'primordial protoplasmic globules' or, as we now tersely put it, cells. It took another thirty years before Meinert gave the first accurate description of the cellular structure of the cortex. However, nerve cells – usually known as neurones – are quite unlike the other cells of the body. Each has a process, a thread sometimes several feet in length, along which the cell-body can transmit an electrical impulse.

This process is known as the axon and terminates on the surface of another cell. In the brain, neurones receive impulses in this way from hundreds or even thousands of other neurones. When a neurone receives more than a certain minimum of stimuli, it in turn emits an electric impulse, or 'fires', as physiologists say. If it fires, its threshold of sensitivity is lowered, so that on the next such occasion it fires more readily. Even if it does not fire, the arrival of impulses may reset its threshold so that, on some future occasion, it will fire more readily when stimulated. Furthermore, general chemical changes in the brain, including those caused by drugs, may shift such thresholds in whole blocks of cells. In addition to axons, neurones are provided with a branchwork of fine threads, known as dendrites, which contact cells in their immediate neighbourhood. The general character of the brain is thus of an elaborate network, in which each unit is receiving information about the state of thousands of other such units. One thing I must add: while some neurones encourage those they are in touch with to fire, others have the opposite effect and block their firing (inhibition). Thus whether a neurone fires or not may be the upshot of, so to say, a large number of votes – some saying 'yes', some 'no' – which it summates.

It is not necessary for our purpose to go into the nature of the electric impulse, except to say that it is different from an ordinary electric current and travels much more slowly. Nor need I discuss how, at the point of contact with another neurone, there is a cleft known as the synapse, into

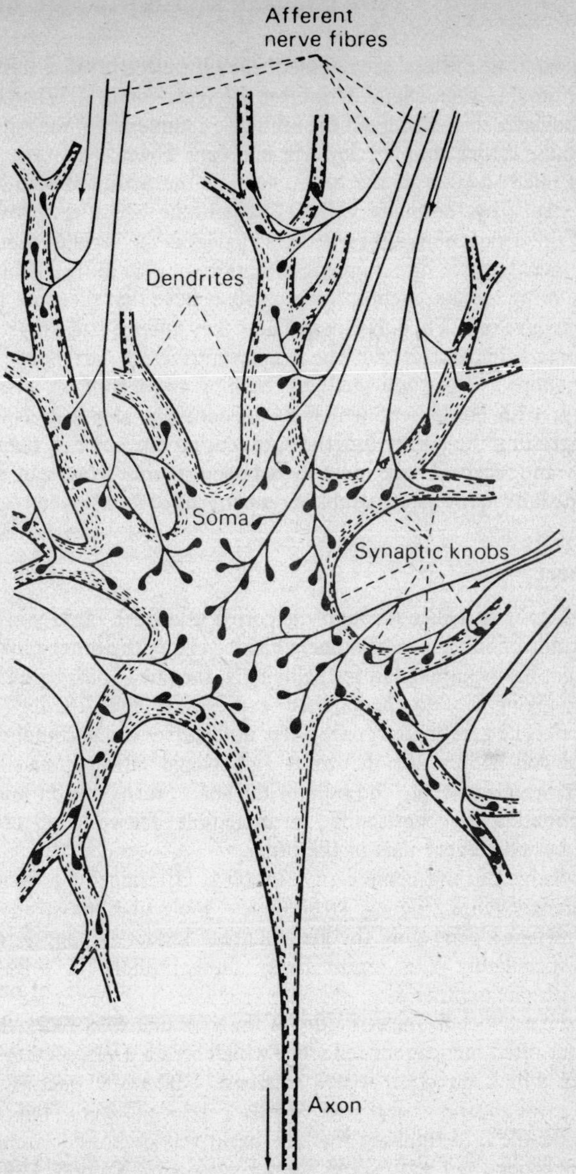

The main body of the neurone receives hundreds – in some cases thousands – of inputs from other neurones; some of them encourage it to respond, others discourage it. Thus every neurone continuously takes decisions.

which chemical 'transmitters' are released when the electric pulse arrives: these neurohumours then excite or inhibit the receiving cell. What I do want to do, however, is to bring out the immense complexity of the pattern into which these rather simple relay-like units are woven.

The early microscopists of the brain, such as the Spaniard Ramón y Cajal, were struck by the many varieties of neurone which they found, but many of these variations appear to be as trivial as the variations in the human race, accidents of development, situation, or role in life. When it comes to the crunch, many neurophysiologists believe that there are only three basic types of cell. Though why and how they differ is still a mystery. Thus the remarkable fact is that the brain contrives to carry out such different functions as sight and smell, as thinking and feeling, as wishing and deciding, with equipment which is substantially identical. Not to mention controlling the bodily functions, executing movements, regulating alertness and sleep. There must be a lesson in this. How can consciousness in all its many aspects subsist on patterns of interlinked relays?

Only Connect

If you take a razor and slice through the cortex of a fresh brain you will reveal two kinds of substance, the one whitish-yellow, the other pinkish. After the brain has been fixed in formaldehyde, the one appears grey, the other white, giving rise to the popular expressions 'grey matter' and 'white matter'. The grey matter, only a few millimetres thick, contains all the neuronal cell-bodies, the dendrites and axonal terminations. The white matter, which takes up the bulk of the space, turns out on microscopic examination to consist of an incredible feltwork of cross-connections between every part of the brain.

This knowledge did not come easily. In 1861, Griesinger was writing of 'an apparently homogeneous, structureless molecular mass, an unusually fine network', meaning the grey matter. As late as 1897 Krafft-Ebing was speculating '. . . most likely these millions of cells are connected with one another'.

Within the cortex itself, the structure of the grey matter is everywhere so similar that often one cannot tell from which area a given section has come, nor in which direction it was oriented. Under the microscope, when sliced through, the grey matter reveals a series of layers. This fact long misled people into thinking that the brain was organised laterally, a notion which persisted until some twenty years ago. Vernon Mountcastle showed that the cortex consists, functionally, of a million vertical columns, packed together like the cells in a honeycomb. Signals are shuffled up and down these columns, in which the various types of cells give rise to the layered appearance. Though each column influences its neighbours through its dendrites (and perhaps in other ways) the main intercommunications are by the axons, running in bundles beneath the grey matter.

Scientists are tracing the paths of these bundles by very laborious methods. A favourite one is to make a lesion in the brain of a living animal: this causes the axons arising from the damaged cells to degenerate or die away. After days or weeks, depending on the method used, the animal is killed and its brain preserved, stained and sliced in very thin sections. By using dyes which only stain injured or dead neurones, the course of their connections can be traced. And, while we are on the subject of staining, let us mention the method devised by Cajal's great rival, Camillo Golgi. He discovered a stain which has the peculiar property of filling some neurones with a red-black precipitate, but leaving the rest unstained. Thus the splendid photographs one sees in illustrated works about the brain give an entirely false impression of the density with which the neurones are packed. Without staining, it would be impossible to see the trees for the forest. With staining, one or two trees are left standing in majestic isolation, so that their branches can be clearly distinguished, but the forest as a whole has become invisible.

I recall these facts in order to set the stage for an excursus on the incredible complexity of the brain, complexity of a very special kind. If any of my readers has a taste for staggering statistics, I can now satisfy it. The number of neurones in the cortex alone is commonly put at ten thousand million, which can conveniently be written 10^{10} – an easy figure to remember. Unfortunately also an inaccurate one, based on an investigation made in 1896 and copied from work to work ever since, even by neurologists themselves. Later studies have put the figure as high as fourteen thousand million and as low as two thousand six hundred million. In any case it is a phenomenal number: around thirty-five thousand cells for each square millimetre of surface, each contacting about six hundred other cells and making 10^7 synapses. Incidentally about one-tenth of these cells are occupied in analysing data from the eyes.

But though this enormous figure of 10^{10} is so often quoted, one could easily cap the quotation. The cerebellum, for instance, contains some forty thousand million granule cells, and God alone knows how many cells there are in the limbic system and the brain-stem. Perhaps a hundred thousand million would be nearer the population of the brain as a whole. If cells were people, they would populate twenty-five planets like the earth. Small wonder that the brain consumes about one-third of the body's total oxygen supply. (In addition there are as many supporting cells, neuroglia, as there are neurones.) As Professor Donald Kennedy has remarked, with noble understatement, 'These vast populations of cells present a formidable challenge to biologists.'

But if I quote these astronomical figures of cell numbers, it is not simply to make you gape, but rather to prepare the ground for the more interesting question of how they are interconnected. It is hardly an exaggeration to say that every group of cells in the brain is connected with every other group. The various parts of the cortex are connected not only with each other, but with the basal nuclei of the limbic system and with the brain-stem, to say nothing of their connections with the muscles and the sensory organs. For instance, the frontal lobes have close connections with the limbic system, a fact which you acknowledge when you say, 'The very thought of it makes me feel sick.' More than a million nerve fibres run from the eye to the brain. A single segment of spinal cord controls the few muscles it operates through several thousand motoneurones. Nature is prodigal, and can afford to be.

The most substantial connecting tract is the one which joins the two halves of the cortex, the corpus callosum. The number of fibres it contains in man is unknown, but in the cat some patient technician has counted seventy thousand fibres to the square millimetre.

Altogether, the axons of all the brain's neurones would stretch, it has been estimated (though I should not care to attempt such a feat) three times as far as the distance from the earth to the moon. That is, the axons of one human brain. The axons of the brain of all living persons would stretch to the nearest galaxy, a hundred light years away. The point I am hammering at is that connectivity, not quantity, is the secret of the brain's success. The human brain, at one thousand four hundred and fifty grams or so for men and one thousand three hundred and fifty grams for women, is piddling compared with the five thousand grams the elephant can boast or the mighty six thousand eight hundred grams of the blue whale. But when it comes to interconnections, the human brain has a clear lead.

The axons of which I have written are, of course, the links between relatively distant cell groups. In addition, there are the dendrites, a dense fuzz of local connections. Valentino Braitenberg has suggested that we should talk of A and B systems of connection, the local connections which co-ordinate cells within cell groups, as distinguished from the connections between groups. No one knows much about dendritic patterns, and the study of the 'local circuit neurones' which link nearby cells (or maybe separate them) has only recently become a recognised discipline. A few years ago, a Californian scientist named Stephen Zamenhof fed growth hormone to pregnant rats. Their offspring were brighter than average at running mazes and such-like tricks; and when their brains were examined proved to have a richer growth of dendrites than usual. Connectivity, in fine, is the basis of intelligence – not brain weight or neurone count.

I said that the complexity of the brain was of a special type, and now I think I have said enough to make this statement clearer. The brain is built of very simple, repetitive units of a very few kinds. It is not complex in that sense. It is the processes which are complex. A great many different things are happening at the same time in any one place. Every neurone is influenced directly by hundreds or thousands of other neurones, and in several different ways. Indirectly, every neurone is influenced, or may be influenced, by every other neurone. Every part of the brain, to put it more picturesquely, knows what the other parts are doing. There are no man-made mechanisms of which this is even approximately true.

Thus the paradox of the brain is that it is both localised and generalised. It analyses, but at the same time, and with the same equipment, it synthesises. It is hard for us to grasp the kind of thing which is continually going on as it matches nothing in our ordinary experience.

And now I have to push this rather difficult conception one stage further. The brain is able, unlikely as it might appear, to distribute its activities among the available equipment in a very curious way, or perhaps several curious ways. In the most obvious of these ways, it simply mobilises the available equipment, rather as the larger computers do.

Suppose you are driving a car and talking to your companion. Suddenly you have to do a tricky bit of overtaking. You fall silent for a few moments while you 'concentrate' on the driving problem. What has happened? You have called in the parts of the brain which were handling your thoughts and remarks to assist the parts which were processing the driving task. The additional equipment makes it possible – thanks to the parallel processing set-up – to process the data more rapidly and more accurately. This phenomenon suggests that the brain must have – just like the larger computers – a central command unit which distributes the equipment as required. In computers these units have a 'noticing order' programme which assigns priorities to different operations. Karl Pribram believes that he has shown that animals likewise have 'noticing order' programmes. Nevertheless, no such unit has been found and I am inclined to believe the result is achieved in a subtler way. I suspect that all the traffic of the brain carries a priority tag – it might be the amplitude of the signal or the die-away rate or the internal structure of the pulse-code; we need something of this kind to explain why some things seem urgent and important, others less so, if not downright dull. (It could even be that priorities are assigned to cortical material by re-inforcement from the hot brain.) If this is correct, the priorities would sort themselves out; certain neural patterns would swamp others, as big waves at sea ignore little ripples.

As each neurone discharges its tiny pulse, the total effect is detectable as an electric field outside the skull. When the brain is inactive, the cortical cells discharge in unison, producing the 'alpha rhythm' of which much has been heard recently. When the brain is concentrating on some problem, the synchrony of discharge vanishes, as different groups of cells pursue their own purposes, and more complex rhythms are detectable. In deep meditation even the ten to twelve per second alpha rhythm dies away, to be replaced by a slower four to six per second rhythm known as the theta rhythm.

It was a German psychiatrist, Hans Berger, who in 1925 first recorded the human 'encephalogram' (EEG) from the scalp of his young son. To begin with, he pushed platinum wires into the boy's scalp, but later found that metal discs taped to the skin would serve as well. Berger was a shy, rigid man, who kept his results to himself until 1929. His report was ridiculed at first: it was thought to be absurd that the brain should be in constant activity. It was Lord Adrian, at Cambridge, who realised the importance of his findings and invited him to work with him.

Eventually, opinion swung from scepticism to the other extreme: the analysis of these brain waves was going to explain everything. The reality has been disappointing. True, the waves do seem closely related to what the brain is doing; thanks to special techniques it has recently proved possible to detect the difference when a person looks at a chequered field as compared with his looking at a uniform one, for instance. Evidently, the rhythms are indicating something, but just what is unclear and shows little sign of becoming clearer. They have proved valuable in the clinical field, however, since abnormal rhythms may warn of an impending epileptic attack, while localised abnormalities may indicate the location of a tumour or blood-clot. They also have a role as a research tool, since probes thrust deep into the brain can record the rhythms from small areas and reveal how their activity is affected by drugs or mental disturbance. But the great breakthrough in understanding the brain which many expected has not occurred. The EEG resembles the noise coming from a house which might tell us that a party or a concert was going on inside, but who is present and what part they are taking we can only guess.

The Brain as a Whole

But even this does not exhaust the account of the brain's connectivity. For though neurologists have long focused on the electric transmission of data through axon and synapse, it is now becoming clear that there are other types of transmission in the brain. The eminent Professor Valentino

Braitenberg, of Freiburg's Max Planck Institute, lists no fewer than five types. Among them – and I suspect of great importance – is electrotonic transmission. Whereas the type of transmission most commonly described (known as the action potential) fires with undiminished strength into all its ramifications, and travels at uniform speed, this other kind dies away and loses speed as it does so. Direct electric coupling can also take place between closely aligned cells. There are also chemical forms of transmission. Thus while the action potential gives the brain a faint resemblance to a digital computer, which works with all-or-nothing pulses, some of these other forms smack more of the analogue computer, which echoes fluctuating forces in the real world with fluctuating electric potentials. This opens up a whole new aspect of brain function.

One more puzzling fact: the sticky stuff inside the axons is known as axoplasm. It flows gently along, taking days to reach the tip. No one knows what this is in aid of. And of course the axons are wrapped up in special cells called neuroglia, which roll round them like a rug. They may insulate them, or feed them, or they could even be the repository of memory. No one knows.

As if this were not enough, that remarkable man Lancelot Law Whyte has made a further intriguing suggestion. Lance Whyte was a polymath: a philosopher who was also an engineer, a financier, an author and a mathematician. We used to meet after the war – his book *The Next Development in Man* had given him a public reputation – in Kensington cafés or in his book-lined study in Hampstead and discuss the borderlands between science and philosophy. He published a small book called *Internal Factors in Evolution* which was largely ignored, despite enthusiastic comment from a few percipient scientists. Very recent developments in genetics have shown that he was on the right lines and I am sorry he did not live to see his ideas vindicated. I, therefore, take all the more seriously what he had to propose about the brain.

'How is memory stored?' was the question he addressed. There are three main theories – that it depends on the wiring diagram of the cells, that it depends on chemical changes within the cells, or that it depends on the interface between cells, changes in the efficiency of the synapse. But why assume that it is determined by *cells*? Why not by the direction of propagation of the pulses? Let us regard the cortex, he said, as a mass of neural cytoplasm, through which waves pass, independently of its division into cellular units. Within the cytoplasm are proteins and we know that a small change in the mobility of electrons in proteins is such that it can affect a whole sheet. Perhaps these proteins, initially oriented in a random manner, became oriented in the direction of the electron flow? If so, learning would have occurred.

I do not want to discuss here the application of this idea to memory: memory is such a big subject it calls for a chapter to itself. I shall only observe that, if Whyte is right, the brain contains a whole new order of complexity on an even more micro-miniaturised scale, namely the molecular. This would make it even more emphatically the most complex structure known. Perhaps the unknown ramifications of the oriented proteins can account for some of the phenomena which at present we find so mysterious.

Up to this point I have treated the brain primarily as an electrical switching device, for this is how scientists have persisted in thinking of it. The biggest change which has come over brain research in recent years, however, is the realisation that it is also a complex chemical system. Though it is over a century since Thudichum, the German refugee who worked at St Thomas's Hospital in London, founded the study of brain chemistry, it is only in the last two decades that neurochemistry has become a science, thanks to the devising of recondite methods of identifying the presence of very small amounts of particular substances in specific small areas of the brain. At least forty such neurochemicals are now known to exist, and their connection with mood and behaviour is slowly being unravelled.

The idea that nerve cells could secrete hormones – chemical messengers which could travel to another cell and affect its behaviour – was slow in coming. The suggestion that they might do so came from a student at Cambridge at the beginning of the century, T. R. Elliott, following experiments he had made with the newly discovered hormone Adrenalin. But his professor, the eminent physiologist J. N. Langley, discouraged these wild speculations and the idea languished. Not until 1946 was nor-Adrenalin identified as the transmitter-substance of the sympathetic nervous system. Even then, no one expected to find such substances in the brain itself. At first only two 'transmitters' were thought to exist, nor-Adrenalin (now usually known as norepinephrine, since Adrenalin is a tradename) and acetylcholine, working in opposition. Today more than forty active substances are known to be present. Among them are the catecholamines (like dopamine and norepinephrine); the indoleamines (like serotonin and tyramine); the amino-acids (like taurine); the prostaglandins; the small peptides; the endorphins; the purine nucleosides; the brain hormones; and various odds and ends such as P-substance, histamine, and sundry substances with unpronounceable names.

Some of these substances are neurotransmitters, facilitating the actual transmission of neuronal impulses. Others are neuroregulators which modulate the sensitivity of target cells to such substances. Others may control the rate at which key substances are produced or reabsorbed.

Some, at least, seem to be arranged in opposing systems (like the flip-flops I mention later, see p. 58) so that if the level of one is depressed, the level of another rises in compensation.

Brain chemistry is now *the* field of study, but brain chemists are somewhat appalled by the enormous amount which remains to be learned; only a handful of these substances are reasonably well understood. As Seymour Kety, one of the fathers of this new field, has recently observed, neurochemists are like people looking at a jigsaw puzzle. Twenty years ago very few of the pieces were even on the table. Now most of the pieces seem to be there, but only a few have been fitted together: there are one or two islands of knowledge, but how they will fit into the eventual pattern cannot be foreseen.

What is very evident, however, is that these substances regulate, or perhaps even create, emotion. Changes in the levels of neurochemicals are found in schizophrenia, alcoholism, affective disturbances, sociopathic behaviour and perhaps in autism. Some, when administered to normal humans, produce euphoria, or depression – but when administered to disturbed people may produce an entirely contrary effect. Hopes for a breakthrough in treating mental disease are high, although there has been modest progress so far.

While the chemists are looking, naturally enough, for a clinical pay-off, I am more intrigued by the fact that the chemical state of the brain seems to be the substrate of emotion. Here the link between brain and mind seems unusually close. If the riddle is to be resolved at all, surely it is here the key must lie. There are substances which will make mice wildly aggressive, turning them into killers; others which will tame the most vicious rats. There are substances which improve the speed of learning, others which boost memory. Recently there has been excitement about the discovery of the 'endogenous opioids' – substances resembling morphine and heroin naturally present in the brain which are involved in the experience of pain. It begins to look, too, as if a special substance is involved in sleep. More mysteriously, the psychedelic drugs affect perception by altering brain chemistry. One of them, MDA, actually induces 'out of the body' experiences.

There seem to be differences in the distribution of some of these materials as between men and women; I will hazard the guess that changes during the course of the lifespan will soon be found. It is too early to assess their significance in relation to mind, but clearly it is fundamental.

Quite distinct from these neuroregulators are the hormones or chemical messengers which the brain – to be exact, the hypothalamus – emits. They regulate the pituitary gland, which lies below the hypothalamus and in turn emits other hormones which regulate certain bodily functions. The idea that the brain used hormones to control the supply of other hormones was regarded as incredible when first suggested. It took nearly twenty years of effort to isolate any of the hypothalamic hormones: the first two were isolated in 1972. The pituitary, it turns out, regulates other glands – the thyroid, the sex glands or gonads, and the adrenal cortex.

The isolation and identification of these master-hormones has been a titanic task, for which a Nobel prize was recently awarded. It took about five hundred tons of brain tissue to yield one milligram of the hormone – about the weight of a postage stamp. Once isolated, the structure was determined and a method of synthesis devised, so that these hormones are now available in gram quantities. The task took twenty years.

While many of these substances facilitate transmission of the nerve impulse (i.e. boost it) others have recently been found which inhibit or block it. So the long-standing assumption that the brain was primarily concerned with transmitting impulses turns out to be only one side of the coin: it obstructs them too, and in the next chapter we shall see how important this is.

Conversely there are hormones produced in the body which radically affect the development of the brain. The gonadal hormones seem to be necessary for masculine performance and not merely for masculine motivation. Presumably they enter the nucleus of the brain cells and remain there, bringing about changes in its neural or neurosecretory activity, but all this is still mysterious. Some males seem to be unable to utilise male hormone. Though on examination their chromosomes prove to be male, they look like girls and are so brought up.

Chemical substances move slowly compared with electric pulses. They mediate changes over hours rather than seconds, sometimes much longer. Their action is probably not indiscriminate but targeted to particular cells. A reassessment of our whole conception of how the brain functions is in train as a result of these discoveries.

In this chapter I have sought to give you a picture of the structure of the brain which will prove helpful in our further discussions. But it is a basic principle of biology that for every structure there is a function and for every function a structure. In this chapter I have said only a bare minimum about function and then only to clarify an aspect of structure. In the next, I want to consider the functioning of the brain as a topic in its own right. It is an area where our ideas have changed radically and will no doubt continue to do so.

4

Paradoxical Brain

NOT VERY BRIGHT

Between 1945 and 1948, Seymour Kety, who was later to become head of Psychiatric Research at Massachusetts General Hospital, together with co-workers showed that the total power consumed by the brain was about twenty watts – one-fifth the power consumed by an ordinary electric light bulb. He also showed that the difference in power consumption between full consciousness and deep coma was only a matter of seven or eight watts. Why, then, is thinking such hard work?

Source: S. Kety, 'Energy Metabolism of the brain during Sleep', CIBA symposium *The Nature of Sleep*, p. 376, Eds G. E. W. Wolstenhome and M. O'Connor, 1961.

Misleading Analogies

In a famous experiment, the American psychologist Karl Lashley removed increasing quantities of the brains of rats which had been taught to run in a maze. He found that, provided he did not remove the visual cortex and thus blind them, he could remove up to ninety per cent of their cortex without significant deterioration in their power to thread their way through the maze. There is no man-made machine of which this is true. Try removing nine-tenths of your radio and see if it still brings in a signal! It would seem that each specific memory is distributed in some way over the brain as a whole.

Similarly, you can remove considerable amounts of the motor cortex without paralysing any one group of muscles. All that happens is a general deterioration of motor performance. The evolutionary advantages of such an arrangement are manifest: when pursued, it is better to run clumsily than not at all. But how this remarkable distribution of function is achieved we do not really understand. We see, at all events, that the brain relies on patterns of increasing refinement and not (as man-made machines do) on chains of cause and effect.

The fact is, the brain is not comparable with anything else. In the seventeenth century, the only means of transmitting power for any distance was by means of liquids in pipes: hydraulic power. Consequently the physiologists of the time likened the nerves to pipes and imagined some kind of 'spirits' flowing through them. When the telephone exchange was invented, the brain was promptly compared with a telephone exchange. People are readily hypnotised by their own analogies, so the brain was at once conceived as a focus for messages from the organs and as a control centre which could send out messages to the muscles. Quite what role the operator played was left rather obscure. Then, when the computer was invented, the brain was compared with a computer. It is true that the programming and structure of computers show certain analogies with what goes on in the brain. But we may be sure that, in the twenty-first century, when some sophisticated machine the existence of which we now scarcely contemplate has become commonplace, the brain will be compared to that.

The brain differs from the machines with which we are familiar in other ways. One of its unique features is its extraordinary capacity for self-repair. After severe brain damage, from shell-fragments or the surgeon's knife, the victim may be incapacitated for a while but often recovers, over a period of weeks or months, many or all of the lost capacities. Not only does the brain rewire itself, but it redistributes its equipment, borrowing (so to say) from other functions some of their spare equipment.

Not only does it adapt to damage, it adapts quite remarkably to changed circumstances: after a few days in space, for instance, astronauts learn (largely unconsciously) how to cope with weightlessness. The psychologist G. M. Stratton fitted himself with spectacles which inverted the world for him. After a few days, the world suddenly swung the right way up, in his perception; when he removed the glasses it was upside down again. Thus it is not merely at the level of mechanical adjustment but also at the subjective level that such adjustment occurs.

The late Warren McCullough, the sage of the Massachusetts Institute of Technology, once told me how he was taking off a pair of heavy boots and putting on a pair of moccasins when he was interrupted. He stumped out wearing a boot on the right foot and a moccasin on the left to cope with the problem; afterwards he found that his judgment of weight held in the hands was affected. Of two similar hammers the one on the same side as the moccasin felt heavier. The brain had reset the bias on the left side of the body so as to equalise the performance of the legs and had mistakenly assumed (if I may so put it) that a corresponding adjustment was required for the arms too. (This suggests a nice experiment. Try putting one foot in hot water and one in cold, and see if your judgment of the temperature with the hands is affected.)

While the brain can adjust to temporary changes in circumstances by resetting certain thresholds, rather as we turn a thermostat up or down, it can also adapt – during its early development – to the kind of world it has to live in. A kitten brought up in an environment with no horizontal lines does not develop the ability to discriminate horizontals, but is very good at verticals. It is for this sort of reason that, if you wish to be a pianist, you must practise conscientiously while young: by so doing you force the brain to develop additional 'wiring' and equipment to perform this function. Similarly, of course, for any other specialised activity.

As Professor Richard Gregory has said, the brain achieves remarkable reliability despite being built of unreliable components. Neurones sometimes fire for no very obvious reason – probably some chance local change in the chemical environment. In engineering terms, the system is 'noisy'. The brain defends itself against such random errors by averaging. Broadly speaking, any one neurone receives stimuli from at least a hundred others before it fires. Thus one or two random pulses will make little difference. One consequence of this 'averaging' is to protect the brain against damage and decay. Even if fifty neurones were incapacitated, there would still be fifty left to do the job, with a somewhat larger chance of error. It is easy to see that if you carry out a mathematical operation – say, solving an equation – and get a single figure wrong, the answer will be incorrect, perhaps wildly so. But if you make the calculation a hundred times and average the answers, even two or three errors will hardly affect the result. We call this 'parallel processing'.

Taking the idea still further, we can see that this results in the brain opting for the most probable interpretation. The brain, so to say, is constantly calling for a show of hands. We therefore call it 'probabilistic' – in contrast with most computers and man-made devices which are 'deterministic'. Now any machine which assesses probabilities is *ipso facto* a classifying machine, sorting data into two categories, probable and improbable, acceptable and unacceptable. We know, naturally, that brains do classify and now we see that they have the right kind of structure for such a function.

Spacecraft have to be equipped with computers which will continue to function effectively for months and even years without attention. Designers of such equipment are beginning to borrow from the logic of the brain to design computers sufficiently reliable and envisage, for the even longer space voyages of the future, computers based extensively on parallel processing, which could carry on even if a micrometeorite rips through their innards.

But while the brain achieves remarkable reliability, in the sense of being able to carry on despite damage, it also contains an element of chance. Where two interpretations are about equally probable, the brain may jump either way, influenced by chance factors – fatigue, associated ideas, or even minor physicochemical shifts within individual cells. As Delisle Burns says in his excellent book, *The Uncertain Brain*: 'I am after all an unpredictable machine.' That is something many people find comforting.

Inquisitive Filter

Always keeping in view our objective of seeing whether the mind-brain identity theory makes any sense in relation to the neurological facts, I must tell you a good deal more about how the brain functions – especially since scientists' conceptions are changing so radically – before we can attempt an assessment. The brain is a very unusual machine in more ways than one.

Another major defect of the telephone exchange analogy is that it depicts the brain as inactive, as waiting inertly for a 'stimulus' before emitting a 'response'. But the fact is that the brain is incessantly active – even in sleep. At the behavioural level we can see this in the form of curiosity and inquisitiveness. The brain is always asking questions, seeking to find patterns. That is why when we look at the clouds, or the embers in the fire, we find it easy to visualise landscapes, animals and so forth. As Michelangelo said: 'I only have to throw a pot of paint on the wall to find there fine landscapes.' The brain seems constantly to be checking what it sees against what it has on record, to see if a match can be made. And it detects even very incomplete similarities, as it does when it recognises a face in the half-dozen bold strokes drawn by a cartoonist.

The restlessness of the brain is also detectable when we study it in detail. 'The first thing which strikes anyone who inserts a micro-electrode into the grey matter of the "resting" spinal cord in the decerebrate animal,' says Delisle Burns, 'is the large and continued traffic of activity and the essentially unpredictable behaviour of the cells encountered.' Scientists have only become aware of this firework display of activity in the last twenty years or so. It was not until 1951, when Bernard Katz and a colleague inserted the newly invented micro-recording pipette into the brain – a pipette with a tip so fine it could be inserted into a single cell – that the unpredictability of the brain was demonstrated.

The origin of the electrical rhythms which the brain is continually producing remains rather mysterious. They seem to arise in the dendrites, and even a single cell will produce a rhythm. Sometimes all the cells throb together; that is when they have nothing much to do. Give them a job, and the pattern breaks up, different cell assemblies beating at different rates and amplitudes. I am reminded of the 'carrier wave' emitted by a radio or television transmitter, on which the subtle vibrations of speech sounds or music can be superimposed. But when the microphone is disconnected, the smooth regular carrier wave continues to ripple the ether and can be detected by suitable equipment.

The analogy with television may be quite a close one. If you had to transmit simultaneously the hundred thousand or so picture elements of which the image on the screen is effectively composed, you would need an equal number of radio channels to do it. But scanning the picture and transmitting each spot in succession – though all within the space of one-fifteenth of a second – the picture is compressed into a single channel. The brain may make a similar economy. The penalty of such a system is that brief flashes will appear as spots or lines on the screen. So it is suggestive that when the eye is presented with brief flashes at about the same frequency as the alpha rhythm, strange geometrical shapes are seen.

And this brings us to the brain's central problem: how to cope with too much information. We cannot take in, much less remember, all the information available to us. The brain has complex filtering arrangements to cut down the load. The most obvious is the one we call 'attention'. When we 'concentrate' on something we 'shut our ears' to everything else. It had long been taken as Gospel that nerves from the sense organs invariably ran to the brain, but Sweden's Ragnar Granit showed that nerves also run from the brain to sense organs (efferents) and serve either to damp them down or key them to a higher pitch.

However, it is not only the sense organs which are involved in attention. The brain distributes its equipment, calling in more for difficult tasks, which is why we dislike being distracted by noise or conversation when listening to music or trying to perform a calculation in our head. The interruption reduces the amount of brain we can apply to the main task.

The question of how we decide what features of the environment merit special attention is an interesting one. It is difficult to avoid the almost incredible conclusion that everything is submitted to the cortex for recognition and preliminary assessment at the unconscious level – on the strength of which the arousal system damps down both sense organs and channels, as well as the analysing equipment, for those which are of lesser interest and boosts those which are needed for the more interesting data.

That the brain is constantly refining the amount of information it absorbs can be deduced from the fact that when we look at an object or a scene, we normally carry away only a general impression of the most striking features. And as time goes by, our memory is simplified still further, various minor details being suppressed. Really dull details, like phone numbers once heard, are jettisoned in a matter of a few seconds.

This too tells us something significant about the way the brain works.

It deals with hierarchies, or, better said, with nested structures. If you have a picture and part is destroyed, you lose that part totally and keep the rest; but the brain keeps the whole picture, just blurring the details. This parallels what we said earlier about performance: after general damage, you do not lose all performance of some one function, but rather do everything slightly less well. (There are exceptions to this, where damage is quite local, as we have already seen.) There seems to be no word for this general degradation of function and its converse, the finding of pattern within pattern within pattern, which is awkward as I shall have more to say about it. I shall call it the hypermorphic method as opposed to the anamorphic methods with which we are more familiar.

Where There's a Way There's a Will

Next time you find yourself walking on the seashore, you might like to try a simple experiment in inhibition – or perhaps I should say demonstration. Find a nice fat starfish and turn it on its back. It will thrash about, waving its five arms vigorously but ineffectually. Soon it will discover that by bearing down with two of them and stopping with the other three it can manage to flop over into its normal position. Whereupon it will hurry away, cursing.

The technical term for deliberately not contracting a muscle is inhibition. Or rather, for not blocking the nerve impulse which would cause it to contract. If you had been so unkind as to drip strychnine, which blocks inhibition, into the poor creature's nerve-net (it has no brain), it would have been unable to stop three of its arms thrashing and so would have remained upside down indefinitely. In this simple way you will have demonstrated the importance of *not* doing something in order to achieve your ends; in a word, of inhibition. When you raise your forearm by contracting your biceps muscle, you must at the same time relax your triceps muscle or the two will strain against each other, and you will say that you have cramp. A beautiful mechanism known as reciprocal inhibition normally arranges this very satisfactorily.

Strychnine being, as I have said, a blocking agent for inhibition, the effect of a large dose is to throw you into convulsions: all your muscles contract wildly. From which some neurophysiologists infer that muscles are always ready to contract, once the brakes are taken off, a startling reversal of the usual conception. Tetanus and lock-jaw are more limited examples of the same effect. Epileptic convulsions also display an inhibitory failure at work. In contrast, the state of immobility known as cataplexy would seem to result from excess of inhibition.

Inhibition of motor nerves has long been recognised, but it is only recently that neurologists have begun to see that inhibition, in addition to working in the body – in muscles and sense organs – is also a major feature of the brain. To visualise the brain as an inhibitory system is, I believe, a shift of fundamental importance. For instance, obsessive behaviour – such as worrying – can be regarded as an inability to stop attending, a failure of inhibition. Schizophrenics, likewise, often complain of 'having too many thoughts'. As one told the psychologist A. McGhie: 'I just can't shut things out . . . Everything seems to grip my attention.' In short, our problem is not so much to attend, as to *dis-attend* to what is not relevant.

That the brain is almost invariably treated as a facilitatory mechanism is perhaps a legacy of the telephone-exchange analogy. Electrical impulses are conceived as arriving at neurones and causing them to 'fire' and so transmit further pulses, much as happens in man-made computers. It is known, of course, that some of the inputs arriving at a neurone are inhibitory – they discourage it from firing. Indeed, there are neurones which seem specialised for blocking impulses: the 'inhibitory interneurones' which are situated, like gate-keepers, between neurones of other types. It is also known that the chemical substances, called neurotransmitters, secreted at the junction between nerve-processes of one neurone and the body of another are of two kinds: facilitatory and inhibitory. Despite this, the role of inhibition in the brain has received very little attention. As I suspect this may be one of the reasons for our failure to break through, I would like to pursue the point a little further.

Inhibition works not only at motor but also at sensory levels. Our sense receptors are normally held below their level of maximum sensitivity but when we want to, we can sharpen them by disinhibition. 'He pricked up his ears', we say, to indicate not merely closer attention to auditory input, but also a raising of the level of sensitivity. I have reached an age when I find it difficult to read in a bad light. I find it hard to read the numbers in a phone directory at night, in an ill-lit call-box. But if I make an intense effort, I can usually bring them into view. Perhaps what I actually did was to lessen the inhibition?

Though it is not often noted, in a motor cortex of the brain are found 'sensory suppressor strips' – they were discovered in 1937 – and hence it is reasonable to suspect there may be similar suppressor zones in the sensory cortex. These have not been demonstrated, but there are suggestive facts. For instance, patients undergoing brain operations have reported that 'one ear goes deaf or partly deaf' when the surgeon was stimulating their auditory cortex.

We adapt to continued stimuli. We become unaware of the pressure of the chair on our rump, unaware of the ticking of the clock. We fail to notice the chest vibrations of our own voice. These, too, are demonstrations of inhibition. Indeed, attention in general must be an inhibitory process, for attention means blocking out all uninteresting material so that the interesting material can be processed without distraction. Repression, too – perhaps the whole idea of the unconscious, in the Freudian sense – suggests the inhibiting of certain material from rising to consciousness. Freud, by training a physiologist, used the word 'inhibition' in keen awareness of its practical meaning, and this leads to the thought that remembering may consist in the removal of an inhibition, which would help to solve another mystery, and it is inhibition we appeal to when we say, 'Make your mind a blank.'

In short, to perform an action, we do not have to will, we merely have to choose. And that is just what computerlike systems are very good at. I am reminded of the indicators which used to be found in the kitchens of great houses to show which bell had been rung. The current did not haul the flag into position – it merely removed a catch which allowed it to fall. All the flags were poised to fall under the influence of gravity. The message simply had to disinhibit one of them. Thus a small signal could produce a large effect.

I do not doubt that what is true of motor actions is true in a larger sense of all the decisions we make. We plan various alternative courses of action; then we disinhibit one of them and say, 'I have decided what to do.'

As I have already said, the older textbooks divide the subject of psychology into three sections, known as Cognition, Conation and Affect. In less pretentious language: thinking, willing and feeling. Of these, we can now delete 'willing'. We do not have to will because the brain is willing to do anything it knows how to do, all the time. All we have to do is decide what is to be done, and take the brake off. Where there's a way, if you will allow me the fancy, there's a will. Thus we do not need a ghost in the machine to account for volition.

Of course, we also use the word 'will' when we force ourselves to do something we do not want to do. A part of the brain sees the long-term advantages of some action, another part sees the immediate disadvantages – or it may be that we have to weigh the advantage to others against the sacrifice of our own interests. If we have made a habit of self-abnegation, we shall have facilitated certain circuits and are more likely to decide on self-sacrifice another time. We might call this 'training the will'. But we shall be talking about a different mechanism from the volition by which we, having decided what to do, actually do it.

This mechanism, as you will perceive, echoes the mechanism at the level of the muscles themselves, but at a higher organisational level. Since the brain is a system of hierarchical structures (we shall see this in more detail shortly), it may be that this pattern repeats all the way up to the top. This would make the brain a device for *not* doing things, in a context where doing everything is possible. So, if we desire to explain Omega Effects, and conceivably such effects as telepathy, perhaps we should be thinking in terms of the brain as a device which blocks these possibilities (most of the time) rather than as a device which generates them.

If this seems at first sight too wild an idea, I would point to the simple analogy of a switch in an electric light circuit. All the circumstances required to produce light are present – power station, transmission lines, electric bulbs and so on. What the switch does is prevent the phenomenon occurring, until it is thrown. In the same sort of way, Omega Effects may not be (as they seem to be) a function of the brain itself. The brain may be just the switch, the final link in the chain. We may have to understand the total system of the universe to understand how they arise.

If I have convinced you that inhibition is a concept of critical importance you may wonder why scientists have been so dilatory, even reluctant, to embrace the idea. It has been around a long time. Aristotle noted that you can't talk and listen to flute music at the same time. John Locke commented on 'the power to forbear'. In the nineteenth century, inhibition was first seen in modern terms as a neurological function. The brilliant English neurologist Charles Bell had a clear concept of inhibition, though he lacked the word for it. Other workers noted how some nerves damp down, rather than stimulate: thus the vagus slows the heart, the splanchnic nerve immobilises the gut. But it was Pavlov's forerunner, the great Russian physiologist Sechenov, who first actually demonstrated inhibition in the brain, applying a salt crystal to frogs' brains and showing that their muscular activity increased instead of subsiding. Sechenov, the son of a peasant woman and a landowner (which perhaps explains his lifelong interest in the education of the poor and especially of women) entered the army in order to get a free medical training. But his frankness to the braggart son of a senior officer caused his dismissal before the course was completed. He starved in St Petersburg, eating (as he noted in old age) meat twice a week only, and having tea – Russians attach great importance to tea – once a month, and it was in St Petersburg that he performed a noble self-experiment. He wished to see if a higher stimulus would inhibit a lower one. So he dipped a finger into acid, while his girl friend tickled him. (I take a liberty in assuming that it was the future Mrs Sechenov who carried out this service for science. But Sechenov, who normally was good about giving the names of his assistants, is curiously silent – and somehow I do not see him asking a Russian lab-assistant to engage in slap-and-tickle with him.)

Sechenov eventually published his seminal *Reflexes of the Brain*, in which mind was dealt with deterministically; the censors thought that a book which treated the brain as a machine might unsettle non-scientific readers and it had to be withdrawn, to be republished in a scientific journal.

By the end of the century, the idea of inhibition was widely accepted and appears in the works of William James. Charles Sherrington demonstrated its importance in bodily contexts – his *Integrative Action of the Nervous System* might equally well have been called *Inhibitory Action of the Nervous System*. But he lacked the imagination to extend the concept from body to brain. Then the behaviourists came on the scene. There was no room in their black box for inhibition. The job of stimuli was to evoke responses, not to inhibit them, and the word ceased to be heard. It is only in the last decade or so, as behaviourism slowly crumbles into the limbo of lost causes, that inhibition has been given a new lease of life. The new techniques to which I have referred, by revealing the presence of neurones specialised for inhibition, in sensory and motor systems and in the brain itself, have made such recognition inevitable. Even more decisive has been the discovery of inhibitory chemical substances, as I have already mentioned.

Before I leave the subject of inhibition, however, a few words about the reciprocal kind, which I mentioned in connection with muscular action. It runs on the brain too. In your brain, down in the hypothalamus, there are two centres which regulate how much you eat and when. There is a hunger centre which flops into the on position when your blood sugar level (and other clues) indicate that you need refuelling. You then eat, if God permits, until your satiety centre says: Enough! and switches the hunger centre off. (At least, this is what happens in rats – *you* may be on a slimming course.) Conversely, when the hunger centre flops 'on' it switches the satiety centre 'off'. This mechanism, which is known as reciprocal inhibition, mirrors the relationship between opposing muscles, to which I have referred. Thus it is not the case that there is a single eating centre which detects hunger and gradually becomes ineffective as blood-sugar builds up; instead there are two centres in a flip-flop configuration, very like two oscillators feeding one another in an electronic circuit. This explains, incidentally, why *L'appetit vient en mangeant*. It explains why we continue to eat once we have started and often carry on longer than is wise.

I mention the matter because the brain seems to use a lot of flip-flop instead of using volume-controls. Sleeping–waking, alertness–relaxation, aggression–co-operation, approach–withdrawal, pleasure–unpleasure, are some of the many systems which are almost certainly controlled by flip-flops, perhaps domination–submission is another.

A House Divided

As is now widely known, the limbic brain contains pleasure centres: an area which, when electrically stimulated, causes intense satisfaction, often sexually toned. Rats implanted with an electrode in this area and provided with a bar to press which delivers an electric pulse to the electrode, stimulate themselves many thousands of times before they collapse in exhaustion. They will brave powerful electric shocks in order to get at the pedal which gives them so much reward. Human beings have occasionally been implanted in the same way, usually to relieve the pain of cancer, and stimulate themselves with equal enthusiasm. Perhaps the future will see healthy people thus implanted: several have already asked for such an operation. It has been suggested, not too seriously, that the sexual act of the future may consist of a man controlling a girl's stimulator, while she controls his.

While scientists have been busy exploring the effects of stimulating the pleasure areas and trying to relate them to theories of motivation, none have stopped to ask the big philosophical question: what is there about these particular tiny areas of brain which has such a unique and powerful Omega Effect? The cells in the relevant regions look no different under the microscope from any other brain cells. I cannot find that anyone has made a Herculean effort to find a difference, and I rather doubt whether they would succeed if they tried. The brain, as I have tried to indicate, doesn't seem to work that way. Or, if it does, then the mechanisms lie at a level which eludes all existing techniques.

Be this as it may, the existence of these centres presents materialists with a direct challenge, which they have studiously ignored. If the brain 'is' the mind, then septal cells 'are' pleasure. And that is clearly nonsense.

When James Olds and Brenda Milner published their famous paper on the pleasure centres in 1958 it caused a sensation, for it completely wrecked the 'drive theory' on which many psychologists, and certainly most American psychologists, had rested their hopes. Animals, including man, were supposed to behave as they do because they are animated by certain ill-defined 'drives' which were alleged to be reduced by their actions. Thus the 'sex-drive' was reduced by performing the sexual act, the hunger drive by eating and so on. No one knew how many drives there were or what structures produced them, or how. Olds and Milner, having demonstrated that many different behaviours were keyed to pleasure, reported bluntly: 'There are no drives to reduce.'

The importance of the pleasure centres has been pushed to wild extremes, notably by Campbell in his book *The Pleasure Areas*, in which he declares, 'Mutations endured when they increased the animal's chance of obtaining pleasurable and avoiding displeasurable [*sic*] sensations,' and not its chance of surviving. He also says: 'A sensory input only has meaning if it activates the pleasure centres.' This is certainly untrue: anything which causes pain has meaning, and arguably pain-avoidance is a more powerful motive than the lure for pleasure.

Not far from the pleasure area lie 'punishment centres' or 'unpleasure areas', stimulation of which causes unease mounting to wild attempts at avoidance, accompanied by fear and rage, as the voltage is increased. Unpleasure is not the same as pain, though the two may be associated. The feeling which preoccupies us when extremely hungry, thirsty or sexually frustrated is not pain; nor is our reaction to a cacophonous noise or the sight of another person in pain, and it is certainly not pleasure.

The discovery that there are two distinct motivational centres – pleasure and unpleasure – is more significant than may at first appear. As everyone knows, many mechanisms have controls which operate on either side of a balance point. More treble if you turn the knob to the right, more bass if you turn it to the left. The brain's arousal system is like that: turn it up for extreme alertness and activity, down for relaxation and sleep. Nature might have provided such a control for motivation: up for pleasure, down for discomfort. The fact that she provided *two* controls allows the possibility that both can be activated at once: that pain can be pleasurable (as in masochism), that pleasure can be painful. (It's too much – I can't bear it.)

Much human behaviour is more easily understood when we bear in mind that we have *two* motivational systems which can be in opposition. We constantly trade off losses and gains: the effort of climbing a mountain against the pleasure of reaching the top.

The eminent animal psychologist Theodore Schneirla, from his base in the American Museum of Natural History, traces all behaviour to the two responses, approach and withdrawal. We approach what causes pleasure, withdraw from what causes unpleasure or pain. When the same objective offers both at once we are at a loss. The child who seeks love from its mother but is rejected or ill-treated is a classic example. We solve such conflicts when they become severe by repressing one or other emotion and thus neurosis is born, by stages which Freud has detailed. Here, at least, psychoanalytic theory finds an adequate physiological basis.

Charles Fair, a pharmacologist who has thought about the relationship of brain structure to its function, has analysed mental function in a slightly different way. Some of the time, he points out, we are busy surviving: we seek food, warmth, friendship, etc., in order to maintain ourselves. Pleasure is the aim. At other times, however, we have to rise to emergencies – to cope with instant threats to our whole existence. Fear of mutilation, maltreatment or death is the motive. Emergencies take priority over survival. The deer engaged in feeding, when it sees the approaching tiger, abandons its meal and flees. The body also is prepared to sacrifice long-term interests to urgent short-term ones. Rising to an emergency may cause stresses which shorten life – but that it is better than death immediately. The lizard abandoning its tail in order to escape a predator prefigures the complex stress responses of man.

This dualism is echoed in the autonomic (self-governing) nervous system. It was in 1845 that a German scientist, Weber, discovered a nerve – the vagus – which slowed the heart when it was stimulated. From this small beginning grew the realisation that many of the internal organs are under the control of a nervous system which is, at least in part, independent of the main nervous system represented by the brain, spinal cord and its sensory and motor termini: in short, not under conscious control. The network of nerves has affinities with the nervous systems of the animals which preceded the vertebrates in the evolutionary sequence. It looks after the humdrum body activities: nutrition, breathing, excretion, fluid balance and so on.

Though not under conscious control, the autonomic system is linked to the brain through the hypothalamus, which is closely associated with our emotions. We shall discuss the emotions later. Here I wish only to say that the autonomic nervous system is divided essentially into two opposing parts, known as the sympathetic and the parasympathetic systems. The former marshals energy for instant use (emergency), the latter seeks to conserve and restore bodily resources. Animals with damaged autonomic systems cannot react to emergencies or restore themselves after over-exertion. They cannot withstand oxygen lack, temperature extremes, loss of blood or shortage of blood sugar. A shift to the sympathetic leads to alertness and then to aggression and manic activity. Stimulate the parasympathetic and you become calm, sleepy and, in the long run, depressed. We are therefore essentially divided individuals. Man is that great and true Amphibium, as Sir Thomas Browne said.

Functioning of the Brain

Feedback has been called nature's most important invention. Instead of just responding to a stimulus, you correct your response in the light of how effective it is proving. When Norbert Wiener formalised this idea under the name of cybernetics in the 1950s, the favourite illustration was an automatic pilot, which detects if the boat or aircraft is diverging from course and corrects it. Another often cited example is the thermostat, which turns the heating on if the house cools and off when it becomes too hot; or rather, when the temperature falls below a preselected point or rises above it.

Such mechanisms may be said to have a purpose or aim. The pilot aims to keep the boat on a particular course; the thermostat's 'purpose' is to keep the house environment at a chosen temperature. Such adjustments closely resemble the responses made by animals and even by plants. Nature is replete with feedback loops in which the output of a system is monitored and used to correct the input. You aim to hit the nail on the head; when you see you are hitting too much to one side, you slightly adjust your muscular programme so as to hit it fair and square. Or to take an even simpler example, when you burn your fingers you withdraw your hand, automatically.

The brain contains countless feedback loops, but the significant feature is that they are nested hypermorphically. Each level sets the aim for the level below. In this way, the brain parallels purpose, which is also hierarchic. You want to drive to the city – so you want the car – so you must unlock the garage – so you must grasp the key of the garage door, insert it and turn it. But at each level there is a certain amount of room for caprice, a certain amount of 'play'. Your thermostat does not hold the temperature exactly at seventy degrees. It must fall to about sixty-five before the heating comes on, rise to about seventy-five degrees before it switches off.

But scientists have recently discovered a curious fact about the manner in which the brain monitors the movements of its body. It relies not on what the muscles do, but on what they are *told* to do. You can temporarily paralyse the lower half of a person's body by an injection in his lower spine. If he then tries to raise one leg (provided he cannot see it) he will believe that he has actually done so, although the leg is in reality still hanging helplessly paralysed. If he can see it, he will be deeply shaken by the disparity between what he sees and what he feels. (Here again is an Omega Effect: he is conscious of what he sees but somehow even more conscious of what he feels.)

There are, then, two contrasting brain systems: an analytic one which dissects the environment into units of information, and which works, so to say, upward; and an intentional one, which uses that information to affect the environment, and works, we may say, downward. The first system is causal, in the normal sense, the second is purposive. Its causes lie in the future. Purposiveness is what distinguishes living organisms from dead structures, and the implications of this for man are something we shall have to return to later. As Karl Pribram has shown, there are definite areas in the fore-brain which underlie each of these functions, the analytic and the intentional.

Of course this is far from being an exhaustive account of brain function, even in its most general aspects, but it will serve our present purpose.

Further Mysteries

Scientists have adapted to the idea that the brain is not only an electrical but also a chemical device. They have hardly yet absorbed the notion that it may have a third, wholly unexplored, aspect. It may be a magnetic device. Hamer, Gavalas-Medici and Bawin have made an attempt to study the effect of electromagnetic fields on the brain. The results are curious and unexpected. For example, monkeys shorten their time estimates when exposed to fields alternating about seven times a second, though the effect is much smaller at ten cycles per second. Cats were sent to sleep by waves modulated at 150 cycles/sec. and, what was much odder, if they had been conditioned, it took two months to extinguish the reflex.

Doctors have noted that admissions to mental hospitals rise just before a magnetic storm, and arctic explorers have reported extreme irritability at these times. There are indications that stress diseases in general are associated with high sunspot activity, which of course causes magnetic storms on the sun and later on the earth. Like straws in the wind, such disparate facts suggest that the brain has realms of complexity beyond our imagining.

Research is difficult, for the magnetic fields are faint so that the subject must be screened more elaborately from any local fields existing at the time, as a result of electrical equipment. It may be some time before we really know whether a whole new chapter has to be opened before we can say that we understand the brain.

Then again, the brain contains clocklike mechanisms which are responsible for our feeling sleepy or wakeful in a regular daily rhythm. A fascinating subject which need not detain us here, though I would risk the guess that the relationship of time factors with the brain will prove increasingly important. How can we recognise a tune? Only by some kind of analysis extended over time. How do we time a complex movement, like hitting a tennis ball, so that it culminates at the right moment as well as in the right place? How is it that many people can waken themselves at the precise time they wish to? And as I have already said, it is the time-pattern of neuronal discharge which conveys the message, not the intensity.

And then there is the very strange fact that we are sensitive to variations in the light level. Strong lighting raises our spirits, feeble lighting depresses them. The pineal gland, or 'third eye', is directly responsive to light in birds and amphibians, lying as it does under a thin lamina of skull. In thick-skulled men, and other mammals, it has learned to use information picked up by the eyes, but still continues to exert odd chemical effects. For example, if you blind a hamster, its testes become smaller – but if you also remove the pineal gland, this does not occur. Again, if female rats are kept continuously in the light, they remain in oestrus – persistently – but this can be prevented by injecting pineal extract.

Long before this was known, in the 1930s, it was shown that the body tonus is raised by high light levels: we brace ourselves up in the sun. I have often noticed in a television studio, how everyone slumps down when the studio lighting is switched off at the end of a scene; and how they perk up when it comes on again. A logical step was to see if other sensory inputs had the same effect. It was found that 'bright' sounds and 'dull' sounds and even bright and dull smells also braced or relaxed. This was dramatically shown in a soldier who had an injury to his cerebellum (which would normally have restrained his response). When a high E was played on the violin, his arms involuntarily rose; when a low G was played, they sank down again.

I have made so many points in this chapter that perhaps a recapitulation will be helpful. The brain is not a telephone exchange; it is active and inquisitive. It is also a filter, choosing what it will admit. It works by inhibition of pre-set patterns more often than not. It is hierarchically organised. It prefers to balance opposing systems instead of using volume controls.

Since so much detail obscures the view, to conclude the chapter let us pull back and try to see the wood rather than the trees.

In a broad sense, one might say that the brain mirrors the environment. Since the wiring and the thresholds are specified by the kind of world that exists, there must be some kind of homology between the two. It is a homology of transition probabilities. Similarly the brain mirrors the internal world. It is the brain's task to try to reconcile the macrocosm with the microcosm. Moreover, the brain models the world not only spatially but temporally. Prediction is one of its essential attributes – I shall argue the point in more detail later – and the laws which govern the chain of events are mirrored in the brain as well as the events themselves.

The brain is constantly busy monitoring the discrepancies between its predictions and what is happening.

However, my object in this chapter and the last is not just to reveal the brain as an incredibly sophisticated piece of machinery, more complex by far than any mechanism known to us. It is rather to show that it is a mechanism of a different kind. It differs both quantitatively and qualitatively. Hence we are simply not in a position to say what is or is not possible to such a unique system, or to dogmatise about what properties it might exhibit.

Professor F. O. Schmitt, who is head of MIT's Neurosciences Research Program, after a career embracing London, Berlin, Washington, Chicago and Valparaiso, is a man who speaks with a certain authority. He says that the circuitry we know looks like a service mechanism for a higher function and concludes bluntly: 'The enormous complexity . . . of the interactions possible . . . suggests that . . . output may not be predictable on the basis of unit properties alone.'

The brain is capable of being in millions of different states, and these states are modified every few milliseconds. Not only is the electrical connectivity constantly altering but so are the chemical balances and sequences. Sir John Eccles, the Nobel Prize winner, has declared that for every mental event there is a unique brain-state.

We should be arrogant indeed to assert that such a mechanism could only exhibit the sort of properties found in the vastly simpler mechanisms which we construct ourselves.

PART TWO

Consciousness

5

On Knowing That You Know

TAKING THE INTENTION FOR THE DEED

There is a chemical substance called succinyl chloride which has the remarkable property of disconnecting the nerves which activate the main body muscles. In 1964 American scientists tried the heroic experiment of injecting it into the spinal columns of five volunteers. The experience was so traumatic that it could only be maintained for a hundred seconds. The men were seized with terror because, of course, they were unable to breathe, and sought frantically to claw the recording electrodes from their heads and to escape. All that the experimenters could see, however, was a slight quivering. Yet – and this is the curious part – the subjects were convinced that they had made large movements. They were 'conscious' of something which in fact had not happened. Classic theories that motor output is essential to perception were proved wrong. But what was proved right?

Source: Campbell, *et al.*, 'Characteristics of a conditioned response in human subjects, etc.', *J. abn. & soc. Psychol.* (1964) *68*:627–39.

The Blindsight of Helen

It was in 1967 that Nick Humphrey and Lewis Weiskrantz, then at the Cambridge Psychological Laboratory, reported an astonishing discovery. After some trouble getting Home Office permission for the experiment, Weiskrantz had removed from two monkeys the part of the cortex concerned with vision – the striate cortex – and in consequence they were blind. The strange thing was that they gradually recovered a limited but effective amount of sight. Weiskrantz christened this surprising phenomenon 'blindsight'.

One of these monkeys, Helen by name, was studied intensively for another eight years. She was then sacrificed and the brain was examined to make sure that the operation had really and truly removed the striate cortex. It had.

For the first three years Humphrey tested Helen solely in her cage, but in 1970 he moved to the Sub-department of Animal Behaviour at Madingley, where there was no testing-room available, but where there was access to a large field and wood. Here, at the instigation of an assistant, Mireille Bertrand, he put Helen on a leash and took her for walks in the open. 'In the context of this new-found freedom,' Humphrey told me, 'she began to exploit her vision in quite unexpected ways.' At first she often bumped into obstacles and several times fell into a pond. 'But then, day by day, there was an extraordinary change in her behaviour. On the one hand, she began systematically to anticipate and skirt round obstacles in her path, while on the other she began actually to approach the trees in the field, turning towards them as we passed by, walking up and reaching out to grasp their trunks. There was an old elm tree which she especially liked to climb, and, with her perched in a hole in its trunk, I would hold up bits of fruit and nuts for her to reach for; and now she did something else she had not done before – she would reach out when the target was within arm's reach but ignore it if it was too far away. It was clear that, given at last the experience of three-dimensional space she was quickly developing a kind of three-dimensional vision.'

Now a room was made available for tests indoors, with an area in which she could move around. 'The game was for her to pick up small bits of chocolate or currants from the white floor. She soon learned, for instance, to run straight to a tiny currant 2·5 m. [eight feet] distant from her. Her vision was in fact so acute by this time that it was hard to keep the floor clean enough to prevent her trying to pick up specks of dirt. When twenty-five currants were scattered at random over an area of five square metres, she took only fifty-five seconds on average to pick up every one.' However, she was regularly deceived by small squares of sticky tape and tended to go for more conspicuous objects first. She also proved capable of avoiding various kinds of obstacles placed in her way. She could not recognise a carrot, or even the experimenter's face. Both monkeys reacted more effectively to moving than to stationary objects, and, if over-excited or distracted by commotion, tended to reach wildly.

In recent years the existence of this second, more primitive kind of vision has become generally accepted. This 'blindsight' is not as inexplicable as it might sound. It had long been known that there is, in addition to the main visual pathway from the eyes to the cortex, a secondary pathway to a structure known as the superior colliculus, and hence to the associative cortex, but the great Klüver, in a series of classic papers in the 1940s, had reported that monkeys deprived of their striate cortex could only discriminate 'total luminous energy'. They could tell only whether they were in the light or in the dark. It was also noticed that animals, the cortex of which had been stilled by general anaesthesia, could still react to light.

The story might have ended here, but chance played a role. Luck favoured Humphrey when a consultant at the National Hospital noticed something similar in a human patient. This was a man, who, due to an obstruction of the blood supply in the right half of his cortex, had become blind in the left visual field, a condition known as hemianopsia.

(By a quirk of nature, the nerves from the left half of each retina run to the right half of the cortex, and those from the two right halves to the left cortex. Hence, if the right cortex fails, it is not the left eye which becomes blind, but the left halves of both eyes.) When this man was shown a light to his left, he could point to it quite accurately.

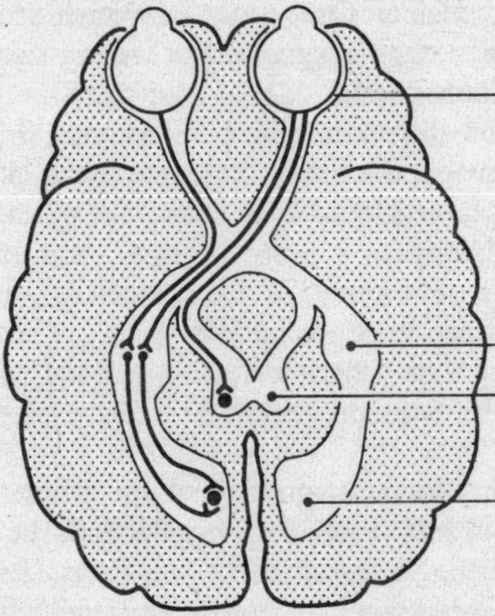

The two paths from the retina to the two brain areas concerned with vision: the visual cortex and the superior colliculus. Note how some fibres cross to the contrary side of the brain, while others do not.

He could also distinguish a cross from a circle, or horizontal from vertical lines. But this was all outside his *consciousness*. When asked how he knew, he said he was only guessing. Actually the vision in his blind sector proved, on test, to be only slightly worse than his normal sight. (He did have a small patch where the vision really was poor.) He was not much good at discriminating colours and could only tell red from green stimuli (for instance), because green felt 'brighter' than red.

Subsequently, further instances of human 'blindsight' were discovered in France and America.

The fact that such people are unaware of what they are seeing (which could not be inferred from animal experiments), is profoundly interesting, not to say amazing. To begin with, it suggests that we all take in more than we are conscious of observing. Actions which we perform on a hunch, or on impulse, may in fact be quite closely keyed to clues in the world around us, of which we are not consciously aware. (Smells of which we are unaware, for instance, may change our mood.)

Obviously, we must be very careful in using terms like 'conscious' and 'aware' – distinguishing conscious awareness from unconscious awareness – and confining the word 'conscious' to the higher state.

In point of fact, this is one of the most significant elements in the story I am telling and, now that I have plunged you into the middle of it with a vivid anecdote, we need to step back and review the whole subject more carefully. For there is a great deal of data, much of which scientists regard as disturbing and prefer to deny or ignore. But we must start by trying to define what we are talking about.

What then have we discovered about consciousness? First, I think we can be confident that it does involve the brain. This may seem obvious, but philosophers have sometimes sought to deny it and the philosopher U. T. Place's paper, 'Is Consciousness a Brain Process?', has become famous in the narrow world of philosophy. (Place decided it was, and showed where the philosophers had gone wrong.)

Second, we have established that consciousness is not the same as awareness; although they are both brain processes. So we have two things to explain.

Third, neither of them seems to be a function of the whole brain, neither are they functions of neurones. Professor Ivan Beritoff, the doyen of Russian neurophysiologists, believes that imagery, at least, is a function of the squat, star-shaped neurones known as stellate neurones found in layers III and IV of the cortex; and of the interneurones which link them; and that emotion is specifically a function of the stellate neurones which are found in the mid-brain. We may be near the day when it will be possible to stimulate these rather small neurones selectively, which might provide an opportunity to test this idea experimentally. For my part, I am inclined to think that whole patterns of neuronal firing (in which stellate neurones may certainly play a major part) are more likely to be the basis of consciousness, for that seems to be the way the brain works.

Lastly, it is hard to agree with those philosophers who declare that consciousness is an unnecessary hypothesis. I would rather side with a neurophysiologist like Roger Sperry when he says that consciousness is an emergent: something which arises in the course of evolution as a result of increasing complexity.

Consciousness and Awareness

Of all the problems which arise in connection with the notion of 'mind' the most difficult is the fact of consciousness itself.

Consciousness is often defined as awareness – awareness of self and of the environment – but this does no more than substitute one word for another, since we are equally unable to explain the subjective aspects of awareness. But even if we have to take the fact of awareness as a given, just as we take light or gravity as givens, we can still usefully ask certain questions, such as: where in the brain is awareness, or consciousness, located? Is it a function of the whole brain or only of part? Is it a property of neurones or nerve cells? Is there more than one kind or level of consciousness? What does it mean to be unconscious and what mechanisms determine whether we are conscious or not? In recent years, some of the answers to these questions, which have puzzled thinkers for ages, have begun to receive answers and the nature of consciousness is becoming a little clearer. It is these answers and this new data which I shall now try to bring together.

Confusion arises right from the start because of our strange habit of using the word 'conscious' and its opposite 'unconscious' in two very different senses. Sometimes we mean the state which follows a severe blow to the head: complete lack of awareness of what is going on coupled with inability to plan or execute movements or motor responses of any kind, except a few primitive reflexes. But sometimes we say something like: 'I suppose I was unconsciously trying to avoid meeting him,' or, 'I was not consciously aware of the fact.' Here we seem to distinguish two parts of our mind. While Freud has made the idea of an 'unconscious' mind widely known, the notion is much older. Although the idea that we can have thoughts and feelings of which we are not consciously aware has been denied and derided repeatedly, there is overwhelming evidence that something of this sort occurs, quite apart from anything Freud may have had to say on the subject.

Let us start, however, by considering the distinction between consciousness and unconsciousness and ask whether any part of the brain is particularly implicated.

Descartes located consciousness in the pineal gland. Half a century ago the outer part of the brain, the cortex, as the seat of the higher faculties, was the favoured site. Then the mid-brain, seat of emotions, became favoured. In a moment of facetiousness, Professor William Barrett went so far as to say: 'I think there is not much doubt that the soul is located in the basolateral amygdala.'

However, it seems beyond doubt that if consciousness is located in any one place, it must be in the oldest part of the brain, the brain-stem. Back in 1892, the Polish physiologist Friedrich Goltz succeeded in keeping dogs alive for several years after removing their cerebrums – that is, the whole of the roof brain. Before the days of antibiotics, massive surgery of this kind was liable to lead to infection and death, so that Goltz's achievement was without precedent. These dogs walked about, ate, slept, rejected bitter food, and so on, so they could hardly be called unconscious. On the other hand they showed no fear and had no memory. As I have already mentioned, human infants are sometimes born without cerebral hemispheres and they too exhibit this limited degree of consciousness. They show pleasure when sung to or when stroked, displeasure when hungry or cold. They wake and sleep. Some have survived twenty years in this condition, which is technically called idiocy.

An extraordinary case of a girl with very little cortex, a so-called microcephalic, came into the hands of Professor Beritoff a few years ago. This girl, apparently between the ages of eight and ten, was found by a policeman, but as she could not speak it was impossible to discover her origin. Beritoff began to study her about two years later and christened her Peta because she resembled the early hominid Pithecanthropus. Peta displayed the ordinary emotions, but could not dress herself or sweep out her room. She easily reverted to scratching and screaming if she did not get what she wanted. Beritoff taught her to recognise a few simple commands such as 'Sit' and 'Go'. In one series of experiments he led her behind a screen where sugar was available to her, then took her round the other side. It took one hundred and sixteen exposures of this kind before she got the idea that she could get sugar by going round. Out of sight was out of mind. When Beritoff placed two screens 25 cm. (ten inches) apart she stood helplessly in front of the gap which she could easily have passed through by turning sideways. Remembering Professor Koehler's apes, which discovered how to hook bananas into their cage when given hooked canes, Beritoff gave Peta canes, and placed food within reach, but she never got the idea even when shown how to do it.

Peta died soon after and a post-mortem examination was made. Her brain weighed four hundred and ten grams, about as much as that of a chimpanzee, and its surface area (actually a more significant measurement) was about one-third of what it would normally be in a girl of her age. The convolutions of the surface were less developed than in a new-born baby, suggesting that the arrest of development had occurred before birth. The brain-stem was almost normal.

Clearly Peta was conscious, but not at the ordinary human level.

There is other evidence of the brain-stem's crucial role which adds a further dimension. Professor W. Feldberg of the National Institute of Medical Research recounts the case of a boy of fourteen who fell and ruptured the meningeal artery in his brain. He became unconscious and remained in this condition until an operation was performed, and a blood-clot was found to be pressing on his brain-stem. As soon as the pressure was relieved, he woke up 'and became embarrassingly lively'.

The crucial area for consciousness appears to be the swelling of the brain-stem known as the pons. Operations on the brain are usually performed with the patient conscious, since the brain feels no pain when touched or cut and the co-operation of the patient is needed by the surgeon. In one such operation, the patient, a woman, jerked her head backwards causing the surgeon's probe to enter some three centimetres into the pons. She immediately became unconscious for about ten to fifteen seconds and later reported that her past life had flashed before her. The surgeon, of course, at once withdrew the probe: consciousness was almost immediately restored. It is also known that haemorrhage into the pons, or into the medulla which lies below, causes deep coma – although, strangely enough, tumours of the pons do not do so.

As recently as 1950 most neurologists believed that unconsciousness was due solely to cerebral anaemia, that is to say, to a reduced supply of blood to the brain – and of course, this will produce unconsciousness. The observations just noted, however, suggest the presence of something very different: a kind of switch blocking and unblocking awareness. Consciousness thus cannot be a property of neurones as such.

Manipulation of the anterior wall of the third ventricle – the central space in the brain – also has this all-or-nothing effect on consciousness. Tumours of the thalamus and hypothalamus may also cause unconsciousness, but as they are linked by many fibres to the brain-stem, this is, I fancy, an indirect effect.

Experiments show that if you expose persons to a noise of increasing intensity, they report a conscious experience, at precisely the level at which their brain rhythms change, which suggests consciousness is a function of discharge patterns, rather than of discharges as such. Similar experiments by Libet show, moreover, that there is a delay of thirty milliseconds before anything happens, and a delay of seventy milliseconds before the peak of the response is reached; there are also responses with much longer delays. Shagass and Schwartz got similar results for visual stimuli, but found that the neurones responded equally well to similar stimuli when the subject was under anaesthesia.

It seems to be the after-discharges which are detected in conscious, but not detected in anaesthetised subjects, which provide the basis of conscious experience.

Since you respond to a stimulus in less than half a second – the time it takes to register a conscious experience – it follows that you can respond to a stimulus before you know you have perceived it. Not only that: an epileptic can perform elaborate actions without conscious awareness. In a well-known case, a doctor examined patients and prescribed for them perfectly efficiently without any awareness of what he was doing. At least, he had no recollection of his actions, which raises the question: can one have consciousness without memory?

Consciousness is not, as is often assumed, an all-or-nothing business. Thus the brain surgeon Hugh Cairns once described how a soldier who received a serious head wound in Normandy on 16 July 1944, and was deeply unconscious, slowly recovered. On 17 July, though still unconscious, he cried if interfered with. On 23 July, when addressed by name he opened his eyes, but no more. On 26 July he was comparatively alert, but unable to speak coherently. By 5 August he could hold short conversations, though partially paralysed. And so it continued. I think we must deduce from this that brain function is divided into many sub-functions, which recover one after another – and consciousness represents the totality of such functions and the effectiveness with which they function.

We see the same sort of gradual loss of capacity and its gradual recovery in clinical anaesthesia, though of course it takes place more rapidly. The capacities are lost in the reverse order of their evolutionary development. Sight goes before hearing, movement next. But even at this stage reflexes remain, and the patient withdraws his foot if the toe is pinched. If still more anaesthetic is administered, even these reflexes disappear and finally basic life processes – breathing and heart-beat – begin to weaken. I can recall recovering from a major anaesthetic. I lay there, suddenly aware of voices and also conscious of the fact that my feet felt icy cold. I was quite unable to ask for anything to be done about this, and for quite a while (I cannot judge how long: it seemed like ten minutes but may have been much longer) it did not even occur to me that such a move was possible. I was simply aware. I was quite unable to move or even to entertain the notion of moving. I probably looked unconscious, but in fact I was not. Deep heart surgery patients have recently reported similar symptoms.

We are all familiar with drowsiness and the confused state in which we find ourselves when suddenly woken from deep sleep. Too much alcohol also modifies our consciousness in a quantitative way. I know of no one who has tried to analyse what happens here. I have the impression that there is a failure of attention. Most of us have had to cope with a drunk man who is totally preoccupied with some immediate objective and cannot be brought to see the implications of his behaviour or the wider obligations upon him. There may also be an actual slowing of the mental processes. Some forms of mental disturbance are marked by confusional states of a rather different kind, to which I shall refer later.

Consciousness thus seems to be displayed at several levels; more particularly, there is a contrast between awareness and attending – and when we attend, we start looking for associations and implications, we plan and execute responses and so on. We are, as people often say, switched on.

One of the few people to look closely at this contrast is Ronald Shor, an American psychologist who particularly studies hypnotism. He has drawn attention to an aspect of normal consciousness which is best conveyed in his own words:

> 'I had been awake for a number of hours. My level of body tonus was fairly high and my mind clear to dream-images so that I believe I was not asleep but rather in some kind of trance-like state. At that time I was not conscious of my personal identity, nor of prior experiences, nor of the external world. It was just that out of nowhere I was aware of my own thought processes. I did not know, however, that they were thought processes or who I was or even that I was an I. There was sheer awareness . . . sheer existing. After a time a "wondering" started to fill my awareness: that there was something more than this, a gap, an emptiness. As soon as this "wondering" was set in motion there was immediately a change in my awareness. In an instant, as if in a flash, full awareness of myself and reality expanded around me. To say that "I woke up" or "I remembered", while perhaps correct, would miss the point of the experience entirely . . . suddenly all the specifications of reality had become apparent to me. At one moment my awareness was devoid of all structure and in the next moment I was *myself* in a multivaried universe of time, space, motion and desire.'

Shor calls this frame of reference which gives meaning to all experiences – the 'generalised reality orientation' (GRO). A whole framework or background of relationships became available by which to interpret what was happening. This makes sense to me.

Shor considers that this GRO is only maintained by a certain effort and that it is quite easy to drift back into the unoriented state. This happens in going to sleep, when one is absorbed in music or some similar interest, in mystical states, while engaged in deeply creative activity, and also in hypnosis. He adds that in the developing child the GRO is gradually established, citing the Swiss child psychologist Piaget's findings and those of others in support.

Thus there seem to be two principal states of consciousness: one, so to speak, in which the engine is idling and the gears are disengaged, and one when it is in gear and functioning.

Another account of consciousness at the moment of waking is worth mention. It concerns a man who, for a moment, saw the room in different colours from normal; or rather, it seemed drained of colour. This is a different observation from Shor's but does suggest that consciousness is by no means an unambiguous state.

Of course, anything which depresses the action of the cerebral hemispheres causes defects of consciousness too. Doctors speak of 'clouding of consciousness', and note that patients become easily distracted from the task in hand, however simple – they may strike a match but fail to light their cigarette with it; or, having lit it, fail to put it in their mouth. They misjudge and cannot think clearly. They forget what has just been said or done. In some diseases this progresses to stupor, defined as a state from which the patient can be aroused by a violent or repeated stimulus, then to coma, from which he cannot be aroused, and eventually death.

Distinct from such crude modifications of consciousness are such 'altered states of consciousness' as hypnosis, mystical experience and perhaps the states induced by psychedelic drugs. These I discuss in the next chapter. For the moment let us continue the exploration of normal awareness.

Summing up so far, two things seem to me to be clear. First, consciousness is not a single entity but varies in kind as well as degree. The most primitive consciousness may reside in the mid-brain; the cortex elaborates it – provides, so to say, a Technicolor version of the primitive black and white representation. Second, it cannot be a property of neurones as such, since there are many neurones, notably those in the spinal column, which do not display consciousness. Also, it is possible to remove considerable parts of the frontal cortex without appreciably affecting consciousness. It must either be a property of some particular neurones, or of certain electrical or electrochemical patterns produced by large assemblies of neurones. But there is more to it than that. Down in the brain-stem, below the pons, there is a kind of on-off switch known as the reticular activating system.

Paying Attention

One of the most far-reaching of recent advances in our understanding of the brain was the discovery in 1949 by the Italian Giuseppe Moruzzi and the American Horace Magoun, at Northwestern University, of an arousal system in the brain-stem. They found that stimulating this area with a small electric current would cause a sleepy cat to wake up. Recordings of its brain waves as well as its behaviour indicated that the awakening was not an alarm reaction but just normal arousal. Microscopic examination of the stimulated area revealed a network of cells which they christened the Ascending Reticular Activating System, usually abbreviated ARS. This system starts down in the spine and runs up into the mid-brain.

This discovery transformed sleep research, until then almost at a standstill. It was observed that a transsection of the brain-stem below the pons resulted in permanent wakefulness. But if electrical stimulation resembling the brain's normal sleep pattern was applied, the animal fell peacefully asleep. It seemed, too, that anaesthetics might work by depressing the reticular arousal system. Conversely, strong stimulation of the ARS causes a keyed-up state. 'All my senses were on the alert,' we sometimes say, when we are expecting danger. This is the arousal system at work.

Russian workers have studied what happens when you are alerted by some unexpected event such as a loud sound. Immediately your pupil dilates and your visual threshold falls, so that you can see more sharply. At the same time your auditory threshold falls – by as much as ten decibels in man – so that your hearing becomes acuter. Your blood vessels contract and after a short delay your breathing speeds up. Your heart rate chases up and down. Your brain rhythms speed up but their amplitude reduces.

But the arousal system, it transpires, has two components, a diffuse one which projects (sends signals) to all parts of the cortex – this is the one I have so far been talking about – and a specific one working through the hypothalamus which seems to bring about concentrations on a particular subject; that is, it explains the phenomenon we call attention. I suspect it does so not only by stimulating the part of the cortex which handles the kind of input we are, at that moment, interested in, but also by inhibiting or blocking off all other processing. As we all know, it is practically impossible to attend closely to two things at once, it can only be done by switching rapidly back and forth.

According to a recent newspaper report, a boy aiming his gun at a bird succeeded in shooting his father. He said afterwards, 'I never even saw him.' That may well have been literally true. Experiments have shown that one is slower to notice a tactile stimulus when having an intelligent conversation, but such experiments are hardly necessary, since we all know such things from our own experience. Entranced by music, we do not notice the hardness of the chair. Or, as the old joke has it: the honeymoon is over when you notice that the apartment is unheated.

Conversely, the brain actually sharpens up sense organs when receiving signals that interest it. The sensitivity of the ear, for instance, rises by as much as ten decibels when you listen hard.

A curious aspect of this heightened perceptiveness was discovered accidentally by Professor W. R. Hess of the University of Chicago about 1960, when he was lying in bed reading. His wife noticed that his pupils were much enlarged and thinking that the light-level must be inadequate suggested that he should switch on another light. Hess, realising that the light was as bright as usual, deduced that another factor must be at work, and in laboratory experiments demonstrated that fact in detail. Hungry people dilate their pupils at the sight of appetising food; homosexuals dilate at the sight of attractive members of the same sex, and so on.

Still more interesting, it seems that we are unconsciously aware of these dilations in people we are speaking to. Hess' students rated photographs of young people which had, in some cases, been retouched so as to enlarge the pupils. They assessed the retouched faces as 'more attractive' than the unretouched ones. This, one can be sure, is why in the Renaissance women put belladonna in their eyes, for belladonna enlarges the pupils. A man finds the woman who looks at him with evident interest (or seems to do so) more attractive than the one who seems bored with him. (Ingenious of nature to go to so much trouble to increase the probability of procreation occurring!)

The problem in all this is: what triggers the specific arousal system? How does it know what to bother about?

In Oxford, Anne Treisman was carrying out some ingenious experiments on attention which certainly made the whole question a good deal more obscure. Her method was to feed speech from a tape to one ear through one headphone and different speech to the other ear through another; the subject was then asked to attend to one ear only. It turns out that, though he may notice a *major* change in the speech in the unattended ear, such as a woman's voice being substituted, or the use of a foreign language, he will in general recall nothing from the text.

Yet, if his own name is mentioned, he will detect it. So it must have been listening to the 'unattended' channel after all. This was a bombshell.

In a variant of this experiment, lists of words were read to each ear, so arranged that if you took a word from each ear alternately, they would combine to make a meaningful sentence. It turned out that the subject immediately spotted this and could report the sentence. So we are forced to the conclusion, and it is a very radical one, that much, if not all, of the input to our brains is monitored at the unconscious level, and filtered, before the interesting bits are supplied to consciousness.

Now the only mechanism capable of making such a fine discrimination is the cortex itself. So we are driven to conclude that the data reaches the cortex without conscious awareness, and is then examined; when something of interest is found, a message must go down to the arousal mechanism in the brain-stem, which then fires back a 'wake up' instruction to the cortex to pay heed. This is quite heterodox, but no alternative theory has been offered. In fact, everyone has kept very quiet on the subject.

Anne Treisman's discovery became known as 'the cocktail party phenomenon' in reference to the familiar fact that at a party, if your own name is mentioned in another part of the room, we often notice the fact, even though we are busy talking to someone else, and may start to monitor the other conversation. Any signal which has special meaning for us or which indicates danger can have this effect of breaking in on our attention. I recall that once, when I was having dinner in a restaurant, chatting with three other people, suddenly hearing the word 'death' spoken at the table behind me. My ARS had decided that this was something which merited my immediate attention.

So efficient is this warning system that it even works while one is asleep. It is well known that a mother will wake from sleep if her child cries, while sleeping undisturbed through the noise of passing traffic. Her husband, who is undisturbed by the baby's whimper, may waken suddenly to the smell of smoke. Experiments conducted in the Psychology Laboratory at Oxford showed that most people, when asleep, respond to familiar names and especially to their own name with changes in brain waves, heart-beat and skin resistance, even when they do not wake. Some subjects were more liable than others to waken to their own name.

A novel stimulus is arousing but a continued stimulus quickly becomes boring. This is known as habituation. However, if there is a very slight change in the stimulus, we at once become alert again. For example, if we are listening to a humming sound, it soon becomes unnoticed, but if the note changes, we at once observe the fact. When the mill stops, the miller wakes, as an old saying has it.

Here again, we perceive that the brain must have been monitoring the note all the time or it would not have noticed the change. It was thus only at the higher levels of consciousness that the note was unperceived.

Why the Theatre Felt Cold

There is an experiment devised by Russian psychologists, in which a random series of numbers are read to the subject by a tape-recorder. Every time one particular number – let us say 'five' – is pronounced, a puff of air is blown at the subject's eyes, causing him to blink. After a few repetitions he will blink when he hears 'five' even if no puff of air is discharged. He has been conditioned, in the language of Pavlov. Now comes the pay-off. The volume of the tape-recorder is turned down until the words cannot be distinguished – but the subject still blinks whenever 'five' is being inaudibly spoken. The political advantages of being able to make someone perform an action without being aware of the stimulus are obvious, and no doubt this helps to explain the Russian interest in such work.

In a Western version of the same experiment, a square and a circle were drawn on cards and placed under several layers of tissue paper until they could not be made out. The subjects were then asked to draw a copy of an ambiguous figure. Those who had a square concealed beneath their drawing paper drew it rather squarer; those who had a circle, drew it biased towards circularity. As a check, they were told to look closely and see if they could detect the concealed figure, but they could not, even when told it was there.

This kind of awareness has been called subliminal perception, and a few years ago it became the focus of interest when it was thought to have a commercial application. It had been found that when subjects were asked to describe a face flashed upon the screen, with (at the same time) the word 'happy' or the word 'sad' exposed too briefly for them to detect, they were more likely to describe the face as 'happy' or 'sad' depending on the subliminal stimulus. In another experiment when test pictures were shown and the words DON'T WRITE were projected subliminally, shorter descriptions were written. Such experiments generated the idea that by flashing 'Coke' or 'Jello' on the screen subliminally, the sales of the product might be promoted. An experiment was conducted in a cinema: the word ice-cream was subliminally displayed, in the hope that sales would rise. But all that happened was that several patrons complained that the theatre was cold! Subliminal perception seems to be of a rather primitive type.

The magazine *Playboy* made some very curious experiments in subliminal influence, such as substituting for the dots which go to make up a picture reproduced by a screen process the word SEX printed in extremely small type. Other even more dubious ploys are described by Wilson Bryan Key in his remarkable book *Subliminal Seduction*.

Actually the idea of subliminal influence has a respectable history. Leibniz spoke of 'perceptions insensibles'; the great German physiologist von Helmholtz showed that unperceived stimuli could give rise to perceived after-images. And in a particularly convincing experiment it was shown, as long ago as 1934, that a sequence of repeated subliminal exposures adds up to a perceptible experience. If I seem to labour the point, it is because it is still hotly denied.

In view of all this, it is remarkable that the idea has been ridiculed. The existence of subliminal perception is particularly awkward for the recent branch of knowledge called Signal Theory, which rejects the notion that there is a threshold to (conscious) perception.

In point of fact, subliminal awareness can be demonstrated in half a dozen different ways. For instance, subliminally perceived images often crop up in the subject's dreams; it is almost as if, having failed to surface in waking life, they sought to do so in sleep. This fact, which was known to Aristotle two thousand years ago, goes a long way towards accounting for some of our dream images. 'Why should I have dreamed of *that*?' we say, little realising that we may have seen precisely that, unbeknownst.

The existence of the realm of subconscious life is a matter of such great importance in life – leave alone its central position in any discussion of the mind – that it is strange that there is, as far as I know, no comprehensive review of the subject. I must, however, acknowledge a debt to N. F. Dixon's *Subliminal Perception* which, though narrower in scope, is a classic work and deserves to be better known.

A common psychological procedure is to time accurately how long it takes a person to respond to a stimulus-word by finding an associated word. For most people, for example, the stimulus-word CHAIR readily suggests TABLE, SCHOOL may suggest BORE and so on. Mentally disturbed people produce unusual associations. Words which arouse unconscious fears – in particular words associated with sexual matters – cause prolonged reaction times and also physiological changes, notably changes in the electrical resistance of the skin. It is thought that the person being tested rejects the first association which occurs to him for something more neutral. (So-called lie detectors are based on this phenomenon: it is assumed that questions concerning a crime committed by the person questioned will arouse anxiety and that he will substitute neutral words for the associations which might betray him. Such 'lie detectors' are unreliable, since some criminals are brazen while some innocent persons feel fearful when accused, and because some words may have painful associations for certain people for quite other reasons.)

The unconscious tendency to suppress embarrassing words is known as perceptual defence. Furthermore, such defence-mechanisms may also, it is claimed, extend to perception in general. We sometimes fail to see or hear something which, unconsciously, we do not want to see or hear. We do not *attend*, as the saying goes. Not surprisingly, this idea is even more repugnant to the sceptics than is subliminal awareness itself. 'To say that one can perceive in order not to perceive is a logical contradiction,' declares the American psychologist, J. J. Gibson, an expert on perception. To which one can only reply: 'Then why say it?' The bitterest attacks have come from C. W. Eriksen, who particularly dislikes the idea of learning without awareness. He has dubbed the process 'supersensitive discrimination', but there is no evidence that abnormal sensitivity is involved. In point of fact, physiological confirmation of this phenomenon has been provided. By implanting electrodes in the brains of animals, it has been shown that signals are arriving at the cortex when the animal is presented with stimuli too faint to evoke any behavioural response; moreover, if the stimuli are interesting (e.g. food) the electrical response is more marked than if they are boring (e.g. a coloured light).

What are we to make of all this?

It seems incontrovertible that if a person can see a word like SACRED at shorter exposures than, say, INCOME, his brain must have identified the word in some way before he was consciously aware of it. But critics objected that this effect might be due to some words being more familiar than others. To meet this criticism, two workers at Johns Hopkins, McCleary and Lazarus, devised an ingenious experiment based on ten nonsense words, such as YILIM and ZEWUK. After preliminary training to familiarise them with these oddities the subjects were shown the words at subliminal exposures and given electric shocks to five of them. When you are shocked your skin resistance falls, so the expectation was, after this conditioning, that their skin resistance would fall when shown the 'shock' words without being given any shock. The experimenters found that even when the exposure was so short that the subject misidentified the word, his skin resistance fell if it was actually a shock-associated word. Thus even though, at the *conscious* level, the subject thought it was *not* a shock word, his unconscious mind knew jolly well that it was! That was a tough one for the sceptics.

It showed that we not only detect some stimuli subconsciously but may even have a physiological response as well as a psychological one. It also introduces the idea that subliminal stimuli can not only be detected (I must not say perceived) but can also provide a basis for conditioning.

Another curious fragment of data which has to be fitted in somehow comes from an American psychologist, Ward Halstead (whom we shall come across in connection with intelligence later). During the war he studied oxygen shortage in aircrews and found that a man could report the sight of an enemy plane by pressing a button quite well, in anoxic conditions, without having consciously seen it. This seems an observation which should be followed up with modern methods.

On Certain Conditions

I mentioned earlier a Russian experiment in conditioning to a subliminal stimulus in the form of a word spoken 'inaudibly'. Actually this is only one in a vast array of Russian experiments on subliminal conditioning, some of which are so weird and so little known in the West, that they are worth describing. Gregory Razran, of Queens College, New York, who speaks fluent Russian, spent several summers in the USSR visiting psychological institutes and reading Russian psychological periodicals, and it is to him that I owe this information.

The American psychologist Edward Tolman claimed that all the basic phenomena of psychology could be determined in the rat, and that experiments on human beings were a luxury. The Russians, following a dogma of Pavlov's, have always held that language was of crucial importance – a 'second signalling system' which animals lack – and many of their experiments have been in this area. For instance, having conditioned a thirteen-year-old boy named Yuritz to blink when offered the Russian word for 'ten', it was found that he also blinked when offered the words '83 – 73' as a stimulus, which implies that a conditioned reflex can be formed to the output of a cognitive process. This takes us a long way from the classic conception of a reflex as a simple coupling of an input to an output.

But the story grows more mysterious when we consider some of their strange experiments in 'interoceptive conditioning'. Russian psychologists placed rubber balloons in the stomach (or sometimes the bladder or uterus) of animals and pumped in hot or cold water whenever they were shown food. As in the classic experiments of Pavlov, they salivated, and after five or six exposures formed a reflex, i.e. they salivated whenever the water was pumped in, even though there was no food. Now the stomach (as also the bladder and uterus) has no nerve endings for detecting heat and cold, and, as we know from our own experience, we are not conscious of sensations of hot and cold from these regions. So how then did the brain learn to couple the sight of food to sensations it (presumably) did not experience?

The Russians not only tried many variants on this theme, but even adapted it to human beings. Patients with urinary fistulas were induced to volunteer to have rubber balloons inserted in their bladders. These were connected to pressure gauges which showed the urinary pressure in the bladder. The experimenters, however, faked the readings so as to show high pressure when the bladder was nearly empty and low pressure when it was full. The gauges were clearly visible to the patients and before long they experienced an uncontrollable desire to urinate when the gauge said 'full' although their bladders were actually empty, and inversely. Of course we have a perfectly good built-in mechanism which tells us when our bladders are full: here the conscious brain was apparently overruling the unconsciously perceived sensations.

In another series of somewhat alarming experiments, subjects were exposed to a rather powerful and prolonged electric shock. This, among other things, normally causes the blood vessels to contract, as part of a general emergency response. Occasionally, however, the blood vessels, instead of contracting, dilate. The experimenter arranged for the shock to terminate immediately if this occurred. Although the test was repeated as many as eighty times, if the gauge was not visible, no learning occurred. But if the subject was able to see the gauge which detected the contraction or dilation he soon spotted that the shock would stop when dilation occurred and – somehow – began to induce dilation every time. Thus he was learning a control which was unconscious (in the sense that he had no idea how to set about such a task) as a consequence of conscious awareness of a relevant fact.

After absorbing the nub of a few experiments like these, I find my simple mind in a state of considerable confusion.

The fact that we can learn to control our autonomic system is surprising enough. Neal Miller, Professor of Psychology at New York University, stunned many people in 1971 by training human beings to change their heart rate; one of his students, David Blizzard, trained a thirty-three-year-old woman with high blood pressure (essential hypertension) to raise or lower her blood pressure. Subsequently a group at Boston induced students to shift their blood pressure by the now almost classic technique of showing them centrefolds from *Playboy*. (This is apparently a very powerful stimulus for American psychology students, who presumably had little time for gazing at real girls.) Then Dr Philip G. Zimbardo of Stanford University trained subjects under hypnosis to vary the temperature of their hands. Of course, yogis have been doing this sort of thing for centuries, but that doesn't count. These experiments, started about 1960, made Miller 'perhaps the best known experimental psychologist in the country' according to an American science journal.

But to condition people to control their autonomic system to stimuli of which they are *not aware* is something else again. Is it possible that the body has a system of self-knowledge which does not depend on the nervous system as we know it?

Razran himself followed up some of these experiments with results which made little sense. Back in the 1830s, a Russian named Klestchov had conditioned animals to salivate when they heard the musical interval of a fifth. He found they then salivated when this interval was played in a wholly different key – in other words the actual notes were quite different. The animals were reacting to the relation between the notes, not the notes themselves. When he played them a third, they salivated, but not so much, as if they weren't sure whether this counted. When Razran tried to repeat this with human beings, the results were puzzling, since some intervals proved more effective than others.

Razran reports that 'interoceptive conditioning' is actually more potent than the better-known exteroceptive kind. 'Awareness is not a *sine qua non* of human conditioning,' Razran concludes, pointing out that new-born babes and aments (idiots) can be conditioned.

The implications are vast and alarming. Satellite countries have been brought in on the programme, and a Polish team recently reported attempts to condition people while they were asleep.

But quite aside from the possibility of misusing such a technique for political purposes, there are implications for ordinary life. If you smile at someone every time he uses a certain word, he will begin to use it more often, without being aware of the fact. If you smile when he turns his head to the left or scratches his chin, he will increase the frequency of such gestures. How many of the actions which we perform with what we think is complete spontaneity are due to conditioning? Are we more likely to become church-goers if in childhood we learned to associate churchgoing with reward – or to avoid it for the contrary reason?

At all events, it seems beyond doubt that we are affected by a great range of stimuli which never come to our conscious attention and which, therefore, we cannot rationally assess. Some may be valuable: this, I think one can take it, is the origin of the 'hunch' or what we sometimes express by saying, 'I feel intuitively that . . .' Consciousness is only a small part of our whole psyche.

On Lethe's Shore

The story has one further – and yet more incredible – chapter. It is usually assumed that when you have been anaesthetised for a surgical operation you are unconscious. Yet, in the medical literature, there are quite a number of reliable reports of patients who, having been fully anaesthetised, retained a high degree of awareness. Some of the early reports, dating from the 1960s, concern patients who were being intubated; that is, a tube was being put down their throat, which causes a vomiting reflex. (As I had the pleasure of being intubated during the war without benefit of anaesthetic, I can vouch for the unpleasantness of the experience, which goes on for some time.) However, the introduction of muscle-relaxing drugs made it possible to control the vomiting so that only very light anaesthetics are now usually employed. Light anaesthetics are also used for Caesarean section and some minor operations. Some of these patients reported awareness and even pain or discomfort during their operation, but doctors firstly assumed that they had simply not been given quite enough anaesthetic: people vary considerably in the amount they need.

However, since the reports continued to come in, a study was made.

It showed that seventeen per cent of such patients had unpleasant memories of their experience including feeling real pain, while two per cent could recall factual matters such as words that had been uttered by the staff at the time they were 'unconscious'. Some recalled feeling paralysed and unable to breathe. They felt terrified. The report added that some still felt considerable resentment as a result, whereas others were quite relaxed about it.

But two remarkable experiments, carried out in South Africa, demonstrated that it was not merely a question of inadequate doses of anaesthetic.

B. W. Levinson, a Johannesburg hypnotist, exposed ten patients during surgical anaesthesia to a suggestion indicative of an anaesthetic crisis. At a certain point in the operation the anaesthetist was to say: 'Just a minute, I don't like the patient's colour, he's much too blue – his lips are very blue – I'm going to give him a little more oxygen.' A month later, each patient was hypnotised and told to think him- or herself back to the time of the operation. They were then asked what, if anything, they remembered. Four of them were able to repeat almost the exact words used. Four more became anxious and awoke from the hypnotic state. Two were apparently unaffected, but an examination of brain waves taken during the operation (in one of them) showed abnormalities starting at the time the suggestion was made and continuing for some minutes after. The patients who had volunteered for the experiment were anaesthetised with thiopentione, nitrous oxide, oxygen and ether for dental surgery. A typical transcript reads:

Q. Who is it talking?
A. Dr H. He's saying that my colour is grey.
Q. Yes?
A. He's going to give me some oxygen.
Q. What are his words?
A. (pause) He said that I will be all right now.
Q. Yes?
A. I can feel him bending close to me.

An assistant, Jacobus Mostert, shocked at Levinson's casual attitude, later revealed that in another, similar experiment, the even more alarming words 'the lung is black . . . it comes of living in the city' were used, with similar results. He adds that only alarming material caused reminiscence to occur.

And there is another scrap of evidence.

Hypnosis is sometimes used to help terminal cancer patients tolerate the pain they suffer. In one such case, the patients were asked to place their thumb and forefinger together to indicate that they could hear the hypnotist's instructions. In eight cases it was found that when they were near death and unconscious for all ordinary purposes, they could still oppose their digits when requested. The two patients who failed to respond in this way died within two hours.

Mostert, in a review of the subject, concludes that surgeons require to be very careful what they say during an operation. In view of the crude jokes which young surgeons sometimes make, probably as a way of relieving the tension they feel and taking some of the sting out of the situation, this is sound advice. However, I see rather more to it than that. If the comparatively mild stimuli of spoken words – some of which carry no baleful meaning – can get through the defences and form memory records, one must suppose that the more powerful stimuli of pain do also. The experiment of asking a hypnotised patient to recall the pain has not been tried. (It would also be interesting to place substances with definite tastes on the tongues of anaesthetised persons and see if they could be recalled.) If so, then the body, or rather the subconscious mind, must remember the insults (as doctors call them) of surgery, even though they were never appreciated at the conscious level. That might account for the long time it takes to recover from major operations and the lowering effect of even minor ones.

If it is possible to acquire information without ever being conscious of it, one begins to wonder what else may be so acquired – during sleep or even awake. It does not follow that this mode of acquisition only operates under anaesthesia.

Where is Fancy Bred?

The sage of Vienna made us all aware, with his *Psychopathology of Everyday Life*, that we repress ideas and memories which we find uncomfortable. We conveniently forget about an appointment we do not want to keep. We suppress resentments and are sometimes surprised at ourselves when they emerge in a moment of truth. What is true in everyday life is also true of extreme situations. Soldiers who have undergone appalling war experiences may develop 'hysterical amnesia'. The notion is so familiar that we often say: 'I must unconsciously have done it,' or, 'I wasn't consciously aware of it, but I must have sensed that something was wrong.'

There is a phenomenon known as 'highway hypnosis'. The driver of a car sometimes finds himself in a strange part of the city, sitting in his car, with no idea how he got there. He remembers, perhaps, leaving work and getting into his car, and then there is a blank. Evidently he was fully aware (in some sense) of the traffic lights, other vehicles and the road layout or he could not have driven without accident. This is perhaps an extreme instance of what we normally refer to when we say, 'My mind was on other things.' It is, surely, impossible to deny that we can be aware without being consciously aware, if I may so put it.

It is an extraordinary thing that we don't have an agreed vocabulary for distinguishing the two conditions. I propose, therefore, to speak of conscious and unconscious awareness. Thus, I shall use awareness in a larger sense than conscious. The latter word will apply only to what is accessible on demand to what I think of as myself. It will mean, knowing and knowing that I know.

My decision is an arbitrary one and will certainly annoy some philosophers, for most writers on the subject declare roundly that 'consciousness' and 'awareness' are one and the same thing. Back in the seventeenth century, John Locke said, 'It is impossible to perceive without perceiving that he does perceive,' although his contemporary John Norris said, 'We may have ideas of which we are not conscious.' Since then many have echoed Locke, a few have echoed Norris. Some to whom I have spoken consider that conscious should be used as the more embracing term, awareness as the less embracing. I reject this convention on the practical grounds that it is easier to accept the term 'unconsciously aware' than the term, which we should be forced to use of the alternative plan, of 'unawarely conscious'. This distinction also affects words like 'know' and 'perceive'. Have we perceived something if we only perceive it unconsciously?

Scientists – some of them – may also be annoyed, for quite a few still deny that there is any such thing as subliminal awareness. I wonder why. Thus Arturo Rosenblueth, the distinguished Mexican neurophysiologist and former collaborator of the famous Walter Cannon, declares grandly: 'Since I define "mental processes" as the conscious experiences of which someone is aware, the concept of "unconscious mental processes" is, in my opinion, an unacceptable contradiction in terms.'

Obviously if you choose to define mental processes so as to exclude the unconscious the expression 'unconscious mental processes' becomes a contradiction and you require to find some other label for them. But defining terms does not obliterate facts. I find it enormously puzzling that anyone of Rosenblueth's intellectual calibre can persuade himself that he has disposed of the topic by such a transparent quibble.

The evidence is irrefutable: it is time we based our thinking on it.

6

Unusual States of Consciousness

ROOTED TO THE SPOT

Hester Y. was suffering from the late effects of contracting sleeping sickness. In her moments of normality she was a charming, intelligent woman. But without warning her movements would suddenly be arrested, like a television picture in 'freeze frame'. She might stay thus rooted to the spot for a second or an hour and no effort of hers could break the spell. She told her doctor that during these episodes the world had a weird quality for her. 'Thus everything seems sharp-edged, flat and geometric, with a quality like a mosaic or a stained-glass window; there is no sense of space or time at such times. Sometimes these "stills" form a flickering vision, like a movie film which is running too slow.'

'I have run out of space to move in,' said another patient, 'you see, my space is nothing like your space.' But it was really time which these afflicted women had run out of.

Source: O. Sacks, *Awakenings*, Pelican Books, 1976.

Pleasure Blind with Tears

The great psychologist William James, after taking nitrous oxide and having a numinous experience, wrote: 'One conclusion was forced upon my mind at that time, and my impression of its truth has ever since remained unshaken. It is that our normal waking consciousness, rational consciousness as we call it, is but one special type of consciousness, whilst all about it, parted from it by the filmiest of screens, there lie potential forms of consciousness entirely different. We may go through life without suspecting their existence; but apply the requisite stimulus, and at a touch they are there in all their completeness, definite types of mentality which probably somewhere have their field of application and adaptation. No account of the universe in its totality can be final which leaves these other forms of consciousness quite disregarded.'

It is a leading sign of the revolution which is taking place in our attitude to 'mind' that these alternative states of consciousness are at last being taken seriously by scientists and subjected to detailed investigation. Just in the last ten years or so, a subject which has been more in the realm of myth than science has begun to attain respectability. The legendary accretions are being cleared away, and the underlying physiology and psychology are beginning to emerge. The implications for man's view of his ultimate nature are plangent.

Of course the existence of unusual or abnormal states of consciousness has been recognised since man emerged as a species. Sleep, unconsciousness, confused states, insanity are departures from normal consciousness of which everyone has some knowledge. Trance states, possession and hypnosis are recognised as unusual states even if many people have never witnessed them personally. And it is well known that drugs can alter behaviour and subjective experience in various ways and varying degrees. The difference is that such states – except for sleep perhaps – have been regarded as abnormalities and, in general, undesirable. Certainly, mediumistic trance and religious possession are sought by some for special purposes, though few would wish to remain in such states for long.

How do such states relate to 'mind'? Can we infer anything about mind from them?

The founder of Methodism, John Wesley, carefully recorded several. Thus he writes in his *Journal* for 6 March 1758, when he was at Everton, that he 'talked largely with Ann Thorn and two others who had been several times in trances'. Then he was told that the fifteen-year-old Alice Miller had fallen into a trance. 'I went down immediately and found her sitting on a stool and leaning against the wall with her eyes open and fixed upward. I made a motion as if going to strike, but they continued unmoveable. Her face showed an unspeakable mixture of reverence and love, while silent tears stole down her cheeks. Her lips were a little open and sometimes moved; but not enough to cause any sound . . . Her pulse was quite regular.' In about half an hour, her face changed into fear and pity. 'Dear Lord, they will all be damned!' Wesley heard her exclaim.

About seven o'clock her senses returned. 'I asked her, "Where have you been?" "I have been with my Saviour." "In heaven or on earth?" "I cannot tell; but I was in glory." '

Wesley studied one of these female ecstatics closely, remaining near her for the best part of a day, noting her behaviour and questioning her after she returned to normality. Ann Thorn said that she was at times 'visited with such overpowering love and joy that she often lay in a trance for many hours', an interesting remark, since it suggests that the trance-condition was a result of the feeling of ecstasy, and not the reverse as is often assumed.

Patty Jenkins had enough strength to utter 'ejaculations of joy and praise; but no words coming up to what she felt, she frequently laughed while she saw His glory.' When it was time to leave for Cockaigne Hatley, 'her strength was restored in a moment'. Thus the trance was, apparently, not comparable with intoxication or the effect of psychedelics, from which one cannot withdraw at will. It looks more like a deliberate concentration on inner experience. We find the same in meditative states.

And Let Us All to Meditation

The unknown author of *The Cloud of Unknowing*, a fourteenth-century mystical treatise, gave the following instructions for inducing religious trance: '. . . forget all the creatures that ever God made and the works of them, so that thy thought or thy desire be not directed or stretched to any of them, neither in general nor in special . . . At the first time when thou dost it, thou findest but a darkness, as it were a kind of unknowing, thou knowest not what, saving that thou feelest in thy will a naked intent unto God . . . Smite upon that thick cloud of unknowing with a sharp dart of love.'

In the language of modern psychology, you are to damp down all cognitive or affective functions. And in fact, physiological studies which have recently been made of the meditative state show a damping of the arousal system and also of the autonomic system. The heart and breathing rates decrease; the skin resistance falls. Brain rhythms are marked by the synchronisation which occurs when nothing much is going on – but after a while there are bursts of the theta rhythm, the significance of which is not well understood, and presumably this is the point at which the dark cloud of unknowing is transformed into a mystic experience.

The meditative states of oriental mystics are surprisingly similar to the one just described, except that they lack the 'naked intent unto God' – at least unto a specific personalised deity of the Christian type.

Thus the Zen Buddhist teacher Suzuki describes 'the void experience' in terms not much different from 'the cloud of unknowing'. 'All things have the character of emptiness. They have no beginning, no end, they are faultless and not faultless, not perfect and not imperfect. Therefore, O Sanputra, here in this emptiness there is no form, no perception, no name, no concepts, no knowledge. No eye, no ear, no nose, no tongue, no body, no mind. No form, no sound, no smell, no taste, no touch, no objects . . . There is no knowledge, no ignorance, no destruction of ignorance . . . There is no decay nor death.' And he concludes with an unambiguous statement: 'When the impediments of consciousness are annihilated, then he becomes free of all fear, is beyond the reach of change, enjoying final Nirvana.' He is, in short, a vegetable.

However, the advanced Zen practitioner seems to keep his perceptions and motor abilities to hand; it is recorded how one such master seized a piece of paper as it blew off his table with lightning speed although deep in trance. The resemblance to Patty Jenkins, who snapped back to normality the moment Wesley announced that the time had come to move on, is noticeable.

One of the people who have studied trance directly is Arthur Deikman, of the Austen Riggs Medical Centre, who points out, rather as I have done for Suzuki, the similarity between the instructions given in the fourth century by the Indian sage Patanjali and those of Julian of Norwich in the fourteenth. In one experiment Deikman asked subjects to sit in a quiet room, and contemplate a small blue vase (about ten inches high), standing on a red-brown table, while certain sounds were played on a tape-recorder. The subject was instructed to put all thoughts and sensations out of his/her mind and concentrate passively on the vase . . . to let perception of the vase fill the entire mind. The session lasted five minutes the first day, ten minutes the second, and fifteen (or more if desired) on all subsequent days. Music, prose and poetry were played, at low volume, on the tapes. Some sessions were held in silence. Most subjects commented spontaneously on their experiences, and their comments, as also their answers to questions, were tape-recorded.

Some phenomena were experienced by all subjects. The colour of the vase became more intense, almost luminous. Its outlines seemed to shift or dissolve. Most subjects felt that less time had elapsed than was actually the case. They became increasingly able to keep out distracting stimuli. More unexpectedly, they became very attached to the vase, and were disturbed if it was removed. As one subject commented, 'I was nostalgic . . . it was like saying good-bye to a teacher of a course you had learned something in, and had become involved in and were sorry to leave it . . . the most vivid thing in the room.' All enjoyed the sessions.

Among the phenomena experienced by individuals was a merging with the vase. 'At one point it felt . . . as though the vase were in my head rather than out there . . . it seemed as though it were almost a part of me.' Another subject found a strange difficulty in analysing the view he could see from the window. 'For a long time it resisted my attempt to organise it so I could talk about it.' A third seemed to enter a state of transcendence and of loneliness reminiscent of those described by Suzuki and in *The Cloud of Unknowing*.

Doors of Perception

The group of drugs known as psychedelics produce alterations in consciousness, most of which appear to be explicable as changes in the balance between different sub-systems in the brain.

Characteristic is an increased vividness of all sensory perceptions, coupled with disturbances of space and time sense. Colours are brighter. Walls bulge. The subject's body seems to change in size. Weir Mitchell, one of the first to take peyote, the Mexican plant from which mescal is derived, wrote that it was hopeless to try and describe the beauty and splendour of his visions. 'Stars, delicate floating films of colour, then an abrupt rush of countless points of white light swept across the field of view, as if the unseen millions of the Milky Way were to flow into a sparkling river before my eyes . . . A white spear of grey stone grew up to huge height, and became a tall, richly furnishe Gothic tower of very elaborate and definite design, with many rather worn statues standing in doorways or on stone brackets. As I gazed, every projecting angle, cornice and even the face of the stones at their jointings were by degrees covered or hung with clusters of what seemed to be huge precious stones, but uncut, some being more like masses of transparent fruit . . . All seemed to possess an interior light . . . All the colours I have ever beheld are dull in comparison with these. As I looked, as it lasted long, the tower became a fine mouse hue, and everywhere the vast pendant masses of emerald green, ruby reds and orange began to drip a slow rain of colours.'

Subsequently, he sees a vast stone claw, set on the edge of a cliff. A fragment of stuff hanging from it begins to roll out to an immense distance. There are 'miles of rippled purples' from which float 'soft golden clouds', while things like green birds flutter from them into the gulf below.

Not only perception of the external world, but body-awareness is often altered. After taking eighty micrograms of LSD, one subject reported that he had shrunk to six inches in height: but the room too had contracted, only his two companions remained full size, and he looked up at them, feeling, as he said, like David looking at Goliath. Given a box of miniature Japanese figures, he tried to hide behind one of them, and he was concerned that someone might step on him and crush him to death. In short, the parts of the brain responsible for perception have been affected.

Time/space sense is altered, subjects having little sense of past or future. Time flows fast or slow. Cognitive processes may be reduced or are at a standstill, so that the consequences of actions are ignored.

Unconscious material preoccupies the mind, and anxieties may rise to the surface. A writer and painter, who had taken psychedelics several times before, after consuming two hundred and fifty micrograms, went for a walk. About a mile from home, he began to experience alarming hallucinations. 'He thought that taxi-cab drivers, resembling grotesque charioteers, were trying to run him down. Glass buildings exploded before his eyes and the air around him became filled with countless fragments like flying crystalline needles and knife blades that he feared would slash him to ribbons.' Realising that he was in a paranoid state, he hurried home, lay down and was assailed by a flood of terrifying ideas and images. The account he wrote later contains such passages as: 'Floor a tempest. Sanitorium. No keys, no doors, walls or locks. Who are you? Rashomon swirling on sheets of torture beach. OK, begin. Trilogy of Life faces sea of death. Battalions begin their march down the brain-stem. Spears of red sashes helmeted in Tibetan black . . . Demons, demons, a million of them.' And again: 'Six thousand streets pour with phlegm, each helmet holds a face, each spear a tear. Is this masochism? Where else can I go, can you go? I rip off my shirt and start to sweat. All those karmas. Death house walls me in. Battling eunuchs cut off their legs and roll up their pants, impale catastrophes. Let's have it. Smell like cheese in a gym, woman hiding stained socks. No love.' And so on, for pages. Obviously, cognitive control of thought and imagery has vanished.

In contrast, William Pahnke, after giving psilocybin to twenty students in a calm atmosphere on Good Friday, got reports resembling mystical experiences, and it has been claimed on the strength of similar experiences, that psychedelics confer 'instant religion'. But the truth is that they release unconscious material in the form of images which may be pleasant or unpleasant, uplifting or depressing, depending on circumstances and the mood of the taker at the time.

Undue attention has been paid to LSD-25, probably because it is easy to synthesise and hence comparatively easy to obtain on the underground market. But it appears from the work of psychochemists like Claudio Naranjo that some of the rarer drugs have rather specific effects. Naranjo distinguishes drugs which enhance feeling from those which enhance fantasy. Harmaline, known for centuries in South America, evokes vivid imagery (it is used in the initiation of shamans and witches), and has been called 'telepathine' because it allegedly facilitates awareness of events happening a long distance away. Ibogaine, in contrast, directs attention towards the past: the taker seems preoccupied with remote experiences and may feel anger and aggressive impulses towards people who once maltreated him. In contrast to these fantasy enhancers, there are feeling enhancers like methyl-dioxy-amphetamine (MDA) which is derived from nutmeg and is mentioned in the Ayur Veda as a narcotic. MDA strengthens the sense of ego: the feeling that 'I am I'. There is also enhancement of the memory system, and some subjects regress mentally to the cradle. Naranjo has called it the drug of 'here and now'.

Naranjo has also experimented with the use of 3-methoxy-4, 5-methylene-dioxyphenyl-isopropylamine, more conveniently referred to as

MMDA, which curiously resembles the nepenthe of the Greeks. Some people take it and fall asleep, but others enjoy what Abraham Maslow has called 'peak experiences'. They enter a state in which everything is equally lovable – the state which Freud christened 'the oceanic feeling'. This is an ego-disturbance and I shall be discussing it in the next section. There appears also to be stimulation of the memory for images: thinking takes on a visual, emotional and experiential character.

In general, then, psychedelic drugs appear to shift the balance between brain functions; and the altered states of consciousness which they produce, though qualitatively different from normal consciousness, are not in any sense 'higher' than normal consciousness, as is sometimes claimed, but rather (as one might well expect) a sign of disorganisation. They have value, nevertheless, in therapy, when it is necessary to sensitise a patient to aspects of reality and of his own capacities which he has shut out of awareness.

The situation as regards hypnotic trance, however, is rather different.

Astonishing Spectacles

Apart from sleep, if there is an altered state of consciousness at all, it must be the hypnotic trance, which has been studied with increasing determination for one hundred and fifty years. Yet, even now, there is no agreed explanation of what goes on in hypnosis.

When Mesmer first demonstrated his powers in the eighteenth century, the results were quite different from those we think of today when the word hypnotism is mentioned. As the Commissioners appointed by the French Government to investigate the new-found 'animal magnetism' reported: 'Nothing is more astonishing than this spectacle. You have to see it to believe it. We were equally surprised by the profound calm of some of these patients and by the agitation which animates the others, by the various accidents which occur repeatedly and by the sympathies which are established. The patients seek each other out exclusively, run to one another, smile, converse affectionately, and mutually ease their crises. All of them are subject to the magnetist. They may appear to be exhausted but a word from him revives them. The uninterrupted effects force us to recognise the presence of a *great power* which excites and controls the patients and of which the magnetist seems to be the depositary.'

Later, all but one of the Commissioners decided that the power did not exist and could only have harmful effects. They were particularly exercised by the possibility that a woman could be violated while under the magnetic 'fluence. It was, they said, all imagination. In 1802 Mesmer, despairing of the French, appealed to the Royal Society of London for a fair investigation of his methods. However, despite official opposition, treatment continued to be given and cures were effected. Lafontaine, a Swiss practitioner, was even arrested for 'imitating the miracles of Christ'. It was James Braid in England who took the subject up scientifically and put it on a rational basis. Unfortunately, he changed the name from mesmerism to 'hypnosis', from the Greek for sleep, though as it turns out it has nothing to do with sleep.

Today we think of hypnosis as a trance state, nothing to do with any mysterious power of the hypnotist. People can be hypnotised without the presence of a hypnotist by simply listening to a tape-recorder. An effective method is to play back to the subject the amplified sounds of his own breathing. Light shone through revolving prisms is also effective. People can hypnotise themselves – in Japan it is a popular technique for refreshing oneself. Americans have found another variant: mutual hypnosis, in which two people hypnotise one another. It is also possible to hypnotise a person without his being aware of it.

In point of fact the hypnotic trance takes three distinct forms. The conventional technique is to suggest to the patient that he is sleepy, that he is losing control of his limbs, and so on, while his attention is focused on something neutral – perhaps a shiny object – so that he is not stimulated by seeing anything significant.

His mind detaches from external reality. After trance has been induced, the hypnotist can tell him to brighten up, pay attention, talk, move and so forth, without the trance state dissolving. But it is also possible to induce trance by the opposite approach, namely arousal. The subject paces the floor, while the hypnotist tells him he is keyed up, on edge, that his thoughts and emotions will erupt. He is encouraged to spin round, bend his knees, and attend to the parts of his body beginning with the toes. After from five to twenty-five minutes of this, trance sets in; his face takes on the usual distant expression and the customary phenomena, such as suggested hallucination, automatic writing, etc., are producible. This has been called, misleadingly, 'hyper-alert trance'. It is obviously akin to possession.

Finally, Meares, an Australian hypnotherapist, has reported on what he calls the Y-state, resembling the trance of meditation. (Y for yoga, I suspect.) Finding that some of his patients fell from hypnotic trance into actual sleep as a way of avoiding uncomfortable discussion of their personal problems, Meares took to suggesting simply that they were completely relaxed. 'Utter calm', 'complete security' are the suggestions made. The subject's jaw sags, his eyes close, his muscles become flaccid, his forehead smooth. Then the suggestion is made: 'You are wide awake, completely alert,' and so on. The method works best with introverts and those who are accustomed to practise meditation.

It looks, therefore, as if the hypnotic state is simply a variant on a state of consciousness also widely known in other forms. Any explanation then, to be convincing, should throw light on all these conditions. But before debating the underlying psychology, it will be helpful if I outline the curious phenomena which occur in the hypnotic state, since they bear on what has to be explained. While many of the miracles attributed to hypnosis are imaginary, what has stood up to scientific investigation is queer enough in all conscience.

Rather arbitrarily, I propose to group these phenomena under seven headings. Lengthy books have been written on this subject, and I shall only try to give the cream. In many cases, one group of workers has been unable to duplicate the results reported by another group, and I have used my judgment in selecting what seems to be reliable from among hundreds of claims. (For those who want more detail, Weitzenhoffer's classic review of 1953 gives an admirable survey of the position up to that date. I have added a good deal of more recent evidence.)

1. The best-defined group of effects are the physical ones. Touch a hypnotised subject with a pencil after suggesting it is red-hot iron and his skin will blister. For long regarded sceptically, this is now established as a fact. Allergic reactions can also be induced by suggestion. Two Japanese workers, Ikemi and Nakagawa, caused an allergic rash by telling the subject (who was blindfolded) that he had been touched by a leaf from the Japanese wax-tree, when in fact it was a chestnut leaf. Even more extraordinarily, no weal appeared when they touched his hand with a real wax-plant leaf, saying it was a chestnut. And, as most people know, warts can be caused to vanish by hypnotic suggestion. There is clearly some mechanism connecting mind and body, to which hypnosis gives access. I shall discuss this whole question further when I come to consider psychosomatic disease.

2. Amnesia for events occurring during the trance is regarded by some authorities as the decisive proof of a trance state having been induced. Such amnesia, however, is rarely total and does not last indefinitely. After six or seven months a good deal returns. However, the extraordinary case of an English WAAF, part of a secret British unit working in the US during the war, came to light many years later when she went to a hypnotherapist for help. It turned out that her emotional problems arose from repressed memories of the tragic death of a member of the unit, in circumstances which had caused great resentment at the time. She did finally recall, after much probing, that she had been hypnotised by an American officer and ordered to forget the entire incident. I will not comment on the ethics of this, but simply draw the conclusion that suggestion of amnesia does not wipe out the record, it merely prevents its rising to consciousness. This is further illuminated by the comment of a hypnotised American boy who said: 'I feel that if I thought hard enough, I could remember, but I just can't get down to business.' Another said, 'I do remember but I can't say.' Thus it seems to be a question of the will rather than an actual paralysis of the recall mechanism.

Hypnosis can also be used for the converse purpose: facilitating memory. Hypnotists regularly use it to bring repressed material to conscious awareness. Some analysts prefer to use it to obtain clues, leaving the patient amnesic, then question him in the non-hypnotised state until he recovers the memories for himself. They claim this has a better therapeutic effect. The Israeli police are reported to have used hypnotism to extract details – such as car registration numbers – from bystanders who have witnessed terrorist incidents or the like. By 'racking one's brains' one can often recall details one thought one had forgotten or never noticed. Hypnotic suggestion probably provides the motivation to do this, rather than modifying recall as such.

3. Post-hypnotic suggestion is usually combined with amnesia. M. T. Orne carried out experiments in which a subject was told under hypnosis to scratch his nose every time the word 'experiment' was mentioned. Subsequently, he was asked back to the laboratory on some excuse and the word 'experiment' was introduced into the conversation. Each time it appeared, he touched his nose – but when the word was used by a casual visitor, or by secretarial staff, he failed to do so. It seemed that he was unconsciously distinguishing between the word when used by the experimenter as part of this experiment and situations which he felt were not part of an experiment. He was, of course, unaware of his automatism.

However, in another case the subject was told to touch his hair whenever the word 'seal' was mentioned. Six weeks later he returned to the laboratory with a red patch above his forehead and asked if any suggestion about seals had been made. He had been obsessed by the subject, he said; he had read every book on seals in the local library and had proposed to his wife to buy one and keep it in the bath. Only her objections as to how to feed it had prevented his doing so! There certainly seems to have been amnesia for the making of the suggestion in this case.

4. A demonstration dear to stage hypnotists is the 'human plank'. The subject is told to remain rigid, is placed across two chairs like a plank, and then the hypnotist stands on his stomach. Actually any fit and strong-minded person can do this if so minded, and Professor T. X.

Barber, a sceptic about hypnotism, loves to demonstrate the fact to anyone visiting his lab.

It is also claimed that muscular strength can be increased, but tests show that the increase is no greater than can be produced by a non-hypnotised person who is really trying. Hypnotism just provides the motivation. (However, some feats of endurance the hypnotised subject does better than the normal, if the suggestion that he cannot perceive pain is made.) Of course, it is easy to simulate a reduction in strength. The same is true of attempts to induce exceptional visual, auditory or tactile acuity.

Attempts have been made to change body metabolism and other functions not under voluntary control. It is found that, while suggesting the actual change has no effect, suggesting the appropriate emotion or circumstance does produce a physiological change. Thus you cannot cause enzyme secretion by ordering: 'Secrete enzymes,' but you can do so by saying, 'Imagine you have just eaten a large meal.' And the response is rather specific. If you suggest that a fatty meal has been eaten, lipase – the enzyme which digests fat – is secreted and shows up in the urine. If you suggest, on the other hand, that a high-protein meal has been eaten, trypsin and pepsin are secreted. Similarly, suggestions of anxiety will increase the heart rate, alter respiration and promote sweating. Once again, we are back to the question of the mind-body relationship, rather than hypnosis.

Several attempts have been made to induce blindness, by analogy with the hysterical blindness well known to psychiatrists. The subject puts on a very good show of being blind, but when given sophisticated tests reveals that he or she can see perfectly well. The alpha rhythm, usually absent when the eyes are open, remains absent. The same is true of suggested colour blindness and deafness. This brings us to the question of how far such effects are a form of acting or role playing, but before discussing it, I must pick up the point about awareness of pain, and suggested anaesthesia.

5. Probably no hypnotic phenomenon has impressed people with the magical qualities of hypnosis more than its ability to block pain. There is no doubt that hypnotic suggestion *can* reduce awareness of pain, and hypnotic procedures are used by many dentists and even for minor surgery every day, although its effectiveness depends on depth of trance and it does not work for everyone. Voluntary functions, such as flinching, are controlled. There seems to be some doubt whether involuntary phenomena, such as the electrical conductivity of skin, remain unaffected by the pain under suggested analgesia.

The question is: what is actually happening? Some subjects report that the pain has not actually disappeared – it just does not seem to matter. It is somehow divorced from them personally. This hint of an ego-change is worth remembering, for we shall find other evidence of the same sort. A subject of G. H. Estabrooks who was engaged in automatic writing with his left hand began to write a stream of curses when his right hand was sharply pricked, though behaving in every other way as if he felt nothing! I infer that some inhibitory process in the brain is at work, divorcing the pain-manifesting circuits from the ones concerned with ego functions.

6. In the typical stage demonstration of hypnosis, the subject is asked to enact various roles – to pretend he is a baby or to converse with an imaginary person and so on. Investigators have explored this 'acting as if' capacity in a wide variety of ways, for it raises the fundamental question of how far, and in what sense, the subject is consciously acting or unconsciously faking the result.

Is Hypnosis a Fake?

A common procedure is to instruct the subject to hallucinate a person or thing which is not there, or to hallucinate out of existence (negative hallucination) something which is in fact there. If you ask the subject to hallucinate a chair out of existence and then ask him to walk through the space where it is standing, he hesitates slightly before he crashes into it. And if you ask him to hallucinate out of existence the newspaper you are holding, and then ask him to read certain words to which you point, he will do so. Thus clearly he can see the newspaper and is only 'pretending' not to. (I put quotes round 'pretending' because the exact meaning of the term here requires discussion.)

In another demonstration, the subject is asked to hallucinate the hypnotist's assistant as sitting in the chair opposite him. The assistant himself then walks into view and the subject is asked what he sees. Typically he replies: 'How odd, I see two assistants. One of them must be a hallucination, but which? Ah, I know how to find out. I can will one of them to do whatever I want.' The hypnotised subject shows extreme ingenuity in dealing with such situations. Charles Tart, the Californian authority on states of consciousness, tells how he instructed a subject to imagine himself going downstairs and out into the garden. Here a mole came out of a hole, he reported, so he picked it up. He was then told to return to the room, as part of his mental journey, and stand in the middle of the floor. Tart then asked him to describe the contents of the room, which he did, omitting any mention of himself sitting, as he had been all the time, in a chair. Something like the following dialogue, Tart recalls, then took place:

Tart: Is there anyone sitting in the chair?
S: I am.
CT: Didn't you just tell me you were standing in the middle of the room?
S: Yes, I am standing in the middle of the room.
CT: Do you think it's contradictory to tell me you're standing in the middle of the room and sitting in the chair at the same time?
S: Yes.
CT: Does the contradiction bother you?
S: No.
CT: Which one of the two selves is your real self?
S: They are both my real self.

This stumped Tart until he finally thought of a further question:

CT: Is there any difference at all between the two selves?
S: Yes, the me standing in the middle of the floor has a mole in his hand.

As this anecdote reveals, the hypnotised subject has an unusual tolerance for logical incongruities. The two sub-systems which have formed in his brain co-exist without any integration occurring or being felt desirable.

Another favourite ploy of hypnotists is to ask the subject to move back in time, becoming younger and younger. Now you are twenty, now you are fifteen, now you are twelve, and so on. When one subject reached the age at which he had a serious asthma attack in real life, he began to reproduce all the systems of such an attack in the laboratory situation. Most workers report that it is impossible to regress people earlier than about age six, although one or two hypnotists claim to have regressed people right into the womb. One London worker even reported that his patient heard a regular 'boom, boom', which was supposedly the beating of his mother's heart; then he felt a frightful burning sensation, which was allegedly due to the fact that his mother had attempted to procure an abortion.

In America, Milton Kline has progressed people forward in time and reports changes comparable with senescence. Such tests prove little unless the subject's powers of simulating when unhypnotised are also tested. Rubinstein and Newman at the Yale School of Psychiatry have progressed people forward in time and note that such subjects have sometimes reported unwished-for events, such as death of a son. This, they conclude, casts doubt on the validity of age-regression. It well might. When intelligence tests are given to regressed subjects, their mental age is always revealed as higher than their 'regressed' age. Events which they no longer recall, or never knew about, are not re-enacted. They make statements which can be checked against records, and which prove to be in error, such as saying they were at school when they were not. In one such case, a subject who was born German and learned English later, proved quite able to comprehend questions in English when regressed to an age at which he was monoglot – while explaining to the hypnotist in German that he could not speak English!

From these and many other enquiries it seems certain that all such 'as if' experiences involve an elaborate kind of play-acting. But how far is the subject *consciously and deliberately* acting? Is his ego involved?

Some sceptics regard the whole business as little more than faking. Professor T. X. Barber has repeatedly shown that most hypnotic effects can be obtained with unhypnotised subjects. If sufficiently motivated, they can ignore pain, change their metabolism, respond to delayed suggestions, act as planks and so forth. However, this does not answer the question why hypnotised subjects become willing to do things most people would simply refuse to do, and continue in this state until released. It is all very well for Professor Barber to demand of his students that they should carry out his wishes – they already have strong motives for pleasing him.

Apart from this, the appearance of the hypnotised person is somewhat abnormal: his gaze is glassy, he is humourless, and withdrawn. Furthermore, he feels different. As one of the great French psychiatrist Paul Janet's patients, whom he was using to hypnotise, said to him: 'I am perfectly ready to obey you and I will do it if you choose: but I tell you beforehand that the thing did not take.'

In an attempt to explore the difference in the state of consciousness of the hypnotised person, the experiment has often been done of asking a control group of unhypnotised subjects to perform the same actions as the hypnotised ones, and to look for differences. It is found, for example, that when the control who is simulating a negative hallucination walks into the obstruction, he does not hesitate, in the way the hypnotised person does. When he is presented with the person, in the flesh, whom he has supposedly hallucinated out of existence, he denies seeing him. In a word, the simulator does not have the tolerance for incongruity that the hypnotised person has.

To discover whether subjects were falsifying their reports, L. F. Cooper devised various ingenious ploys; the subjects were almost equally ingenious at avoiding being exposed. Thus when one subject was told that he would see a 'bremfra', he reported seeing a woman with a parcel under her arm. Questioned further, he explained that the bremfra was in the parcel. On another occasion Cooper played tapes of Lithuanian speech and suggested the subject would understand what was being said. The subject subsequently reported that he had indeed understood but was unable to say what he had heard. He did not attempt to fabricate. In this kind of situation, the simulator tends to fabricate a plausible reply. The impression one gets is of a naïve readiness to accept the hypnotist's assertions and to behave *as if* they were true, rather than of conscious 'play-acting'.

On the other hand, Cooper obtained intriguing results when he attempted to compress the subjects' awareness of time. In the fifties, he performed an experiment with a woman violinist, in which she had to rehearse material under hypnosis. She then applied this to her work, and found that she could practise on an hallucinated violin much faster than she could normally. She reported: 'I did passage practice – picking hard passages and playing them in several different ways. Then I went through the whole composition for continuity. In doing this in "special time" I seemed to get an immediate grasp of the composition as a whole.' Subjects trained in this way were often able to complete activities normally taking half an hour in ten seconds. In simpler tests involving writing sentences, the effect was less startling but still impressive; output was sometimes more than doubled, a real time of twenty-seven minutes being hallucinated as ninety-six, in one such experiment.

Numerous theories of hypnotism have been advanced. Most of them strike me as little more than wrapping the subject up in words. To say that hypnosis is 'a state of enhanced suggestibility' is to state the obvious. What we want to know is why such suggestibility has supervened. Many of the theories do not cover all the facts. To say that the subject has adopted the hypnotist's ego as his own and only perceives the world through him fails to explain auto-hypnosis or the carrying out of post-hypnotic suggestions. Seldom has there been a subject on which so many hundreds of thousands of words have been written to so little effect and I shall not burden you with a recapitulation of them. The best that can be said, I believe, is that brain function is composed of sub-systems, and that the ego-system relinquishes control of bodily and sensori-motor systems in hypnosis, just as it does when one is extremely tired.*

* The idea that hypnosis is concerned with splitting mental activity into sub-systems is lent further support by experiments in which multiple personalities were evoked by hypnotic suggestion. H. C. Leavitt evoked secondary and tertiary personalities and exposed them to Rorschach and other psychological tests. He found that the personalities, though quite real, were substructures of the normal total personality. That is what one would expect – and of course the same is true of those multiple personalities which appear spontaneously, as I shall describe in the next chapter. In a word, hypnosis is one more instance of the phenomenon of inhibition.

What is genuinely interesting, I would like to suggest – and the point has not been widely taken – is that hypnosis gives one access to the unconscious and to the levels at which the mind can affect the body. It is, evidently, the ego which suppresses disagreeable information; by-passing the ego enables it to emerge. It also enables intuitive subtleties to emerge which, in normal life, are damped down by the rational faculties. For instance, at the Menninger Clinic, L. S. Kubie found that naïve subjects could interpret the dream symbolism of other subjects more expertly than unhypnotised persons; one of them could interpret the cryptic automatic writing of another – writing which was incomprehensible to the psychologists. Using a form of hypnotic reverie they found neurotic subjects could recall childhood traumas without the guilt-laden feelings evoked in ordinary analysis.

One man, who had made no progress in analysis for two years, was able in three hypnotic sessions to recall his major childhood traumas – falling from a pony, being assaulted sexually, a rejection by his mother, etc. – and was rapidly restored to normality. Not only the facts are revived: the emotions once felt are relived.

I said I would mention seven categories of hypnotic phenomena and I have named only six. The seventh is more dubious, less generally accepted. It is the enhancement of powers of extra-sensory perception. Charles Honorton and Stanley Krippner, who are principally associated with the Maimonides Medical Center in Brooklyn, have reviewed the evidence as well as conducting a number of experiments. The margins of success, though sometimes significant in the statistical sense, are very small, and the experiments are inconsistent with one another. Attempts have also been made to hypnotise people into dreaming the contents of sealed envelopes, with similarly confusing results. Enthusiasts tend to interpret these results encouragingly. If barely significant results are achieved in nine out of twelve experiments, this can be called seventy-five per cent success. It can also be called inconclusive. However, the possibility that access to paranormal powers can be facilitated by hypnosis does not seem inherently improbable, provided that they exist at all.

Levels of Consciousness

How can we bring all these various types of trance into a coherent system? Is there any general explanation which would make sense of what is going on? In view of the long history of puzzlement they have aroused, I think it is a matter of some importance that the answer to such questions is at last 'yes'. A tentative 'yes' to be sure; there is still much to learn. But at least they can be fitted plausibly into the scheme of things.

In an area as complex as mental function, simple answers are inevitably over-simple answers and it is difficult to steer between the Scylla of simplicism and the Charybdis of obscurity. The following must therefore be taken as clues rather than definitive accounts, as forays into a country still only partly opened up.

Start by thinking of mental function as an array of sub-systems. Some of these systems are rather obvious. There is the motor system which orders and co-ordinates our physical movements and actions. There is the exteroception system which provides us with information about our environment: it readily breaks down into sub-sub-systems for vision, hearing, touch and so on. There is an interoception system which gives us data on the state of our body and its organs, the position of our limbs, and so forth. Then memory can be regarded as a sub-system, and so can our emotional responses. There is clearly a system which makes plans and decisions. And there is a system concerned with personal identity, often called the ego, about which I shall write more in the next chapter. I suspect there is probably a system which deals with our time sense and it may be combined with one mediating handling our sense of space – a system which conveys to us such feeling as 'far away and long ago' or 'it all seemed to happen in a flash' as well as handling sequential material such as music and speech.

Professor Charles Tart, whom I introduced to you as a specialist on consciousness a few pages ago, has stuck his neck out and identified ten such systems, adding to the eight I have named, the sub-conscious, and 'input processing', by which he means the abstraction of general ideas and concepts from the perceptions yielded by the intero- and exteroceptors. I suspect the list is too short – where does imagery fit in, for instance? But the real trouble with a simple list like this is that it is too clear-cut. The brain is a subtle device, constantly reorganising itself, and quite capable of using the same equipment for different purposes. Thus one cannot really draw a line between exteroception and input processing: the one runs into the other, and interoceptive data is fed in at the same time. Again, the line between conscious and sub-conscious is fluid. And as we shall see later, perception is very closely linked with memory. Nor can we say that these systems are on a par with one another. The 'ego' embraces, or can embrace, almost all the other systems, or at any rate, much of the data processed by them. On the other hand, the time-space sense, though also feeding into all the other systems, is evidently much simpler and less subtle than 'ego'.

With this caveat, one can proceed to show how such an analysis illuminates the notion of altered states of consciousness. Broadly, individual sub-systems can be damped down, pepped up, or phased out entirely. Thus in sleep the sensory and motor systems are damped down almost to a standstill, and so is the planning system, whereas the unconscious is stimulated to activity.

The application to hypnotic trance is evident: there is a damping down of the planning sub-system; the hypnotist's suggestions are treated as if they came from the subject's ego. There is generally a damping of the memory system too. The hypnotist's suggestion can also damp the sensory system, when it is suggested the subject cannot feel pain. Alternatively, as G. S. Blum has shown, the senses can be hyper-alerted. (Blum tells his subjects that their feelings will increase as he turns up the lights and decrease when he turns them down. In this way he creates a 'volume control' which he can manipulate.)

Let me remind you at this point of what I said earlier about the brain as an inhibitory rather than a facilitatory mechanism. We see here very plainly how inhibition can be applied not merely to single cells but to major cell systems, and even, I suspect, to specific aspects of such systems – so that a cell may be inhibited in respect of one system while still functioning as a component of other systems.

Meditational trance seems to represent a massive inhibition of almost all cortical systems. As I have already described, sensory perceptual and cognitive mechanisms are brought to a stop, and the sense of ego dissolved. Memory, too, is blanked off. As St John of the Cross observed, the soul must strip itself of all forms and manners of knowledge, and it cannot do this 'unless the memory be annihilated as to all its forms'.

Time and space sense also goes. When all the functions performed by the brain as we understand it have been stilled, what remains? Not, as one might suppose, nothing at all, but an amazing sense of deity, to which mystics of all ages bear witness. Can it be that some primitive function lies buried beneath the accretions which, in the course of evolution, the brain has acquired, which has an ultimate character lying quite outside our phenomenal science?

If so, what will be the effect on modern man of the clear realisation that this is the case? While some, naturally, will close their minds to a discovery so inconvenient to their habits and aims, others surely will seek to pursue the path of transcendence, and perhaps bring about a quasi-religious revival of a kind unknown to the history of technologically advanced nations.

The altered states of consciousness which involve 'possession' by supposed spirits or other personalities clearly arise from disturbances of the ego sub-system and I shall deal with them in the next chapter.

Back to Square One

From the time that evolution theory began to affect thinking – say in the 1880s – neurologists tended to assume that the evolution of the brain had been simply an evolution in complexity. With this had gone a transfer of reflex and instinctive activities to planned and consciously controlled activities. Where the bird builds a nest by following built-in patterns common to fellow-members of the species, a man can plan a house and build it to satisfy his personal whims. But there is a counter-theory, dimly glimpsed by Hughlings Jackson in Darwin's time, developed by Freud and others, and restated in a detailed way (as I mentioned briefly in Chapter Three) by Paul McLean in the 1960s, according to which the brain developed through four distinct phases.

As McLean puts it, Phase One was the brain of reptiles, emotion as we know it has not yet appeared; there are simply drives to satisfy immediate needs. Cognitively, there is no understanding of future or past: everything is done on a here-and-now basis. Behaviour is precipitate and changeable. (There are other distinctions, but there is no need to pursue them here.) Phase Two is the paleo-mammalian brain, which comprises most of the sub-cortical systems, mentioned earlier. Anger and fear emerge as emotions. Awareness has a dreamlike quality. Behaviour is no longer controlled rigidly by instinct and responses are less automatic and immediate. Phase Three is the neo-mammalian brain based on the cortex. The external world is analysed in a much more detailed way; emotions are more elaborate; actions are planned to an increasing extent. Finally, in the fourth phase, one hemisphere of the brain is specialised to deal with symbols, and in particular language and speech. Of course these phases do not replace one another with a click! but are stages through which development moves. Moreover, the earlier structures continue to exist. But there is a transfer of functions from older to newer structures, or so it is thought. We can see this distinctly in the case of vision, which is handled by the thalamus in Phase Two but handed over to the visual cortex in Phase Three. Nick Humphrey's monkey, Helen, demonstrated the rediscovery of thalamic vision when cortical vision became impossible, and thereby showed that the more primitive structures retain functional capacity or potential although they have been superseded. Probably earlier structures modify their function when superseded and they certainly remain in close working relationship with the newer structures. It is not so much a replacement as the adding of refinements, and a more detailed specialisation of substructures. This process began when early headless creatures like Amphioxus – a needlelike worm which is the same at each end – evolved into creatures with a head, containing nerve ganglia. This steady drift of control-functions towards one end of the body, known as encephalisation, continued throughout the evolutionary story, and the differentiation of new brain structures is simply the latest chapter.

These facts give us the necessary background to answer more precisely the question: where is consciousness located? The answer is: consciousness is not one thing but a graded series, and the series is distributed through graded structures. And when higher levels of consciousness are abolished, by drugs or damage or self-inhibition, the lower levels remain functional.

Now this is where the story becomes even more interesting. In the development of the individual (ontogeny) the same stages are to be seen as in the development of the species by evolution (phylogeny). The nineteenth-century biologist and enthusiast for Darwin's ideas, Ernst Haeckel, declared that phylogeny repeats ontogeny: that all creatures recapitulate their evolutionary history. This turned out to be a great oversimplification, but has a core of truth. Now this is very odd. It implies, so to say, a memory of a racial history in (presumably) the genes. And not just memory, but an iron necessity which (for example) causes you and me to develop rudimentary gills at one stage in embryonic life, as if, at that stage, we expected to become fishes.

Applying this notion to the development of the brain, we might expect to find the young human being exhibiting at least some parallels with the early phases in the development of Phase Four consciousness. And so we do. The baby has no sense of past or future, sucks and grips instinctively, hardly distinguishes itself from its surroundings, and so on. The child reflects the 'limbic presentational' Phase Two: though more aware of self than the baby, it does not plan far ahead or much heed the past. And though it has a cortex which presents the external world in precise detail, yet it makes few abstractions. Most people can recall that, in their youth, colours were more vivid, experiences more intense and moving, fantasy richer – this was not, as people sometimes say, because the world was new to it but rather because the fulcrum of its life was in the limbic systems rather than in the cortex.

Wordsworth was expressing something of the sort when he wrote:

> There was a time when meadow, grove and stream,
> The earth, and every common sight,
> To me did seem
> Apparelled in celestial light,
> The glory and the freshness of a dream.

In religious conversion, too, we find descriptions of the dramatic increase in the vividness of experience which must have a similar origin. 'I remember this, that everything looked new to me, the people, the fields, the cattle, the trees. I was like a new man in a new world.' It was this heightened awareness which Blake referred to when he urged us to 'cleanse the doors of perception'.

And now we can introduce a further seminal idea: that of regression. Freud, and his psychoanalytic followers, have made great use of the idea of a regression to infantile patterns of behaviour, and even to a womb-like state, as a response to stress. And it has often been noted that people behave in a more primitive way when in a crisis. The panicking crowd runs headlong to safety, without thinking ahead. Or it expresses its fear and hatred in lynching, for example, without calculating the consequences. Today Freud's rather imprecise idea – a mere description of behaviour – is seen to have a solid neurophysiological basis. This can even be demonstrated: in the few cases where both cerebral hemispheres have been removed in man, behaviour of this primitive type remains. And many aspects of schizophrenic behaviour can be accounted for in these terms.

In Deikman's experiment on meditation, which I described a few pages back, we see regression to Phase Two occurring before our very eyes; colours became more vivid, and one subject found it impossible to analyse the view from the window – which I interpret as the breakdown of cortically mediated vision in favour of thalamic vision. He said, rather incoherently, 'I don't know how to describe it, it's scattered . . . The view didn't organise itself in any way. There were no planes, one behind the other. There was no response to certain patterns. Everything was working at the same intensity . . . like a bad painting . . . I didn't see the order to it or the patterning to it or anything and I couldn't impose it, it resisted my imposition of pattern.'

I shall conclude the chapter with a question to which I do not know the answer. The mystical experience, to which all Oriental religions urge us – though Christianity has always been ambivalent about it – implies a rejection of the whole great process of encephalisation to which evolution has been devoted. It demands a regression to the starting point. Is the whole of evolution therefore a movement away from perfection? Are all our ambitions for more intelligence and more delicate perception and awareness misconceived? Or is regression the error? Is the mystical state, or Nirvana, a rejection of all that evolution has achieved in two thousand million years? Or can we have the best of both worlds?

7

I Am Me

WHO WAS GUILTY?

In October 1978 a man named William Stanley Milligan, aged twenty-three, was charged with rape, kidnapping and robbery in Columbus, Ohio, according to the local paper, the Citizen-Journal. *He had been under observation in hospital since March on the grounds that he had ten distinct personalities, each with its own name, its own likes and dislikes, and its own intelligence quotient. They ranged in age from two to twenty-three and he referred to them as his 'family'.*

The intelligent personality was named Arthur, aged twenty-two. He had an English accent and seems to have exerted a good influence on his fellow-personalities. But Ragan, aged twenty-three, was the evil personality – the Mr Hyde to Arthur's Jekyll – though he defended the others, particularly Christene, apparently the only female personality in the group. According to the paper, when he was in gaol, 'Christene' was drawing a picture when a guard spilled water on it. 'Ragan' immediately replaced 'Christene' and made to attack the guard. The names seem symbolic: Rage for the aggressor; Christ for the pure one; (King) Arthur for the virtuous one.

Milligan had had a very disturbed childhood. His natural father had committed suicide when he was three. His mother married a man named Milligan, who adopted him. He had a series of stepfathers and was maltreated as a child. By October, the psychiatrists had succeeded in integrating his personalities sufficiently for him to stand trial.

Source: the *Guardian*, 2 October 1978.

How to Tell Yourself From a Zombie

During the war, the twenty-one-year-old officer in charge of a Commando Unit in North Africa, giving a talk on his unit, suddenly felt as though he was talking like an automaton. After a few hours the sensation wore off, but it recurred every two or three days, sometimes coming on quite suddenly. He began to experience curious bodily symptoms as well as a sense of unreality. Everything appeared flat and lifeless. His movements felt clumsy and unsteady. There was a singing in his ears, and his hands and feet felt detached, as if they did not belong to him. He said that his mouth felt like an 'empty cavern' and when he was eating it sometimes felt as though he were chewing powdered glass. In general his sensations – his sense of taste – his response to tickling, even pain – were feebler than normal, to the point where awareness of the fullness of his bladder even seemed muffled.

When he finally sought medical help, he described his feelings to the doctor in these words: 'I seem to have no personality, as if I had no background, no future and no ties at all with anyone or anything. I feel non-existent as a personality – like a vacuum.'

Or, as another such patient put it: 'I feel as though I am not here at all. My mind appears to be here, but the rest of me seems to have gone. I have to touch things to make sure I am still here.'

Such temporary disturbances of the sense of personal identity are known as 'depersonalisation'. It is, I think you will agree, our sense of identity which gives us the feeling that we are something more than our brain and body. Creatures resembling men and women devoid of such identity are usually known as zombies. If robots resembling people are ever built, they too, I imagine, will be zombies. So it will be interesting to look more closely at the phenomenon of depersonalisation; the fragility of our sense of identity justifies the suspicion that it may not be so fundamental, so unmachinelike, after all. Is the sense of identity just a product of the brain circuitry?

While the cases I have just described were extreme ones, calling for medical help, milder, transient experiences of this kind are not uncommon, especially during adolescence. When, after a lecture on the subject, a group of students were asked whether any of them had ever had a similar experience, nearly half replied that they had. They were asked to write accounts of what they felt. For instance, one nineteen-year-old girl described how she had been for a stroll with a friend. 'Suddenly, as we were walking along, I seemed to be completely apart from myself. I felt I was somewhere above looking down on a scene of which I was part and yet not a part. I was walking and talking as though automatically. I couldn't feel any movement and yet I knew I was walking . . . I was completely unable to tell whether I myself was still present or whether I was the part which had gone. In short, there were two different beings.'

This experience would seem to be somewhat different from the officer's. Here there was a splitting of the ego-system into two systems. Something slightly different again was reported by another girl, aged twenty-three: 'One half of me was watching the other perform in a completely disinterested way. I could hear my voice and that of other people very remotely, although there was no lessening of sound. It seemed rather pointless to reply to remarks being made but I heard my voice doing so. Time did seem to be going much more slowly.' This girl was aware of herself as an ego, an individual, but perceptions and body awareness were not incorporated in the ego-system. The time-space system was also disturbed.

A third girl made a somewhat similar comment, she said that she felt, quite intensely, that SHE was located in her brain, just behind the eyes, but that the rest of her head and her body was just a biological machine and did not belong to her. Here I might make an 'aside' to the effect that it is easy to see how a dualist view could have arisen from such experiences.

These girls, I note, had not actually lost their sense of identity so much as become divorced from reality, from other people, the surroundings and their own bodies. We may comprehend this as an uncoupling of the ego sub-system from the perceptual-cognitive systems, and perhaps from others, such as the time-space mechanism. Of course, these experiences were quite brief and did not display the disturbing features which bothered the young officer.

The distinction between these two kinds of case obliges us to define the notion of ego more carefully. None of the girls had lost the basic feeling, which, for lack of a better term, one might call 'I am me'. For this core meaning, the word 'ego' is no longer appropriate because it has acquired too many other connotations. Dr Nathan Leites in his book on the ego complains, very justifiably, of the looseness with which the term is commonly employed. I am certainly not talking about what Freud meant by that term. For Freud the ego was an executive function, to be distinguished from the impulses of the id and the forces of conscience which he called super-ego. Experimental psychologists and clinicians have, on the whole, gone along with him in regarding the ego as an executive function, and speak of strong and weak egos (in contrast with my use of such expressions) when the will and capacity to act are indicated.

But I have been trying to discuss something more subjective than the integration of functions: when the mountaineer or depersonalised individual says that his body was walking along but that *he* was floating above it, he is referring to this subjective sense of 'I myself'. I therefore propose, from now on, to use in this sense the Latin word Egoge, which rhymes with roguey-poguey and means 'I myself'.

The same vagueness attaches to words like 'self' and 'identity'. As I see it, the accepted use of the word 'self' is to indicate egoge seen, so to speak, from the outside. When we say, 'I have hurt myself', we distinguish I-as-subject and agent from I-as-object or victim. But Jungians, if I understand aright, use 'self' rather as I would use egoge, to mean the central core of ego.

Psychologists also speak of 'self image' and common parlance includes such terms as 'self respect', 'self abasement', etc. Here we refer to something else again: the assembly of attitudes, values, habits, skills, etc., by which we are known and which we recognise in ourselves. This, I believe, is best conveyed by the word 'identity'.

'Identity' is the kind of person other people consider us to be; self image is the kind of person we consider ourselves to be and may or may not coincide with our identity. People sometimes turn up at hospitals or police stations and explain, in some confusion, that they do not know who they are. They have lost their identity. They have amnesia for their name, role in life, place of residence, and so on. But they think of themselves as being someone, the 'egoge' is there, though the memory system is in disarray. Incidentally, they still remember how to speak, how to eat and even how to locate a hospital.

Human beings desire strongly to appear as unique, in the sense of being distinguishable from their fellows; they do not want to be ciphers. Modern society tends to make people into ciphers – the production line worker might die and another person step into his shoes and carry on. His contribution had no unique character. In contrast, writers and artists, performers, those who achieve distinction in any field of skill, are individuals. There is only one Menuhin, one Bonington, one Hitler. The fact that, after a murder, many false confessions are made reflects the desperateness of the desire to achieve an identity. Indeed, much crime may have its real origin in the desire to escape from the ruck and to see oneself, at least, as having done something unusual. Those who seek to order society constantly fail to grasp the need to give expression to this basic need. The deprivation of identity on joining the armed forces is painful to many recruited from civil life, in wartime, and was a deliberate policy in Hitler's concentration camps. It is a neglected factor in prisons also.

If I seem to labour the point, it is because it is so surprising. If the mind is machinery, merely, one would not expect it. Robots are not seen as having an identity. Machinery does sometimes acquire a certain identity with the passage of time, as seen by its users. (One thinks particularly of cars and boats.) But it does not demand identity as a condition of its own effective functioning.

In an attempt to understand the ego, let us look at some further forms of ego-disturbance.

Weirdest of the Weirdest

Poets and mystics describe a state in which the ego seems to encompass all other people, even the landscape, all that is. Byron said, 'I live not in myself, but I become a portion of that around me.' Ralph Hetherington, a Quaker, has written: 'A sudden concentration of attention on a rainy August morning. Clusters of bright red berries, some slightly wrinkled, some blemished, others perfect, hanging among green leaves. Drops of rain glistening on berries and leaves. The experience could not have lasted more than a few seconds, but that was a moment out of time. I was caught up in what I saw, I became part of it; the berries, the leaves, the raindrops and I, we were all of a piece.'

Marghanita Laski has called this an 'intensity experience' – she has gathered together many such accounts in her book *Ecstasy*. Accounts by Emily Brontë and D. H. Lawrence, by Tennyson and George Meredith, by mystics like Suso and Ruysbroek, as well as less famous names. The description given by Bernard Berenson, the art expert, is particularly interesting. He was gazing at the leafy scrolls carved on the door jambs of the church of San Pietro near Spoleto when the experience occurred. 'Suddenly stem, tendril and foliage became alive and, in becoming alive, made me feel as if I had emerged into the light after a long groping in the darkness of an initiation. I felt as one illuminated, and beheld a world where every outline, every edge and every surface was in a living relation to me and not, as hitherto, in a merely cognitive one. Everywhere I feel the ideated pulsation of vitality, I mean energy and radiance, as if it all served to enhance my own functioning. Since that morning, nothing visible has been indifferent or even dull.'

A British schoolmaster, Michael Paffard, recently administered a questionnaire to four hundred and seventy-five schoolboys, schoolgirls and university students, after reading to them W. H. Hudson's account of such an experience in *Far Away and Long Ago*. He found that more than half reported having had a similar experience; he checked their claim by asking them to write an account and eliminating those he felt did not fill the bill. He found that four times out of five the experience occurred out of doors, and most often when the person concerned was alone. The event was slightly commoner among females than males.

In all these experiences, the sense of unity with the environment seems to indicate some kind of weakening of the system which distinguishes me from not-me. It is a suspension of the tagging system, if you like. But the metaphor of 'tagging' is a weak one. One should think rather of a pattern which can be analysed into differing sub-patterns, a kaleidoscope whose fragments fall into different configurations.

But the experience is not completely describable in these terms. It is also marked by a disorder of the significance-tagging mechanism. Further it has a moral quality and an emotive aspect. As Wordsworth puts it:

> To every natural form, rock, fruit and flower,
> Even the loose stones that cover the highway,
> I gave a moral life; I saw them feel,
> Or linked them to some feeling: the great mass
> Lay embedded in a quickening soul, and all
> That I beheld transpired with inward meaning.

Thirdly, it is extremely pleasurable. Fourthly, there is a sense of a divine presence.

And I have felt
A presence that disturbs me with the joy
Of elevated thoughts; a sense sublime
Of something far more deeply interfused,
Whose dwelling is the light of setting suns,
And the round ocean and the living air,
And the blue sky, and in the mind of man;
A motion and a spirit that impels
All thinking things, all objects of all thought
And rolls through all things. Therefore am I still
A lover of the meadows and the woods
And mountains. . . .

It seems almost facetious to pose the question: would Dr Good's android feel a conviction such as this?

At the practical level, then, one can interpret the sense of unity with all things as a loss of 'ego-boundaries' or a breakdown of the egoge sub-system. How is 'ego' formed? The child, according to received doctrine, at first regards all sensations and images as coming from within himself. Gradually he learns which are internal and which external. He 'tags' them appropriately. If the tagging mechanism fails, he will cease to distinguish 'me' and 'not-me'. But this applies not only to brief experiences. It may also affect the whole personality. In *The Angel Makers* I advanced the view that some people are constitutionally disposed either to feel themselves remote and separate from the rest of the world, or to feel themselves sympathetically bound to it. I called the first category 'hard-ego' and the second 'soft-ego'. Puritans, with their sense of being remote from God, and their harsh, competitive approach to their fellow-men, typified the former; Romantics, with their preoccupation with welfare and involvement with the weak and downtrodden, the latter. I argued that these attitudes were determined by introjection of parental figures – of the father in the former case, of the mother in the latter. Why such processes should affect ego formation and functioning is unexplained.

All that gave further support to the idea of the ego, in the central sense of I-myself, as a product of experience and development, and to that extent contributed to a materialist view of identity. But I do not pretend to explain why such feelings should be released by nature, why they should be accompanied by a sense of significance and of deity, or even why they should be so pleasurable. Until the identity theorists and the

Central State Materialists can offer some plausible explanation, I shall feel obliged to regard the matter as open.

Pantheism, as a sense of immanent deity, passes insensibly into Christian mysticism, even though bishops and theologians have sought to distinguish them. The Christian mystic feels, during his ecstasies, a sense of union with God, rather than with nature, and frequently describes it in the terms of sexual union; such mystics sometimes even use 'she' to describe themselves, even though male. In the union of two lovers there is, evidently, a modification of ego-bounds to the point at which each is sensitive to the feelings of the other. Parents, too, may feel the pain of a beloved child almost as if it were their own.

In the religious ecstasies, the sense of union is often preceded by a sense of isolation, desolation and remoteness from love. This kind of reversal, known as paradoxical inhibition, is familiar to psychologists in other fields. Conversion, which is always sudden, from a sense of despair to a sense of euphoria has been many times described. I cited numerous instances in *The Angel Makers*. Thus John Haime describes how he went into a lonely field, and after a bout of passionate weeping 'threw a stick at God, with the utmost enmity'. He tried to curse God aloud, but could not nerve himself to risk it. Suddenly he abandoned the struggle and at once experienced a revulsion of feeling; his heart was filled with love for God.

There is a worrying connection between mystical experience and schizophrenia. How close is the similarity can be seen from the account given by Morag Coate of schizophrenic episodes. At one point she writes:

> 'Suddenly my whole being was filled with light and loveliness and with an upsurge of deeply moving feeling from within myself to meet and reciprocate the influence which flowed into me. I was in a state of the most vivid awareness and illumination. What can I say of it? A cloudless, cerulean blue sky of the mind, shot through with shafts of exquisite, warm, dazzling sunlight. In its first and most intense stage it lasted perhaps half an hour. It seemed that some force or impulse from without were acting on me, looking into me; that I was in touch with a reality beyond my own: that I had made contact with the secret, ultimate source of life . . . It flashed across my mind: "This is what the mystics mean by the direct experience of God." '

There is considerable measure of agreement that in schizophrenia something strange has happened to the ego and in particular to its boundaries. Many schizophrenics say that they are too easily swayed, too suggestible – as if they had no identity of their own.

However, we have not considered all the ways in which ego can be disturbed. It can break up into sub-egos and coalesce again like a droplet of mercury.

My Name is Legion

The film *The Three Faces of Eve* has made many people familiar with the idea of multiple personality. Based on an actual case report, the film portrays a woman who is called Eve White: she is shy, inhibited, unhappy. But from time to time her behaviour changes: she dresses in a sexy manner, uses bad language, gets tight and is generally quite uninhibited. When she comes under analysis, the doctor and nurses note that her whole posture and manner are different, her face more attractive. This personality is distinguished as Eve Black. Eve White does not know what Eve Black is thinking, but Eve Black knows about Eve White's thoughts and problems. Sometimes Eve White wakes up with a hangover, and learns that as Eve Black she has 'raised hell' but has no memory of doing so. Eventually the analyst achieves a fusion of the two personalities and a new, more balanced Eve is stabilised.

Such cases are not especially rare. In 1789, at the beginning of the French Revolution, a stream of aristocratic French refugees arrived in Stuttgart. The doctor and scientist Johannes Gmelin tells how a twenty-year-old German girl, apparently impressed by the glamour of the refugees, suddenly exchanged her own personality for the manners and ways of a Frenchwoman. She spoke French perfectly, and German with a French accent, and imitated French ways. She kept switching between these two persons. As a Frenchwoman she had a complete memory of what she had done in previous French phases. As a German she had no recollection of her French phases. Gmelin could make her shift from one personality to another by a wave of the hand.

In England, from 1815, Mary Reynolds alternated two personalities from the age of nineteen to her death in 1854, and a French case was reported in 1836. Since then there have been many.

Perhaps the fullest report we have is that of 'Mrs G.' who was analysed over a period of three years by Robert Stoller, a Californian psychologist who has made a particular study of personal identity. Like most, if not all, such individuals, Mrs G. had had a very disturbing childhood. As she once commented, 'I was never allowed to be what I wanted to be, you know.' Mrs G. split into:

CHARLIE: This was in effect her conscience, criticising Mrs G.'s selfish and destructive actions.

CARRIE: Her uninhibited self. Carrie was in command of the

situation and would say things like, 'I'm going to be you,' or, 'I can put her on a diet' – meaning Mrs G.

CHRIS: An imaginary adopted baby.

She said of 'Carrie' – 'It wasn't so I wouldn't be lonely, that's what I had Charlie for.'

Charlie allied herself more and more with the analyst. As Mrs G. began to understand the reasons for her sense of resentment and to behave in a more civilised manner, Charlie warned her that he was going to disappear and did so soon after. Fusion of the personalities was achieved.

Whereas Eve White was a deeply inhibited woman whose 'id' broke out, Mrs G. was an uninhibited woman, whose 'super-ego' gradually regained control. Of the cases known to me where sufficient data is available, the former seems to be the commonest pattern.

But there are cases which take more explaining.

In 1919 a Boston psychiatrist, Dr Winifred Richmond, found that a young English teacher named Violet X. could produce automatic writing very rapidly, covering pages and pages of paper. These notes were written in varying styles and handwritings: over a period of three months, seven distinct personalities, plus several minor ones, emerged, each with its own name. Each spoke of itself in the first person, answered questions, gave advice, and a clear account of itself. Often one would interrupt another, even rudely, or comment scathingly on what another personality had said.

The first personality (apart from Violet herself, who was fully aware of what was going on) burst on the scene when Violet wrote in letters three inches high: 'Hello, I am ANNIE McGINNIS.' Violet's hand then proceeded to draw a portrait of a rather tough-looking girl. Annie's story, told in a series of instalments, was that she had been seduced, become a prostitute and died while giving birth to a child. She hated men and wrote long diatribes against them, but also told crude jokes and engaged in blarney.

Annie was followed by Mary Patterson, a quiet and reserved personality not unlike Violet herself. Mary Minott appeared next – a woman of the world who criticised Mary Patterson as a 'puritanical prig'. She had a passion for dress designing and produced numerous beautiful designs of great talent.

Then Alton, a real person, appeared; in life he was a friend of Violet's fiancé and attempted to woo Violet, who repulsed him. He told her she could become a medium. There was a brief visit from Violet's father followed by 'The Spirit of War and Desolation', who urged her to give up automatic writing and become a medium; and finally 'Man', who developed a hatred of Alton and finally drove him from the scene.

When Man was there, Violet felt a need to get up and dance. Man covered the paper with rhythmic lines and the injunction, 'Let's dance, Violet'. Finally Violet got up and began to dance, swaying more and more violently. Finally she cried out, her face depicting tremendous emotion – ecstasy and terror. Laid on a couch, she remained stiff and moaning. Afterwards she explained that she felt another personality was attempting to take over completely. 'I wanted to give myself up to it and yet I didn't want it. I can't describe it, but I felt as though I were two people.'

All seven of these 'personalities' expressed facets of her own personality, clearly a complex one. Possession by even larger numbers is on record.

Such cases make it easy to understand the phenomenon of possession, whether by the Devil or by the souls of animals or dead persons or of spirits, as occurs in many unlettered tribes.

In the case of the possessed nuns of Loudun, in the seventeenth century, made famous by Aldous Huxley's account, one notes that Sister Jeanne des Anges was finding an outlet for her repressed desires in much the same way as Eve Black. Her thoughts, she said in her memoirs, written in the 1640s, 'were often bent on devising ways to displease Him and to make others trespass against Him . . . the demon beclouded me in such a way that I hardly distinguished his desires from mine: He gave me, moreover, a strong aversion for my religious calling, so that sometimes when He was in my head I tore my veils and such of my sisters' as I could lay hands on; I trampled them under foot, I chewed them, cursing the hour when I took my vows.' It will be recalled that she developed these symptoms after falling in love with the handsome Mgr. Urbain Grandier.

The prioress seems to have started by relapsing into attacks of jealous rage, as when, supposing Madame de Brou to have flirted with Grandier, she attacked her shouting, 'Whore! Strumpet! Debaucher of priests!' and drove her weeping from the abbey. When she was told by her director that her behaviour was not her fault, because she was possessed, she must have been delighted to believe it. The seven devils who allegedly possessed her were driven forth by administering an enema – the large brass clyster which eighteenth-century rationalists like Molière found so amusing; as Huxley makes clear, the experience was a symbol of the sexual assault she so much wanted.

Surin, one of the Jesuit exorcists, himself became possessed; he explained his state of mind in terms which make the personality split rather obvious. 'I cannot explain to you what happens within me during that time, and how this spirit unites with mine, without depriving me of either consciousness or liberty of soul. Nevertheless making himself like another me and as if I had two souls, one of which is dispossessed of its body and the use of its organs and stands aside watching the actions of the other . . .' The words are almost those of the girl, the first I mentioned, when discussing depersonalisation.

As William Sargant has emphasised, people in trance are highly suggestible. If it is suggested that their condition is due to possession, they accept it. He tells of a patient admitted to a French hospital, where she was told it was the Devil making her ill. Before long she was seeing visions of the Devil, which she described vividly. The nuns and almoner had persuaded her she was possessed by the Devil because she did not pray enough; the almoner sprinkled her with holy water and made signs over her. Moved to a psychiatric hospital in Paris, her visions soon ceased and she discarded the idea of possession.

If possession was a plausible explanation of such behaviour in the pre-scientific era, mediumistic possession is often an acceptable one in modern times. Strangely enough, few mediums have ever been studied psychologically – as distinct from investigating their alleged paranormal powers. One of the few was Hélène Smith, who was studied by Professor Theodore Flournoy from 1894–8. Hélène Smith was an inhibited thirty-year-old shop assistant when she came to his attention because she claimed to be possessed by the spirit of the once-famous magician Cagliostro, a braggart and a sexual adventurer. After a while, Cagliostro was replaced by the spirit of Marie Antoinette. She also had a five-month spell with the spirit of Victor Hugo but Cagliostro won. The parallel with Eve Black the adventuress and Eve White is rather close, though there is an element of fantasy besides; both Cagliostro and the queen, in their different ways, were in possession of power and were envied. To explain these persons in terms of mediumistic power avoided the risk of being regarded merely as insane. Hélène Smith had no recollection of when these other personalities were in evidence; and in these roles she wrote in a crabbed eighteenth-century manner, unlike her own writing. Flournoy had her productions compared with genuine samples of the writing of Cagliostro and Marie Antoinette. There was no resemblance; handwriting experts said the scripts showed the same basic features as Hélène's own writing, although superficially disguised. Occasionally the Marie Antoinette features appeared in her ordinary writing. Flournoy was struck by how her whole manner and even her way of walking changed to suit each personality.

The desire to escape from one's usual role for a time into a different personality is probably normal. Masquerades of various kinds, from pagan and primitive animal impersonations down to fancy-dress balls, have existed throughout history. It is amnesia for these episodes which distinguishes the pathological from the normal.

Mechanisms of this kind may also account for many cases attributed to reincarnation. The Zurich housewife, Ikara, who recalled her supposed past life as a cave-woman, could be so explained. But the American hypnotist's wife known as T. E., who claimed to reincarnate (when hypnotised) as a seventeenth-century peasant named Jensen, is harder to account for. In trance, she spoke archaic Swedish with a correct pronunciation, though knowing no Swedish. In particular, Swedish observers noted that she could pronounce the Swedish for 'seven', regarded as almost impossible for anyone not familiar with the language from birth. Is it possible that she had learned Swedish (she was born in Russia) and that a hypnotist had given her instructions to forget the fact? Or repressed it spontaneously?

In Chapter Nineteen, I make the point that the humanities explain in terms of agents what science explains in terms of processes. To explain such disturbances of personality as due to 'possession' is an explanation in terms of agents. A more scientific explanation would be that the mind contains various idea systems which normally are integrated, but if the disparities are too great dissociation takes place. The mechanism of such dissociation is not far to seek: it is inhibition, in the neurophysiological sense: a closing off of certain neuronal pathways. Thus I feel forced to conclude that the sense of 'egoge' is an Omega Effect arising from such systems, rather than something which exists in a metaphysical sense.

The growing conviction that egoge is an epiphenomenon receives powerful reinforcement from the extraordinary work of Roger Sperry and his colleagues. This is surely one of the investigations which will go down in medical history.

Two Minds in One Cranium?

It was in the early fifties that Roger Sperry, then at the University of Chicago, launched intensive studies on the splitting of the brain. The cortices of men (and of animals, except the most primitive) consist of two symmetrical halves, linked by a massive web of nerve fibres known as the great cerebral commissure, or corpus callosum, and by several smaller links. Physically, the two halves are pretty much mirror twins, the right brain presiding over the left-hand side of the body, and the left over the right side. Functionally, as I have already mentioned, there are differences.

At that time the precise role of the commissures remained a mystery. In the late thirties, surgeons had tried severing them in an attempt to prevent epileptic attacks being transmitted from one side of the brain to the other. These attempts were rather successful; the odd thing was, there was no noticeable loss of performance, so what were the commissures for? For that matter, some people are born without commissures, but seem to function normally. It seems unlikely that these vast nerve tracts were provided by nature for the sole purpose of transmitting epileptic seizure from one side of the body to the other, as Warren McCulloch satirically suggested in 1940.

Sperry suggested to one of his students, R. E. Myers, that for his degree he try to separate the visual systems of cats, so that each eye fed one half of the brain. Myers managed to do this, and found that he could teach such a cat one lesson through one eye, and the opposite lesson through the other. It could learn, for instance, on the left that it would get food if it depressed a certain lever and on the right that it would get a shock by doing so. Whether pussy pressed the lever then depended on which eye was open.

What would happen in a human brain thus divided, Sperry wondered. Could each half think separate thoughts, feel separate emotions?

Though Sperry could not, for obvious reasons, sever the visual pathways in human beings who had undergone commissurotomy, he could ask them to gaze straight ahead, and then show them objects in their right or in their left visual field, for, as I have mentioned, the right fields of both eyes are connected to the left brain, and the two left fields to the right brain. The experiment was tried. When pictures of objects (such as a pencil, a tumbler, spectacles) are presented to the right brain, the subject says that he sees nothing, yet with his left hand he can correctly pick up the corresponding object.

One of Sperry's more amusing experiments consisted in showing a series of pictures, among them photographs of nude and lovely ladies, to each half of the brain. When such pictures are presented to the right hemisphere, the subjects reported that they can see nothing, but a grin spreads over their face and they chuckle.

In a long series of experiments, Sperry and his co-workers explored the transfer of information within the brain, and the extent to which each half was specialised. It emerged, for instance, that the left brain has *some* information about an object which is being felt by the left hand. It knows there is something there and can form an idea of its size and weight, but cannot identify it or determine its exact shape. Similarly, the right brain only forms general impressions of what the right hand feels.

These experiments were complicated by the shrewdness with which the split-brain patient learns to pick up and utilise clues to overcome his deficiencies. Thus in experiments in which the patient was asked to say which was the bigger of two vertical bars, the uninformed half of his brain could detect his vertical eye-movements as he looked at each bar and deduce from this which was the bigger. Again, if a wrong answer caused the patient chagrin, the uninformed half brain would detect the emotional

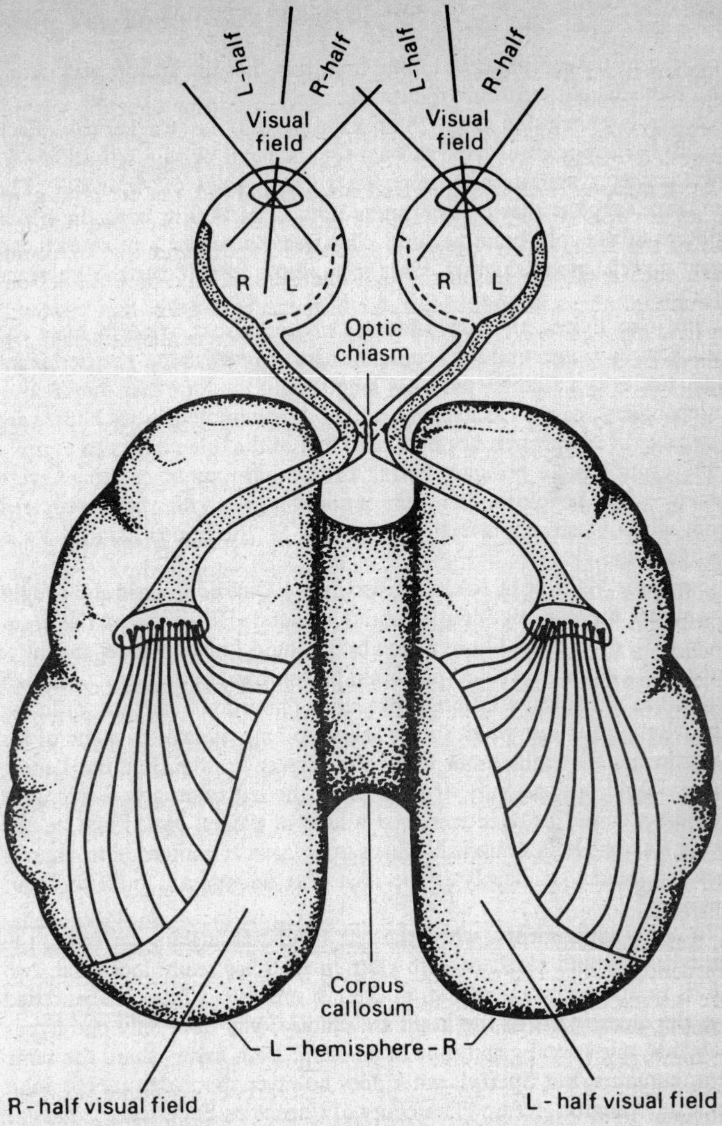

The Split Brain

Since the left half of the retina sends fibres to the left brain and the right half to the right brain, cutting the interchange station – the optic chiasm – has the effect of sending left-eye data only to the left hemisphere, and right-eye data to the right. If the connecting links between the two brain hemispheres are also cut, they cannot compare what they see.

reaction in the old brain and infer from this that the answer was wrong and immediately substitute the correct reply.

Sperry's conclusion from these experiments was categorical. 'Each hemisphere appears to have its own separate and private sensations, its own concepts and its own impulses to act,' he wrote in 1966. 'The evidence suggests that consciousness runs in parallel in both the hemispheres of the split-brain person.' This was a bombshell, of course, and most unwelcome to dualists, since it appeared to rule out the existence of a soul.

Sir John Eccles, the world-famous neuroscientist, tried to meet the difficulty by suggesting that consciousness only exists on the dominant side. Eccles is a Catholic and has long sought to show that mind exists independently of the mechanisms explored by neurologists. But there are a number of cases where the dominant half of the brain has been entirely removed in human beings suffering from brain-tumour or other severe damage: these people function almost normally when they have recovered from what is certainly a major operation. So the minor hemisphere is certainly conscious.

Professor MacKay of Keele University is a Quaker and has also sought to counter mechanistic interpretations of mind. He advanced the argument that, even if the halves of the brain could function independently, one could only say that the split-brain person had two minds if each half of his brain displayed different priorities for actions and had different aims. But this is just what Sperry seems to have shown. In some of his experiments the right brain knew the correct answer (but not having speech could not speak it). It then heard the left brain give a wrong or stupid reply and at once triggered a look of pained annoyance on the owner's face. (It is remarkably hard to construct sentences to express these situations, so deeply is the idea of a unitary self built into our language.)

In some experiments, when the left hand was making an error, the right hand would reach over to restrain it. That really looks like two minds in one body. Of course, in the last analysis it must be conceded that the oldest parts of the brain are unitary: you have only one hypothalamus, one pineal gland, one brain-stem. Both halves share the same neurohumours, but Sperry's work does however show, despite Sir John Eccles' Eddington lecture 'The Unity of Conscious Experience', that the cortical and thalamic aspects of behaviour are products of neuronal assemblies and differ when the experience of the two assemblies differs.

This does not mean that, in unoperated human beings, the two half-brains are identical. Man has improved his performance by specialising their functions, and not only in the sense that that the left brain is concerned with language. A young Californian psychologist, Robert Ornstein, has achieved a wide reputation by arguing that the right brain is concerned with reason, the left with intuition – a view which gains much of its popularity from the current revolt from reason. If one is not very bright, or has been too lazy to study, it is no doubt comforting to be told that our society overstresses intellect, and that one must develop the marvellous powers which reside in the neglected half of one's cerebrum. A disciple, Joseph E. Bogen, finds support for this idea in the fact that the Bagobo people of Malaysia believe that everyone has two souls – a right-hand soul known as Gimokud Takawanan which is good, and a bad left-hand one known as Gimokud Tebang.

Ornstein asserts that one half of the brain engages in 'propositional thinking' the other in 'appositional thinking', whatever this may mean.

However, there seems to be no decisive change of intellectual style in persons who have a hemisphere removed, while those who have undergone the split-brain operation also carry on much as before. What Sperry's tests did reveal, apart from the lateralisation of speech itself, was more curious. The right hemisphere can handle nouns but not verbs. It can recognise affirmative constructions but not future tenses, plurals, the difference between active and passive, etc. In the child, however, both hemispheres appear to be equally proficient: the left hemisphere specialises in speech. I suspect it does so because it has nothing much else to do: the right hemisphere is handling the non-verbal problems very adequately. The Canadian, Brenda Milner (an associate of Professor Wilder Penfield), has shown that musical tonal and temporal stimuli are handled mainly by the right brain. There are many other intriguing differences; for example, men recognise faces faster with their left brain than women do.

Dr David Galin, of the Langley Porter research institute in the suburbs of San Francisco, has advanced the intriguing idea that the right hemisphere represents the unconscious, in the Freudian sense, and the left the conscious. The experiment in which the girl subject giggled and put her hand over her mouth – but did not know why – when the right-hand half of her brain was looking at pictures of nude males certainly has a Freudian air.

Freud drew attention to the differences between logical thinking and 'primary process thinking', a sort of emotionally toned reverie in which symbolic connections are made rather than logical ones. Galin sees the former as a left-brain function, the latter as a right-brain function. The left brain being concerned with temporal sequence would be appropriate for logical thought, where one idea leads to another sequentially. With a colleague he has demonstrated differences between the EEG pattern of right and left hemispheres.

MacDonald Critchley, the British neurologist, has observed that patients with right-brain damage and left-side paralysis deny there is anything wrong, while in the reverse situation, they are devastated. A curious experiment confirms this; a substance known as ICAT produces a brief paralysis. When administered on one side it produces an euphoric mood, on the other a catastrophic reaction.

One could interpret this as follows: the left brain, which handles concepts, can understand the implications of being paralysed; the right brain only notices that it is receiving no messages from the left body and assumes there is therefore nothing there. Left hemiplegics deny that this side of their body exists.

Galin points to various interesting implications for medical care: such as the possibility of giving electroshock to one side of the brain only.

This account perhaps makes the right/left story seem too simple. There are many odd features to be explained. Sometimes an image, perceived by one half of the brain, will vanish, when it is shown to both. There is certainly a complicated 'cross talk' between the two halves which is slowly being explored; and in people with normal commissures, behaviour is the outcome of a synthesis in which, I do not doubt, messages are passed back and forth not once but several times, being progressively modified, before they culminate in action.

But I am digressing from my theme; I want only to make clear that our sense of unity rests on a tremendously subtle integration of numerous structurally, as well as functionally, distinct processes.

My Eyes are Full Up with Sand

Having now explored the question of egoge to some extent, I would like to return to the phenomenon of depersonalisation, which is probably misnamed, for it certainly includes other factors besides the egoge-aspect.

The young officer whom I mentioned had his first attack after a dispute with fellow-officers, and the subsequent attacks also followed periods of emotional tension. Then when he was given psychotherapy, childhood problems were uncovered: a driving father and a possessive mother. After four months of treatment his attacks ceased and he was discharged. This argues an emotional origin and makes depersonalisation look like an escape of some kind from reality.

In all cases of depersonalisation known to me, a loss of capacity to feel seems to be a factor, and results in a feeling of boredom. In fact, the suppression of an emotional response after some painful experience often seems to be the trigger. For instance, Miss E.H. developed severe depersonalisation symptoms following the breakdown of a love-affair when she was thirty. The man was twenty-five years older than she, and gradually revealed sadistic tendencies. 'In essence, this is a feeling of unreality,' is how she described it. 'Sometimes I lie in bed and feel so unreal that I move just to see if I am . . . I seem so unreal to myself, everyone else seems to have ideas and purposes, but I do not – I'm not part of anything and so nothing seems real.'

Her comment is illuminating. Being 'part of something' is a necessary conditioning for existing as a person. Her doctor described her as a highly intelligent, cultured girl, but hopeless in outlook and terrified of everything.

Sometimes, however, it is not oneself but the rest of the world which seems unreal, a state sometimes distinguished from depersonalisation under the name 'derealisation'. As Miss Z.I. put it, 'Things seem unreal, as though there was something shutting me off from reality, as though I could not look at a thing and grasp it or see it as a whole.' The condition developed after her fiancé's mother had caught her in bed with him, and had made a painful scene. Miss Z.I. complained that her body felt light, as though she were walking on air; she had difficulty in grasping things; she felt 'dead inside', and when her fiancé kissed her she felt nothing.

Any amateur psychiatrist can see how such symptoms express the wish to close the mind to a painful experience. But I am not here concerned to 'explain' such states of mind: I want only to throw light on what we mean by personal identity.

Sometimes the denial of reality spreads to other people. Thus Miss H.G., a shy, good-looking girl, who seemed unduly dependent on her elder sister, was hospitalised. 'Things just seem to go on as though they are not happening to me,' she said. 'In fact, I don't seem to be here at all. I seem different, as though something had gone. I feel changed, lacking something I used to have, as though I had no personality and was only existing.'

In psychotherapy it emerged that her elder sister was an ideal on whom she modelled herself; the sister was more active and socially successful, and Miss H.G. (who was only twenty-two) obtained vicarious satisfaction from her elder sister's success. What threw her was the horrifying discovery that her admired sister was going to have an illegitimate baby. She was unable to accept this: 'It was as though my sister had gone and someone strange had come in her place . . . And I seemed to have disappeared with my sister.' (Here too, psychotherapy effected a cure.)

Mr M.Q. said he felt as if he were looking at the world through frosted glass. Voices sounded different and distant. His bodily symptoms were particularly alarming. Not only did he have pins and needles in his hands but, 'My eyes felt as if they were full up with sand and feel as if they were trying to diverge. The top part of my head often seems to disappear. I often have a feeling of swaying to and fro, or spinning round very slowly in a clock-wise direction. I feel as though I have been drugged, my face often becomes hot and flushes and I stammer very badly.' But his unreality feelings also included a third and more basic feature: he felt (he said) as though the world was not interested in him.

I judge from such descriptions that the sense of personal identity is closely bound up with the ability to feel. These seem to be people who have closed off the channels leading to the old brain in order to reduce the psychic pain of their life-situation and in so doing have closed off emotion altogether, even the pleasantness of sensation. The data gets through to the new brain and is analysed and recognised but it has no personal meaning.

But the subject bristles with intriguing questions. Why, for instance, is there such a marked disturbance of the body image and even of balance? Presumably the inhibition has spilled over into these circuits or at least into the area where they are integrated with other forms of self-awareness.

Then again, what is a feeling of reality?

> 'I seem so unreal to myself . . .'
> 'Things seemed unreal,'
> 'I feel as though I am not here at all.'

Certainly, similar feelings affect normal people in a state of extreme or after stress, or when sad: of eighty-one people George Sedman, a British psychologist, asked, thirty-eight said they had had a similar experience. And it is certainly true that disturbances of the temporal lobes produce such feelings, whether due to a tumour, the onset of epilepsy or stimulation of the brain surface electrically by a surgeon. Dr Brian Ackner has argued that the similarity between these cases is only apparent, since several different neurotic states may be involved – schizoid, hysteric and so on. But not all hysterics or schizoids have the experience of depersonalisation. A great many words have been penned, all saying much the same thing: that the central feature is a loss of ability to feel. As Paul Schilder wrote as long ago as 1928: 'The patients complain that they are capable of experiencing neither pain nor pleasure; love and hate have perished with them. . . . It is as though they were dead, lifeless, mere automatons.' But a more recent writer points out that they do not say 'I am unreal', but only 'I feel that I am unreal, although I know I am not.' And he observes that when they speak of a change in their personality, they seem always to refer to it as a sense of loss.

One woman, aged thirty-nine, who had experienced attacks of this kind from the age of fourteen, when asked if she felt unreal replied, rather revealingly, 'I felt unreal when it first came on at fourteen, but after a time I got used to it and found it was just a sort of emotional block. After that I did not seem to feel so unreal.' Another patient, asked the same question by Brian Ackner, said simply, 'No, it is much the same feeling I get when I am drunk.' (Alcohol, of course, numbs the feelings.)

But if it is an emotional block, it seems to be one which affects the pleasure system, rather than the contrary one. Miss W.D. asked how the world appeared to her, replied, 'Trees seem to be stark and staring and ugly, not attractive any more. I used to see people nice and attractive, now even those that are nice look ugly. Even fair people look dark to me now . . .'

A final thought: there seems to be a link between depersonalisation and the experience of being out of one's own body. The student who felt she was in the air looking down on herself closely resembles the mountaineer watching himself trudging up Mount Everest. Most psychiatrists regard such experiences as coming under the heading 'depersonalisation', although the feelings of pointlessness and isolation are usually missing.

Numerous mutually contradictory, psychoanalytic explanations of depersonalisation are available – it is infantile regression, it is 'loss of narcissistic cathexis', it is denial – but as I have said, these are guesses not explanations. There are psychological explanations: it is a 'failure to assimilate percepts to the conceptual scheme'. There are physical explanations: it is due to brain damage in the parietal area. It has been called a form of schizophrenia, though such experiences are not confined to schizophrenics. According to another authority, it is usually found in uncommonly attractive, intelligent, able patients who continue to cope with their daily duties. Theories (such as the one I have proposed) based on the assumption that the mind is a 'bundle of functions' are obsolete, according to Brian Ackner, the principal authority. But he has nothing better to offer.

Conclusion

The notion of egoge as developing through a series of phases or levels can be usefully applied in several areas – for instance, in understanding the mental development of children. The concept of regression down such a scale helps us to understand the behaviour of crowds. Under the influence of chanting and emotive oratory, the cortical function is suppressed, and the individuals retreat to a limbic-presentational level, at which naked fears and appetites become the dominant motives and consequences are lost from view. This is what happens in a lynching party or in the mass rallies of a Nazi Party. It is also, of course, what happens in revivalist religion, even though here the motives released may be ethically preferable.

At the limbic level, since ego boundaries are weakened, the sense of group solidarity grows stronger. The anthropologist Lévy-Bruhl had advanced the view that many preliterate peoples have poorly defined ego-boundaries and hence identify themselves with their clan more strongly than do more sophisticated peoples. Here, one presumes, people have not advanced beyond the limbic phases in their development. There are other things which could be predicted if this analysis is correct and it would be interesting to examine preliterate cultures to see if their behaviour and cognitive processes fit the hypothesis.

The concept may also have application in understanding certain social changes in the course of history. There seem to have been periods when egoges were sharply defined periods of individualism, periods when they were more fluid and when community was an ideal, as seems to be happening in some quarters today. There were even periods when splitting of the ego, and incorporation of normally non-ego elements, occurred. There is evidence of this in the literary sphere. A strange disruption of the ego, just short of psychosis, seems to have been common among the German romantics of the *Sturm und Drang* movement in the early nineteenth century. E. T. A. Hoffman makes a character in his book *The Devil's Elixir* say: 'My own ego, the sport of cruel accident, was dissolved into strange forms and floated helplessly away upon the sea of circumstances. I could not find myself again.' And he adds: 'At strife with my own ego, I am an unanswerable riddle to myself.' In his book *The Golden Jar*, identity loses all stability. The ugly old Dresden apple-woman is also the beautiful bronze knocker on Registrar Lindhorst's door and is at the same time the heroine's kindly nurse, Lise, and the odious fortune-teller, Frau Rahesia.

The archive keeper is a registrar by day and a salamander by night. At one point in the narrative he steps backward into a bowl of blazing arrack and allows himself to be drunk up. In another of Hoffman's works, *Klein Zaches*, one of the characters finds himself constantly absorbing characteristics from the personalities of those he meets. The literary specialist, G. Brandes, sums up the movement by saying, 'They proceed to decompose the human personality.'

Not surprisingly, these writers were fascinated with the idea of the alter ego, or Doppelgänger, to which I have already drawn attention. Such doubles appear in the works of von Kleist, von Arnim and others.

In their books and plays there are characters who are portrayed as living before their birth; characters speak 'out of character' or argue with the stage-hands. Sometimes there are plays within plays, and even plays within plays within plays, in an endless sequence, so that the characters of one are the spectators of another and speak in each of these roles. Brandes comments, 'They split the ego into strips, they resolve it into its elements. They scatter it abroad through space, as they stretch it out through time.'

How does all this bear on the central question of our investigation? If the ego is, at bottom, the product of neuronal patterns it is easy to see that such patterns might become disrupted by stress or by the disturbance of brain chemistry. The fact that methylene dioxyamphetamine is reported to strengthen the sense of ego – the feeling that 'I am I' – lends weight to this hypothesis. If, on the other hand, the sense that 'I am I' derives from an indwelling soul such disruption seems unlikely and we would have to retreat to the position that its expression through the neuronal systems of the brain was being disrupted. This is, you must agree, a much weaker hypothesis.

8

It's All in the Mind

THE DECISION TO DIE

A doctor named Arnold Cowan wrote to a British medical journal to report that a patient of his, suffering from cancer, told him on a Tuesday that he should not make his usual Thursday visit to see him as he would be dying at 2.30 the following afternoon. He learned later that his patient had summoned the members of his family to say farewell after lunch on the Wednesday. His wife being detained for a few moments, he sent a message for her to hurry so that she would not miss the event. At 2.30 precisely he sighed, raised both hands above his head, smiled, and passed away.

On the strength of this report, several other doctors wrote to report comparable cases. A Dr Cameron told of an Arab in a refugee camp of 17,000 people, who went all over the camp bidding farewell to friends, then walked five miles into Bethlehem to say good-bye to relatives, walked back and then, laying his head on his father's lap, died instantly.

Sources: A. Cowan, 'Premonition of Death', *Brit. Med. J.* (1958) ii.1041; A. Cameron, ibid., p. 914.

Mind to Body

During the war I was so fortunate as to form a friendship with a man named Clifford Troke; among other things, he introduced me to the poems of Conrad Aiken, a quotation from which forms the epigraph of this book. He had been an air-raid warden in London for four years, repeatedly at risk and short of sleep. Among his more stressful experiences were the following. After a heavy air-raid in which more people were killed than the burial arrangements could cope with, an empty school in Troke's district was taken over and the unburied bodies placed in it. The following night a time-bomb fell near the school but did not explode. The health authorities decided that it was an unacceptable health risk to leave the bodies *in situ*. Volunteers were called for to enter the school and rescue not the living but the dead from the expected explosion. One night, after various such adventures and during a raid, Troke was assailed with the feeling that all Hitler's bombs were directed at him personally, and that the German airforce would continue to drop bombs in his vicinity until they got him. He sat down on the edge of the pavement and began to weep.

In hospital next day, the doctor took his blood pressure and whistled.

He told him that if he did not take things very easily from then on he would probably explode himself. In point of fact, he survived a few years after the war, but succumbed, while still relatively young, to a heart attack.

I recall this story to emphasise the point that mental stress can produce physical disease. It seems necessary to emphasise it because the idea evokes such strong resistance; even now, it is denied in some quarters. The eighteenth-century surgeon Sydenham was on the track when he reported that a 'violent commotion of the mind' could cause paralysis; earlier still Harvey, the discoverer of the circulation of the blood, had puzzled about the variation of heart-rate with emotion. The word 'psychosomatic' for bodily diseases of mental origin dates from 1818. But while most doctors now concede that *some* diseases have a mental component, they are reluctant to accept the larger claim that all diseases do so.

Nevertheless, the evidence is mounting that the connection between mind and body is subtler and more intimate than most people realise or are ready to admit. So let us explore the whole question of how mind and body interact.

The least controversial group of psychosomatic responses are those which are associated with a stressful existence. That busy executives are liable to stomach ulcers and high blood pressure is nowadays taken for granted. In emergencies, the body prepares for battle or for flight. The heart beats faster, thus supplying the muscles with more blood; the capillaries contract, making bleeding less likely. It is not too difficult to see how such changes, if induced over a long period, could lead to high blood pressure. The gastric secretion of anxious persons rises, and a connection with stomach ulcers is not inherently unlikely. Of course, there are lots of technical problems. Why do some people show increased blood pressure under stress, and others not? (Studies of a group of air-traffic controllers showed that about twelve per cent of them had very high blood pressures while working, others showed no changes at all.) Some authorities claim that particular kinds of stress produce particular bodily consequences – that arthritis is linked to dominating parents; that colitis follows parental rejection, and so on. Others hold that people react according to their personality – that the same stress will evoke arthritis in one person, colitis in another, and arteriosclerosis in a third, while a fourth person might have a mental rather than a physical collapse. The facts of the matter are still a matter of controversy.

There is also a fairly general recognition that diseases of the skin often have an emotional origin. Thus it has been noticed, in manic-depressives who suffer from psoriasis, that the condition often gets worse when they are depressed and clears when they are manic. That there is some kind of intimate connection between the skin and our feelings is understandable since the skin is formed, as the fertilised egg becomes an embryo, from the same layer of tissue as the brain. The terminus of millions of nerve endings, it is almost an extension of the brain. Many observations confirm this idea. Thus it has been observed that blisters 'weep' more when a patient is sad than when he or she is happy. Even the modest stress of having to do mental arithmetic changes the electrical resistance of the skin. But the nature of the mechanism remains unknown. Doubtless analogous is the sudden greying of the hair, the mechanism of which is completely mysterious. Sir Thomas More and Marie Antoinette are both reported to have turned white while awaiting their execution, to say nothing of less eminent persons.

For some psychosomatic diseases, a symbolic (psychoanalytic) explanation has been offered. Thus the reddening of the face known as Rosacea is interpreted as a disturbance of the normal mechanism of blushing, due to a guilty conscience. Resentment and aggression are held to lie behind the itchy condition known as urticaria. Freud observed how one kind of stress can be converted into another and one can dimly see how the brain, which works in patterns, could substitute one pattern for another, the expression of which was strongly inhibited. A striking instance is the twenty-two-year-old girl who was admitted to hospital with severe whole body eczema, which had started at the age of three; she had had a major outbreak of the disease at fourteen and it got worse when she married. She had a horror of sex and began to itch every time she saw her husband. It turned out that she had been raped by her drunken, brutal father, who had masturbated her from the age of three and threatened to kill her if she told anyone. He beat her and his sons regularly. After four years of psychoanalysis she came to accept her femininity: her skin then cleared completely and remained healthy.

By the same token, it is understandable that allergies, which are skin reactions, can have a mental origin. A classic story concerns the woman who was allergic to roses. Her asthma came on, as usual, when someone placed a vase of artificial roses in the room. Asthma and skin reactions can both be provoked by suggestion under hypnosis that an allergen is present. More intriguing is the fact that allergies can manifest in response to unwelcome situations. Such facetiously intended expressions as: 'I am allergic to my mother-in-law,' are not always as exaggerated as the speaker imagines. None of these cases, it seems to me, is inconsistent with what we know about brain function.

A third group of diseases of a rather different kind, to which even the sceptics grant a mental basis, are those 'functional' disorders such as 'hysterical' blindness or paralysis: the soldier who is blind after some frightful battle experience, the boy whose hand becomes paralysed after he had guiltily masturbated. Doctors call these disorders 'functional' because they cannot find anything organically wrong. (They are also called 'hysterical' though they have nothing to do with hysteria.) Quite often, a cure can be effected by hypnosis or the use of ataractic drugs. If once the painful event which caused the crisis can be brought to consciousness, the disorder is exorcised.

What we are seeing here, I believe, is inhibition at work. Inhibitory circuits or substances in the brain simply block the visual circuits (in the case of blindness) or the motor pathways (in the case of paralysis). What is significant is the mere fact that powerful emotions can generate inhibition of basic sensory and motor pathways, for though the psychiatrist knows this to be the case, the neurologists have been slow to fit the clinical material into their conceptions. We gain a clue about the location in the brain of these inhibitory mechanisms from the odd condition known as 'glove anaesthesia', in which the hand becomes insensitive following some painful episode. In these hysterical cases, the insensitivity does not conform to the distribution area of a particular nerve (as happens when the trouble is physical) but affects the whole area which a glove would cover. This tells us that the insensitivity must be produced by inhibition in the higher cortical centres where the limbs, including the hand, are represented by neural patterns.

But while the existence of hysterical and stress disorders is pretty generally recognised, doctors have been sceptical of the idea that psychosomatic factors might be at work in infectious disease or even in degenerative disease like cancer. There was general incredulity when, twenty-five years ago, Dr D. M. Kissen showed that emotional factors were involved in tuberculosis. Stomach ulcers and skin conditions were one thing; TB was another! Tuberculosis seemed to them essentially a physical illness, the cause of which was understood. But, as always with infectious disease, the question is: why does one person fight off infection and another succumb? To say a disease is infectious does little to explain it. As Professor René Dubos, one of medicine's wise old men, has remarked: 'If the infectious theory of disease were true, there would be nobody here to believe it.' The truth is, the body's system of immune defences normally protects us from infection. We fall ill whenever the system is not fully effective, and this, it seems impossible to deny, can be brought about by mental states.

Subsequently, Kissen showed that emotional factors were present in cancer too, but this was too much for the orthodox to swallow and his work was ignored. Very recently the idea has been mooted again in the light of accumulating evidence.

I should add that the term 'stress' does not necessarily mean extreme pressure, such as Clifford Troke was exposed to; any demand for re-adjustment seems to create a significant measure of stress. A careful study by the American doctor Thomas H. Holmes shows this. With the assistance of a young physicist, Richard Rahe, he devised a scale for measuring the number of changes in a person's life. Had he moved his home? Had he changed jobs or been promoted? Had his parents divorced, remarried, died? Had he divorced or remarried? And so on. They found that people who had experienced marked changes in the preceding year were much more likely to fall ill. Later the scale was tested on a variety of groups, from unemployed blacks to naval personnel. The naval study was particularly valuable, since full sickness records were available, while the men, living on ships at sea, were all exposed to similar risks of infection, on similar diets, and so on. They found that the ten per cent who had experienced most change were almost twice as likely to have been ill than the ten per cent who had experienced least change. While Holmes and Rahe stressed 'illness' in their analysis, it is obvious that all changes impose stresses, and demand adaptations.

And here again the coin has two sides. Sometimes the body shows an unexpected capacity to suppress symptoms.

A Dutch psychiatrist relates how all the symptoms of a severe cold vanished shortly before he was due to deliver an important scientific paper and came back again soon after the job was done. He also had a patient who was seized with hiccoughs after travelling to Paris to give a paper at the Pasteur Institute. They stopped abruptly, however, quarter of an hour before he was due to start and came back about 11.15, after which they continued to plague him for two days, stopping in time for an important dinner.

Professor Groen has also recorded many examples of what he calls 'syndrome shift', in other words, the replacement of one set of disease manifestations by another. Patients cured of colitis may develop gastric ulcers. The psychiatrically-oriented person is familiar with this kind of thing and points out that, if a disease is produced by an unconscious conflict, curing the disease merely forces the unconscious to find another outlet. The symptoms have been cured, not the disease itself. The second disease may, indeed, be more painful or life-threatening than the first. The hackles of ordinary doctors tend to rise when such notions are advanced, since they pull the rug out from under their whole approach.

Scared to Death

The body is in a state of perpetual responsiveness to our aims and interests. Think of food, and your gastric juices will start to flow. Think of something sad, and some people at least can make themselves cry. See a pretty girl, or anything else which interests you, and your pupils will dilate.

Respiration is closely tied to mood, as we recognise when we say: 'He caught his breath,' or 'I breathed a sigh of relief.' This of course has long been known. The sixteenth-century physician André du Laurens noted, 'Melancholoke folke are commonly given to sighs, because of minde being possessed with great varietie and store of foolish apparitions, doth not remember or suffer the partie to be at leisure to breathe according to the necessitie of nature . . .' Freud describes the case of a young girl he met in the Alps, who had repeated nervous attacks marked by dizziness, buzzing in the ears, a crushing sensation in the chest, constriction of the throat, and sensations of impending death. He interpreted it as a consequence of repressed anxiety.

These bodily responses to mental states are mediated through the hypothalamus, of which I have already written, and through the sympathetic and parasympathetic nervous systems. The activities of the automatic system are normally unconscious, though it has recently been shown that these autonomic functions *can* be brought under conscious control. However, I am struck by the fact that the body reacts to emotions of which we are not conscious: it reacts *as if* we felt anxiety even when the anxiety is repressed.

Thus there is no great difficulty in explaining how it is that people are sometimes scared to death. This is no hyperbolic expression. Two American doctors, for instance, described how a Catholic who was seriously ill with heart disease was visited by a priest. Apparently convinced that the priest had come to administer the last rites, the patient was so scared that he suffered a heart attack and died. One can often foretell which patients will die and which recover by testing their level of anxiety.

But the phenomenon known as Voodoo Death appears to be a rather different matter. The victim is cursed by a witch doctor, or perhaps he violates a strong taboo. He takes to his bed, shivering with fear, and dies within hours or days. However, if the witch doctor removes the spell, recovery is immediate. An anthropologist, S. Wavell, tells how he once saved an African from death by convincing him that his own magic was more powerful. Faith is thus a central factor. The great authority on psychosomatic matters, Walter Cannon, interested himself in Voodoo

Death. Tests showed dramatic activity of the sympathetic system, heart rate was doubled, blood sugar up by a factor of five.

But why does the victim die? What is the physiology? Birds will sometimes die unexpectedly after being held immobile so that they can be banded; and other animals have been known to die when constrained so that they can be given a needed medicine. However, if they are first given a tranquilliser, such as chlorpromazine, the proportion dying is much reduced; and this is likewise the case when they are given atropine, which abolishes parasympathetic effects. If parasympathetic stimulants, such as mecholyl, are given, the effect is intensified.

I detect a connection here with the experiments which Curt Richter of Johns Hopkins Hospital once carried out with rats, placing them in glass jars full of water where they had to swim to escape drowning. He found that if he cut off the vibrissae, or whiskers, of wild Norway rats, they would drown within two minutes, but they would swim for more than eighty hours before drowning if this had not been done. Tests showed that the second lot died of a slowing heart and slowing breathing (parasympathetic effects) and not, as one might think, from accelerating effort.

These rats were in a hopeless situation: they could neither fight nor fly, the standard reactions to a threat. If they were rescued from time to time, showing the situation was not hopeless, they would try harder to survive. Men, I am sure, are no different in this. Every surgeon knows of cases where a patient 'turns his face to the wall', and gives up the struggle. Thus Voodoo Death seems to belong in the hopelessness category rather than the shock category. Sometimes after successful surgery, a patient will die for no obvious reason. I remember the prominent heart surgeon Norman Barrett telling me that the hardest part of his job was not performing the operation but going round the wards afterwards imbuing the patients with the will to live. That was how he put it. The American surgeon Professor J. M. Tinney habitually refused to operate on any patient who was afraid of the results of surgery.

Coroners have reported cases of people who died after rather trivial wounds or from taking doses of sleeping tablets well below the level normally considered dangerous. Perhaps these, too, were cases of what has been called 'give-up-itis'. Psychologists have written in rather vague terms about the possible existence of a general 'coping mechanism' in the brain, but how it is constituted, if it exists, remains unspecified.

But even queerer manifestations of the brain's power over the body await our attention.

On Having Faith

The most baffling example of the effect of the mind on the body is, quite certainly, the appearance of stigmata: that is, marks on hands and feet resembling the wounds received by Christ. Less often, bleeding from the head or side has been reported. There are about fifty cases in the literature. No satisfactory medical explanation has ever been offered.

There seems to be no case of spontaneous stigmatisation before that of St Francis of Assisi. Among the more recent cases, where the evidence is reasonably reliable, are those of Gemma Galgani, who died in 1903, and Louise Lateau, who was examined in 1873. In the latter case, which was investigated by a Dr G. Molloy, blood forced its way through the skin, and he could see, with a magnifying glass, minute punctures. In the former case, red masses appeared on Thursday, burst on Friday and vanished on Sunday.

A variant on this theme is provided by those girls who claimed to have been selected as 'brides of Christ', and who produced stigmata resembling wedding rings. Observers saw 'a red coral ring under the skin' in the case of the Breton peasant girl Marie Julie Jahvenny (1873), and the same thing in the case of St Catherine de' Ricci – but she said she saw a gold ring with a big cut diamond in it. (Not to be outdone, Barnardine Floriana said her ring had *five* diamonds in it!)

In some of the recorded cases, the wounds were clearly self-inflicted, but some were certainly psychic: those of another stigmatic, St Rita, promptly disappeared when she was told that her condition made it impossible for her to go to Rome. Fr Thurston, who investigated this subject in great detail, concluded that self-induced extravasation of blood through the skin was possible.

A particularly well-observed case was reported in 1974 by two San Franciscans, Loretta Early and J. E. Lifschutz. A religiously-minded black child, aged ten and a half, began to bleed from her left palm in school. She was herself unaware of the onset of bleeding. She was taken at once to the school doctor. She continued to extravasate blood four to six times daily over the next four days: it was Easter week. She bled from her right palm, then the bottom of her left foot, her right thorax and finally the middle of her forehead. This was seen by teachers, nurses and others. On one occasion, blood was seen to start welling from her hand while it was being held by an observer. The girl herself was quite cheerful and friendly. She had never heard of St Francis and his stigmata, but had been reading about the Crucifixion. Occasionally she heard a voice saying such things as, 'Your prayers will be answered.'

The report has been criticised on the grounds that the extravasated fluid was not identified as blood by a haematologist. However, even if it was only coloured lymph, the occurrence is sufficiently remarkable and raises once again baffling questions about the mind/body relationship.

A few years ago two American doctors reported observations of a number of women who had developed spontaneous bruises, apparently because they had become allergic to their own blood corpuscles. It was known that such an allergy could occur, but here it seemed to have a psychosomatic origin. All these were 'angry women' with multiple complaints: headache, vomiting, dyspepsia and so on. Also studied was a woman who began to bleed from her hip whenever she saw her handicapped son put on his hip-brace. Though the bruising was quite different in appearance from stigmatic wounds, these cases seem to confirm the existence of a mechanism which we cannot begin to understand. (I might add that bruising can also be produced by hypnotic suggestion.)

But several much more recent cases in the medical literature take the matter a good deal further and raise additional problems. As they are very little known I will describe them in some detail. They were reported by Dr R. L. Moody in the *Lancet* in 1946.

An army officer aged thirty-five was admitted to hospital complaining of sleep-walking and of uncontrollable aggressive impulses. He told how, back in 1935 when he was in India, he had been ill in much the same way, and when in hospital had had his hands tied behind his back to prevent him assaulting the staff. Now, in 1944, he was observed one night writhing about in bed, as if trying to free his hands, which he held behind his back. He crept into the hospital grounds, his hands still held behind his back. Dr Moody decided, on this occasion, not to follow him, and twenty minutes later he returned. Next morning the patient was found to have weals on his arms, resembling those produced by ropes, and they persisted for two days. That night he was given Evipan, a drug which often helps people to release repressed material, and reduces them to a drowsy state. In this condition, he began to re-enact the events of 1935, and as Dr Moody watched he saw the weals appearing spontaneously on his arms. Moody recognised the purplish red spots caused by blood accumulating beneath the skin. Again the officer crept from the hospital, returning later in a normal frame of mind. Moody had a photographer standing by who photographed the weals, and I have seen the photographs.

In another wartime case, the patient re-enacted under a narcotic the scene in which his home had been struck by a flying bomb and he had been hit by a falling beam. As he told the story, a bruise appeared on his forehead and his ankle began to swell. A third case seen by Moody was a merchant seaman who had been in the water a long time after his ship was sunk. As he re-enacted the scene his extremities became pale and bloodless.

Yet another case concerns a woman of thirty-five who had had a riding accident when she was ten. The bruising and pain recurred at the old site. German physicians have recorded similar cases involving gangrene, urticaria, blisters and other symptoms.

A few months later Dr Moody was able to report an even more striking case. This was a woman of thirty who had had a sadistic father who had thrashed her unmercifully. After she had told how she had been thrashed with a whip at the age of eight, large bruises appeared on her buttocks – and when she recalled how the whip accidentally landed on her shoulder a bruise appeared there too. These psychosomatic wounds were so severe they had to be dressed: twenty minutes later the dressings were stained with blood. Moody noted that the wounds also cleared up phenomenally rapidly. After she told how she rushed through a sheet of glass, trying to escape her father, her legs displayed red streaks. When she recalled fracturing her wrist, her wrist swelled and became engorged with blood. In all, Moody saw these psychosomatic wounds on more than thirty occasions.

We are thus forced, it seems to me, to accept a number of very strange conclusions. It is not simply that the brain has the power to change the general condition of the capillaries, or, for that matter, to alter gastric secretion. Apparently it can change them quite specifically, altering tiny areas and leaving others, a few millimetres away, unchanged. It is inconceivable to me that the memory of the exact position (and nature) of the impressions from a rope could be stored in the brain in such a way that the trauma could be reproduced. There has to be a local body memory of the original insult (as doctors term any event which damages the body) and this memory must endure for thirty years, if not indefinitely, to be released by the brain whenever the original feelings are reactivated. This has weird implications. Further, it seems that repair mechanisms can operate with amazing speed. Surely we have here the opening of a whole new chapter in medicine?

Very recent work suggests the existence of a 'muscle memory' in addition to this 'skin memory'. But if the entire body really remembers, mind must be conceived to be a property of the entire body and not just of the brain! There's something to chew over.

The Original Snake Oil

'We should use new remedies quickly while they are still efficacious,' said the great Edwardian physician and heart specialist Sir William Osler. He meant by this, of course, that if you think a medicine will do you good, it probably will, even if it is pharmacologically useless. Coloured water, harmless powder or other 'medicine' given by a doctor to a patient to satisfy him is known as a 'placebo', from the Latin 'I shall please'. Placebos often work. For instance, placebo competes well with morphine in relieving pain in about forty per cent of cases. Doctors have known this for a very long time – at least since the Greeks – though the term only entered medicine in the nineteenth century. No doubt it was on this principle that the horrible concoctions of many witches and witch doctors depended, and of many mediaeval doctors too.

Today, the placebo effect presents a real difficulty in the testing of new drugs. Unless they are more effective than placebo, it is hard to be sure whether they are contributing anything. To complicate matters further, much depends on what the doctor says at the time he prescribes. A positive suggestion can intensify the effect, a negative one can counteract it. An idea of the difficulties can be obtained from experiments which showed that the appetite-depressing drug phenmetrazine was no more effective than placebo, provided the doctor did not say what it was expected to do. But phenmetrazine with instructions was more effective than phenmetrazine alone. Did the drug potentiate the placebo or vice versa?

Even the colour may make a difference. In 1972 an investigator at a London hospital carried out an experiment on medical students, all of whom had been carefully taught about the placebo effect. He gave half the group red pills, and half blue ones. Both were inert and he made no suggestions. Many of the students, nevertheless, reported that the blue pills had had a calming effect, the red ones were stimulating!

Actually, medical students are *more* prone to the placebo effect than you or I. Again, bitter placebos tend to be more effective than sweet ones. (Shades of Calvin! If it's nasty, it must be doing me good.)

Doctors are totally at a loss to account for these effects. Behaviourists have tried to advance an explanation based on Pavlovian conditioning. Pavlov once noticed that when he was preparing morphine injections for some dogs which had received many such injections previously, they became sleepy and sometimes vomited. Pursuing this clue, Herrnstein injected rats with scopolamine, which depresses their responses. Then, when they were conditioned to this effect, he injected them with saline solution (salt water). Their responses were again depressed. Subsequently, Pihl and Altman performed a similar experiment using amphetamine, which is a stimulant. Soon, salt water stimulated the rats too. Unfortunately, when they repeated the experiment with the tranquilliser chlorpromazine, nothing happened.

One might question whether being stimulated or slowed down has anything in common with curing a disease. But a more fundamental defect of this behaviourist kind of explanation is that placebos work first go off, before any conditioning has occurred; and – as with the red and blue pills – in the absence of any pharmacological effect to act as stimulus. The plain fact is that, as Dr O. Shapiro sadly concluded in the *Journal of the American Medical Association*: 'The etiology of the placebo effect is not yet understood.'

The one clear idea which I get from all this is that we are dealing with a form of suggestion, so that any explanation must come in terms of a general theory of suggestion, and this would certainly embrace hypnotic suggestion.

Hypnotic suggestion has measurable physiological effects. For example, it can change the rate of formation of blood-platelets (structures concerned with blood clotting). What is in some ways more extraordinary is the production of blisters by hypnotic suggestion to which I referred in Chapter Six.

By far more puzzling than the power of suggestion to cause damage is its power of curing it. The removal of warts by hypnosis is well attested. Indeed, warts can be removed on one side of the body and not on the other by suggestion. But the suggestion need not be hypnotic. Many years ago, I had a wart on the side of my index finger which became objectionably large. I went to a specialist who said: 'If you were under ten years old, I should put some red ink on the wart and tell you to go into the next room and touch a piece of equipment I should have left running. The wart would infallibly go. I treat all children in this way. Unfortunately, you have had an expensive education and cannot be taken in by magic, so I shall have to cut it off with an electric cautery and charge you three guineas.' This he did.

Hypnosis (like placebos) can often relieve pain. It can cure asthma and even skin diseases. A case which has become celebrated in medical literature is that of a man who suffered from the appalling skin disease ichthyosis. His whole body was covered with scales. No cures for this condition had ever been reported. But Dr A. A. Mason cured him completely by hypnosis, to the amazement of everyone.

Swellings can be reduced, bleeding stopped and even gangrene arrested.

Scientists have made surprisingly few attempts to study the underlying physiology of such phenomena, though there has been a great deal of work to establish whether they genuinely occur. One of those who have tried to go below the surface is the professional hypnotherapist Stephen Black, who made skin reactions his special subject and did rather extensive work at the Medical Research Council laboratories and elsewhere. If psychotherapy or hypnotic suggestion relieve allergies, what happens in the skin when this occurs? was the question he put to himself.

Dr Mason (the man who cured the patient with ichthyosis) had a patient, a Mrs R., who for twelve years had suffered from severe asthma and hay fever during May, June and July. Treatment with ephedrine and other drugs had been unsuccessful. Her eyes ran, her nose was blocked, she had long bouts of sneezing. She could not perform her household duties and became a chronic invalid. Investigation showed that pollens, especially grass pollen, were the prime cause. Mason gave her hypnotic suggestions: 'This year you will have no difficulty with your breathing, either at night or during the daytime – this year you will not have a blocked nose, your eyes will not run, there will be no itching round the eyes and you will not have sneezing attacks.' These words were repeated for half an hour every week for ten weeks, up to 8 July 1957. For the whole of this time, Mrs R. was completely free of symptoms of asthma and hay fever for the first time in twelve years. This was no surprise to Mason, or to Black. It was not the first such success.

Black's contribution was to apply pollen extracts to her arm at intervals and see if a weal resulted. As a check he also applied them to himself, and in a moment of inspiration also made some tests on one of Mrs R's legs. To his astonishment, he produced no weals on Mrs R's arms but he did produce weals on her leg, and of course on himself. The hypnotic instructions had, it was clear, suppressed the mechanism (or part of the mechanism) in the skin which constitutes the allergic reaction – as far as the arms were concerned. But it had not done so in the leg. Everyone had assumed that, if the mechanism could be suppressed at all, it would be on an all-or-nothing basis. Further studies, made with John Humphrey, the leading immunologist at the MRC laboratories, showed that while the reddening due to changes in the capillaries had been prevented, the local chemical releases were still occurring. This made sense, since the capillaries are controlled by the brain, whereas the chemical response is not.

When Mason and Black reported their results in the *British Medical Journal* the point was completely missed; the report was treated as a claim to have cured an allergy by hypnosis, which was hardly new. They were told you couldn't claim a system of cures on the strength of a single patient. The significance of the differing local response in arms and legs, which was the novel element, was ignored.

What we are talking about, let us admit, is faith-healing. It is ironical that many doctors who concede the existence of the placebo effect are wholly sceptical of faith-healing. When the British Medical Association conducted an enquiry into faith-healing it reported that all cures observed *could* have been due to ordinary medical attention. This was hardly the point.

However, genuine cures are certainly rare. Dunbar estimates that of sixty million pilgrims who have visited Lourdes, two hundred may have been cured of their illness. Between 1938 and 1948, the papal authorities only accepted twelve cases as being extra-medical cures. In 1948, fifteen thousand eight hundred pilgrims visited Lourdes; eighty-three claimed to have been cured and of these nine were accepted, and not all these were regarded as miraculous. An earlier investigation of 'touching' by King Louis XIV disclosed five persons claiming to have benefited out of two thousand four hundred.

L. Rose investigated ninety-six cases in Britain and found that none were clear-cut permanent cures, though there was often temporary relief of pain. Relapses after a few months were common. In any case, most patients were also receiving normal medical attention. He found that cures were largely confined to lameness and bone-disease, blindness and deafness, dermatitis and skin disease, epilepsies and paralyses. (The blindness and deafness were doubtless hysterical.) Claims for the cure of infection and malignancies were fairly rare, while cures of physical injury – broken bones and so on – were even rarer. There seems no need, therefore, to invoke the miraculous, if by this we mean the suspension of natural law by divine power. The cures are evidently psychosomatic, which is quite strange enough. The role of the healing figure, whether human or divine, is to inspire the necessary faith. But why should faith – an attitude of mind – have such a magical effect on the body?

Body to Mind

So far all I have said has concerned the action of the mind, or the brain, if you prefer, on the body. Can the current flow the other way? Can the body influence the mind? (Apart, of course, from Omega Effects and physical damage to the brain.) There is some evidence that it can, but the underlying mechanism is quite mysterious.

We say to a child who is crying or a friend who is being gloomy: 'Come on, cheer up, smile!' as if the act of smiling would induce the appropriate frame of mind. We say to a schoolboy: 'Sit up and pay attention,' as if the physical alertness would conduce to mental alertness. There is evidence that the body's muscles initiate reafferent discharges to the brain – even the facial muscles do so – so it is not out of the question that posture should influence mental attitude. Nietzsche certainly thought it did: look friendly and you become friendly. Unfortunately the mechanism is unknown.

Certainly, we stand proudly when we feel proud: it is difficult to feel proud if we are in a posture of humility, though it can be done for a while. Blaise Pasquarelli and Nina Bull of New York's Psychiatric Institute sought to demonstrate this experimentally. They hypnotised five students and told them that a word indicating an emotion would be uttered and that they would then feel the emotion and adopt an appropriate posture. The words employed were Disgust, Fear, Anger, etc. The students were to describe their feelings. When students had adopted the posture for one emotion, they found it impossible to switch to another, unless they were allowed to change their posture accordingly. I'm not sure that I regard the experiment as convincing, since the students were only simulating the emotions concerned. Would a person who was genuinely in a mood to be triumphant because of some personal achievement be forced out of that mood by being compelled to adopt an unsuitable attitude? That is the real test.

Leaders of men certainly operate on the assumption that the external world influences the internal one. Army leaders assume that a unit which is smartly turned out and drills well will have high morale; and that a unit which is slack in attitude will be slack in discipline too. And they do not see the slackness merely as a symptom, for the first step in raising the morale of the poor unit is always to set new standards of physical behaviour.

Thus it may be that when the loser of a war kneels to his conqueror, the kneeling not only symbolises his submission but even helps to reinforce a submissive attitude. One might extend this idea by suggesting that the hampering clothes of Victorian women effectively fostered a submissive or inhibited attitude. Conversely, the small boy with his Batman or Spaceman suit feels bigger and more powerful as a result of donning it.

One more fragment of information may be fitted into the pattern. It is certainly the case that stroking the skin has a relaxing effect on the mind as well as the body. Even the anencephalic child coos when stroked. Rocking, likewise, is soothing; hence the invention of the cradle. Rocking calms schizophrenics and Alexander Lowen has shown that lack of tactile stimulation is an important factor in schizophrenia.

It seems obvious to me that mind and body – or, if you prefer, subjective states and organic states – are related in a far more intimate way than we are at present willing to concede. In addition to the kind of phenomena I have described there are isolated facts which are so difficult to accommodate that they are quietly ignored. The fact, for example, that neurotics have poor night vision. The fact that multiple sclerosis (a virus infection) attacks people of a particular personality type. Even resistance to bacterial infection is altered by stress. There is nothing inherently unlikely in all this. Emotional states unquestionably alter hormonal outputs. I suspect that they also alter electrical fields. We know practically nothing about the forces regulating growth and development at the cellular level; they may be involved. All disease has a dual aspect.

But the medical profession has been extraordinarily reluctant to concede this – while Professor Skinner, the behaviourist, declares that psychosomatic disease does not exist! In reality, any conception of the brain running the body like a rider controlling his horse is obviously misleading and inadequate. The natural history of the mind implies the natural history of the body too.

Having examined the mind in general, let us now look more closely at its contents: the thoughts and feelings, sensations and perceptions which form the traffic of our mental life.

9

Traffic of the Mind

THAT CERTAIN FEELING

According to Joseph Zubin, Chief of Psychiatric Research for New York State Department of Mental Hygiene, some doctors report that they rarely make a diagnosis of schizophrenia – formerly known as dementia praecox – unless they experience what they call 'that praecox feeling' while examining the patient. I cannot but feel that such feelings are a significant element in our mental life.

Cited by Brian Inglis, *The Scientific Study of Abnormal Behaviour*, 1966.

The Stuff of Dreams

A dream I had some years ago started a train of thought which has long fascinated me. I made a careful record of this dream and later of many others. Since it is closely relevant to the question of what populates the mind, the simplest thing will be to start by telling you the dream.

It was evening, and I was walking along a road in the heart of the country. There were no houses or signs of human life; it might have been in southern Ireland. I had been all day in the hills, walking, and was pleasantly tired but with a sense of satisfaction about the day. I knew I would come shortly to the house of friends, after which I had to go off to my right towards my own home, where my wife would be preparing the evening meal. It was a summer evening and still light; the sky was clear and there was no wind. I seemed to be the only living thing. The next thing I remember was knocking at the door of my friends' house and getting no reply. I looked up at the first-floor windows – the front of the house was covered with creeper – in case they should be upstairs; then I threw some pebbles up at the window to attract their attention, but in vain. Rather downcast, for I had been looking forward to the stimulus of chatter and a drink, I set off on the long five-mile slog to my own home.

What struck me about this dream was how little visual content, how little action, it had. Just me walking along a road; then me looking up at the first-floor windows. All the rest – by far the greater part – consisted in what I can only call 'feelings': the feeling one has had a satisfying day, the anticipation of a meeting with friends, awareness that I had a second thing to do after I had done the first and so on. In most accounts of dreams there is a lengthy narrative and when dreams are represented in films they consist largely of actions. My dreams are seldom like that. I began to keep a record of my dreams to explore the point and soon realised that there was a great range of these specialised 'feelings'. For instance, I remember a dream which started with me walking along with a friend, and knowing that his wife and my wife were walking behind us. At no point in the dream did I look round and see them. Obviously this is a familiar experience: one carries, as temporary mental furniture, knowledge of this kind. Many of my dreams embody the knowledge that I have a train or a plane to catch. In one particularly elaborate one, I was packing three suitcases in a hotel room. I knew that I had to leave by a door in the corner, go along a corridor, past the hotel desk, enter another bedroom where there was a fourth suitcase and then redistribute my belongings more sensibly between the various cases, pay the bill and travel to my own home in another part of the town – seven actions. The dream as such never got as far as any of this and was limited to difficulty in closing one of the cases.

A common variant on this kind of 'situational awareness' is knowledge of identity. I see a white cat and know it is my cat Isabella, although in real life Isabella is a black cat. In the dream, of course, no incongruity is perceived. I am in my own house – I feel it is home – but it looks quite different from any house I have actually lived in. I talk to someone I know is my sister, although my sister does not actually look anything like the person in the dream. I enter a pub and think, 'Oh, I know this pub of old.' Perhaps the commonest of all such feelings is the one of acute embarrassment. There I was in the middle of Piccadilly with no trousers! Or, as happened to me in a recent dream, I was swimming nude in a lake which was suddenly invaded by schoolgirls, and then the water level began to fall.

Thus I am inclined to the conclusion that dreams consist primarily not of images or actions as is generally assumed, but of these 'feelings'. Images and situations are then brought up from the store to give expression to the feeling. The images may be picked up from experiences of the previous day, but the selection is by no means random. Images compress a great deal of symbolic information in an amazingly apt way. For instance, I dreamed recently I had a suitcase which, to my surprise, I found contained a smaller suitcase as well as various other articles, and it seemed strange that there was room for it. On waking, I at once realised that the suitcase stood for my book *How To Avoid The Future*, which contains within it an analysis of how society is losing cohesion which is complete in itself and might well have been issued as a separate book.

Of course Freud has made us all familiar with the symbolic aspect of dreams. But Freud saw them as expressing desires, usually sexual. It seems to me that all kinds of feelings and even situational assessments (for lack of a better phrase) are expressed in dreams.

And from this it is but a short step to recognising that in waking life too our mind is taken up with this special kind of emotionally-toned assessment. It is a major part of the traffic of our mind. There are scores of easily recognised mental situations – for instance, I have met you before but I can't remember your name. Will the drink hold out? Now I see how to solve the problem. You're pretending to be friendly but I don't trust you. I've dropped a brick. Home at last!

Since this is all quite obvious, I find it very curious that the literature of psychology seems to contain few speculations or descriptions of this kind of mind furniture (as distinct from recording dreams for purposes of therapy) and does not even provide us with a name for it. William James, who seems to have thought of everything, comes near to making my point when he says: 'We ought to say a feeling of *and*, a feeling of *if*, a feeling of *but* and a feeling of *by* quite as readily as we say a feeling of blue or a feeling of cold.' But his examples – blue and cold – are sense impressions, whereas I am speaking of a combination of knowledge with emotion. Nevertheless, particles like 'and' and 'if' may well be part of the same traffic.

Sunday is Different

As the twentieth century opened, the most original group of psychologists in Germany was working in Würzburg under the Latvian-born Oswald Külpe. (Originally a historian, he had fallen under the spell of Wundt, the father of psychology, during his time in Leipzig.) The man who was in due course to succeed Külpe was Karl Marbe, and in 1901 he was studying how people judge weights. They do not seem to make an intellectual comparison, he found to his surprise; there seem to be no images or sensations, just some vague feelings, which he called Bewusstseinlagen. It was to become the trade mark of this school. A difficult term to translate, it could perhaps be rendered as 'the content of consciousness'.

About the same time a very different approach was being employed by the Frenchman, Alfred Binet, who had become renowned by developing the first intelligence tests. But Binet's interests were much wider, and among other things he used to question his two small daughters, Armande and Marguerite, about their mental processes. Marguerite often used to say something like: 'I had a feeling it was someone near to me.' Or, 'I felt it was something I should refuse.' This was in the course of explaining how she had come to make some remark or other. These refer, quite evidently, to 'feelings' in the special sense I have described.

Again, the great British psychologist Sir Frederick Bartlett, the only psychologist to be regarded as worthy of an FRS, noted in the course of his experiments on memory that many of his subjects spoke of feelings or impressions. When shown pictures of faces, they made comments like, 'It looks as if he were a martinet,' or, 'As if he had been in bad weather,' and they appeared to modify the image they retained to suit these impressions. Another subject, justifying her interpretation of an inkblot, said: 'You seem to feel different on Sunday afternoon, somehow, and I felt like that.' Another, explaining why the inkblot reminded her of the Crown Jewels in the Tower of London, said: 'I didn't see myself there, but I *felt* as if I were there.' As Bartlett pointed out at the time, half a century ago, all structural relationships were constantly described as 'felt'. Remarks like, 'I had an impression that the figure was symmetrical,' or 'I had the feeling that the figure was growing more complex,' were constantly made.

Dr L. F. Cooper, in discussing the feeling of time-distortion which can be induced by hypnotic suggestion, refers to the 'meaning tone' of sentences and seems to be thinking of much the same effect. For instance, he says, 'Some nocturnal dreams consist largely of meaning tone.' Cooper was concerned with the case of hypnotic subjects who are asked to report information which they have not actually got. Told that he has seen a book, the subject has a conviction of having seen it, but cannot describe the book. What the subject does, Cooper concludes, is to feel what he is told to feel.

It has recently been shown that sometimes a *relationship* between two stimuli can be grasped even when the stimuli themselves cannot be consciously detected.

I keep finding support for this notion of feelings (in this special sense) as the stuff in which the traffic of the brain is chiefly conducted in many different fields. For instance a German psychologist, Professor Heinz Werner, who has made a particular study of mental development, back in the 1950s drew attention to a curious feature of the speech defect known as aphasia, in which the sufferer cannot find the correct word for what he wants to say but tends to light on another word in the same general area of meaning. For example, if you hold up a cigar and ask him what it is, he will hesitate and finally say SMOKE or something of that sort.

Werner holds that before we learn verbal labels for objects, in our childhood, we have already formed some general rather woolly ideas about them. To test this theory he exposed pairs of words to normal (not aphasic) subjects for only one-fiftieth of a second. He repeated these exposures until they started to identify the words and he noted down their comments. As his subjects, and hence the words, were German I will make use of the English equivalents. Thus, when the words were the German equivalents of GROAN and WHIRL, the subject said: 'The first part impressed me as something depressing, distressing, torturing. The second word was not grasped.' Again, when the words were HOWLING GALE, he said: 'I have an impression that in general I am on the right track,' and then suggested the word was BLOWING. In short these subjects had, to use Werner's own words, 'feelings of word meanings' and 'inner experience in the semantic sphere . . . prior to any specific articulation of the words'.

Of course, some of these 'feelings' have a much more subtle character than the rather clear-cut instances I have just cited in order to make my point clear. There is, for example (I quote from my note on a dream dreamed on the night of 30/31.12.72), 'A sense of being aware of the details without actually having them in mind at the moment.' Or again: 'This is habitual communication with someone very close to me, so there is no need to go into all the details.' At the other extreme, feelings include such elementary – what shall I say, flavours, tints, overtones? – as: 'this is deeply familiar'; 'this is very strange'; 'this is boring'; 'this is significant'; 'this is ominous'; 'this is fun'.

The numerous connections which run between the older part of the brain which is concerned with feelings and the newer part which handles facts and ideas, provide a physiological basis for the observation that there are few ideas which are not emotionally toned. And probably for the reverse proposition, that feelings soon find ideas through which to exhibit themselves. Psychologists have tended to treat emotions as if they existed in limbo; and philosophers have treated ideas and concepts in the same way. What the mind actually operates with, I suggest, is a very detailed currency of thousands of ready-made coins composed of an amalgam of the two elements.

I Have Been Here Before

One such 'Situational Assessment' known to everyone is déjà vu, the feeling one has been here before. It also appears in other forms: déjà entendu, I've heard this before; déjà fait, I've done this before; déjà vécu, I've been through this before, and so on. Many people report having felt, during a dream, that they had dreamed it before – déjà rêvé. I have never experienced this myself, oddly enough, but it makes good sense in terms of an explanation of 'tagging' experience.

This type of experience often follows injury to the temporal lobe, and is a feature of temporal lobe epilepsy, which suggests that the 'tagging' mechanism is situated in, or linked to, this area.

Probably as common, though less commented on, is the feeling of unfamiliarity we sometimes have about something which ought to be familiar. Usually, we simply say: 'I've completely forgotten it.' Only when it is something we couldn't conceivably forget – such as our own home or a near relation – do we recognise a sense of strangeness. Jamais vu, jamais entendu, jamais vécu. (I have seen it asserted that such impressions never occur in normal people and are a sign of mental disturbance. Having questioned numerous friends and acquaintances without finding a single instance of such 'normality' I am convinced that this assertion is nonsense.)

An American psychologist, R. Efron, has suggested that déjà vu arises because information is transferred from one side of the brain to the other, a process taking some thirty milliseconds; in consequence, he suggests one side learns what the other already knows. But in that case we should experience déjà vu all the time. Moreover, this explanation does not account for déjà vécu, and still less for the 'this is new' character of jamais vu, jamais vécu. I suggest that the brain contains a mechanism which 'tags' every item with a label 'familiar' or 'unfamiliar', and that sometimes this mechanism makes an error.

Various other explanations have been put forward, not always very helpful; for instance: 'This phenomenon (déjà vu) is a kind of brief derealisation and it points to a predominance in the object of its mnemic (i.e. cognitive) aspect. In other words, déjà vu is the momentary experience of an incomplete object formation. The feeling of familiarity develops out of the greater immediacy with the cognitive matrix within which the object (any object) develops.' This is a fine example of the 'private codes' used by psychologists. Another interesting variant of this theme is the impression that something of unusual significance is occurring. As we saw in Chapter Seven, this feeling is a major feature of mystical and pantheistic experiences. But it can also be evoked chemically: nitrous oxide seems especially to upset the brain's evaluation of significance. William James experimented with inhalation of nitrous oxide and wrote an account of his experience. Under the influence of the gas, he arrived at various profound ideas which he wrote down. Viewed later in cold blood, they looked less significant. He had written, 'That sounds like nonsense but it is pure onsense.' Then came a sentence worthy of a German philosopher: 'There are no differences but differences of degree between different degrees of difference and no difference.' It was O. W. Holmes who said, 'The key to all the mysteries that Philosophy has sought in vain to resolve flashed upon me,' and he had written: 'A strong smell of turpentine pervades throughout.'

To me this looks just like an evaluation mechanism which has gone out of control – a mechanism which tags experience 'significant', 'trivial', 'possibly significant', etc. This raises the question whether the sense of significance reported by mystics has any ultimate validity, or is just a temporary disturbance of the tagging mechanism.

As one thinks about it one sees that more and more of the traffic of the mind can be fitted into this framework: a system of 'impressions' which are assignable to sensory data. In particular it illuminates memory. For example, this morning – shortly before writing these lines – I said to my wife: 'I know I intended to ask you a question before starting work, but at the moment I cannot recall what it was.' The knowledge that 'I'm due to ask a question' is clearly a feeling in the sense I have described. This feeling must, it is evident, be generated automatically when the question arises in one's mind and the decision is made to propound it to someone; but equally clearly it continues to exist in the consciousness, or is immediately available for recall, even when the question which provoked it has been repressed or forgotten. When we come to consider memory I shall take the position that a great part of the traffic of memory also consists of such feelings and not solely, as is sometimes assumed, of facts. Yet another feeling in this special sense is nostalgia: the feeling that something very sweet happened long ago. Proust has given us a classic instance in the episode of sponge-cakes dipped in tea which recalled not simply thoughts but also feelings from his youth in Combray. Let me however give a personal instance because there is a little more to it and I can draw only on my own experience. Driving back from the city yesterday, as I passed through the village where I live, I noticed an inhabitant walking up the hill. I then experienced for a brief moment a feeling which is hard to describe. Perhaps I can say that I suddenly saw in this simple image a settled pattern of life, free of real psychological insecurities, even if not free of material ones. I immediately went on to think that such security hardly exists any more; and perhaps it never did; that what I was experiencing was a longing for a golden past that existed in the imagination only. As Freudians would no doubt explain, it may have expressed a longing for the security of the womb. Nevertheless, in contrast with Proust, it did not affect me as a romanticisation of my own past, and though one could still label it nostalgic what I am trying to pin down is something larger. Nostalgia is only one facet of it. A number of times recently – is the experience more common as one grows older? – I have had these brief bursts of emotionally toned awareness. The emotion itself varies; sometimes it is sad, sometimes gay; sometimes it is a sense of achievement or failure; of companionship or loneliness; of imprisonment or escape. Often music induces it. Or an act of true friendship may. Or a symbol. Or a smell.

One is told that such inexplicable emotional 'auras' are experienced in epilepsy or when one has a tumour of that part of the brain known as the rhinencephalon. However, I doubt whether either applies to my case. If I am unworried, it is because I suspect that artists have such powerful feelings constantly, and that is why they become artists, by which I mean creative workers in any sphere. What for me is a rarity, comparatively, is for them a daily experience.

It seems that in schizophrenia too, the victim experiences similar surges of feeling, which sweep over him and die away without warning, demoralising him. In this sense, maybe, true genius is to madness near allied. I know, too, that some of these experiences are so sweet that if there were a drug which I knew would induce them without unpleasant or dangerous side or after-effects I might become wholly addicted to it. How odd, then, that we know so little of something so personally significant! How many people have such experiences? How often? How do they compare? And how inadequate are accounts of the mind which ignore them, treating it only as a control mechanism, an input-output device.

'Feelings' play a major part in mental disturbance, as the autobiographical accounts of people like Morag Coate show very vividly. In her book *Beyond All Reason* she describes how she often felt she was on the verge of important discoveries. Or again she records, 'I was aware a meeting between the directors of different solar systems had taken place.' She felt the nurses were the agents of alien powers. Nowadays we all know something about the clinical condition called persecution mania or paranoia. The sense that others are treating one unjustly is also a 'feeling'.

If, as I shall argue later, the contents of the mind, like the brain itself, are structured in ascending hierarchies, then I suggest that 'feelings' are, with images, sensations and thoughts, the basic blocks which go to make up the complex experiences which psychoanalysts study, which we all live by, and about which poets write.

They call for further study, but it would be easier to discuss them if we had a less ambiguous name for them. 'Feelings' has too many shades of meaning. It is curious that something so basic has escaped being re-christened. Since the prefix 'meta' means 'beyond' or 'behind' or 'sharing with', perhaps we could agree to call them meta-thoughts or meta-feelings.

If there is one feeling which is more basic to our existence than any other, I suppose that it is our awareness of the state of our body and the position of our trunk and limbs, and to this topic I now turn.

PART THREE

Inputs

10

Images of Reality

LET ME LEND YOU A HAND

DOCTOR: *Is this your hand?*
PATIENT: *Not mine, doctor.*
DOCTOR: *Yes, it is. Look at that ring: whose is it?*
PATIENT: *That's my ring. You've got my ring, doctor.*
DOCTOR: *No, I haven't. It's your hand. Look how different it is from mine!*
(Patient seems bewildered; feels her left shoulder, then her left upper arm and follows it downward to the wrist. Then says):
PATIENT: *It must be my hand.*
DOCTOR: *And do you still say there's nothing wrong with it?*
PATIENT (confused): *It seems I am wrong.*

Source: P. H. Sandifer, 'Anosognosia and disorders of the body scheme', *Brain* (1946) *69*:122–37.

Phantom Limbs

In the majority of cases, when a limb is amputated, the unfortunate patient, waking from the anaesthetic, feels that his limb is still there. He even feels he can move it. Only repeated inspection and touching convinces him that it has gone, and sometimes he forgets this and tries to stand on the missing leg when he gets out of bed, with the result that he falls to the ground.

The 'phantom limb' persists for many years, though often it gradually seems to shorten until (in the case of the arm) the hand seems to be inside the body, where it seems sometimes to be in violent motion, the fingers opening and shutting. Since phantoms of the nose, breast and penis are not experienced – and since phantoms are not reported when limbs are lost in the first few years of life – there can be little doubt that it is the kinaesthetic sense – the sense of the position of one's limbs, which is derived from special receptors in the muscles – which is the main basis of this phenomenon. (Actually, there have been one or two reports of phantoms following amputation of the breast, which Marian Simmel has investigated. She found that what women reported was not an actual phantom so much as lack of awareness of any difference; this probably accounted for 'yes' responses given to some early surveys.)

The famous sixteenth-century surgeon Ambrose Paré noted the presence of phantom limbs, but they were not taken seriously by modern medicine until 1871; and it was not until the 1920s that neurologists began to explain them in terms of a 'body image' or 'body schema' located in the parietal lobe of the brain, the lobe which, you recall, handles motor and sensory experience. Obviously, awareness of one's body goes much further than awareness of the position of one's limbs. This is vividly brought out when one studies the distortions which the body image can undergo when the parietal area is injured by wounds or tumours. Dr MacDonald Critchley, a consulting neurologist who is associated with the National Hospital, Queen's Square, and is the world authority on the parietal lobes, has made a close study of these distortions. They take an amazing variety of forms.

The body may seem abnormally large, or small, or completely absent. There may be supernumerary limbs; limbs may seem detached from the body or missing, or strange. 'I know that they look like mine,' said one patient, 'but I can feel that they are not and I can't believe my eyes.' And she added: 'My eyes and my feelings don't agree and I must believe my feelings.'

Sometimes only part of the body is involved. One patient felt that his head was too narrow and that the left half was filled with bricks. Gerstman, a German doctor, reported a patient who could not recognise her fingers – and who could not count. One reflects that in English 'digit' means both finger and number, and this is true in many languages; counting starts with fingers.

Where one arm is paralysed, the owner may declare that it is short, ugly, shapeless or snakelike; or he may declare that it is not the proper one, and search for his own arm elsewhere, ignoring the arm he can see. Similarly, when one half of the body is paralysed, it may be ignored. Critchley tells of hemiplegics who have shaved one half of their face, women who have combed only half their hair and made up only half their face, and who have stepped out of the bath with only one leg and fallen. Then they dry only one half of their body. Yet the patient who puts on only one glove may use the other hand to do it with. Moreover, some of these hemiplegics seem quite unconcerned by their condition: often they deny that the paralysis really exists and question the sanity of anyone who refers to it. (Freud tells us that people often deny unpleasant facts, even to themselves.) At the neural level we can see this as an inhibitory process such as we have already discussed. But is the hemiplegic's denial only at the level of ideas? After all, he actually lacks the neural data on which he can build an image of part of his body.

Where the whole parietal lobe is involved by the damage, his body may seem to the victim to be rotting away or to have ceased to exist. A Russian doctor tells of a patient who tore off his clothes and rolled in the snow, apparently in a frantic attempt to convince himself he existed by a powerful stimulus. Clearly we are not far removed here from the depersonalisation I discussed earlier.

Parietal lesions can also evoke feelings that limbs are moving when they are not, or are very light, or are in a different position to the one which they really occupy. Or the patient may feel he has a supernumerary arm, which only moves when he moves the one on the opposite side. (Evidently signals from one half of the brain are being transferred to the other half.) Not surprisingly, such people have difficulty carrying out normal movements and may fail to complete movements they have begun to make. The smoker who strikes a match may fail to use it to light his cigarette and merely hold it till it burns his fingers. Even walking may be difficult to do properly. Asked to draw a clock-face, the hemiplegic can only put figures on one side of the dial. This same defect makes him unable to tell the time. In short, we should not dismiss hemiplegia as simply paralysis: the 'mind' is also involved.

These sensory disturbances 'are just torture,' reports one victim. It is so hard for us fortunate ones to form any idea of them that I will quote more: 'The right side of my body behaves quite normally but the left side is like a very troublesome and most irritating foreign body which shouldn't be there. Often it seems that I have no left side and this feeling can cause great distress. Sometimes the leg or arm appears to be in a different position from what it really is. Many times, while engrossed in something else, I have bent to scratch an irritation of the leg and then discovered that I was scratching my other limb or the leg of a nearby chair! . . . I seem to possess a head double the size it really is . . . It seems as if a small but strongly tentacled octopus is inside, using its suckers to pull hundreds of tiny brain cells together into a tight bunch, and the pull is often so strong that my head is tilted to the right, an ear almost touching the shoulder, causing the neck muscles to ache in sympathy.' To my mind, these horrifying aberrations embody particularly clearly what I have called the Omega Effect. Purely neurological damage is experienced by the sufferer in subjective forms which are highly detailed and specific. We do not operate by means of 'cognition' and 'affect' as the textbooks have it, but by quite clear-cut 'feelings' of protean character. But even this does not fully explain the situation, as we see if we look more closely at the phantom limb experience.

The amputee can tell the doctor: 'Now my hand is open. Now I am touching my thumb with each finger in turn.' Yet the nerves which convey to him the subjective impression that he is performing these actions have no end-organs. Sometimes the phantom hand, however, is immovable; it may be bunched up most painfully and the patient will complain: 'The doctor forgot to straighten out my fingers before he took my arm off.'

Does the Body Remember?

One of the great students of this phenomenon was Bill Livingston, an outstanding American physician, who included hunting, fishing and playing the clarinet among his talents. In 1929, a friend (also a doctor), lost an arm from infection and suffered severe pain thereafter. For a long time he said nothing, believing that the pain was 'imaginary'. His fingers seemed pressed over his thumb, his wrist flexed, while every so often it felt as if a scalpel was being driven into the ball of his thumb (at a point where he had once been inoculated). Alternating with this was a burning sensation. The pain sometimes brought him to the point of nausea. One day he told Livingston about it. He bent his friend's fingers over the thumb, flexed his wrist and raised his arm into a hammer-lock position and kept it there. 'After five minutes I was perspiring freely,' says Livingston. 'My hand and arm felt unbearably cramped and I quit.' 'But you can take your hand down,' said his friend.

Livingston decided to make the study of pain his aim in life, became a world authority and wrote a book – published in 1943 when most people had little leisure to read – which was much before its time.

But there are still more curious aspects of the story. Some amputees report that they can feel something in their phantom hand, saying it feels like a watch, a penny or a handbag mirror. (Sometimes, too, when holding such an object in their real hand, they feel a corresponding phantom object in the phantom hand.) One of Livingston's patients was a railway man, whose arm was taken off by a passing train when he was working on the track. Just before the impact, he felt some gravel in his glove, and he continued to feel this gravel at his fingertips after amputation. It annoyed him more than the pain. This remarkable report suggests that the body has some kind of memory for stimuli which may persist indefinitely. It is an idea quite outside the normal sphere of physiological debate, but we shall come across it again.

The limb which is not felt and does not obey commands is not felt to be part of the self. Paraplegics often give their crippled limbs derogatory names like 'Old Useless' and address them: 'Come along now, old useless, don't get in the way like that.' The same may be true of hemiplegics. One such patient claimed the inert half was his brother, lying in bed with him, offered it a cigarette and asked it questions. A hemiplegic nurse said the paralysed arm belonged to her friend, who was also a nurse. She described it as being heavier, thicker and darker than her own arm. Thus perception is influenced.

Other patients deny the whole problem, as we have seen. In other words, we only accept as egoge those parts of our system which are contributing to the total neural pattern in our brain.

I also observe that the whole issue is heavily invested with emotion, and even erotic feeling. One patient had erotic sensations from his own left side which he imagined belonged to a woman lying beside him. Here again we see how closely the various aspects of the psyche are integrated.

Finally, it is worth noting that schizophrenics often suffer disturbances of the body image which are even more chaotic than those mentioned. Migraine sufferers likewise. As one reported: 'Today my body is as if someone had drawn a vertical line separating the two halves: the right half seems to be the size of the left half. I wonder how I am going to get my hat on when one side of my head is so much bigger than the other.' Even worse was this case: 'I experienced the sensation that my head had grown to tremendous proportions and was so light it floated up to the ceiling, although I was sure that it was still attached to my neck. I used to try to hold it down with my hands.' The phrase brings out how convincingly real the feeling was.

Psychedelic drugs, like LSD, also disturb the body image: limbs seem to lengthen and shorten, the head balloons, and so on. In hypnotic experiments in which the subject is instructed to think himself back to earlier and earlier periods of his life, even as far as the womb, reports are sometimes given which suggest the body image is dissolving and that, at the same time, the boundaries between the subject and other people are dissolving. A psychoanalyst, Andrew Peto, who works at the Einstein College of Medicine, Yeshiva University, reports on a patient who hallucinated a gradual shrinking of her body, turning into a baby and then being cuddled by her analyst. Then (she said) the analyst's whole body softened up, lost shape and became jelly-like; the patient's body, which had also softened and was now minute, penetrated the analyst's body or merged with it.

On another occasion, this imaginative lady felt herself enlarging until she engulfed the analyst and the whole room.

The reason I report such delusions and fantasies is not simply to amaze you but because they raise serious issues related to the Omega Effect. They show the extraordinary range of subjective experience which is keyed to neural disturbance.

The idea of the body schema, as proposed by the physiologist Henry

Head, was taken up by psychoanalysts, notably Paul Schilder, who elaborated it to include one's mental conception of one's body as handsome, vile, misshapen and so on, and also one's ideal of oneself. I have used the term however only in its original sense, though it is sometimes hard to draw a line between the two. The conception of one's body as glorious or corrupt can only be an imaginative elaboration of one's basic awareness of it.

There are plenty of other mysteries here: for instance, why when half the brain is removed does the body image remain intact? Or conversely, if awareness is regularly transferred from one side of the brain to the other, why do hemiplegics not get some compensation for their parietal damage?

The image of the body is perhaps our most basic perception; we know about ourselves before we know about the external world. But there is another kind of signal our consciousness receives about our physical condition; namely, pain. Let us explore this phenomenon next for it reveals unusually clearly how complex is the mechanism of our perceptions.

11

The Puzzle of Pain

'PAIN IS A STATE OF MIND'

When the British landed at Anzio in Italy in 1943, a young soldier received a frightful wound from a mortar shell. It was five hours before he reached a hospital and when doctors were finally able to examine him, it was found that he had 'a meat-cleaver-like wound cutting through his fifth to twelfth ribs near the vertebral column. He had bled a good deal and was cyanotic [turning blue]. Obsessed with the idea that he was lying on his rifle, he struggled to get off the litter. He appeared to be wild with pain. His wound supported such a belief', wrote the surgeon afterwards.

Since he was thrashing about so much that it was impossible to examine him and the oxygen tube kept coming out of his nose, he was given the only sedative available, sodium amytal. The dose – 2½ gr. – was insufficient to control pain, but quietened him. It was then found that not only were eight ribs sliced in two and his body-cavity open, but a broken rib-end had lacerated one kidney and one lung. Yet the moment he received the sedative his condition, which had been deteriorating, began to improve and his colour returned.

The surgeon who operated was Lt.-Col. H. K. Beecher; he was so struck by the absence of pain in this and similar cases that he subsequently questioned 225 soldiers with severe wounds in five categories whether they felt pain; if so, how much? Finally he asked, 'Do you want something for it?' Three-quarters of the patients did not request analgesics! As a check, he later questioned civilians with similar, though usually less severe, wounds: eighty per cent did *want analgesics. 'Great wounds are blocked by small doses of morphine; experimental pains of little significance are not,' noted Beecher later. 'Morphine acts on the significant pain, not on the other.' Beecher concluded that pain is not a state of body but a state of mind.*

Source: H. K. Beecher, 'Pain in wounded men in battle', *Ann. of Surg.* (1946) *124*:96.
See also: H. K. Beecher, *Measurement of Subjective Responses*, 1959.

Patterns of Pain

There is one further kind of sensory input, different from all the others, which has a unique claim on our attention; namely, pain. Even when we are preoccupied, pain signals break in on our awareness. They have, in all ordinary circumstances, a high priority. If the pain continues, we notice it more not less: we do not habituate. Yet, surprisingly, we can sometimes ignore pain. The subject of pain is baffling and leads us into the heart of the mind/body problem.

Though pain is often contrasted with pleasure, it is not the opposite of it. In fact, pain may become a source of pleasure, as in masochism.

Pain is an unique experience, which can be associated with pleasure, its opposite unpleasure, or with neither, as we shall shortly see.

Wrongly, we tend to assume that pain only occurs after injury and is proportional to the damage done. Most people, including some surgeons, appear to hold a sort of 'telegraph' notion of pain; they seem to assume there are special pain nerves which convey messages to the brain, which are perceived as pain when the nerve endings are stimulated beyond a certain point. Surgeons have repeatedly sought to help patients suffering intense pain by severing nerves or inserting alcohol blocks. Unfortunately, this only works half the time and sometimes makes the pain worse than before; or new pains develop. Even stranger, sometimes severing the nerve *beyond* the point at which the pain originates will relieve pain.

Sometimes minor injuries will evoke unexpectedly severe pain. The late Bill Livingston, the American specialist in pain, whom we met in the previous chapter, describes how a 'bruise, a superficial cut, the prick of a thorn or a broken chicken-bone, a sprain or even a post-operative scar', which both patient and doctor regarded as minor, may give rise to intolerable pain. He describes how he treated a fifty-eight-year-old woman who fell and injured her foot: it was bruised but not fractured. She began to have attacks of pain which grew more and more severe as the months passed, so that years later she was back under medical care. She said that her toes felt 'as if bursting and on fire'. The lightest touch on her foot was intolerable.

Livingston cured her by a method which, on the face of it, doesn't make sense. He made a series of Novocaine injections at the base of the toes. Each injection stopped the pain completely for a while. The attacks returned at ever longer intervals until, a year later, they had ceased altogether. Livingston also treated other similar cases successfully by this method. But, of course, the effect of Novocaine wears off in a few hours, so why was the pain stopped for much longer periods? Livingston reckoned that the injections were breaking some kind of vicious circle. He achieved many other successes by this method, so clearly the telegraph theory of pain won't wash.

The frightful pain which (as in the case just mentioned) sometimes follows a trivial wound or bruise and which continues long after the damage has healed, if not indefinitely, is known as *causalgia*. The victims often describe it as 'blazing' or 'fiery'. In such cases, it often happens that a light touch on another limb, or on the head, will suddenly bring on pain in the limb which was damaged. Indeed, even a loud noise can trigger an attack of causalgia. When Livingston was in charge of the peripheral nerve injury ward of a US Naval Hospital, he had to ask Washington to issue a special order forbidding airplanes to fly over the site, since the noise produced screams of agony from his patients. Even a strong emotion can trigger causalgia. Both these facts strongly suggest that the key lies in the brain, and not in the spinal or peripheral nerves.

To me these extraordinary phenomena strongly suggest a system which is only just in equilibrium. Like a house of cards, a mere touch destroys the balance and the structure crumbles. Pain must result from patterns of nerve impulses becoming unbalanced. This is, indeed, the modern conception of pain. But before we discuss theories there are further facts to be taken into consideration.

One of the oddest is the strange response of people suffering from tabes dorsalis, sometimes known as locomotor ataxia. This disease, fortunately no longer common, is a consequence of syphilis: it erodes the spinal cord, disturbing gait and posture, among other things, and causing severe pain. Now if a tube containing warm water is applied to the skin of a tabetic several successive times, it appears hotter each time, until finally it is experienced as burning, where an ordinary person would feel only successive applications of warmth. It is as if the stimuli were piled on top of one another. Stranger still, a considerable delay may occur before any pain is felt from a blow or wound. Professors of neurology, in order to impress their students, used sometimes to end a demonstration by pinpricking a tabetic patient, who would show no response. The professor would close his lecture, put on his coat, say good-bye and then suddenly the patient would cry out. Facts like these are clearly incompatible with a telegraph theory of pain.

Any comprehensive theory of pain also has to explain why some people feel no pain while others feel too much. There are people who develop so extreme a sensitivity that any bright light, slight noise, even a puff of air causes them agony. More than a century ago, the case of a young lady was described: she had to spend all her time in a dark room, almost motionless. Doctors were at a loss.

In contrast with this there are people who cannot feel pain at all, or scarcely at all. The best known case was a young Canadian girl, the daughter of a doctor, who was able to arrange for her to be studied by experts. As in several other such cases, she had burnt herself unwittingly. (One such girl was only awoken to the fact that her leg was being burnt by a radiator when she smelled roasting flesh.) When examined in the laboratory, she felt no pain in almost boiling water, in an ice-bath or when given powerful electric shocks. Other tests included injecting histamine under the skin, which normally produces intolerable itching. She never sneezed or coughed and the reflexes which protect the eyes were absent. The side effects of pain, such as sweating and rapid heart rate, were absent. She developed serious trouble in her hips and spine, probably because she did not shift her weight when standing or sitting, nor did she turn over in bed. She died at the age of twenty-nine of massive infections. During her last month of life she finally began to experience what she so long had missed: tenderness and pain in the left hip. Interestingly enough, this pain was relieved by analgesics in the usual way.

In some cases such insensitivity to pain runs in a family, and is due to a genetically controlled defect in the development of the nervous system. Usually such people are insensitive to temperature too, which suggests that pain and heat-sensitivity are connected, whereas their response to pin-pricks may be only slightly diminished.

Finally, we must recognise that pain is not just 'pain'; it comes in many forms. One of the leading authorities on pain, Ronald Melzack, has studied this. Leaving aside words which describe degrees of intensity (tenderness, sickening, vicious, unbearable, etc.), Ronald Melzack and W. S. Torgerson found about eight quality categories, indicated by words like pulsing and throbbing; pricking and stabbing; cutting, gnawing, tugging, burning, smarting, tingling, stinging, itching . . . I suspect that it is the specialised nerve endings which assist in making such distinctions by contributing their quota to the total nervous pattern of pain.

For a long time, some physiologists expected to find special nerves devoted to conveying the sensation of pain, but it turns out that pain is signalled by the same nerves that subserve ordinary sensation. If you expose your arm to heat, the experience, which is pleasant at first, then unpleasant, becomes definitely painful at about 45° C, which is the temperature at which cell damage starts to occur. People vary little in this respect. The question is: what has happened to the signals indicating warmth to make them indicate pain too? The answer is far from clear. Let us look at the physiology.

Pathways of Pain

Nerves are of several kinds, ranging from thin ones which conduct quite slowly to thick ones which conduct much faster. Neurologists divide them for convenience into three groups, A, B and C. A is thick, C is thin. The speed of conduction is about walking-pace in the slow, about as fast as an express train in the B group and almost as fast as an airplane in the A group. If you stub your toe, you note at first a sharp pain, then a moment without pain, and then a dull aching pain. These are known as 'fast' and 'slow' pain respectively.

There are three main pathways which ascend through the spine to the brain. It used to be thought that one was particularly concerned with pain signals, but it now seems highly probable that all three are involved at the same time.

Livingston explained the continued pain from wounds which had healed as a feedback process in which the neurones in the spine affected those in the skin, which in turn drove the neurones in the spine. (He noted that in such cases the skin was often discoloured, colder and sweated more. Amputees often find their stumps several degrees colder than the rest of the body.) He attributed his success with Novocaine to breaking this vicious circle. His pupil, Ronald Melzack, took the idea further, arguing that impulses arriving at the spine from one source might block the passage of pain signals from another source. This 'gating' theory would explain why we scratch an itch, rub a bruised limb and clench our hands when in pain. It could also explain, or help to explain, the effectiveness of acupuncture.

Acupuncture is quite puzzling; the analgesic effect often does not start for twenty minutes or so, and during this time the needles may be twirled or an electric current may be passed between them. One Western visitor, Dr E. G. Dimond, saw a man's stomach removed with the aid of acupuncture; four needles were inserted in the flap of his ear. A six-volt 150-cycle current was applied to them. The patient, who had also received a mild analgesic (sixty mg of meperidine hydrochloride) chatted away throughout the operation, noting some sensation when the surgeon actually pulled on his stomach.

But what happens when the complex of signals through these nerves arrives at the brain itself? They go to three destinations. First, the reticular system which arouses us, so that we shall do something about the cause of pain: it is this arousal which explains why it is difficult to sleep or even sit still when in pain. The arousal system is saying, 'Do something.' Paths run to the cortex, which tells us where the pain is and perhaps analyses what kind of pain. (Actually nerve-tracts run to five different destinations in the cortex; three of these are knocked out by anaesthetics and one is not; the fifth is somewhat affected. To me this suggests that some pain awareness persists during anaesthesia, as I have already suggested.) Paths run to the thalamus, the area mediating between mid-brain and cortex, which seems to evaluate and so, presumably, creates awareness that the nerve signal is unpleasant.

This notion is confirmed by the fact that damage to parts of the thalamus can sometimes give rise to pain – called 'central pain', since no peripheral nerves are involved. Surgeons have attempted to cure intractable pain by making lesions at certain points in the thalamus. Such operations are often successful at first. But, after a year or so, pain often returns; as with other injuries, the brain manages to find ways of getting round the deficit. Removal of part of the cortex adjacent to the thalamus may then help. Sometimes these operations make the pain worse. We simply don't know enough. Prefrontal lobotomy has the curious effect that the patient is still aware of pain, but it no longer seems to matter. Moreover, such a patient will still complain about a pin-prick or a mild burn. So what makes pain unpleasant?

The neurones of the entire nervous system are in a state of dynamic balance; some groups stimulate others to fire, some restrain them. (This balance is not only spatial but temporal.) Upset it by destroying some of the inputs and the whole thing distorts. It has been shown (in cats) that severing a certain nerve will cause other cells to fire and to continue firing for as much as thirty days. Neurones not only fire when stimulated but produce after-discharges for some time after stimulation has ceased, and pain appears to be associated particularly with these after-discharges.

If pain is thus a disturbance of the whole pattern of nervous discharges it is easy to understand why cutting a nerve often makes pain worse rather than better. 'Operations have been performed for pain at nearly every possible site in the pathway from the peripheral receptors to the sensory cortex, and at every level the story is the same: some encouraging results but a disheartening tendency for the pain to recur,' write two Australian surgeons, Sunderland and Kelly. 'At whatever level pain is attacked, the impression is conveyed that the whole nervous system makes a co-ordinated effort to re-establish the pathway.' And as Ronald Melzack points out, cutting a nerve permanently disrupts normal patterning, may result in irritating scars and neuromas, and destroys channels which may be potentially useful for the control of pain by 'gating' methods.

For this is the modern approach to pain control. Just as you scratch an itch, seeking to restore the nervous pattern, so nowadays electric stimulators can often be used to block pain. Interestingly, a short period of stimulation blocks pain for many hours, no doubt because of the after-discharges which are evoked. Melzack, like his British colleague Patrick Wall, has shown how vibrating the skin mechanically can also modify pain, sometimes assuaging it, as in rubbing a bruise, sometimes making it worse, as I have described causalgia.

I want to bring out how very sophisticated the sensory system is, so I will add one more fact which is not well known. The receptive fields of nerves (the area of skin served) actually change in size and shape from moment to moment. Descending fibres from brain to skin control field size and, I suspect, sensitivity-level. There are also descending 'message modifying fibres' from the cortex to stations in the spinal cord. (You will recall that there are also efferents to eye and ear.) But even more astonishing is the recently discovered fact that the cortex continually modifies its own wiring, handling the incoming signals first with these neurones, then with those.

A Japanese team inserted recording electrodes in the thalamus and worked out where the signals they recorded were coming from. Then they anaesthetised this part of the skin with a local anaesthetic. The signals stopped. But soon, long before the anaesthetic wore off, they restarted and proved to be coming from another area of skin. So it seems the nervous system can rewire itself in a matter of minutes. It may even be that in daily life our circuitry is constantly changing in detail while subserving the same overall purpose. This is a thought we shall meet again in another context. It certainly helps to show why cutting nerves is no reliable way of blocking pain. (As Livingston once said, the best neurosurgeon to consult for intractable pain is one with no arms.)

It is difficult to discuss pain without discussing sensation, since the two are mediated by the same nerves. And touch also has its subtleties. So now let us look at these.

The Sensibility of Henry Head

One of the classic experiments of physiology was carried out by the English physiologist Henry Head. On 25 April 1903, a surgeon, at his request, severed two nerves in his arm. The nerve ends were immediately sewn together again and the wound closed. Naturally Head at once lost sensation over the whole area served by these nerves. But gradually feeling returned; the surprise was that it returned in two stages. At first Head could feel crude differences in temperature and pressure, though he could not localise them. Painful stimuli were experienced as a dull general kind of ache. An odd feature was that, the morning after the operation, he noticed, just outside the area which was dead to feeling, an area which was abnormally sensitive. It was 'most difficult to account for', he said.

It was only some weeks later that normal discrimination began to return. And now there was another odd feature. There was a small area on the back of his hand which never recovered at all. Even stranger was the fact that he noticed on his wrist a triangular patch which was quite insensitive to being pricked, but which could detect stroking with a wisp of cotton wool.

However, the fact which struck Head most was that sensation came back in two stages. He named these two kinds of sensibility *protopathic* and *epicritic*. He thought there must be two kinds of nerve fibres specialised to handle touch: one, developed early in evolution, reporting to the thalamus a crude sense of pleasantness and unpleasantness; another, more able to discriminate and locate the stimulus, reporting to the cortex. Neurologists have failed to find two distinct kinds of nerve fibre, but the basic sensory distinction cannot be denied. (It is believed that protopathic pain is transmitted by the C fibres, epicritic pain by the A fibres and perhaps B. Both A and C transmit temperature, while C only transmits touch. There are also subdivisions of these fibres: that's how complicated the system is!) Later, other scientists repeated this heroic experiment. Among these were Trotter and Davis, who noted that, at the time when epicritic sensation is coming back, cooling the skin causes reversion to the protopathic type of sensibility. Another puzzle.

According to the textbooks, sensation is registered by specialised nerve endings scattered throughout the skin. There are 'cold spots', 'pressure spots' and so on. The several types of end-organ are named for their discoverers, Pacini, Ruffini, Mazzoni, Krause, Golgi and Meissner, and allegedly respond to distinctive stimuli. The Meissner corpuscles are said to register touch, the Krause end-bulbs cold, the Ruffini end-organs warmth, while the free nerve endings handle pain. But the textbooks are, as usual, behind the times.

The outer ear contains only free endings, yet can register touch, temperature and so on. So the new idea is that the free endings culminate in highly specialised neurones which (in the case of warmth) fire not just for warmth but for specific temperature. Thus a neurone might start firing at 44° C, reach a peak of activity at 45° C and tail off at 46° C; another might peak at 46° C, and so on. Moreover, some neurones seem to register whether the temperature is rising, others that it is falling. Thus the nervous system reports not merely that it is hot, but how hot and whether it is likely to become hotter. Furthermore, different neurones cover areas of varying size. The story is much the same for pressure-sensors.

This is an appealing picture, since it parallels the set-up in the eye, which has specialised receptors for edges, for the change from dark to light, etc. Thus we might think of the skin as an enormous kind of retina, spread all over the body, with the brain integrating the totality of messages received into a coherent impression of the environment. Furthermore, the branching networks in which free nerves end interpenetrate and overlap, so that even a sharp point will activate at least two nerve fibres.

The only trouble with this account is that it explains a bit too much. If free nerve endings are sufficient, what are all the end-organs with the fancy names doing? They must be there for some good reason.

Some areas of the body lack certain kinds of sensitivity. Thus the penis is not sensitive to pressure – has only protopathic sensibility – while the conjunctiva of the eye are not sensitive to heat. (There is a clue in the fact that when Head was recovering from his self-inflicted injury he could detect touch but not warmth.) Even odder is the fact that the corneal sensitivity of women is reduced at the time of menstruation, as is the touch sensitivity of the middle finger. This weird fact emerged in the course of studies by Michel Millodot, of the University of Wales at Cardiff, on how well people tolerate contact lenses. He also found that brown-eyed people tolerate them better than people with light coloured eyes, since the former are less sensitive to pain. People with hazel eyes and green eyes have corneas which are more sensitive than brown, but less sensitive than blue-eyed. Moreover, coloured people are much less sensitive than whites in this respect. Since the Chinese are dark-eyed, could this explain why they accept acupuncture so readily?

While the primary cause of pain is certainly an unbalancing of the nervous system in its electrical aspect, the fact that neurones may continue to fire long after the stimulus has ceased suggests that chemical changes may also be involved.

One of the most exciting of recent advances is the discovery that the brain has its own chemical mechanisms for abolishing pain. As I briefly mentioned in Chapter Three, substances akin to morphine and hence christened endorphins (meaning 'internal morphine') have recently been discovered by John Hughes and colleagues at the Unit for Research on Addictive Drugs in Aberdeen. No doubt it is to these substances that we must look for the temporary insensitivity to pain of the severely wounded. They also could account for the analgesia bestowed by acupuncture.

It is not difficult to see why such a mechanism should have evolved, for there are advantages in being able to ignore pain in desperate situations. Better to escape the wild beast pursuing you, regardless of a broken ankle, than to spare the ankle and lose one's life. This explains too why boxers and other athletes manage to fight on despite injury.

The endorphins have raised hopes of a new and more effective analgesia, but, just like morphine, they are addictive. When we understand better how they work, something valuable may result. Judging from their distribution in the brain, they are something more than pain-relievers – a distinct chemical system acting within the total pattern of the brain. As if this were not enough complication, there are signs that the brain contains a pain-causing substance: Substance P. Its role is unknown. In biology, everything is more complicated than you think.

I Hate What I Fancy I Feel

Various fragments of evidence suggest that the painfulness of pain signals varies according to our state of mind. If we are concentrating on some problem, we often forget about minor pains – even toothache may almost vanish from our awareness. We do not notice how stiff a limb is getting in the theatre or cinema until the performance comes to an end. It has been shown, too, that a continuous loud noise largely blocks awareness of pain and dentists have made use of this. It would seem, therefore, that we can inhibit the pain signals from reaching that part of the brain which, presumably, constitutes 'I myself'. This is a curious matter for the philosophers to digest. The pain is there, but it is not part of us. Can it then be the case that the 'mind' (defined as awareness, in the manner of Plumb and Posner) shifts about in the brain; even that the brain can block off parts of itself from 'mind'? To me this suggests, rather, that we have got our notion of mind wrong.

Women in childbirth are commonly given an anaesthetic, such as pethidine, which leaves them more or less conscious. They report that they are aware of the presence of pain, but that it doesn't seem to matter. A comparable indifference to pain is displayed by patients who have undergone leucotomy (the severing of fibres connecting the fore-brain with the mid-brain). Normally employed to relieve depression, this operation is sometimes used to help people to cope with the pain of terminal cancer. What can we infer from this? Perhaps the feedback between cortex and mid-brain is a necessary condition for pain to be experienced as distinct from known about.

Christian saints and mystics are said to have gone to torture or slow death without showing signs of pain, and this has also been reported of some witches burnt at the stake. Can it be that intense concentration on spiritual matters and a long habit of ignoring bodily discomfort, not to say pain, had enabled them to ignore even the pains of torture? Perhaps the object of self-flagellation was to train the mind in ignoring the claims of the body, rather than to inflict pain as a punishment for sin. There is a ready parallel here with Eastern fakirs, such as those who sleep on beds of nails or adopt painful positions indefinitely. Perhaps also with fire-walkers and those who go through painful initiation ceremonies in a trancelike state.

During the war, H. K. Beecher observed the behaviour of soldiers injured in battle. Only one in four asked for morphine, though they had suffered wounds which had they received them in civil life would have caused severe pain. They were not in a state of shocked insensibility, he considered, because they complained at minor pains such as an ineptly done injection. Questioned, several of them said that it was not just that they felt indifferent to pain, but that they actually felt none. Beecher thought it was their joy at having survived which preoccupied their attention and produced this effect. But I doubt this. Once when I was run down by a taxi on a pedestrian crossing but escaped with bruising,

I not only was unaware of pain for about half an hour but did not notice that my clothes were badly torn and my leg bleeding until I was in the train on my way to keep an appointment. In much the same way, sportsmen, explorers and others manage to carry on despite injury and only become aware of pain when arousal subsides and the effort is over.

I have already described how giving coloured water or an inert powder to patients requesting medication will often produce the desired result and this also applies to pain-control. But it is surprising to find that no less than thirty-five per cent of cancer patients gain relief from pain on nothing but placebo medication.

The use of hypnosis to control pain is a similar phenomenon, although it too works only in a proportion of cases.

It is certain that anxiety increases the painfulness of pain. In experiments in which an electric fire slowly approached experimental subjects they allowed it to approach much closer when they could control its stopping than when they had to trust the experimenter to respond to their request. Since anxiety seems to reflect a constant dwelling on a problem, and thus the very opposite of the inhibitory process I have discussed, this is consistent with the theory. It has been shown that merely hearing the word 'pain' used before undergoing a test will increase the degree of pain reported by the subject.

So it seems that the famous faith-healer of Deal, in the limerick, who declared that pain was not real, was not completely off-beam. Pain is real enough, God knows, but we do have powers of detaching ourselves from it. And that is an Omega Effect all right.

Recently biofeedback has been employed to help people tolerate pain with some success. As many people now know, the brain produces a regular rhythm of electrical pulses some twelve to eighteen times a second when it is relaxed and the mind is blank. The presentation of any interesting matter causes this smooth rhythm to break up as different parts of the brain go to work and produce their own rhythms. Biofeedback reports to the subject whether he is producing alpha or not and he soon learns to do so at will. Pam was a thirty-four-year-old American woman who suffered chronic pain from inflammation of the kidneys, which she had endured since the age of sixteen. She was taking rather heavy doses of analgesics. After twenty training sessions in biofeedback she no longer needed medication, except at times of acute urinary infection; both the frequency and intensity of her pain were much reduced. This is how she described the experience to her physician: 'The process of going into alpha eliminates or withdraws attention from the environment and even from the sensations of your own body. As a result you become unaware of a lot of things around you – you are much more centred inside your own brain. It's a passive experience – you let yourself out of a state rather than put yourself into one.'

A curious detail is that she found she could increase the effect by visual imagery. Not only did she imagine herself relaxing in an airy room, but, 'I imagine telephone wires transmitting pain and I manufacture a big pair of scissors and cut the wires.'

In all this we can see the inhibitory capacity of the brain at work. Barry Wyke, a British authority on low back pain, is so overwhelmed by such facts as to declare: 'Contrary to long-standing traditional views, pain – as a phenomenon of human experience – is not a primary sensation in the sense that vision, hearing, smell, taste, touch, pressure, thermal sensitivity and kinaesthesia are. On the contrary it is a *disordered affective state* that is called into being by the development of mechanical and/or chemical changes in various tissues of the body.' Though he subsequently says it is evoked by 'unusual patterns of activity in specific afferent systems', which is correct, he goes too far in saying it is not a sensation. As we have seen, the pattern may, or may not, evoke an affective state. At the same time what we see, hear, smell and so on, can also evoke an affective state. At the same time what we see, hear, smell, and so on, can also evoke pleasure or the reverse. Pain is not just an emotional state; it is unique. Why we perceive it as we do is just as much an Omega Effect as any other sensation.

One curious point remains. Melzack suggests, like Livingston before him, that there may be a memory for pain. Could we explain the persistence of pain after a lesion has healed by the presence of remembered pain? This would have to be not just a cognitive memory of the fact of having suffered – we all have that and it is curious how rapidly we forget what pain really felt like. Women who have borne a child often comment on how their memory of the pain faded, so that they approached a second parturition without apprehension. It would have to be a thalamic not a cortical record. Since I believe – as I shall describe when I come to discuss memory – that all brain action leaves records, I find this suggestion plausible. And perhaps it would account for the lowering effect of a major operation. Though, thanks to anaesthetics, we remain cognitively unaware of pain, it may be that at more primitive levels the body remembers the agony it has been through.

Melzack, who has called the subject 'one of the most fascinating problems in medicine and biology', sums the situation up by saying, 'Pain is a function of the whole individual.'

Now let me turn from our awareness of our body to our awareness of the external world – from our interoceptors, to use the technical jargon, to our exteroceptors.

12

Sensational News

'YOU SMELL, I STINK' – Dr Johnson.

R. W. Moncrieff, an expert on perfumes, tested odour preferences at various age-levels in man, using ten odorants. Though people of both sexes agreed that strawberry and vanilla were nicest, rape oil and chlorophyll least pleasant, there were curious differences between the sexes. Under age eight, boys rated vanilla higher than girls; girls rated almond essence higher than did boys. Between eight and fourteen, boys up-rated musk lactone (which has sexual connotations) while girls, rather surprisingly, started liking the smell of naphthalene (mothballs). They also fancied orange blossom. From fifteen to nineteen, girls went off vanilla and began preferring lavender. The men stuck with vanilla and musk. Between twenty and forty, strawberry declined in popularity with both sexes, while over forty, as sex became less important, women's preference became much the same as men's, except that men stuck with musk and developed a minor preference for spearmint.

Moncrieff concludes that, while sexual factors decline in importance with women, men 'are still attracted by the sweet sexy musky smells long after they have passed forty. That some of our olfactory preferences, in the prime of life, derive from sex interest and requirements there can be no doubt.'

Source: R. W. Moncrieff, *Odour Preferences*,
Leonard Hill, London 1966, pp. 147ff.

The Rabble of Senses

The Omega Effect is nowhere seen more clearly than when we experience a sensation. Somehow a physical stimulus is converted into a unique subjective experience. The first problem which presents itself to us when we try to make sense of this is one of variety. Trains of nerve impulses which seem to be pretty much of the same kind are generated by quite different sense organs and, on reaching the brain, are experienced in totally different ways. A taste is completely different from a sound; a smell is completely different from a colour.

Because the fact is so familiar we tend to take it for granted, so perhaps the question with which to start is: how many possible types of subjective experience are there? The number seems to be indefinitely large. We have Aristotle to thank for the wholly misleading belief that we have only five senses. To begin with, the word 'touch' covers a whole range of senses. The nerves described as 'tactile' detect heat and cold, mechanical deformation, pressure. Nerves which clasp the roots of hairs detect a faint stroking. Other nerves detect the stretching of muscles, including the kind of stretching which leads to stomach ache. Yet others tell us what position our limbs are in. Furthermore, we can integrate impressions over time to get another unique sensation. Thus roughness is detected by moving one's hand across a surface and noting the *changes* in sensation which take place. We assess weight by hefting an object, softness by squeezing it. We are extraordinarily good at estimating whether an object is truly level or truly vertical. We know when we are out of balance. Often we combine data from several sources into a single experience, as in tasting food.

And, as if that were not enough, we have blood-sugar and salt-level detectors, mouth-dryness detectors, bladder-distension detectors and various other sensors which contribute their quota to such experiences as thirst, repletion and so on.

Nevertheless, man's capacities are only a fraction of what is possible. The bee has wind-detecting bristles between its ommatidia (eye units). Prawns have depth detectors sensitive to a few centimetres. Worms are sensitive to faint vibrations, and elephants, horses and some other animals seem sensitive to trembling of the ground, as before an earthquake. Fish have a lateral line which responds to the bang of a door a hundred yards away. Gymnarchus, the electric eel, can distinguish tap-water from distilled water, thanks to an electric organ sensitive to a billionth of an ampere lasting twenty milliseconds. It obtains information from an electric field by detecting distortion of the field lines. Migratory birds detect the magnetic field of the earth and the Coriolis force. Not only bats and dolphins, but probably rats, voles and dormice use echolocation. Snakes detect infra-red and ultra-violet light; bees analyse its polarisation. One must presume, I think, that these sensory systems do not just provide data, they must create unique experiences just as our own senses do.

In short, what we have to explain – but cannot – is not just consciousness but why consciousness takes such a wide variety of quite distinct forms.

Scientists and philosophers have long puzzled about the source of these differences, some saying that the experience was determined by the nature of the receptor, others that it was determined by the brain area to which the impulses were conducted; more recently, others assigned it to the way the impulses were electrically coded. In 1842 the great Johannes Müller declared that it was something about the 'nervous energy' which determined the nature of the sensation. But when the neurologist Magendie touched the eyeball of a conscious patient and caused him to see a flash of light, it looked as if the nature of the receptor determined the nature of the experience. This was known as the 'local sign' theory. The truth proved more complicated.

As this is not a textbook of physiology, I shall simply point out to you a few awkward facts which no one has been able to explain.

It used to be thought there were taste receptors for sweet and sour, for bitter and salt. But it turns out that some nerve endings are activated by acid alone, some by acid and salt, some by acid and quinine. Thus our subjective experience seems to be concerned with a *pattern* of responses not a 'local sign'. There is a substance known as potassium bromide. In a weak solution it tastes sweet. Double the strength and it tastes bitter-sweet. At four times the strength it begins to taste salty too. And at twenty times the original concentration it is simply salty. So the subjective experience is clearly not determined by the end-organ or by the part of the brain which it serves.

The human skin contains five types of specialised nerve endings, in addition to 'free endings' which just trail away into nothing, as you will recall from the previous chapter: the Pacinian corpuscles, the Ruffini end-organs, the Meissner corpuscles, the Golgi-Mazzoni corpuscles and the bulbs of Krause. It was long supposed that one kind handled heat and cold, another pressure, another pain and so on. But now that we can trace nerve paths in more detail, we find that several different end-organs project to the same neurone; conversely, each type of end-organ projects to many neurones. Once again, it looks as if the sensation is extracted from an analysis of the *pattern* – the relative contribution – of all the types. When I was discussing pain, we found further reason to suppose that pattern is what matters. And that puts the problem of the Omega Effect in a new light.

But at this point I must describe some of the other aspects of sensation which a theory of the Omega Effect would need to explain.

Experiment shows that if you increase the energy causing a sound by a factor of ten, it appears, subjectively, to double in loudness. Why is that? There is a simple experiment you can do yourself which illustrates the difficulty of relating experience to data. Take three basins and fill them respectively with hot, tepid and cold water. Put one hand in the hot and one in the cold for several minutes, then move both hands into the tepid water. You will find that the hand which was in the cold water feels it is now in hot water; conversely for the other hand. In short, the same tepid water is perceived by the brain as both hot and cold simultaneously. However, there is more to it than that. On the skin of the back there are widely spaced 'hot' receptors and 'cold' receptors. If you touch a 'cold' receptor with a piece of metal warmed to 44° C (say 120° F, or about the same as the hottest tea you can drink) it feels cold!

The relationship between stimulus and experience is also complicated by the question of pleasure. What determines whether a stimulus is pleasant or unpleasant? For example, an air temperature which is rated pleasant by a cold person may be rated unpleasant by a hot subject. Again, if you drink solutions of sugar at increasing concentrations, at first you will find each one pleasanter than the last, then less pleasant and finally quite unpleasant. However if you do not swallow, but merely taste, the glucose, the pleasure does not vanish. Likewise, some strong perfume essences are rated disgusting, although delightful when highly diluted.

There also seem to be great individual differences. 'My wife . . . likes . . . the smell of the jonquil type of narcissus and they are often described in gardening books as sweetly scented,' wrote a reader of the *New Scientist*. 'I have never been able to detect anything sweet about them. To me they have a strong smell which is no more pleasant or unpleasant than, say, geranium leaves.' He went on to say that, when he was working for his doctorate, his supervisor was exceptionately sensitive to the smell of cyanide. 'On entering the laboratory he could tell if a bottle of KCN was open. None of the other students or staff were as sensitive.'

But, why, if there is a relation between stimulus and experience, does it vary not only between individuals but in the same individual at different times? Drugs like LSD seem to increase the intensity of perception. As we said when discussing pain, there are pathological conditions in which the subject becomes so sensitive that he or she must remain in a dark room and will scream with pain at a slight noise. (Some hypersensitivity often follows alcoholic overindulgence.) But increases in sensitivity can also be made by deliberate effort. We have all heard too of the acute awareness of the Red Indian tracker, accustomed from infancy to notice the tiniest indications in the life of the forest. More impressive is the account given by Jim Phelan who, after fourteen years in gaol, wrote: 'The tyro . . . in gaol has to develop new senses, become animal keen in a thousand ways not known to civilisation. Long before the end of my second year, I could tell one warder from another, in the dark and at a distance, by his breathing, by his scent, even by the tiny crackings of his joints. Presently I could smell the cigarette in another man's pocket six feet away, hear a lip-still muttering in church even when a trained warder missed every sound . . . A long-sentence convict is not a person; he is an alert, efficient and predatory animal.'

Paying Attention

One more fact – it is a major one – modifying the usual over-simple picture of the mind as a kind of camera, automatically taking in whatever is presented to it, is the fact that we 'pay attention' and only perceive what we attend to. Conversely, we get used to things ('habituate' is the psychologists' word for it) and cease to pay attention to them.

I have already described the neuronal mechanisms underlying attention in Chapter Three. I told how the arousal system alerts the whole brain in emergency but can also alert specific parts of the cortex when advisable. I also described how nerves from the brain to the sense organs raise or lower their thresholds of sensitivity. I mentioned how the thalamus evaluates input.

In Chapter Five we discussed unconscious awareness and how we seem to inspect material unconsciously before becoming conscious of it. There is another example of this which is interesting just because it is so simple. Donald Mackworth, when he was at the Applied Psychology Unit in Cambridge, devised a method of tracking just what a person's eyes were looking at. One use to which he put this equipment was to explore how a person searched for a given figure in a table of figures. The curious fact emerged that the eye would often stop on the desired figure for a few milliseconds, the conscious brain would fail to take in the fact that success had been achieved, and the eye would move on to search elsewhere.

The obvious comparison for a system which passes some items and rejects others is a filter, and Donald Broadbent, who succeeded Mackworth in his job, gained a lot of attention a few years ago with his filter theory of attention. The problem is: what criteria does the filter apply and how? Experiments show that we can attend to a male voice and ignore a female one, attend to a high note and ignore a lower one, and much else of this rather obvious kind. What is harder to explain is that if we are listening to two messages of similar content, trying to concentrate on one, we tend to muddle them. This shows that the filter (if it is a filter) is working at the level of ideas as well as the level of superficial characteristics of the signal; that is, in the higher layers of the cortex as a whole.

This is confirmed by the fact that if strings of words are fed to each ear, so arranged that a meaningful sentence can be constructed by taking words from each ear alternately, then we generally hear the sentence. This implies an even more sophisticated treatment of the material at the preconscious level.

The idea of attention leads on to cognate ideas such as curiosity, vigilance and the 'orientation reaction' to which I've already made a brief reference. But these are specialised topics, which would lead me too far from my theme.

The brevity of these remarks should not mislead you about the importance of attention. Any breakdown in the mechanism is disastrous. In fact, it has been said that *all* mental illness can be construed as a defect of the attention mechanism. Certainly this seems to be true in schizophrenia.

It is often said that we cannot attend to two things at once – and naturally the whole object of attention is to select one thing for analysis and reject others. However it is also true that we perceive many things simultaneously. We look at an object and perceive its colour as well as its shape and other details. Nowhere is this more true than in listening to speech; to recognise language involves attending to some ten features: vowel or consonant, stopped or continuant, voiced or unvoiced and so on.

Experiments have been done to discover how much we can manage. If we wish to identify one of a set of objects which differ in a single aspect, we can cope with about eight. But if you listen to notes of four different degrees of loudness and five pitches (of which there are twenty combinations) you can only discriminate about ten or twelve of them.

Human beings, it seems, make many measurements simultaneously but do a crude job on each one, unlike scientific instruments which measure only one thing at a time but do it with great accuracy. It obviously has survival value to keep an eye on everything that is happening even if we lose accuracy in doing so. This trade-off is part of the phenomenon of attention.

Another problem in this field is how we look for things. How is it that we can pick out a familiar face in a crowd, or a wanted word in an index so fast? I have often had the experience of hunting through a book for information: the word one is looking for seems to start out of the page before one has read it. Readers in press cutting agencies attain speeds of one thousand words a minute, after a year's experience, searching for twenty or more items, with only ten per cent of errors. We seem to form a picture in our mind of what we hope to see and then try to match it. But the process is mostly unconscious and incredibly fast.

The Doctrine of Immaculate Perception

There has been a long controversy in psychology between those who claim that our senses represent the world to us as it really is and those who believe that we construct a view of the world from our sense data. The former are known as Nativists, the latter as Empiricists. The idea that we receive stimuli quite passively is sarcastically known to empiricists as the doctrine of immaculate perception. I can tell you with confidence that it does not hold water.

There are many quite simple experiments which demonstrate this and also some sophisticated ones.

Harvard's Jerome Bruner, one of the liveliest brains in psychology, persuaded a manufacturer of playing cards to print some for him with the conventional colours interchanged; that is, the hearts were printed in black and the spades in red. He then briefly exposed such cards, one at a time, to various of his students. (In the trade they are known as Subjects, or Ss, but in practice they are almost invariably the professor's own students, who think it would be tactless not to volunteer to help.) Shown a black ace of hearts, some of the Ss – presumably those more interested in colour than form – reported that they had seen an ace of spades. Others, more interested in form than colour, reported that they had seen an ace of hearts. Some of them added that there seemed to be something funny about the card, but they couldn't say quite what. A few, however, and this is the bit I find fascinating, reported that the 'pip' was purple or brownish in colour.

As this demonstrates, our perception of colour is only loosely related to what we see, a fact we have already noted when discussing colour vision. But in this case, the important point is that the people who saw brown were fusing internal expectation with external observation.

Nor is this subjectivity confined to vision. For instance, if a person is given an electric shock every time he hears a particular musical note, he begins to report that it sounds 'different'. Even the taste of things he eats can be affected, and by something as tenuous as the general level of light in the room.

These distortions I have just mentioned are at the level of sensory input; but subjective influences intrude even at the highest levels of awareness. For example, if coins are shown to poor children and to richer ones, the poor ones estimate the size of the coins as being larger than the rich ones do. But there are subtler effects than these. A. Ames built a room which, when viewed through a peephole, appeared normal but which was in fact of an unusual shape, with the result that people appeared to change size as they moved about in it. In a variation of this, two people look through windows opposite the observer, and seem to have faces of different sizes. But Ames found a curious exception to this. One of his subjects, Honi by name, failed to experience the illusion when it was her husband's face she was looking at. She had been happily married to him for twenty-five years and the constancy of her idea of her husband counted for more than Ames' legerdemain. This has become known as 'the Honi effect'.

Something similar has been found in experiments in which people were disguised to look as if they had lost a limb. It turned out that wives were less likely to notice anything wrong when it was their husband they were looking at than were strangers. In another similar experiment, enlisted men were shown both officers and enlisted men thus altered. It was found that they were less likely to notice the apparent mutilation when looking at officers than when looking at 'other ranks'.

The subjective nature of perception is also shown by the effect of brain injuries. Strange disturbances of colour perception have been noted in people who have suffered a stroke. Thus some patients could not distinguish, visually, silver from copper coins, pickles from jam. Others found their vision gold-tinted, red-tinted, or abnormally vivid or dim as regards colour. Some patients, who felt quite normal, nevertheless called a red object brown at one time, blue at another – though this may possibly have been word-blindness rather than a visual defect. In three cases where an autopsy was performed damage was found in defined areas corresponding to Brodman's Areas eighteen, nineteen and perhaps thirty-seven. These areas, we must hence assume, not only analyse the signals reporting colour but create the colour-sensation itself.

To summarise all this, let me quote Professor Richard Gregory, who says: 'Perception seems to be a matter of looking up information that has been stored about objects and how they behave in various situations. The retinal image does little more than select the relevant stored data . . . We can think of perception as being essentially the selection of the most appropriate stored hypothesis according to current sensory data.' The drowning sailor who sees a non-existent ship on the horizon demonstrates, however, that it is not always the most probable but sometimes the most desired hypothesis that we seem to perceive. Gregory is thinking of visual perception. The point is even more obvious in the case of hearing: we hear what we expect to hear, making a plausible interpretation of remarks partly drowned by other noise. Actually, experiments show that old people, in particular, do this: when listening to a list of nonsense words they frequently hear actual words. Such guessing is often unavoidable when there is no context to guide you. Thus you may hear 'stress' as dress, choice, Joyce or even as florist.

More than this, 'It appears that there are records of visual input which can be consulted before anything at all is seen, in order to determine the proper framework for perception.' I am quoting Professor John Ross of the University of Western Australia, whose ingenious experiments would take too long to describe. 'We adopt a perceptual attitude in order to comprehend the world.' Plato, then, was almost right when he supposed that we carry a stock of 'ideal forms' by virtue of which we recognise actual forms.

But although empiricism has triumphed, Professor James G. Gibson has fought a valiant rearguard action for the nativists, making some useful points in so doing. He claims that the senses provide information without the intervention of a consciousness process. As an example, he says that when you use a pair of scissors, your hand tells you the position of the parts, not just the pressure of the metal on your skin. So it does. More than that, you learn something about the texture of what you are cutting from the ease and smoothness with which the cut takes place. But this only shows how efficiently the brain interprets the data, a proposition with which no empiricist would disagree. At bottom, the difference (it seems to me) is only one of emphasis – the nativist stressing the fact that we do contrive to discover how things really are, most of the time, with extraordinary success. The empiricist stresses that we manage this by virtue of stored data and beliefs and sometimes come to grief in the process. (As to Gibson's reference to a *conscious* process, we have already seen how much depends on what you mean by the word conscious.)

Philosophers often talk about 'raw feels' – an inelegant expression for sensory data as it first appears to us before interpretation. But we have seen that analysis starts already in the retina and in the cochlea (in the cases of sight and hearing). What reaches the brain is already transformed several times by different nerve nets. Thus there are really no 'raw feels' on the one hand, and no final 'perceptions' on the other. The whole thing is more complicated and it is time the philosophers read up the facts.

We reconstruct the data. We integrate it with material from memory. We load it with emotion and positive or negative affect. We combine sensory material in one half of the brain with abstract, word-based material from the other. It is now clear that there is a phenomenal amount of traffic between the two sides of the brain.

It is this enormously complex feltwork of processes which, taken together, comprises consciousness. Consciousness is not, one can say with confidence, a property of neurones as such. Consciousness is generated by brain processes: to this extent the nativists are right.

It's Only a Play

Anyone who reads through a scientific journal devoted to perception – for example *Perceptual and Motor Skills* – must be struck by the unrealistic nature of most of the experiments in vogue. Subjects are exposed to inkblots, flashes of light lasting a hundredth of a second, electric shocks, different messages in each ear, and a hundred other things which no one experiences much in ordinary life. These approaches have their place, to be sure. But psychologists seem to overlook the fact that real life perception is mostly concerned with long sequences of meaningful material. We perceive in order to survive. What we perceive has meaning, motivates us to action, has varying priorities. It arouses emotions. Furthermore, what we perceive depends on our past experience and the lessons we have learned, as well as on our aims and expectations for the future. Perception is not an end in itself, but one stage in a sequence of mental operations and physical actions. Nor do we perceive passively: we attend, we search, we hope. Perception as studied in the laboratory omits all these aspects.

R. W. Leeper, of the University of Oregon, at Eugene, has asked a question it might be worth answering, which illustrates very effectively the subtlety of the process we are discussing. How is it that, when watching a play, we become involved emotionally without losing sight of the fact that it is only a play and we are not expected to intervene? I do not pretend to know the answer.

There is one sense mode which exceeds the others in subtlety by a large margin: namely, vision. Its pre-eminent position is confirmed by the fact that it is mediated by about one-tenth of our total stock of brain cells. Nowhere is the uniqueness of the Omega Effect more striking. Vision deserves a chapter to itself.

13

Seeing and Believing

A BLACK OUTLOOK

At the National Hospital for Nervous Diseases in Queen's Square, London, Dr R. W. Ross Russell had a brain-damaged patient, a forty-four-year-old customs inspector, who exhibited symptoms so curious that the surgeon, J. C. Meadows, wrote an account of them for the bible of the profession, Brain.

Mr P. said that everything looked black or grey to him: the world was drained of colour. He found it difficult to distinguish a silver sixpence from a copper new penny, and had to feel whether the edge was milled or read the inscription to do so. Stamps presented a similar difficulty. When given visual tests, he often reported bright red objects as black; bright blue cards he called black, but green ones he sometimes called green, sometimes blue and sometimes black.

He was an enthusiastic gardener, but when pruning bushes often cut off live green shoots in mistake for dead brown ones. Worse, he had difficulty recognising his friends, and insisted on being told who was coming before anyone visited the house. He became reluctant to go out. To test this further, Dr Russell asked Mr P.'s wife, when she came to the hospital to visit him, to put on a white doctor's coat before going in to see him. Mr P. totally failed to recognise her. So Meadows asked him to describe his symptoms, and after a few seconds, amused by some contretemps, his wife laughed. Mr P. at once recognised her.

He had suffered damage in a part of the brain known as the anterior inferior occipital lobe, on both sides.

Source: J. C. Meadows, 'Disturbed Perception of Colours associated with localised Cerebral Lesions', *Brain* (1974) 97:615–32.

What the Eye Tells the Brain

'I'd always remembered this window. It had a design of blue grapes and yellow leaves against a diamond of red. I must have spent hours at it, as a kid, peering out at the garden through the different squares of coloured glass: changing the scene, at will, from colour-mood to colour-mood, and experiencing the pure pleasure of sensations which need no analysis . . . How had red felt, at the age of four? What had blue meant? Why was yellow? Perhaps, if I could somehow know that now, I should understand everything else that had happened to me in the interval. But I should never know. The whole organ of cognition had changed and I had nothing left to know with. If I looked through that window now, I should see nothing but a lot of adjectives.'

Christopher Isherwood's words gave me a pang of recognition, for I too, as a child, gazed at the garden through coloured glass; in my case the panes were simply diamonds of glass, on either side of a little entrance porch. All memory of where and when is gone, but the sensory impression remains vivid to this day. This is pure sensation – if anything is – as distinct from perception. I suspect it is the mid-brain at work, almost without intervention by the cortex.

Perception, which I take to be the new-brain function, is more complicated, and an enormous amount of scientific work has been done on it. Philosophers have asked questions about it. Is the tomato red, or is 'red' only something in your mind? I shall try to handle it by arbitrarily taking four or five aspects which seem particularly relevant to my theme. Let us start by looking at what occurs when we see something.

In the past twenty years there have been at least four major advances in our understanding of vision, which have quite transformed the scene. It is well worth trying to understand them, for they bear closely on our theme.

The popular approach to vision was embodied in a television film which Walt Disney made for the Bell Telephone Company. Inside a schematic cross-section of the human head was shown a chamber containing a little man watching a television screen, connected to the eyes. As an explanation of vision this does not get you very far. Presumably inside the head of the little man is an even smaller man watching an even smaller television screen, and so on ad infinitum.

Philosophers and neurologists, I regret to say, were – until recently – not much more sophisticated in their approach than Disney's scriptwriter. They tended to assume, more or less overtly, that somewhere in the brain would be found literal models or representations of what the brain's owner was looking at. Thus if he were looking at a square, nerve cells arranged in a square formation would be activated. If an orange, then a sort of ghostly orange would appear. This view seemed to be supported by the fact that painstaking studies of the path taken by single nerve fibres from eye to brain has established that the visual cortex was laid out in about the same way as the retina. That is, nerves from the centre of the retina run to the centre of the visual cortex, nerves from the top left quadrant run to the top left quadrant of the visual cortex and so on.

This simple conception began to crumble when Jerome Lettvin and his associates at MIT published their classic paper entitled, with more gaiety than is usual in this field, 'What the Frog's Eye Tells the Frog's Brain'. They revealed that it does not convey a picture, it tells it four things: whether there are any sustained contrasts, whether there are convexities, whether there are dark edges and whether there is net darkening over the bulk of the field. Naturalists note that frogs turn away from any large dark object but are attracted to small, more or less circular, moving objects which are darker than background. When I talked to Lettvin in his darkened laboratory, not long after the publication of these findings, he called this mechanism, reasonably enough, 'a bug detector'. He was peering through a microscope at one of his frogs, in which he had been inserting recording electrodes, and I couldn't avoid thinking of the well-known belief that people possess features in common with the animals they associate with. A heavily built man, who speaks only after thoughtful silences, he can move with speed and precision when he wants to.

Each of these types of information is transmitted by a separate group of nerve fibres, distributed across the retina, and largely independent of the general level of illumination. Thus the classic assumption that the receptors simply measure light intensity at various points proved quite false. Receptors pick out specific features, such as a sudden change from light to dark, and compare them with reports from neighbouring receptors, to establish direction of movement, curvature of the edge and so on.

Earlier work by H. K. Hartline and H. B. Barlow had paved the way for Lettvin's contribution by showing that the eye of the horseshoe crab has on/off detectors: nevertheless the impact of Lettvin's paper was tremendous. 'It shows,' his paper said, 'that the eye speaks to the brain in a language already highly organised and interpreted, instead of transmitting some more or less accurate copy' of what is seen. The tectum of the frog's brain contains, so to say, four maps, superimposed in perfect registration, each recording a particular quality. Thus the image on the retina is transformed from a set of discrete points to a space in which each point is described by the coincidence of particular qualities.

But between eye and brain a further transformation is interposed. In a neuronal relay station known as the lateral geniculate nucleus the whole signal is put through what mathematicians call a 'Fourier transform'. The information is preserved, but the pattern becomes totally different. Searching for an analogy with which to convey this I can only think of a library in which the books are, to begin with, arranged in alphabetical order of authors' names, and afterwards, rearranged in order of titles. The books themselves are unaltered but their placing has become quite different. In the case of vision, the arrangement is now by intensity and phase – the amount by which one signal lags on another.

What happens when this transformed set of signals finally reaches the cortex?

The answer was published in the *Journal of Physiology* in the same year as Lettvin's paper, and by two men working only a few miles away across the Charles River, in the Medical School of Harvard University. I went to see D. H. Hubel and Torsten Wiesel after my visit to Lettvin. They were recording from single nerve cells in the brains of lightly anaesthetised cats. In a large, bare room, a cat, its eyes immobilised by a muscle-relaxant, gazed on a screen on which were projected black bars, the length and slope of which could be varied. They were moved about until a position was found which caused the brain cell under study to fire.

The retina of the cat, they had found, is less specialised than the frog's, reflecting its wider range of interests. A cat is not restricted to the detection of mice and the avoidance of large objects. Nevertheless, the visual cortex of the cat also extracts features from the environment, notably straight lines of definite length and orientation. (Assuming that the human eye is not far different, which is not unreasonable, this would explain our preoccupation with contrast and contour.)

And now I must refer to another change of viewpoint, also earth-shaking in its tiny world, which has occurred in the last twenty years. Ever since the lynx-eyed Spaniard Ramón y Cajal discovered how to stain nervous tissue selectively, it has been known that the cortex is made up of six or seven layers of cells of different types, and neurologists have consequently tended to think of it as organised laterally. As I described earlier, thanks to the works of Vernon Mountcastle and others, we now know that it is organised in vertical columns, rather like a honeycomb, though the columns are only half a millimetre across. In each column cells feed their signals to cells higher up. Each of these columns seems to be a 'feature detector'. To put it in a schematic and simplified way, if a hundred adjacent receptors report, 'I am detecting the edge of a black area', and all are wired to a master cell, then the latter specifically responds to an edge of that length orientation. If three of these second level cells energise a cell at a higher level, this last reports, 'There's a triangle.' One of the things which Hubel and Wiesel showed was that, in the cat, cells are wired up precisely so as to detect long, thin, contrasting objects of various slopes and orientations. Thus the visual cortex is revealed as a classifying mechanism.

Thus the original image, broken down into little items of data in the eye, converted into electric pulses, transformed again in the geniculate, integrated again in the columns, finally re-emerges in our experience as an image bearing a close resemblance to the original, thanks to the Omega Effect.

We can see a little further into the Omega process thanks to recent work on how depth and colour are perceived. A major mechanism in depth perception is stereoscopy: the fact that each of our two eyes presents to the brain a slightly different image. So efficient is the brain at detecting these discrepancies that if you take a page of print from early in the printing run and another copy of the same page from late in the run, and place the two on a stereoscope, so that one is presented to the left eye, the other to the right eye, a stereoscopic effect is experienced. The slight differences caused by wear of the type, though quite invisible to ordinary inspection, are detected by the stereoscopic mechanism and interpreted as differences in depth. It now is known that nerve fibres from corresponding points in the two eyes lead to adjacent columns. How each column compares its signal with that from its neighbour is still mysterious, but from this comparison the subjective experience of depth arises.

Much the same is true of colour. As many people know, there are three types of colour-receptor in the eye. One is chiefly sensitive to blue light, one to green, one to red. And as Newton showed, the spectral colours are made up of mixtures of these primary colours. S. M. Zeki, of London University's University College, has shown that columns responsive to each of the three primary colours lie alongside one another. So here again, it is their *mutual relationship* which gives rise to the subjective impression of a particular colour. (I shall return to the subject of colour in more detail shortly.)

I have simplified, of course. There are cells which are particularly interested in movement, regardless of what is moving. It has been known for some years that, in the eyes of some creatures, there are cells which will respond to movement even at levels of light too low to cause them to fire for the illumination as such. This fits well with the extreme sensitivity to moving objects to which I referred earlier, and which is so convenient for prey and predator. Later work with rabbits and ground squirrels showed that not only frogs but mammals can have specialised retinas – the squirrel is particularly fitted to detect the direction of motion of small objects. The rabbit has 'fast' detectors and 'slow' detectors far more sensitive than man's.

This remarkable specialisation seems to be brought about by the creature's experience after birth. Thus kittens brought up in a 'world' containing only vertical bars do not seem to develop detectors for horizontals, and kittens brought up in a grey and featureless environment prove almost unable to distinguish objects at all when removed to normal surroundings. It is perhaps comforting to reflect that if we were transported to a planet which contained some life-form quite unlike anything known to us – say, clouds of intelligent coloured gas – our children would have little trouble in identifying the aboriginals, however baffled we ourselves might be. It seems then that we see what we have learned to see, and this means that we all see slightly differently – apart from any other reasons there might be, such as age or infirmity. When the German biologist von Uexkull attempted to draw pictures of the world as it might appear to a horse or a fly, he had taken the point that their world would seem different from ours, but he could not visualise just how different. Just as we cannot imagine what it would be like to be an electric eel, detecting our surroundings by sensing magnetic perturbations.

Quite recent work has shown that the principle of 'feature extraction' also applies to hearing, and presumably therefore to other senses too. Thus the bat emits sound-waves which are frequency modulated: they fall and rise again, rhythmically. The ears of moths are specialised to detect the range and frequency of these rhythms and, to no one's surprise, they turn out to be specially good at detecting just those sound-patterns which bats emit and which are of life-and-death importance to moths.

To sum up: what the senses tell the brain is already analysed into specific kinds of information and this is further analysed in the cortex; what arrives at the interface with the mind is not a picture or a tune, or a smell, but a bundle of specialised bits of data coded into nerve impulses. This is the material with which Omega Effect has been produced. It is luminously clear, then, that the long arguments of the philosophers about whether or not there is an orange in the skull are about as relevant as the celebrated (and probably apocryphal) debate upon angels dancing on the point of a needle.

Add to this the fact that we do not yet know how the light falling on a receptor gives rise to a series of pulses, the frequency of which is related to the intensity of the light, and you can see how far we still have to go.

Seeing and Recognising

The humble frog does not seek to understand what it sees. Like the British sportsman of old, its simple motto is: If it moves, kill it! But creatures of a higher order such as ourselves attempt to identify and understand what they perceive and to do this they compare the patterns they see (let us confine ourselves to vision for the purposes of this discussion) with some kind of stored representation or memory of similar patterns in the past.

A blind man to whom sight has been restored cannot immediately see but has to learn to relate what his eyes show him with his experience. In 1959 Professor Richard Gregory and Jean Wallace had the fortune to observe such a man, the first such study since 1904. (Since then some other cases have been investigated because, thanks to a new grafting technique devised by Professor Benedetto Strampelli, it has become possible to plant acrylic lenses into the cornea without the graft being rejected.) Gregory's subject, S.B., had been blind from the age of ten months. After the operation, he could identify things he had learned by touch, such as upper-case letters which he had learned in blind school,

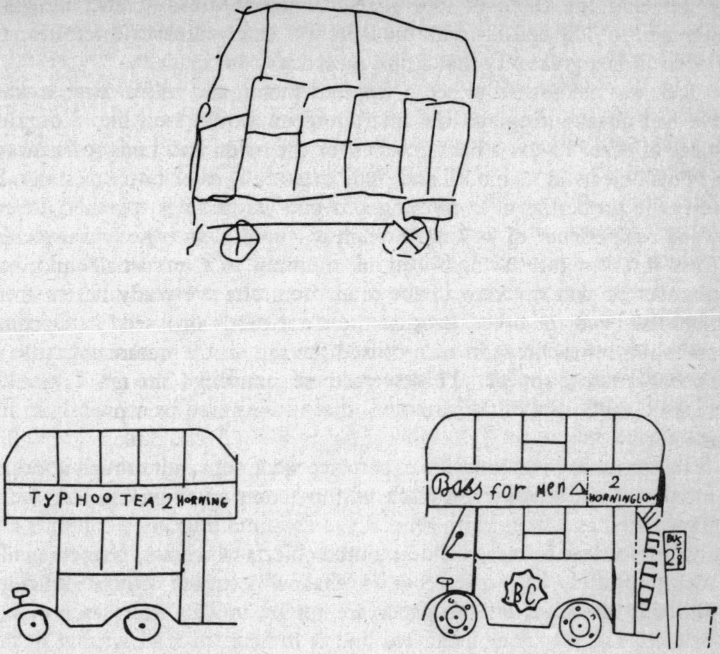

Too Hot to Touch

Blind from soon after birth, Mr S.B.'s sight was restored by corneal grafts when he was over fifty. But he had to learn to see. Here are his attempts to draw a bus forty-eight days after the first operation and a year later. Since he never felt the engine with his hands when blind, he still does not draw it.

but had trouble identifying drawings of objects, and objects which were unfamiliar. As he had a long-standing interest in machinery, Gregory showed him a screw-cutting lathe, and asked him to say what it was. He was quite unable to say anything about it, except that he thought the nearest part was a handle. He seemed rather agitated. He was then allowed to touch the lathe. 'The result was startling; he ran his hands deftly over the machine, touching first the transverse feed handle and confidently naming it as "a handle", and then on to the saddle, the bed and the head-stock. He ran his hands eagerly over the lathe with his eyes tight shut. Then he stood back a little and opened his eyes and said: "Now that I have felt it, I can see it." He then named many of the parts correctly and explained how they would work, though he could not understand the chain of four gears driving the lead screw.' Gregory comments, 'The episode with the lathe was extraordinarily interesting to watch: it is a great pity that a film record was not made.'

S.B. was astonished to see a crescent moon, and asked what it was. He had always imagined the quarter moon would look like a quarter piece of cake. So too a baby reaches for the moon and finds it far away. It puts objects in its mouth and finds they are hard or bitter or slimy. It tests the properties of everything and puts its findings together. Isherwood's experience of looking through coloured glass is a vivid instance. I can just remember lying in bed one morning, as a very small child, and discovering that my view of the room from one eye was different from the view from the other, because the sheet partly obscured it. Opening and shutting each eye in turn caused the jug on the washstand table to appear and disappear. This seemed so amazing (though I quickly realised the optics of the situation) that it registered permanently in my memory.

In consulting our previous experience we accept quite rough approximations when necessary. A circle with two dots and a line in it is readily interpreted as a face. More generally, a few lines indicating contours and shadows suffice to recall solid, coloured objects which are, phenomenally, totally different. We can recognise 'shadow' lettering without difficulty, although the lines on the paper are totally unlike letters as normally printed. On the other hand, we find it difficult to read writing upside down or reversed left-to-right. We need to have in our brain a neurone which has specialised to detect just that pattern, and reversed writing is not a pattern we are normally trained to analyse.

Presented with the diagram opposite: we infer the existence of a white triangle – indeed we almost seem to see it; the triangle seems whiter than the surrounding paper. Our triangle-detecting neurone has alerted its fellows which, were it an ordinary triangle, would be busy reporting the edges, and their enhanced activity gives us a sub-phenomenal feeling that the rest of the triangle is there.

And while we perceive, we analyse. A pattern like this: 'Ø' is at once analysed as a circle crossed by a bar, since we have detectors for those shapes; it is not analysed as two P-shapes placed back to back. Similarly a circle with a bit left out is seen as that – for circles with a fragment obscured or damaged are commoner than curves which are not quite closed. In short, in case of doubt, we go for the most probable interpretation in terms of our experience.

Richard Gregory had made some casts of human faces and has then mounted them, so as to create a 'face' which is concave, not convex. In the right lighting, it is virtually impossible to see the face as hollow since

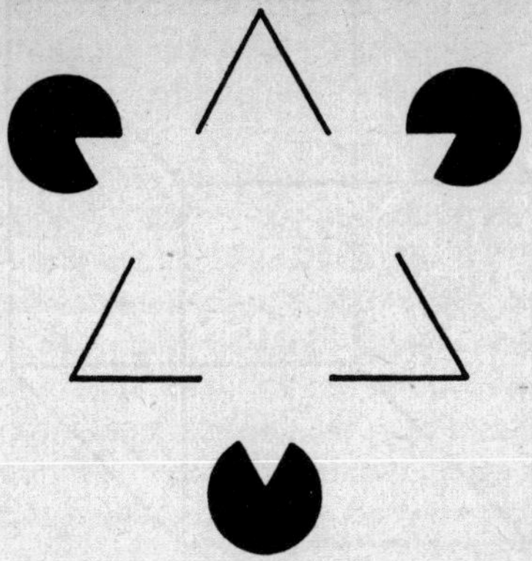

this flies in the face of our experience. But moving one's head at once gives the game away. So do the unnatural shadows caused by normal lighting.

What happens when two interpretations are equally plausible? Many so-called optical illusions – they are really just optical jokes – depend on devising ambiguous pictures; a well-known example is the picture of a pretty girl which can also be seen as an elderly hag. (It is often known as the wife and mother-in-law picture.) In real life, of course, we should have other clues which would enable us to decide: it only works as a picture.

Back in 1832, the Swiss crystallographer, C. A. Necker, was peering through his microscope at crystals, when he realised that he could not decide on the orientation of some of them. Indeed, they seemed to switch. Today this effect is known as the Necker cube, and usually appears as shown on page 198. Actually, Necker's original drawing was a tilted oblong; personally I find the original figure exhibits the effect more readily than the tidied up version favoured by modern psychologists. Are we looking at the cube from above, or from below? The brain cannot decide, and as one gazes the subjective impression switches. Since Necker's cube does not show the perspective effect one would get from a real cube – the rear edges of a real cube would be, on paper, slightly shorter than the near edges – the brain is dissatisfied with the first interpretation and tries another, only to find it equally deficient.

Some people find it difficult, I am told, to make these figures reverse. For my part I find it easy. I just tell myself: You are looking at the cube from above, or from below, as the case requires. My impression is that I summon up a schema or frame of reference and fit the perceived lines

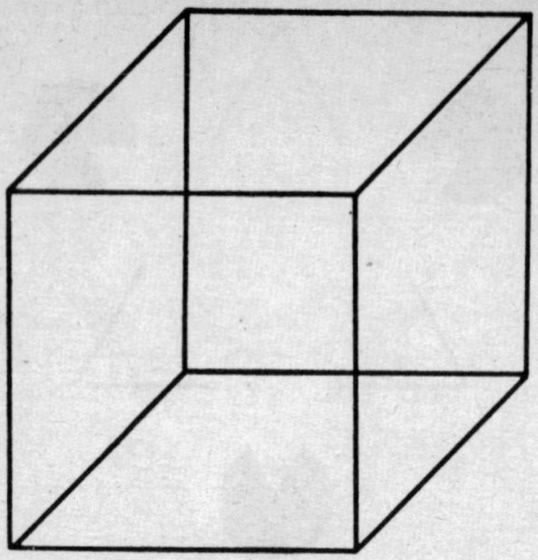

to it. But my real point is that out of all this analysis does not come an empty concept of a cube, or an intellectual doubt as to its orientation. What comes out is a strong feeling, in the sense earlier noted, and this is consciousness.

An illusion which combines both ambiguity and the property of reversal is found in the vase which can also be seen as two faces in profile. Here the crucial question for the brain is what to treat as background and what as 'figure', as the psychologists call it. The picture is carefully drawn so as to provide no clues. Add a few details and the ambiguity vanishes. As Gregory said, we interpret what we see by referring to internal models.

It seems to be the case that we treat the whole scene, normally, as ground, and the details which interest us as figure. Thus we often, looking at the moon across which clouds are drifting, have the impression that the moon is riding through stationary clouds. As a boy, I remember standing on a bridge, staring at the water below, which occupied my whole field of vision. Suddenly I felt that I, the bridge and the whole town were sweeping upstream at six or seven miles per hour. The effect, which many others have noted, was quite dizzying. Since this goes against our cognitive-intellectual experience it demonstrates that our feelings are derived from our analysing systems, and may fly in the face of reason.

A similar illusion is often experienced in a railway train about to start, and as this is such a common, yet puzzling experience, it justifies a small digression. One would expect that the carriage in which we sit, which occupies most of our visual field, would be treated as ground, and the small bit of the other train seen through the window would be figure. But in my experience, the illusion usually occurs in the form of supposing

that my train is moving, when it is really stationary. Despite the silence and lack of vibration, which should be enough to enable the brain to pick the right interpretation, the illusion persists for an uncanny second or two. I have enquired of others, who tell me they have had a like experience. Could it be that one is 'set' to expect the start of one's own train? Probably, but I am intrigued by the vividness of the illusion. During these seconds, though I *know*, cognitively, that I am at rest, I 'feel' that I am moving. I am bound to conclude that awareness does *not* mean, as almost every writer assumes, cognitive awareness.

In real life, we use numerous clues from various senses to check out our interpretation, and the visual illusions I have mentioned only 'work' because in a drawing we can suppress such clues. One would never be in doubt about vases and faces in reality, because colour, texture, movement and the whole context would point emphatically to the right interpretation.

This multimodality of perception is worth stressing if only because so many psychologists have conducted their tests in situations which have excluded all modes except the one in which they are interested. Thus when we estimate the distance away of an object, we use up to eighteen clues: eye-focus, stereoscopy, comparison with nearby objects of known size, intervening objects of known position, the haziness of the atmosphere, and so on. (Mountains look small on a clear day because the clarity causes us to underestimate their distance. Conversely on a foggy or hazy day they loom enormous.)

If, in a dimly lit room, you slowly blow up a white balloon, a person watching will often assume that he is watching a ball which is approaching him. If you alternately inflate and deflate it, he will have the impression of a globe approaching and receding. This is not difficult to understand, since in ordinary life (as opposed to the abnormality of a psychologist's laboratory) we very rarely see things which change in size as we watch, while we often see things which *appear* to change in size because they are approaching or receding. So movement is the most plausible interpretation. It is perfectly true that we also judge that an object is approaching from other clues, such as the increasing detail which becomes visible, the obscuring, successively, of different parts of the background, and so on. Consequently, the illusion described is quite difficult to bring off. The background must be featureless, the light too dim for texture to be perceived, and so on. Yet, when it works, the subjective impression is quite convincing. Once the brain has made its interpretation we feel (meta-feel) it to be true.

The moral is, perception is a cognitive process. We do not simply perceive things as they are, as many philosophers have supposed, but use our think-box to interpret them. This is beautifully brought out by another experiment in which a wheel is made to cross a darkened room, carrying on the rim a small light. The observer sees only a light which seems to descend to the ground and rise again in a series of bounds. Now the experiment is repeated with the modification that a second light, on the centre of the wheel, is also illuminated. The observer now at once perceives the first light as revolving round the second and deduces, without conscious thought, that a wheel is involved. It makes better sense this way.

Obvious as the point may seem, the cognitive nature of perception is quite a recent idea in psychology, and Ulric Neisser's book on the subject, *Cognitive Psychology*, published as recently as 1965, is regarded as something of a classic.

Once we have 'made sense' of the data, it becomes very difficult to see it any other way. This is well brought out by a picture devised by one K. M. Dallenbach in 1951. He called it 'A Puzzle Picture with a new principle of Concealment' and I reproduce an improved version here. I have shown this picture to scores of people, but have found no one who could see, without help, what it represented. Once they are told that it shows a white cow with a black muzzle and black ears, they usually have no further difficulty and then find it impossible to see the picture in the naïve way they did originally.

Some psychologists dislike the idea that we compare what we see with images, but for me this demonstration points unequivocally to the

Can you see what this is? (See text.)

existence of a 'library' of images (and therefore, I suppose, also a library of sounds, of smells, of tactile sensations and so on) with which to make comparisons.

Of course this black-and-white picture contains much less information than would a view of a real cow. Colour, depth cues, most of the texture, movement – to say nothing of sounds and smells – are missing. Presented with this stripped-down paradigm, the mind hunts madly through its records for something which will fit the available data. This 'something' amounts to an 'internal representation' and Dallenbach's picture convinces me at least that I am employing, if not an image, at least a coherent totality to make sense of the picture. I do not sit there enumerating details but apprehend the pattern as a whole.

These stored patterns may be what the British psychologist Frederick Bartlett meant when he spoke of 'schemata' being employed for memory.

Be Constant, O! My Soul

As I try to pin down this moment of miracle when the computerlike processes of the brain crystallise into an Omega experience, I see a beautiful example in what psychologists call constancy mechanisms. When an object approaches us it seems to grow bigger – but we do not really believe it has grown larger. Our brain allows for this, and we call the effect 'size constancy'. According to the anthropologist Colin Turnbull, when men from a forest tribe which he studied first went out into the plains and saw cattle five miles away, they said: 'What are those strange insects?' Unused to the diminishing effect of great distance, and with no memory records of cows for comparison, they were misled. Even we, with much more data to go on, experience this effect to some degree when we first look down from the top of a skyscraper and see people 'looking like ants'. Because we have no previous experience of this vertical view, and because there are no familiar objects to provide a sense of scale between them and us, we tend to look at what we see naïvely.

Scaling mechanisms may be located not in the visual system but in the temporal lobe, for prior to an attack of temporal lobe epilepsy people often experience size distortion, seeing part or all of the visual image as too small or too large. However, damage in the parietal areas has the same effect. After the war two distinguished American experts on perception, N. B. Bender and H. L. Teuber, examined twelve cases of men injured in battle whose spatial sense was disturbed in a way which could be explained by then-current theories. All had injury in the parieto-occipital region.

One was a twenty-two-year-old lieutenant in the Marines who was hit by a shell fragment in the invasion of Saipan on 15 June 1944. When he recovered consciousness three days later, he felt that his left side was not there. (Later, he recovered some awareness of it, but it felt abnormally cool and sensitive.) He had several visual disturbances, especially in the lower left visual field, where things appeared too small, causing him to misjudge how far away they were, and looked dimmer than in the rest of his visual field. His visual field shrank with the distance of the object looked at. Other defects were that the boundaries between coloured objects were blurred, while there was abnormal persistence of after-images.

Though his right motor cortex was lacerated by bone fragments, and an abscess developed, I am happy to relate that after twelve months he had recovered so well that he could type and even fly a plane.

Another of their cases was a radio operator, injured in the right occiput. He reported that people looked small and far away. Things in his left visual field fluttered, making him feel dizzy. He could not distinguish triangles from circles, and, strangest of all, when he looked at a revolving disc, the right side seemed to be going slower than the left, the lower left going faster than all. Evidently his movement-detecting neurones were out of kilter. Also odd was the fact that, while his after-images were uncoloured, he developed eidetic imagery for coloured objects such as the American flag.

Even though we cannot yet dissect out all the mechanisms involved, these cases convey to us rather convincingly, it seems to me, that our visual mechanisms comprise numerous quite specific analysing and compensating mechanisms which normally work so harmoniously together that we readily think of vision as a single process. The same could be said, of course, of the other senses, of movements and actions, of speech and writing.

When we look at a *picture* in which depth is important, say a street receding from us, we naturally apply scaling and interpret small human figures as being the same size but further off than larger figures, ignoring their 'real' size as measured on the surface of the paper. This leads to a well-known illusion, in which solid bars of equal phenomenal length are placed across a pair of receding railway lines. The upper bar naturally appears larger than the lower, and if it was really part of the picture it would indeed have been larger. In a sense there is no 'illusion'. The only question which arises is whether we are expected to treat the picture as an object (and not apply scaling) or as an impression of a scene (and apply scaling). It is a discrimination we often have to make. When a picture restorer examines the cracks in the paint, or a critic the brushwork, he is treating the picture as an object. The railway lines 'illusion' succeeds inasmuch as it leaves the brain in doubt which stance to adopt.

Professor C. K. Mundle has discussed these two ways of looking and introduced the practice of writing look$_{ph}$ or see$_{ph}$ (where $_{ph}$ stands for phenomenal) for exact attention to what we see, as distinct from how we interpret it.

If you look at a coin lying on the table from any position except plumb overhead what you see$_{ph}$ is an ellipse, though you instantly, without conscious effort, make allowance for perspective and identify it as a circular disc. Curiously enough, however, if you set this up formally as an experiment, presenting people with an inclined disc, at a predetermined angle, and giving them a family of ellipses to match with it, different people choose different members of the family as a match. Most people choose ellipses rather fatter than the geometrically precise equivalent, ranging all the way up to an actual circle. Constancy correction, in short, is subjective.

The delicate margin between seeing and seeing$_{ph}$ is even more vividly illustrated by colour constancy.

Throw a piece of shiny self-coloured material down in a heap, and what do you see? Viewed objectively, the colour will seem darkest in the shadowed parts of the folds, lighter where the illumination is stronger and almost white where there are highlights, and a painter would so paint it. Yet you do not conclude that the material is of a varying hue. Experience enables you to make a good estimate of the 'real' colour. By 'real' colour, we usually mean viewed in daylight – but actually our perception of hue changes with intensity, so that in strong lights colours look paler. Thus the question arises, is there any sense in which an object has a 'real' colour?

Let me offer one more puzzler for anyone who thinks that things have real colours. Professor Ivo Kohler devised spectacles with a red filter on the left half of each lens, and a green one on the right half. To the wearer everything to the left looked red, everything to the right looked green. After a few days, he began to see colours normally again. But when he removed the spectacles, the side which had been green looked red, and vice versa. This was quite unforeseen. One must conclude that the colour effect is determined in the brain. So colour is *not* a product of receptors in the retina, as we have been taught. It is an Omega Effect.

Outlandish Colour

Perception is a topic which brings us very close to the origins of subjective experience, and this is particularly so when we come to consider how colour sensations are produced. The textbooks tell us of the three-colour theory first proposed by Newton and formalised by Young and von Helmholtz, to which I referred briefly a few pages back. But the almost magical experiments of another young man from MIT, Edwin Land, have shown the textbooks to be wrong. Also of course all the philosophers who thought they understood about colour too.

But before we come to Land, a word is in order about von Helmholtz, since even his account of colour is frequently misunderstood. One reads, for instance, that a red object, say, a tomato, is not really red but simply reflects a certain wavelength of light, so that for each wavelength a different shade of colour will be seen. But the fact is that the colour receptors in the eye are not really specific for red, green and blue. They respond to a range of wavelengths, most strongly at one particular wavelength and with declining strength to wavelengths on either side, as the diagram indicates. Thus each receptor is naturally responding to all three colours, but in differing proportions. It follows that there is an infinite number of wavelength combinations which will evoke a given subjective colour-impression. Hence objects with differing wavelength-absorbing qualities may look the same colour. In this respect, at least, our senses fail to tell us what the world is 'really' like.

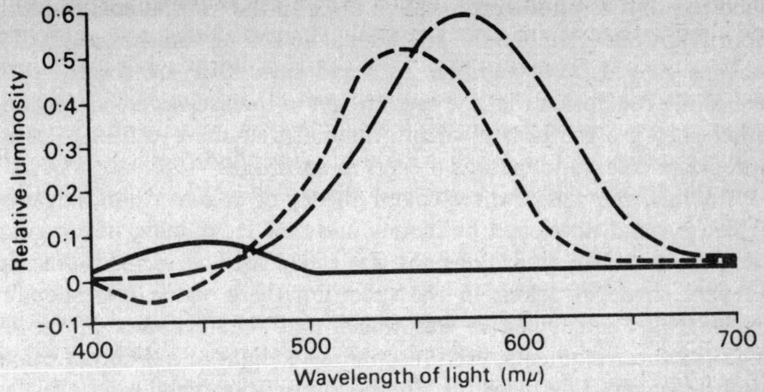

How the Retina responds to Colour
These three curves show how the three kinds of colour receptor respond. At most wavelengths of light all three types are affected to differing extents. The subjective experience of colour is thus derived from a synthesis in the brain of three distinct sets of information. (*Blue: solid line; Green: dash; Red: long dash.*)

So much has long been known. Edwin Land was twenty-eight when he founded the Polaroid Corporation, but the war diverted his efforts and it was not until 1947 that his colour camera emerged to become the biggest novelty in the photographic field since film replaced plates. Not content with inventing the Polaroid camera, he also conducted experiments of great originality, the outcome of which continues to intrigue scientists to this day.

In the 1950s, I went to see a demonstration which Land gave in London of his discoveries. The one which impressed me most – to be more accurate, it left me absolutely pop-eyed – was this. Land took two black-and-white transparencies of the same scene (actually they showed a number of parked cars of different colours) and projected them by means of two beams of yellow light so that the images were superimposed. The scene then appeared in full colour! Slightly washed out, like a slide projected in a room which is not completely dark, but unquestionably displaying a full range of colours. It is true that the transparencies were not identical; one had been taken through a red filter, one through a green, so that parts of one were slightly darker than the corresponding parts of the other. True, the beams of light were not quite the same shade of yellow. Nevertheless, all that each transparency could do was to pass more or less of the yellow light. The only light falling on the screen was yellow, yet the picture appeared to us who were looking as coloured.

In a variant of this experiment, Land projected red and white beams, which combine to pink on the screen. Drop in the transparencies and the colour leaps out. Remove the red filter; the colour vanishes again. The audience gasped quite audibly. As Land says: 'We are forced to the astonishing conclusion that the rays are not in themselves colour-making. Rather they are the bearers of information that the eye uses to assign appropriate colours to various objects in an image.'

With this, the classic three-colour theory of colour-vision, advanced by Newton and developed by Young and von Helmholtz, lies in ruins. When the wavelike nature of light was established, it seemed clear that for every shade of colour in the spectrum there was a corresponding wavelength. Then, when it was found that the receptors in the eye contained three pigments, each responding to light of a different colour, the three-colour theory seemed to be copper-bottomed, and the rival theory of Hering, which called for only two colours, went into the discard.

The full implications of Land's shattering discovery have not yet registered, and many scientists prefer to carry on as if it had not happened. Professor W. A. H. Rushton, of Cambridge University, is currently the world-expert on visual pigments, having devised incredibly ingenious methods of studying these pigments in the living eye. In describing Land's work, Rushton comments that it should be possible to scale the intensity of two lights of different compositions so that they will be absorbed equally by any one pigment; to do this so as to fool all three pigments is much harder, but, once this is achieved 'no one – not even Land – has the magic to show as different what all three cone-pigments agree is the same'.

The pigments may – poor, simple things – *agree* that they are the same, but no one – not even Rushton – has the science to show that what is by definition different, is actually the same. So the question of why it is *perceived* as being the same remains unanswered.

I feel tempted to parody the well-known epigram on Einstein:

> Colour and colour's laws lay hid in night.
> God said: 'Let Newton be,' and all was light.
> It did not last. The Devil shouting 'Ho!
> Here's Edwin Land!' restored the status quo.

As Land, pursuing his own discovery, has shown, the colour balance is unaffected by varying the intensities or wavelengths of the two projection lights, provided the same proportion is maintained between them. On the other hand, if you insert a 'wedge filter' – that is, a piece of glass graduated in density from clear to opaque – in one of the beams, the colour vanishes. One is forced to conclude that the eye-cum-brain computes an average light intensity for the scene and then compares the intensity at every point with this average. As Land puts it: 'Colours are determined by the relative balance of long and short wavelengths over the entire scene.'

To look at it another way: the eye does not make absolute judgments of colour. In this case, as in other forms of perception, *it makes only relative judgments* – and then treats them as absolute. Elsewhere, we shall come across further examples of this: generally ignored, it is of philosophical importance.

What put everyone on the wrong track about colour was the assumption that the mind is interested in wavelengths, when what it is really interested in is the comparison of warm and cool colours. Historically the error was compounded by a series of experiments in which observers were required to match patches of pure colour. Such matching does depend simply on the wavelength of the light and the absorption characteristics of the retinal pigments, so the results appeared to confirm the three-colour theory very convincingly. In real life we are not much concerned with matching; we are busy extracting meaning from what we see and colour is only one of the cues to meaning on which we rely.

All this, you will appreciate, is very relevant to the questions I set out to explore – the relation of the objective world to the subjective experience, or, as we say, of mind to body. In colour vision, we have a range of different subjective experiences produced by three physiological processes. But if we can perceive a mixture of red and blue as purple, or of yellow and red as orange, why cannot we perceive a mixture of red and green as some new colour? And why is there no yellow-blue?

We can understand this better when we look at the neural basis of colour vision. Confining ourselves to the cones, we can say that we have three receptors the outputs of which are converted to 'spikes', or electric pulses, and coded. But what is sent up to the visual cortex is not three colour signals. It is a luminosity signal based on the inputs to all three types of receptor, plus a two-colour difference signal. (There is also a second luminosity signal from the rods.) The first colour-difference signal reports red against blue, the second yellow against blue. The yellow is derived by compounding the red and green inputs. So it turns out, as so often happens, that in the long battle between the three-colour theories of Young and von Helmholtz and the two-colour theory of Hering, both parties were partly right.

It may be easier to see why nature adopts this seemingly unnecessarily complex system by looking at colour television, for TV engineers also transmit colour as difference signals. This takes up less channel-width – about half the frequency-band which a three-colour system would require.

I find it interesting that a system which starts out, at the physiological level, by adding together three components is converted at the psychological level to two components in opposition – for, as we have seen earlier, the brain appears to prefer such opponent systems.

Perceive it for Yourself

One of the long-standing puzzles in the field of visual perception is the phenomenon of the after-image. You have almost certainly gazed at bright sky through a window and then, looking away, have seen a dark rectangle with light cross bars, which reversed to a light rectangle with dark cross bars. Or, looking at a bright coloured surface and then shutting the eyes, you may have seen the complementary colour. That is very odd. We see red, perceive green.

For two centuries, psychologists debated whether this effect took place in the eye or in the brain. In 1940 the controversy seemed to have been settled by that almost legendary figure Kenneth Craik. (Craik was killed in a senseless accident, on the eve of VE day, at the age of thirty-one: in his short life he had made brilliantly original contributions and his work is still read. He was riding home from his Cambridge college on a bicycle when the door of a parked car was suddenly opened. Craik collided with it, and was thrown into the path of an oncoming car. He never recovered consciousness.)

Frederick Bartlett, the grand old man of British psychology, was his professor and has described his first meeting with Craik in 1936, when he was twenty-two. His immediate impression was 'of a tall powerful frame; a face pale but full of life; a firm chin, straight mouth, singularly attractive dark eyes, and above a shock of black hair.' And he added, 'He knew, and within a very few minutes I knew, of the power that was within him.' He had studied classics at Edinburgh, including philosophy, but knew when he came to Cambridge that psychology was the subject he wanted to study. He got his doctorate in 1940 and spent the war working on military problems, winning the confidence of generals and admirals, industrialists and mechanics, to say nothing of professors and lab. assistants. That fate did not give him the chance to devote his whole energies to pure psychology is tragic.

Before the days of 'big science' it was almost a point of pride to solve problems by ingenuity, rather than engineering. It was in this spirit that Craik investigated after-images by making one of his eyes temporarily blind for about a minute, by pressing firmly on it and so cutting off its blood supply. After looking at a bright light with the blind eye he found that he perceived a negative after-image, on looking at a white wall, when the eye recovered its sight. Since during the period of blindness his brain could not have received any messages from the blinded eye, this showed that the after-image was due to something which happened in the eye itself, rather than in the brain. As we now know, there are central processes involved in many after-images too, but Craik's self-experiment proved that part, at least, of the mechanism must be in the eye. Until he had his brilliantly simple idea, no one had managed to think of a way of studying the topic.

Craik performed an even more heroic self-experiment when he looked for two minutes at the summer sun at noon, with his right eye, thus burning a small hole in the retina. A Frenchman had looked at the sun fixedly in the previous century and had rendered himself permanently blind, a fact of which Craik must have been aware. Craik reported that the brightness of the sun's disc fell steadily until it was almost completely black, surrounded by a bright halo. Among other effects he noted was a very bright after-image in the left eye and a slight positive after-image in the right, which persisted for several days. The burned patch, or scotoma, that evening, looked like a dim orange disc, across which flitted tiny jet black points, or, more rarely, bright sparks.

Two days later the scotoma was subjectively 'filled in' with the prevailing colour of the background he happened to be looking at, though small objects – full stops on a page or birds against the sky – were invisible when fixated with the right eye alone. But he found, which was quite new, that the filling in did not occur immediately, while, if you waved your hand back and forth, it became continuously visible, with a flickering appearance.

Craik made highly original observations of what I have called the Omega Effect in this connection. To use his own words: 'The unconscious nature [of the scotoma's infilling] could be further demonstrated by the following paradoxes:

1. A black circle, such as a printed O, held at such distance that the black ring just overlapped the edges of the blind area, was seen under favourable circumstances as a uniform dark-grey disc.

2. A ring or triangular pattern of white spots on a darker ground, when similarly placed, was seen as a white area, with a considerable "flare" or brightness, and equal in size to the blind area. In both these cases one was perfectly aware of the true nature of the figures, but this appeared to make little or no difference.'

He was baffled to get a coloured after-image of the scotoma on a strip of paper held close to the eye and moved up and down – red if it appeared above the paper and green if below. 'What is the explanation?' he asked.

He continued to make observations of his damaged vision, which recovered to something like normality in six months, except for some distortion and magnification of images. But four years later he was debating why the brain could marry the magnified image from his right eye with the relatively much smaller image from the left. He found an ingenious way to measure the discrepancy between the two images accurately and reported that it reached a maximum of thirty-eight per cent.

However, the subject of after-images proved more complex than Craik supposed. Some after-images persist for months, and can therefore not be explained by bleaching of retinal pigments. I was once hag-ridden by a crescent of light which appeared briefly to my right every time I passed from a bright area to a dark one. I found that it could be made to recur by shifting my eyes quickly from one side to the other. I have consulted experts for an explanation but none was forthcoming. There are other mystifying observations to account for.

Years ago a biologist, S. D. Porteus, reported being driven very fast 'along a narrow concrete road, fringed by thick bushes. Suddenly a child stepped out on the road just ahead of the car. We were travelling too fast to admit of swerving to avoid her. Fortunately, she drew back just in time. A moment after, we flashed past a store on the plate-glass window of which was printed WAIAKEA MILL STORE. For some minutes afterwards I retained an extremely vivid image of those letters as if printed on the windshield of the car instead of the store window as a background. In its persistence this after-sensation resembled an hallucination.'

Thus there seems to be a kinship between hallucination and after-images. The British philosopher Hume said that images and percepts differed only in intensity: Hoffding, the German psychologist, denied this, and Porteus' experience suggests that, sometimes at least, they are equally vivid. But the subject of imagery is so large that it calls for a chapter to itself.

14

Just Imagine!

THE VERY SPIT AND IMAGE

'What a yellow and crumbly voice you have!' said the Russian mnemonist Sherevsky to the psychologist Professor L. S. Vygotsky. For Sherevsky, sounds had colour and taste and were tangible. Conversely, colours might taste sour or feel sharp. 'Music changes the taste of everything,' he said. When he was working as a professional memory-man, any noise in the auditorium appeared as a splash or puff and obscured the words he was memorising from a chart or blackboard. When he imagined a 500-watt bulb shining in his eyes, his brain rhythms changed as if there were really a bright light. He could accelerate his pulse by imagining himself running and could dispel pain by imagining himself to be someone else.

Source: A. Luria, *Problems in Psychology*, Moscow, 1960.

Pictures in the Mind

The inventor Nicola Tesla is said to have had such vivid imagery that he could test the wear on a machine part by making a mental model, letting it run for thousands of hours while he got on with something else, and then taking it apart and looking for the wear.

A tall story, I fear, but it is certainly true that some people have quite exceptionally vivid imagery. Sir Joshua Reynolds' successor at the Royal Academy, for instance, could paint a portrait by copying the remembered image of his sitter. First studied by the Czech physiologist Purkinje in 1819, the subject was only picked up again early in this century by a German psychologist, Erich Jaensch, who christened it 'eidetic imagery'. Many experiments were done on it in the 1920s; then psychologists lost interest. About ten years ago Norman Haber of Rochester University revived the topic. Examining five hundred children he found twenty who had this photographic kind of mind. He seated them before an easel carrying a card of neutral grey, over which a picture was placed for inspection, then removed. The results were impressive. Briefly shown a picture in which the word HAUSWIRTSCHAFT appeared on the fascia of a shop, these English-speaking children could spell out this unfamiliar word by reading off from their mental image after the picture had gone. Shown a picture of a cat in a tree, one boy was asked, after the picture had gone, 'Do you see something there?' He replied:

'I see the tree, grey tree with three limbs, I see the cat with stripes around its tail.'
'Can you count those stripes?'
'Yes' (pause). 'There's about sixteen.'

He was right. He then described, in answer to questions, other details, ending up with the experimenter asking: 'Is the image gone?'

'Yes, except for the tree.'
'Tell me when it goes away.'
(After a pause) 'It went away.'

The images persisted for a few minutes in the case of young children but lasted as much as thirty minutes in the case of older children. Several of them mentioned that if they actively attended to the details in the picture, naming them or rehearsing them, no image would persist after the picture was taken away, or, at best, a very poor one. That is very hard to explain.

The faculty seems to fade with age, as a rule, but not always. There's a professor on record who was astonished that people needed a stereoscopic viewer to look at stereoscopic pairs of pictures, since he could easily create the stereo-image by simply recalling them.

Speaking of stereo-images reminds me of an ingenious series of experiments devised by Bela Julesz of the Bell Telephone Labs. He programmed computers to produce patterns of ten thousand black and white dots, as seen here. The two patterns differ slightly, in such a way that, when viewed through a stereoscope, a figure or letter can be seen. The brain's visual system, it emerges, can detect and interpret very slight differences too insignificant to appear to ordinary inspection. Two Harvard psychologists used such stereograms to test eidetic imagery. The

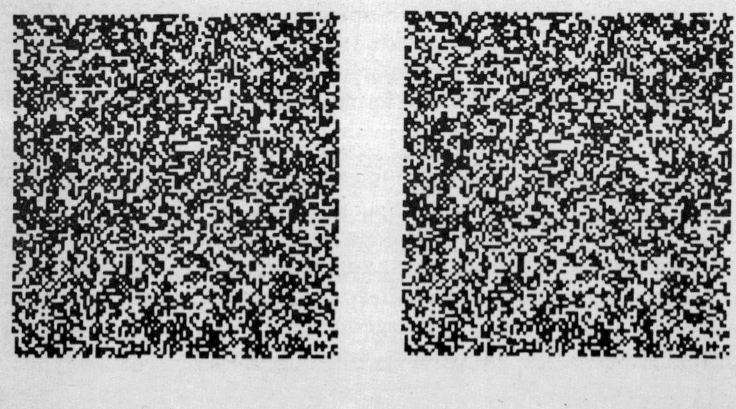

observer was a woman of twenty-three, a teacher at Harvard, with remarkable imagery. She could copy a page of poetry in an unfamiliar language from bottom to top as fast as she could write.

She scanned the left Julesz pattern with the left eye for one minute; then, after a ten-second rest, the right pattern with the right eye and unhesitatingly announced that she could see a 'T' coming in depth towards her. Subsequently the interval between presentation to each eye was extended to ten minutes, then to twenty-four hours, with four minutes for each scan of the picture. She could still resolve the embedded image. There was even partial success when the experiment was repeated after a lapse of three months. Unhappily, she became tired of being treated as a phenomenon and declined to be the subject of further experiments.

When eidetikers gaze at a blank sheet of paper, or a wall, and recall an image, their eyes move about as if they were looking at a real image. But, unlike a real picture, they can cause the figures they are seeing to move, or a carriage to drive out of the picture. When asked to move their image from one piece of paper to another, they spontaneously observe that when it reaches the edge it falls off. One child, visualising a donkey, was surprised to see it start eating!

No one has any explanation of these phenomena, which have been almost wholly neglected for thirty-five years. As Haber says: 'Much more work needs to be done. Imagery is an important characteristic of many cognitive tasks, and it should be opened to serious scientific investigation.' It would be odd enough if everybody could visualise in this way. I find it odder that only a few can. As the faculty tends to decline with age, it may be that some of us have forgotten how – perhaps because our education stressed words and concepts rather than imagery.

Not only is the eidetic image 'out there' but if an eidetiker visualises, say, a black square, he will subsequently see a white after-image, as he would after looking at a real square. Again, eidetikers have been tested with optical illusions. For instance, if parallel straight lines are placed over a web of radiating lines they will appear bowed. An eidetiker can produce the bowing by looking at the parallel lines and imagining the radiating ones.

That's very suggestive: it argues that the neural patterns which convey remembered images and those which convey real ones are of the same kind and share the same circuitry. If so, the philosopher Gilbert Ryle was wrong when he declared: 'To see is one thing; to picture or visualise is another.' There may be another clue in the fact that eidetic imagery is reportedly commoner in brain-damaged children, while adults who have suffered occipital damage (that is, damage to the visual areas) report an increase in the vividness of their imagery.

One might expect that if such vivid imagery is found for vision, the other senses should exhibit something similar; and in fact there are a few similar reports of hearing and touch. I am inclined to think this may account for the way in which a good orchestral conductor can pick out a single misplayed note from the web of sound produced by a full orchestra. And perhaps some wine-tasters owe their superiority to the fact that they can recall more vividly than most of us the exact taste of a wine drunk on a previous occasion, for comparison with the one they are now drinking. What an attractive field for experiment!

Verbalisers and Visualisers

Sir Francis Galton was a polymath who made many highly original observations towards the end of the nineteenth century. Perhaps his most endearing enquiry was into the longevity of English monarchs, in order to see whether the many prayers offered up on their behalf had had any effect on their average life expectancy. (They hadn't.) He was the inventor of statistical method, but I introduce him to you because of his study, perhaps the first ever, of imagery. He estimated that six per cent of the population had vivid imagery – not necessarily eidetic, of course, for the concept of eidetic imagery had not been propounded.

A century passed without anyone attempting to establish more accurate figures, much less trying to explore ethnic or national differences or the breakdown by age, sex and personality type, in any comprehensive manner. A bouquet, however, to Ann Roe, who surveyed American scientists and came back with the news that biologists and physicists were primarily visualisers, whereas psychologists and anthropologists were verbalisers: that is, depended upon words to think with.

Some authorities have asserted that no thought is possible without imagery, but that is almost certainly false. It was Professor Bartlett, at Cambridge, who, in the course of studying memory, came to the conclusion that people fell into two distinct groups: visualisers and verbalisers. The late Dr Grey Walter, the encephalographer who worked at the Burden Neurological Institute near Bristol, brought a little more scientific accuracy to the subject when he estimated, on the basis of the brain waves he studied, that fifteen per cent of the population think exclusively in visual terms, fifteen per cent exclusively in verbal terms, while the rest employ a mixture. But it is not established that the two faculties, which presumably reflect the functions of the two halves of the brain, are reciprocally related. In other words, some people might be strong on both, others weak on both; most people would have other combinations. Perhaps some of those who firmly deny that they ever enjoy imagery may simply be ignoring it. The question of how such people cope with tasks (like map reading or tying a knot) which involve imagery has not received an answer.

It is an odd, totally unexplained fact that visualisers breathe more regularly than non-visualisers; moreover verbalisers breathe more regularly than is usual for them when engaged on spatial tasks which presumably demand their visual powers. Furthermore, high imagers are more relaxed, more creative, more mature, and more flexible than low-imagers. Put that in your pipe and smoke it! We have a clue in the fact that absence of imagery is correlated with strong defences against impulse, while such people experience more dream fantasy.

Visualisers find it hard to form abstract concepts and find it difficult to communicate with verbalisers. I myself am strongly visual and I certainly find it hard to follow the writings of philosophers, which are highly conceptual. As I argue elsewhere, verbalisers tend to operate in a domain of concepts which have, all too often, only the vaguest relevance to the real world. I suspect that many lawyers, legislators, bureaucrats and administrators have the same defect. Unfortunately, we live in a world which is biased towards the verbal and conceptual, so that they do not feel their deficiency, while the visualiser feels frustrated and left out of account. In education, particularly, the verbal individual is frequently at an advantage. When I was at school, I vividly remember, I had no difficulty with geometry, because I could always recall the figure and derive the proof of the theorem from it. The fact that the square on the hypotenuse of a triangle equals the sum of the squares on the other two sides has remained with me because I recall the diagram. On the other hand, algebra and calculus I found extremely difficult, and only those parts which could be graphically represented could I retain. I distinctly remember the flash of illumination which struck me when, after an incomprehensible discussion of the algebraic formula for a parabola, the teacher drew a diagram on the the blackboard, and showed how it came about. Yet educators still make no effort to determine which of their pupils should be given visual and which verbal instruction; much less do they offer a choice of examination methods.

Perchance to Dream

When I go to bed, as soon as I have closed my eyes, a series of vivid images presents itself. Scene replaces scene, like a series of lantern slides; or, rather, short lengths of movie film, since the images are not static. For instance I may see a girl's face, from a position above, as if I were in a bus looking down, or on a low terrace. I may note the way her hair is done or the exact shade of her lipstick. Suddenly this is replaced by a view of something like the Piazza of San Marco in Venice, on a rainy day, with a figure in a yellow raincoat crossing from left to right. I am puzzled by the long white balcony which seems to cross a series of different buildings – could it perhaps be a long banner? Before I can decide, there is a man getting into a car. Several times, after several hours of weeding plantains from the lawn, I have seen nothing but plantains, a foot or two from my eyes. (I have heard of someone who kept seeing raspberries, after a day raspberry picking.) I can still remember a night, when I was about nineteen, when these images succeeded each other so recklessly that for two or three hours I could not sleep. I turned on the light and opened my eyes in order to dispel these frantically distracting images: oriental processions, wedding cakes, executions and I know not what. I may get a similar effect when I wake in the morning, though briefly; and I have known it to happen when drowsing in the afternoon. Such images are called hypnopompic when they occur in the morning and hypnogogic when they occur at night, a futile distinction.

About twenty per cent of the population is said to experience them at one time or another, but in questioning my friends I have found that fewer than one in ten know what I am talking about. David Foulkes and various colleagues at the University of Wyoming seem to be almost the only team to have investigated this type of imagery experimentally. They report that it is associated (I am delighted to say) with a healthy ego structure.

Such imagery, in my experience, is much more vivid than the imagery I can construct from memory. I imagine it to be like eidetic imagery, but curiously enough there is a negative correlation of ·27 between the two faculties; i.e. eidetikers are rather unlikely to have hypnogogic imagery and vice versa. Moreover hypnogogics do not get imagery in sensory isolation experiments. It is much like ordinary perception, though not quite as vivid. It is 'out there' to the extent that one feels in a spatial relation to what is seen, but not to the point of supposing it to exist, as in a hallucination. Finally one is not personally involved, which puts it in sharp contrast with dreams, which are always about one's own activities and feelings.

However, as I have argued in Chapter Nine, dreams are not wholly and perhaps not even primarily visual experience, despite the common assumption to the contrary. Moreover, they have a narrative character, which is not the case with hypnotic imagery, in my experience.

It is now fairly well known that during the course of a night's sleep there are several periods during which the eyes move rapidly (REM sleep) interspersed with others when they do not (NREM sleep). The electroencephalographic pattern is also different in the two kinds of sleep. When a sleeper is wakened during REM sleep he almost invariably reports that he was dreaming, and it has been noticed that the eye-movements seem to correspond with what he is 'seeing'. If it was a car or a train, they move sideways; if a waterfall or a rocket launch, they move vertically, and so on. This has given rise to the idea that NREM sleep is dreamless sleep, but this is not so. Foulkes has found that dreams are often reported, but more often there is a kind of long worrying process of a conceptual kind. We all know, I suppose, those nights in which we revolved a problem endlessly in a semi-conscious state; and we tell our friends, 'I did not sleep a wink last night.' Actually we did, though perhaps not very fruitfully.

It looks as if the image-making faculty has a fairly precise location in the brain; since cases of people who have lost it on injury are known. As long ago as 1883, Charcot described an eminent classical scholar who lost all imagery including dreams. He could not visualise his wife, his children, or his home, but his memory and intelligence remained perfectly normal. Two British psychologists, Humphrey and Zangwill, reported three cases of people who ceased to dream after injury to the parietal lobe of the brain, while their imagery became dim; there were also other symptoms. In one case dreaming returned after five years. But other brain areas may also be involved. Sir Francis Walshe, the neurologist, had a patient who lost the power to visualise after a depressed fracture in the mid-frontal area. He was a thirty-six-year-old manager for a building firm, so this was a handicap, but he managed to resume work by dint of keeping the plans of buildings he was concerned with constantly at hand.

Two doctors at the Radcliffe Infirmary, Oxford, reported vivid dreaming while awake in a patient who had undergone the operation known as cingulectomy – removal of a portion of the brain which envelops the great commissure. He described it as 'sort of waking dream . . . even with my eyes open', a phrase which supports the idea that dreams, day-dreams, and imagery are all of a piece. 'I have been having tea with my wife,' he told the doctor. 'Oh, I haven't really. She's not been here today. But as soon as I close my eyes the scene occurs so vividly. I can see the cups and saucers, and hear her pouring out – then, just as I am lifting up the cup for a drink, I wake up and there's no one there.' This persisted for about three days. Vivid dreaming may also follow lesions of the temporal lobe, and much the same effect is sometimes produced by the tranquilliser, Chlordiazepoxide (Librium).

An American doctor reported that sixteen per cent of patients on this drug reported vivid dreams, nightmares and dreams which continued after waking. As one patient, a black girl, put it, 'The dream wouldn't stop.' She was aware that the dream was subjective; but the fifty-two-year-old psychiatrist who screamed with rage because two little green boys were sitting on the bureau and demanded that they be removed was evidently hallucinating. Once again, the slightness of the distinction between the various kinds of imagery is evident. Dreams which continue into waking life must surely be akin to hallucinations.

Now You See It – Now You Don't

Back in 1905 a Cornell psychologist named C. W. Perky performed an experiment which was to prove a classic, constantly cited even today. He seated subjects in front of a screen and told them to imagine a tomato and to describe the image they saw, if any. Unknown to the subjects, behind the screen was a projector which was throwing an image of a tomato on the screen too faintly to be seen, and the image was oscillated slightly. This was repeated, substituting for the tomato, in turn, a book, a banana, a leaf and a lemon. Twenty-seven subjects were thus studied. In three cases the projectionist inadvertently gave the game away, and so these were excluded. All the remaining twenty-four subjects gave descriptions which matched the slides being projected but believed that the image was in their minds. Perky concluded, therefore, that there is no fundamental difference between an image which arises subjectively and one which is evoked objectively.

In 1964, S. J. Segal of the Center for Research into Cognition and Affect in New York, decided to repeat this extraordinary experiment, wondering if it was really to be relied on. He found that the students of his day, whom he roped in as subjects, were smarter and more suspicious than those of some sixty years before, and tumbled to what was happening after a few trials. But until the truth dawned, they too were unable to distinguish internal and external imagery. So it is not too difficult to accept that hallucinations are internal imagery mistaken for external. But I would add that normally internal imagery is much fainter than external; a stepping-up of vividness must occur, giving them an eidetic quality. Perhaps it is emotional loading which has this effect, since hallucinations seem to be predominantly of images which arouse strong feelings.

Sometimes people report, 'I knew it must be a hallucination,' or words to that effect; sometimes they are deceived into thinking the hallucination 'veridical' – to use the convenient term suggested by Professor A. J. Ayer. The dictionary tells us that we ought to use the term 'hallucination' only for the case where the subject is fooled into taking what he sees 'for real'. If he knows he is 'seeing things' it should be called a pseudo-hallucination. In my view, this distinction is misleading. The image-forming process is the same in both cases, but in the latter the cortex tests (as it is always doing) the plausibility of what is perceived. If the image is of a dead person, for instance, it knows it cannot be veridical. It is precisely in cases where the cortex is confused, drugged, or exhausted that this reality-testing fails to occur – as in the case of alcoholics. Sometimes people report that they could see the room *through* the hallucinated people or objects – and it is a familiar convention that ghosts are represented as semi-transparent in drawings. I suspect that it is not so much that the hallucinated figures are transparent as that both are present in the visual cortex simultaneously, rather like two slides projected simultaneously or a double-exposed photograph.

The fact is, it is remarkably difficult, sometimes, to distinguish fact from fancy. 'I get confused between true and false memories,' said one patient, while a schizophrenic explained: 'I cannot remember whether things have really happened or not.' A third is reported as saying: 'I can't distinguish between dreams and reality.' A thirty-one-year-old school-mistress: 'Ever since I left the [operating] theatre, I just can't distinguish between phantasy and reality.'

Ritchie Russell, the Oxford brain surgeon, has described a patient whose hallucinations affected only his right visual field – which means that only the left half of his brain was involved in the hallucination. While watching a film, this man could see various objects from his hospital ward to the right of the screen, while the film he was watching continued to the left. On another occasion, in bed in the ward, 'he suddenly saw a motor cycle and then a convoy of lorries passing from right to left in his right visual field. They appeared to be passing over the end of the bed, which he could still clearly see in his left visual field.'

We need not infer from this that hallucination was generated in the left cortex, but merely that it was failing to suppress the imagery arising from the mid-brain, while the right hemisphere was continuing to do so.

There appear to be three or four distinct situations in which hallucinations occur. The first is lack of interesting sensory input. Lindbergh, flying the Atlantic alone, experienced several hallucinations. Regular airline pilots will tell you that they sometimes hallucinate 'the clanks' – as the thumping of clear-air turbulence is known in the trade. In much the same way, long-distance truckdrivers have reported red spiders on their windscreens, among other divertissements. In sensory deprivation experiments, hallucination is fairly common. There is an interesting technique of complete visual deprivation in which the subject's head is placed inside a translucent dome (the illumination of which can be varied) so that in every direction he sees nothing but a completely featureless field of light; this is known to psychologists as a Ganzfeld. Deprived of all meaningful visual input, the brain, which is always searching for patterns, turns to internal imagery to occupy itself. Likewise in the experiments in which the subject floats in a tank of warm water, preoccupation with internal material – ideas and feelings as well as imagery – develops, as the delphinologist John Lilly vividly describes in his book *The Centre of the Cyclone*. There seems to be a parallel between the man with his head in a bowl and the polar explorer or mountaineer who has travelled for hours over featureless snowfields – and whose cortex is functioning minimally owing to exhaustion. Thus the hallucinations I mentioned in Chapter One are cases in point.

The second situation which provokes hallucinations is an intense need or desire for the object hallucinated, as in the thirsty desert traveller who 'sees' an oasis or a lake and the shipwrecked mariner who 'sees' a rescue vessel on the horizon. This also applied, no doubt, to people who see loved ones after their death. Havelock Ellis' mistress, Françoise Delisle, told me how, after Ellis' death, she once saw him pass through the room and out into the garden; this impression was so vivid she followed him, but he disappeared.

Thirdly, we are easily deceived when a strong suggestion is made, whether under hypnosis or not. In another key experiment, the Swedish-born Carl Seashore, who was Dean of Psychology at Iowa State, asked subjects to walk down a corridor, telling them that they were to stop when he switched on additional lighting. In fact, he did nothing to the lights, but most of the subjects stopped anyway. It is, of course, a common experience, if one is expecting a phone call or a visitor, to imagine one has heard the phone tinkle or the door bell ring.

When I was producing the *Horizon* programme for BBC Television I carried out an informal demonstration of this effect, involving not vision but smell. We built some impressive equipment and persuaded the late Professor S. Tolansky of London University to join in the fun. He explained to viewers that it was now possible to broadcast smells. He put chopped onion into one end of the equipment, did a splendid cod explanation of how the vibrations were picked up and transformed into electrical signals, and told viewers to sit exactly opposite their screens and concentrate, when they might smell onion. He then did the same for coffee. Anyone who smelt anything was invited to write us a letter, to arrive by *April the 1st*. Hundreds of letters arrived from people who had smelt coffee and onion, together with one from a smeller who said he had smelt not coffee but violets. At least two viewers said that they had been completely taken in until they noticed the date.

The Swiss psychologist James Leuba demonstrated that hallucinations can also be evoked by associations. At first he used hypnotised subjects;

later he found the effect occurred with unhypnotised subjects almost equally well. He paired two stimuli, in different sensory modes: for instance, he rang a bell while giving the subject creosote to smell. Then he suggested that the subject would forget all about this and roused him from trance. Then, when he suddenly rang the bell, the subject said: 'What's that curious smell? It's like creosote.' In a variation, the subject's hand was pricked when the bell was rung. Later he reported a sudden shooting pain in his hand. In another variant, he showed the subject a card bearing the letter N, while giving him a mild electric shock. Later, when again shocked after waking from trance, the subject exclaimed in amazement that he could see the letter N on the paper before him. So coincidental stimuli may in ordinary life evoke hallucinations in predisposed persons. And since conditioned reflexes can be made to moods and feelings, such affective states, recurring later, may evoke a hallucination of the circumstances in which they first were felt.

Hallucinations can be evoked by alterations of brain chemistry, such as are produced by the psychedelic drugs. The hallucinogens are diencephalic stimulants. Professor R. G. Heath has extracted from the blood of schizophrenics a substance christened taraxein; injected into normal subjects, this evokes hallucinations. And, as everyone knows, alcoholics are apt to see snakes and pink rats. So it is not surprising that abnormal diets, especially a shortage of vitamin B_6, can favour hallucination. Since starvation deprives you of B_6, starving people often hallucinate. Early Christian anchorites, living on a marginal diet, naturally were given to hallucination, as the record shows. Aldous Huxley has suggested that changes in blood chemistry resulting from suppurating wounds could have a similar effect. After ritual flagellation, such changes might well occur.

Equally, hallucination can be evoked by suitable electrical stimulation, particularly in the hippocampal area. Stimulation of the temporal lobe produced hallucinations of a curious kind: they seem to be 're-runs' of a memory, rather than constructions of the unconscious mind. For, if the point is stimulated again, the same hallucination occurs. Thus one patient, a lady, heard a tune being played and thought it was the radio; when it recurred, on re-stimulation, she decided it must be a record-player. The incident reveals the convincing 'out there' quality of the experience. In epileptic attacks, when the point in the brain responsible lies in the temporal lobe, very similar hallucinations occur just before the attack.

The conclusion to which all this tends, I am inclined to think, is that the production of imagery is going on all the time in the older, more primitive part of the brain, but is normally ignored, or shut off by the cortex. It is one more example of the inhibitory function of the brain. Only when the cortex is numbed or unoccupied – or when the fantasy is strongly amplified by emotional loading – does it break through into consciousness. We must suppose that animals, and perhaps primitive people, live in a sort of dream world to a much greater extent than we do. There seems to be some evidence for this: for instance, primitive peoples accept the presence of spirits and the ghosts of the dead as existing in the external world and interacting with it, as if the two planes were one.

In schizophrenia something similar may be happening – though hallucination is by no means invariably a feature of this condition. Professor Silvano Arieti, an authority on schizophrenia, has suggested precisely this: a breakthrough of the fantasy world at the expense of the external world.

It is worth stressing, however, that hallucination is not, as many people suppose, a mark of insanity. ('I must be going bonkers, I'm beginning to see things that aren't there.') It is practically a normal occurrence. It is only when reality-testing fails that a pathological condition may be present; and even then the cause may be chemical and the disturbance temporary.

So far all has been plain sailing. But now I must mention one or two forms of hallucination which are harder to explain. The first is autoscopy: the hallucination of seeing one's own double. This is not uncommon. Goethe, after leaving his fiancée, had a vision of himself: so did Poe, Hans Andersen, d'Annunzio, Dostoevsky and many others, including Aristotle. I have described two or three cases in detail in the opening chapter. One man claimed to be able to summon his double at will. Such Doppelgängers are usually reversed left-to-right, and some are cut off at the waist, which suggests that they arise from seeing oneself in a mirror. As with other hallucinations, they are frequently (but not always) associated with disease, alcoholism, epilepsy, brain tumour or with a feeling of anxiety and grief. One woman saw herself bending over a bed, wearing the clothes which she had worn three months before when her child was dying in the same bed.

The counterpart of autoscopy is the out-of-the-body experience, in which one's body is seen from outside. I mentioned several cases in the opening chapter, such as that of Augustus Hare who, when a boy, thought himself up near the transom of the door looking down on himself. I once had a similar experience, lying, rather tired, on a bed in the Clift Hotel, San Francisco. I was trying to imagine how I would look to myself; I constructed, so to say, an image of myself in the air above me, when, suddenly, I was up near the ceiling, in the image, looking down at myself. I interpret this realistically: I think the egoge system got linked to the image instead of to my body scheme, owing to the intensity with which I was visualising. A friend has told me that, when in labour in hospital, under pethidine, she had the impression of leaving her body (which she saw straining on the delivery table) and going to Paris for a walk beside the Seine. Others recount still more elaborate journeys 'out of the body' and Celia Green of the Institute of Psychophysical Research has collected many of them and analysed them. Professor Charles Tart, in California, experimented with a man who claimed to be able to do this regularly. He was to acquire data while out of the body – such as reading a message left on a shelf or visiting the next room to see what was going on. On returning to normality, he was to give an account of what he had learned. Unfortunately, few of the experiments were wholly convincing.

Another curious illusion is known as palinopsia: the persistence of a visual sensation after the stimulus has ceased. It occurs with some brain tumours. In one case, simply a colour persisted: after looking at a pink blanket, everything appeared to the patient to be pink. In another case, the image was of a picture which she had not seen for eight or ten years. This sensory persistence can occur with other senses. Thus a man felt his hand being gripped by a hand, many minutes after it had ceased to be. But it is quite normal to feel the pressure of a hat after it has been removed, or the feeling one is wearing a ring, which has been removed. And after being on a ship the solid ground may seem to heave for some hours. These are sensory after-images. Where a tumour is present, the mechanism may operate with unusual force.

Oddest of all are the Lilliputian hallucinations reported by the French alienist, R. Leroy. Miniature people and animals co-exist with normal-size tables, chairs, etc. The figures occasionally speak in Lilliputian voices. Alfred de Musset, when ill in bed, and talking to his brother, saw four genies come and rearrange the room as it had been before he was ill. He complained that it had formerly been dusty. A miniature figure then appeared distributing dust. Alcoholics have described seeing regiments of artillery, theatrical scenes, processions, smiling girls and so forth. They hide under furniture, jump out of the window, climb ladders or feast. One old man, in an advanced state of paresis, saw files of people entering by the window and disappearing into the frieze on the wall. Anatole France has described something of the sort in *Sylvestre Bonnard*. Thus the brain can combine real with fancied imagery.

Mythopoeic Faculty: The Mind's Eye

'My eyes make pictures when they are shut,' said Coleridge, in his poem 'A Day Dream'. This may have been hypnogogic imagery, but for many writers the pictures are a source of material – not just of inspiration but of quite detailed stories.

There is a particularly clear account by, of all people, Enid Blyton, the well-known writer of stories for small children, in a letter to the psychologist Peter McKellar: 'I shut my eyes for a few minutes, with my portable typewriter on my knee; I make my mind a blank and wait – and then, as clearly as I would see real children, my characters stand before me in mind's eye . . . The story is enacted almost as if I had a private cinema screen there . . . I don't know what is going to happen. I am in the happy position of being able to write a story and read it for the first time at one and the same moment . . . Sometimes a character makes a joke, a really funny one that makes me laugh as I type it on my paper and I think, "Well, I couldn't have thought of that myself in a hundred years!", and then I think: "Well, *who* did think of it?" '

The feeling that their material comes from elsewhere has occurred to many writers: Stevenson, for example, spoke of his 'Brownies' who worked while he slept. Rosamond Harding collected many examples of this in her book *An Anatomy of Inspiration*, originally published in 1940, from which I will quote: 'Dickens declared that when he sat down to write "some beneficent power" showed it all to him. Thackeray says in the *Round-about-Papers*, "I have been surprised at the observations made by some of my characters. It seems as if an occult Power was moving the pen. The personage does or says something and I ask: how the dickens did he come to think of that?" '

And again, Blake, referring to his poem 'Milton', in a letter to Thomas Butts, says, 'I have written this poem from immediate dictation, twelve or sometimes twenty or thirty lines at a time, without premeditation, and even against my will.' Goethe looked upon his genius as a mysterious power; his poems came to him of themselves and at times even against his will. 'The songs made me,' he says, 'and not I them; the songs had me in their power.' The description of Apollo in the third book of *Hyperion* seemed to Keats to have come 'by chance or magic – to be as it were something given to him'. He said also that he had often 'not been aware of the beauty of some thought or expression until after he had composed and written it down. It has then struck him with astonishment and seemed rather the production of another person than his own.'

The evidence is strong, but the phenomenon is so odd that I want to cite George Eliot, who puts the matter particularly strongly. She told a friend, J. W. Cross, 'that, in all that she considered her best writing, there was a "not herself" which took possession of her and that she felt her own personality to be merely the instrument through which this spirit, as it were, was acting.'

It is not only writers who are thus inspired, or 'possessed'. Musicians, too, such as Elgar, who looked upon himself as 'the all but unconscious medium' through which the works were created. Tchaikovsky and Parry likewise.

Many of these reports also reveal a sense of compulsion, even obsession. Dickens, writing *A Christmas Carol*, 'wept over it, and laughed, and wept again, and excited himself to an extraordinary degree . . . and walked, thinking of it, fifteen and twenty miles about the black streets of London' when most people were in bed.

Contrary, therefore, to all those wiseacres, from Hughlings Jackson to Max Rosenblueth, who assert that to speak of an unconscious mind is a contradiction in terms, we must accept that very extraordinary powers of recombination of experience exist at a non-conscious level – or else we have to accept that inspiration comes from a psychic world. Not from whimsy did the Greeks, who liked to personify their concepts, suppose that there existed Muses from whom, if you humbly attended them, inspiration might come.

In much the same way, scientists have had intellectual problems solved for them, so to say, by their unconscious: Lord Kelvin, Edison, even Einstein. Alfred Wallace, co-discoverer of evolution with Darwin, said: 'Ideas and beliefs are certainly not voluntary acts. They come to us – we hardly know *how* or *whence* . . .' The French mathematician Poincaré tells of worrying over an obscure mathematical problem (whether there were any functions analogous to Fuchsian functions) and having found there were, 'At this moment I left Caen where I was then living, in order to take part in a geological conference arranged by the School of Mines. The incidents of my journey made me forget my work. When we arrived at Coutances, we got into a brake to go for a drive, and, just as I put my foot on the step, the idea came to me, though nothing in my former thoughts seemed to have prepared me for it; that the transformations I had used to define the Fuchsian functions were identical with those of non-Euclidean geometry. I made no verification and had not time to do so, since I took up the conversation again as soon as I had sat down in the brake, but I felt absolute certainty at once. When I got back to Caen I verified the result at my leisure to satisfy my conscience.

'I then began to study arithmetical questions without any great apparent result and without suspecting that they could have the least connection with my previous researches. Disgusted at my want of success I went away to spend a few days at the seaside and thought of entirely different things. One day as I was walking on the cliff, the idea came to me, again with the same characteristics of conciseness, suddenness and immediate certainty, that arithmetical transformations of ternary indefinite quadratic forms are identical with those of non-Euclidean geometry.' Then a third problem arose from these; he was called up for army service and one day, crossing the street, the answer again occurred to him, though he did not have any opportunity to fathom it until his service was finished. Then, 'I had all the elements and had only to assemble and arrange them. Accordingly I composed my definitive treatise at a sitting and without any difficulty.'

I have no idea what the mathematical problem signified, but one does not need to be a mathematician to perceive that something very odd was going on. And one may be rather envious of an unconscious which so conveniently provides you with ideas which lead you to world fame.

There seems to be a close kinship between the internal cinema screen of people like Enid Blyton and the curiously coherent dreams which Celia Green, the parapsychologist, has christened 'lucid dreams'. Only the night before I sat down to write these lines, I found myself involved (in a dream) in a sequence of adventures in a Middle Eastern country which would have served as part of a thriller. (Unfortunately, I was awoken before the mystery was solved and I cannot recall the earlier part of the dream.) Unlike most of my dreaming, which is episodic and very tedious – I usually seem to be trying to make a deadline with too many tasks to carry out in the time available – this dream was full of incident, mysterious threats, unexpected clues, and sinister characters. Even the clothes they wore were photographically clear. On another occasion, I was involved in a personal scene with a film actor (known to me in real life) and his bodyguard. Such dreams have a strong dramatic plot, unlike every-night dreaming.

The poet who wrote under the pseudonym A.E. felt that 'our dreams and visions come into our sphere out of other spheres of being and are not built up from memories of earth . . . I walk out of a strange city, steeped in the jewel glow of evening, or sail in galleys over the silvery waves of the antique ocean . . .' he said, and asked, 'is it only on earth that there has been this long ancestry of self?' He was aware of 'elemental beings, shining creatures of water and wood, or who break out in opalescent colours from the rocks or hold their court beneath the ponderous hills'. And he adds, 'I know I have not been alone in such imaginations. I have spoken to others.'

He describes one such experience thus: 'I was meditating about twenty-one years ago, when my meditation was broken by a series of pictures which flashed before me with the swiftness of moving pictures. They had no relation I could discover to the subject of my meditation.' He was taken to a wooded valley, where a vast figure, aureoled with light, descended from the sky and assumed human shape. The figure vanished and next he saw a woman in a blue cloak, with a child on her lap, with light rays converging on her. This was followed by a shot of a royal coronation (he might well have seen religious pictures suggesting the first two images, but, as the year was 1898, there had not been a coronation in his lifetime). The sequence then became apocalyptic, with burning cities and the whole of Ireland lit up, followed by a pantheistic experience.

A dream in which both narrative and problem-solving are features was related by H. V. Hilprecht, an archaeologist working at the University of Pennsylvania; it is of such interest that I shall tell it in detail. Hilprecht had been struggling to decipher a cuneiform inscription on a broken clay cylinder from the Assyrian site Nippur. Going to bed at midnight, exhausted, he dreamed he was visited by a priest of some non-Christian religion, aged about forty and clad in an *abba*. The priest led him to the treasure chamber of a temple, and into a small, windowless room where there was a large chest; scraps of agate and lapis lazuli lay scattered on the floor. The priest said to him: 'The two fragments which you have published separately on pages twenty-two and twenty-six belong together; they are not finger rings and their history is as follows: King Kurigalzu [who, Hilprecht knew, lived *c.* 1300 BC] once sent to the temple of Bel, among other articles of agate and lapis lazuli, an inscribed votive cylinder of agate.

'Then we priests suddenly received the command to make for the statue of the god Ninib a pair of earrings of agate. We were in great dismay because there was no agate, as raw material, at hand. In order to carry out the command there was nothing for us to do but to cut the votive cylinder into three parts, thus making three rings – each of which contained a portion of the original inscription. The first two rings served as earrings for the statue of the god; the two fragments which have given you so much trouble are portions of them. But the third ring you have not yet found in the course of your excavations and you will never find it.' With this the priest disappeared.

'I awoke at once,' Hilprecht relates, 'and told my wife the dream that I might not forget it. Next morning – Sunday – I examined the fragments once more in the light of these disclosures and to my astonishment found all the details of the dream precisely verified, insofar as the means of verification were in my hands. The original inscription of the votive cylinder read: "To the god Ninib, son of Bel, his lord, has Kurigalzu, pontifex of Bel, presented this".'

But although Hilprecht had a plausible solution to his problem, actual verification was still to come. In August of the same year he was sent by the University to Constantinople (now Istanbul) to catalogue further objects retrieved from Nippur. He took the opportunity to tell the director of the Museum of his dream and was given permission to look for the missing fragments. Sure enough, he found the fragments – they were in two different cases, as the Assyriologist who had arranged the collection had not realised that they belonged together. Hilprecht put the two bits together and, bingo! they fitted.

The psychologist Gardner Murphy, retelling the story, comments that Hilprecht had all the necessary data; it only needed his unconscious to put it together. But he does not explain why the solution came to him in such dramatic form.

The faculty for making stories might be dubbed 'the mythopoeic faculty'. It also emerges in automatic writing, as we see from the case of 'Patience Worth'. A Mrs John Curran produced a string of novels about the seventeenth century, much praised in their time but, to my jaundiced ear, pretentious historical flummery, full of unconvincing phrases like: 'Saw-drip would build thy head,' and unheard-of formations like 'a-there' and 'a-neath'. She claimed – if you think it was her mind which was animating the ouija-board – 'Many moons ago I lived. Again I come. My name is Patience Worth.'

Unfortunately, among the gadzookery were some modernisms like 'check', in the sense of 'verify'. Thus the origin was not psychic; it was the mythopoeic faculty. And from Patience Worth it is only a short step to the elaborate fantasies of Hélène Smith, who claimed (you may recall) to be a reincarnation of Cagliostro, Marie Antoinette and others. She gave a detailed account of her journey to the planet Mars, and what she found there, including specimens of the Martian language. For example: 'Dodé né ci haudan té mess métiché astané ké dé mé véché,' which means: 'This is the home of the great man Astane, whom you saw.' Language experts pointed out that the structure of this language was basically French; still, to invent an entire language is quite a feat.

The psychoanalyst R. Lindner also had a patient who reported visiting Mars and gave most detailed accounts of that planet – accounts which are not, I need hardly say, borne out by the pictures sent back from the spacecraft which landed there.

In the circumstances, I feel that we have to regard the reports of those who claim to be reincarnations of people who lived earlier with some distrust: the capacity to fabricate (quite unconsciously, without intentional deceit) a convincing yarn must be fully allowed for. A case in point is the American girl who claimed, under hypnosis, to be the reincarnation of an Irish girl, Bridey Murphy, who lived in Dublin early in the nineteenth century. It later turned out that she had picked up her Irishisms, and even the name Bridey, from a beloved Irish nurse. Even so, the story she told was so detailed and plausible that for a long time no one could pick a hole in it.

Conclusion

We have so much information about imagery that one has the impression that we must be on the verge of understanding what goes on, yet the answer remains tantalisingly elusive. Are hallucinations dreams which force their way up into the waking state, as Dr Roy Whitman, of Cincinnati University, thinks? Alcohol inhibits dreaming – but alcoholics are not the only ones who hallucinate.

Is thought impossible without imagery, as some claim, or are images mere ghosts without functional significance, as the behaviourist Watson insisted?

Personally, I side with Alan Paivio of Western Ontario, when he says that there are two systems: a visual imagery specialised for spatial tasks and a verbal system for symbolic ones – to which I would add that there is also a system of meta-feelings, all three contributing to thought.

Another question which arises is: how are visual images stored? A rough impression, or a detailed photograph, or the details individually? Perhaps the last. Many schizophrenics go through periods in which they are unable to perceive wholes and seem to break up images into details in a curious way. Looking at a nurse or a doctor, they see only a nose, an arm or an eye. The psychiatrist Dr Silvano Arieti describes a patient who, in an acute episode of dangerous excitement, had been confined in a 'seclusion cell' – a polite name for a padded cell. Afterwards she told him that she could not look at the whole door of the cell. She could see only the knob, or keyhole or a corner of the door. Other patients recalled how, at first, the big unities were divided into smaller units, but as their excitement increased, these were divided into smaller fragments. Arieti believes that the same thing occurs in delirium and perhaps in some normal dreams; but memory fails when the brain is so disorganised, which is why the fact has rarely been reported. He comments that the drawings made by schizophrenics often show a similar fragmentation.

Something quite similar has been described by the great Russian psychologist Aleksandr Luria, only his patient was not schizophrenic but had suffered a brain injury in the occipital lobe, on both sides. I.R. was a forty-eight-year-old bookkeeper who was admitted to the Bourdenko Neurosurgical Institute because he could see only single letters, not words. He could see, when he looked at the road, only one car at a time. 'I know that there are many,' he said, 'but I see only one.' He could not avoid colliding with other people. When, during a snowstorm, he looked at the entrance to the house, he could see the door but not the snow falling. Naturally, he had difficulty writing, often placing one letter on top of another. When he tried to draw a circle, he could not see both the circle and the tip of the pencil at the same time.

He improved miraculously when given a drug which facilitates the transmission of certain nervous impulses – to be exact, an anticholinergic. Luria concluded that I.R.'s condition arose from excessive inhibition in the occipital cortex, resulting in restriction of excitation to a single point. One or two similar cases have been reported by British workers.

(It has been claimed that this case shows that the brain does not carry images, only descriptions, but I cannot see how this follows.)

We do not even understand what regulates the intensity of images – though we know that psychedelic drugs intensify them, and that schizophrenics often report that colours are more brilliant, sounds louder, and so on. (One man's first indication that something was wrong came when the alarm clock woke him one morning: it seemed intolerably loud and to go on unendingly.) If we knew what the mechanism was, perhaps we could understand the difference between memory images, hypnogogic images and eidetic ones.

The German philosopher Karl Jaspers said that hallucinations were quite distinct from imagery, because they were 'out there', clearly defined and persistent. But as we have seen, eidetic imagery is 'out there' and persists as long as many hallucinations. And hypnogogic images are certainly clearly defined. It seems more economical to suppose there is one basic imagery, which can be modified, rather as one can shift the intensity, colour and contrast of a television set by adjusting its controls.

Of course, the biggest problem about imagery is how we store so many images, and how we fish up the images we want so easily and speedily. In other words, we must now consider the whole question of memory.

PART FOUR

Processing

15

Thanks for the Memory

MY PAST LIFE FLASHED BEFORE ME

In 1892, the Swiss geologist Albert Heim, who was exploring in the Alps, fell off a precipice. As he fell, his past life flashed before his eyes. Being a man trained to record his observations, he did what few have done and recorded his impressions as exactly as he could, for he did not lose his life. In the five or ten seconds which he estimated his fall to have taken, he was submerged in a flood of impressions. He watched the news of his death reach his family, and tried to console them in his thoughts. 'Then I saw as if on a distant stage my whole past life playing itself out in numerous scenes. I saw myself as the chief actor. Everything was bathed in a heavenly light and was beautiful and without pain. Also the distant memory of very sad happenings appeared, yet they were not sad.' He felt he was floating painlessly into and out of tender pink and violet cloudlets in a blue sky. Then he suddenly saw the snowfield beneath him and as he hit it 'a black object whooshed in front of my eyes'.

Source: A. Heim, 'Notizen über den Tod durch Absturz', *Jahrbuch des Schweiz. Alpenklub*, Bern 27:327–37 (1892).

The Three Rs

'It seems certain,' says the *Encyclopaedia Britannica*, that the Cardinal Giuseppe Mezzofanti, chief keeper of the Vatican Library from 1833, 'spoke with considerable fluency and in some cases with attention to dialectic peculiarities, some fifty or sixty languages of the most widely separated families, besides having a less perfect acquaintance with many others.'

Extraordinary memories are not all that uncommon, oddly enough, though they are very difficult to account for. There are Jewish scholars, it is said, who can recall the exact position on the page of every word on every page of all twelve volumes of the *Talmud*.

While you and I are stunned and envious at such feats, the memory of we ordinary people is remarkable enough. I suppose that if one were to write down everything one knew, it would fill as many volumes as the *Encyclopaedia Britannica*. There would be a volume of faces and places that we had seen, of town maps and features of roads, there would be the interior of many houses and buildings with the precise location of books, pictures and other objects. There would be a volume of poetry, synopses of plots of books, films and plays. There would be many pages of music to represent all the tunes we can recognise and the songs we can sing. The details of our daily work would certainly call for another volume. Of course, there would be linguistic rules and a fair-sized dictionary. Perhaps another for our hobbies and recreations, with the rules and techniques of various sports and suchlike activities. Our own biography would fill yet another volume. And this is far from exhausting the list. All this data contained in a lump of tissue no bigger than a plum pudding, along with much other equipment, and most of it available on demand within a second or less.

Far from being satisfied with this sophisticated aid to gracious living, most of us complain that we have memories 'like sieves' and would welcome simple methods of uprating them. It has been calculated, in fact, that the brain can only retain about one hundredth of the information it receives in a lifetime. We are thus bound to forget ninety-nine out of every hundred bits of data presented to us. Actually, the situation is a little worse than that, because the information flow-rate often exceeds the rate at which the memory can file the data, so there will be times when we register much less than one-hundredth of what is going on, and this is not compensated by the periods of slow information-flow, when our memories are underworked. But how do we know what to forget? Because of this overload we have evolved methods of clearing the files continuously of what is likely to be least important. This purging process we call 'forgetting'.

Memory, like a filing system, involves at least three processes: information must be entered into the system, stored without deterioration, and recovered when needed. These processes are generally known to psychologists as the three Rs: registration, retention and recall. (Since nowadays it is smart to use computer talk, there are psychologists who choose to say: input, storage and read-out.) Forgetting, accordingly, could be due to breakdown of any one of these three processes. There are those however who claim that the storage system is faultless. Nothing, once entered, is ever forgotten, they maintain. It is simply recall which fails. The file becomes lost, but it is still there, somewhere. Thus Aldous Huxley wrote: 'Reflecting on my experience, I find myself agreeing with the eminent Cambridge philosopher, Dr C. D. Broad, "That we should do well to consider much more seriously than we have hitherto been inclined to do the type of theory which Bergson put forward in connection with memory and sense perception. The suggestion is that the function of the brain and nervous system and sense organs is in the main *eliminative* and not productive. Each person is at each moment capable of remembering all that has ever happened to him and of perceiving everything that is happening everywhere in the universe. The function of the brain and nervous system is to protect us from being overwhelmed by this mass of useless and largely irrelevant knowledge, by shutting out most of what we should otherwise perceive or remember at any moment, and leaving only that small and special selection which is likely to be practically useful." '

Dr Broad was a leading member of the Society for Psychical Research, and leaned towards such a theory since it would provide a basis for thought transference and the seeing of 'phantasms of the living'. I am rather sceptical of such universal *perception.* What we now know of perception runs quite contrary to this, and it is hard to fit it into the evolutionary picture. Presumably animals, with their smaller brains, would shut out less, and unicellular creatures would know everything! Thus the end towards which evolution would tend would be universal ignorance. Memory may be another story: the eminent psychiatrist Paul Schilder believed that nothing was ever lost.

Certainly, there is good reason nowadays to believe that we remember more than we know. Under hypnosis, it is possible to recover 'repressed' memories – that is, painful memories which record events of which we were conscious at the time they occurred. But, what is much more surprising, it is sometimes possible to recover memories we never knew we had. As I have already mentioned, various police forces are now regularly using hypnosis to recover such material, and they have come up with such details as the numbers of cars which they claim not to have been aware of – rather as one might take a snapshot of the scene and only on studying the print discover details one had not noticed at the time the snapshot was taken. The American police now regularly use hypnotists in this way.

The Fourth 'R'

The mystery of memory is further complicated by the fact that there is a fourth process, recognition, which does not seem to be quite the same as recall. One may recognise the long-forgotten face of a person seen many years before, or have a sudden sense of familiarity on visiting a house one had quite forgotten visiting.

Professor Ralph Norman Haber of Rochester University is one of the few people to have attempted experimental studies of recognition. He exposed two thousand five hundred and sixty slides showing a range of photographs to volunteers at the rate of one every ten seconds. (In some cases, there were two-hour sessions on four consecutive days; on others, two four-hour sessions. It made no difference to the results.) The subjects were then shown two hundred and eighty pairs of pictures, one of which was drawn from the series already seen, the other similar in nature but unfamiliar. Asked to say which of the two was familiar, the subjects were right nine times out of ten. Even when the familiar pictures were shown reversed, left-for-right scores declined only slightly. These results suggest, Haber comments: 'that recognition of pictures is essentially perfect. The results would probably have been the same if we had used twenty-five thousand pictures instead of two thousand five hundred.'

Such results are baffling and bring stock theories of memory into confusion. Haber went on to show that the pictures he displayed could not have been stored in memory in the form of words, and concluded that linguistic memory is different from pictorial memory. Not a surprising finding, in itself. (Incidentally, the word 'memory' properly refers to the storage system and not to the items stored.)

However recognition is not confined to the visual. We can recognise a tune as familiar, and even a taste or a smell. What kind of substrate can bear the impress of such different inputs? Some such substrate there must be, but researchers have so concentrated on visual and verbal memory they overlook the scope of the problem.

Verbal memory is certainly distinct from visual and auditory. In cases where patients have had the temporal portion of one hemisphere removed in an attempt to control epilepsy, it is found that, when the left side is removed, verbal memory – both for spoken and written material – is impaired; where the right side is taken, it is memory for complex visual or auditory patterns which suffers. Presumably recognition is similarly distributed. But these are not the only memory systems.

I have no doubt also that there is a third memory system concerned with physical skills, the so-called kinaesthetic memory, and since physical co-ordination is effected by the little brain or cerebellum, I would take a modest bet that this is where it is located. Not long ago, while attending a meeting in Austria, I had occasion to ride a bicycle for the first time in thirty years. For a minute or two, though I was riding it perfectly successfully, I experienced a slight lack of confidence. I felt that I must concentrate my attention on what I was doing, since I could not wholly rely on my automatic reactions. But this soon passed, and I found myself riding as if I had been doing it every day for years. This well-known experience, which also applies to playing the piano and many other skills, suggests that kinaesthetic memory is less troubled by forgetfulness than verbal memory, and hence may be distinct from it. Moreover, people who lose their memories after a blow on the head not infrequently retain their skills unimpaired.

Curiously enough, psychologists have given no attention, so far as I know, to the possibility that there is also a separate memory for emotions.

Do we remember the *emotion* we once felt – the rapture of love, the grinding of anxiety, the shock of fear – or do we merely remember the *fact* of having experienced it? Certainly emotions fade. However, as we shall see, each part of the brain seems to carry the memory appropriate to the function it performs. So, as we have a part of the brain concerned primarily with feelings, it is logical to suppose that it remembers them. Without such an arrangement, it would, I think, be unable to know what emotion it was feeling at any given moment. The majority of psychologists are all too apt to talk about memory as if there were only one kind. In particular, they draw conclusions from studies of verbal memory and assume very readily that they apply to other forms of memory too.

I was interested to find, therefore, as I researched for this book, that a Russian psychologist named Blonsky, who has made memory his special subject, also considers that there are four levels of memory: verbal, visual, emotional and motor (or kinaesthetic), which complements my own impression. Blonsky examined school-children at various ages from this point of view and showed there were marked age differences in ability which varied with the different modes of memory.

It is even possible, I think, that there may be a fifth memory mode, namely conceptual memory. The fact that we can reproduce the content of a story accurately, but in different words, shows that we do not necessarily store it in words, or like a tape-recorder does. It is possible, I suppose, that we achieve this either by forming suitable images – we see a mental picture of Little Red Riding Hood visiting her grandmother – or, in some cases, by promptly translating the story into a condensed paraphrase.

There may also be a spatial memory: cells have been found in the hippocampus of trained rats which only fire when the rat is in a certain position in the maze. Perhaps there are even more than six memories. One psychologist has listed as many as twenty-three types of memory. It certainly seems that we should be cautious in speaking of memory, *tout court*, and should perhaps speak of memory systems. And we should think twice before generalising from facts learned by the study of a particular form of memory. On the other hand, I cannot believe there are as many as ten or twenty distinct systems. I can imagine more easily four memories: kinaesthetic in the cerebellum; verbal in the dominant hemisphere and visual in the minor hemisphere; and some cruder non-visual, non-conceptual system in the mid-brain. Something of this kind would account for a good many of the discrepancies. But there is also another puzzling distinction which exercises psychologists considerably.

How Many Memories?

Sergei Sergeivich Korsakoff was a brilliant psychiatrist, one of the founders of Russian psychiatry, who died in 1900 aged forty-six. He was among the first to free mental patients from restraint in strait-jackets and is credited with establishing the concept of paranoia. But his name has gone down in medical history as the discoverer of Korsakoff's Syndrome. He observed that chronic alcoholics suffered loss of permanent memory. The victims could talk normally, answer questions about the present, carry out tests of dexterity and so on; but they remembered nothing for more than a few minutes. If a person in this condition is asked a question, and the question is repeated ten minutes later, he has no recollection of the previous query. If the doctor has to leave the room for a few minutes, he is greeted on his return as someone the patient has not met for a long time. One amnesic patient of Professor George Talland's permanently thought she had been brought to the hospital the day before, and still felt convinced of this eight years after her admission. In extreme cases, the patient's entire past life is blotted out; he does not remember that he is married or where he was born. He may think of his wife and himself as being the same age as they were when he was hospitalised many years before.

The condition is caused by failure of the liver to eliminate toxins, and can result from meningitis, from lack of oxygen, from lead poisoning and frequently from excessive consumption of alcohol.

This and other facts have given rise to the idea that memory is of at least two kinds, usually known as long-term memory and short-term memory or recent memory. Recent memory is what enables us to hold a telephone number (for example) while we dial it, and even then we usually have to renew the trace by repeating it to ourself. Recent memory may last as little as ten seconds.

It is a highly controversial point whether long-term memory arises simply by the consolidation or etching-in of short-term memory, or whether two different systems are involved.

Actually, the Korsakoff syndrome is rather more than a failure of memory. The sufferer seems to lose his critical faculties and cannot make use of information available: he seems to be in a dreamlike state and cannot fully distinguish the real world from his thoughts and imaginings. He is confused about the time-order of events, and does not seem to relate what is happening to himself. (In one case, a Mr Bon, it is reported that his verbal memory persisted although his visual memory failed, if not his entire imagery: he could form no image or map of his surroundings.)

However, the evidence for the two types of memory does not depend upon Korsakoff's observations. There are other facts, such as that short-term memories seem to be associated by sound whereas long-term memories are associated by meaning. Or the fact that blocking the synthesis of proteins in the brain (the experiment is usually done in goldfish, the brains of which are easy to get at) impairs long-term memory but not short-term. This experiment also supports the idea that long-term memory has a chemical basis, while short-term memory may have an electrical one. If you teach an animal to respond to a stimulus in a certain way, and then apply an electric current to its head, you find that anything learned in the previous half-hour has gone but that earlier memories remain. Again, if you cool the animal to freezing point and then revive it, the most recent memories are found to have vanished. Since cooling stops the electrical activity of the brain, this gives plausibility to the idea that short-term memory is electrical in nature. On the other hand, you can cool a human being to just above freezing point and he will talk to you quite coherently, yet remember nothing afterwards. This could mean that transfer from short-term to long-term memory is impaired.

Some psychologists argue, rather passionately, that there is only one kind of memory but that the records take some time to 'consolidate'. However, on balance, the evidence seems to be against this. Both electrical and chemical processes are certainly involved. Some workers think the difference lies in the retrieval system rather than in the retention mechanism, while one or two believe there is an intermediate system between short and long. They point to the fact that some short-term memories vanish in seconds, while others last for as much as half an hour. We also have a brief visual memory, lasting less than a second, called iconic memory, but it does not bear on my theme so I omit it.

In short the situation is remarkably confused, and David Rapaport's prophecy, 'A revolution in the theory of memory is in the offing,' seems no nearer fulfilment than it did when he made it a good many years ago.

Yet one more distinction can be made.

You may have had the experience of walking along a street, vaguely aware of the passers by, when suddenly it is borne in on you that one of them was an old friend. You stop, turn round to find him doing the same thing, and apologise for not at once recognising him. 'My mind was elsewhere,' you say. But the fact was you did recognise him, if belatedly, so your mind was monitoring the situation pretty well. Here is the basis of the 'double take' beloved of comedians.

This experience suggested to the pharmacologist Charles Fair, in the fifties, that we have a 'type' memory and a 'thing' memory for specifics.

The 'type' memory is vaguely checking on the environment, observing people, buses, street intersections and so forth. When it needs to know more, it calls on the higher centres to analyse in detail: to say if the traffic lights are at red, for example. Since, as we have seen, neurones are arranged in vertical columns of increasing generality of functions, Fair was happy to locate his type memory in the fourth layer of the cerebral cortex.

After visiting a house, we might say, 'I remember there was a big picture over the hearth,' without being able to say what the picture showed. We have recorded the type but not the thing. Memory, in short, can be at more than one level of generality. And the contents seem to be arranged in time-order.

For my part, I think we should treat this as an aspect of attention, rather than memory. But of course the two are closely intertwined, and to say we have a non-specific attention implies that we also have a non-specific memory.

I apologise for so much preliminary clearing of the ground, but the subject of memory is open to so many confusions that I could not tell the story of its investigation without some definition of terms.

The Associationists

Serious study of memory started when a young German philosopher and historian, Herman Ebbinghaus, was seized with the idea that experimental methods could be applied to such higher mental functions as memory and sensation. After five strenuous years, in which he acted both as subject and as experimenter, his book *On Memory* appeared in 1885 (under the German title *Über das Gedächtnis*) and started a tradition which still flourishes. His work is still quoted in contemporary textbooks. Ebbinghaus wished to eliminate the influence on memory of meaning and interest in the topic; he therefore invented over two thousand nonsense words, such as DAK and VAR and ZUB. Any set of these syllables, he reckoned, would be equally difficult to remember. He set himself to learn lists of various lengths and to see, on trying to repeat them, how far he could go without making an error. He found that he could learn seven syllables at a single reading; but that he needed fifteen repetitions to absorb twelve syllables, and as many as fifty to learn thirty.

There are many variants of this technique. How many syllables can be recalled after an hour, after a day, after a week? How much re-learning will bring the learner back to perfection?

After publication of his path-making book, Ebbinghaus, now a professor, gave up the subject of memory for ever, exhausted (I have no doubt) by the overwhelming tedium of stuffing his mind with GUG, ERK and VOD. He did, however, coin an epigram when he remarked that psychology has a long past but a short history. Epigrams are so rare in psychology that he must be duly credited.

Since that date, countless students have been subjected to like tedium, presented with an inexhaustible stream of nonsense at one-second intervals by revolving drums. Journals have been founded to chronicle these painstaking studies. Yet, after almost a century of effort, no real understanding has been gained.

I find this far from surprising. Memory is a capacity evolved to improve our chances of survival. Accordingly, it is concerned with meanings, with what is pleasurable, promising or painful. We do not just learn by rote but seek to understand a situation. Even the humble rat, when the floor of his cage is electrified, learns how to escape a shock, by one means or another: he does not just learn a set of muscular movements.

Furthermore, it was not until man appeared on the scene that memory had anything to do with words. Hence Ebbinghaus and his long trail of followers, in their desire to study 'pure' memory, 'decoupled' as they like to say from meaning and feeling, threw out the baby with the bathwater. Rote memory is the *least* normal kind of memory.

In the twentieth century, the study of memory was further bedevilled by the rise of associationism: the theory that the brain works by linking a stimulus with a response. I have already made clear what I think about this grotesque doctrine, which was held with quasi-religious fervour. In consequence, memory came to be regarded as an association process, and the learning of lists was dropped in favour of the pairing of words. But what happens if you pair UGH with LAWN on Monday and then ask the victim to pair it with AISLE on Tuesday? He becomes understandably confused. This is known as 'the interference theory of forgetting'.

But is the second pairing interfering with the first, or is it the other way about? Attempts to resolve this problem have merely added to the confusion. Thus if we call the list of pairs first learned List A and the second List B, we find that on immediate test List B is remembered best, but that after twenty-four hours the recall of this list declines although that of list A does not. However, if the subjects (or victims) are given a long and short list to memorise and are tested after a week, they recall the long list better than the short! Experiment suggests that forgetting depends on the length of the list rather than on the number of intervening items, i.e., it does not depend on interference. Recognition experiments also fail to confirm this theory. One of the stalwarts in the field, after reviewing the subject, reluctantly concluded: 'The most obvious possibility is of course that the interference theory of forgetting is fundamentally wrong.' That didn't stop anyone, though.

Recently, associationists have got themselves into the even more recondite question of how we remember the order in which things are presented: they like to believe that each word is associated with the one which precedes it.

Thus 'serial order' studies were expected to provide support for associationism. But here too they met with disappointment. As the same authority sadly concluded: 'The outcome of such tests can be summarised only too briefly. With a few scattered exceptions, the deductions from the theory failed to be supported.'

There is a phenomenon in psychology known as perseveration: it means going on doing what you're doing, even though it is getting you nowhere. Physician, heal thyself!

After seventy-five years of barking up dead trees, the whole field of memory is wide open for a new, more pragmatic and less doctrinaire attack.

Forgotten Aspects of Forgetting

A more enlightened approach was that of Frederick Bartlett of Cambridge University. His most important book, *Remembering*, was published in 1932 and is still in circulation. Starting with a study of the real-life recall of battle experiences in the First World War, he showed conclusively that people do not simply register passively what is presented to them, but select and interpret the material in terms of their current attitudes and interests and, when they remember, they often consolidate two memories into one, or alter details unwittingly, and they progressively simplify it. For instance, if the subject is presented with a picture of a square-jawed face, he may remember it as a 'grim, determined face' and later recall it in profile, so that the jaw line is emphasised, even though he originally saw it full face.

Bartlett also gave students stories to learn and tested them at various intervals afterwards – a week, a month, six months. Analysing the results, he considered that we fit specific memories into larger patterns he called 'schemata'. For instance, a story of prejudice might be fitted into a scheme of 'racial intolerance'. 'The schema is where and why consciousness come in,' he said. It is extraordinary that so few attempts have been made to follow this lead. If nothing else, it shows the naïveté of 'storehouse' conceptions of memory. What makes the heart sink is the enormous waste of time: generations of effort and hecatombs of rats have been sacrificed for almost no return.

It is quite obvious that memory records ('engrams' is the official term) are not stable traces like the grooves in a gramophone record but are repeatedly modified, simplified and amalgamated after they have been formed; information is gradually lost. 'I can remember that we went, but I can't recall anything else about it.'

It is also clear that we remember best what is meaningful. If a chess-board, showing a position from an actual game, is exposed to a Master or Grand Master for a few seconds, he will reproduce it without error, getting some twenty to twenty-five pieces right, where ordinary players will only get about six pieces right. But if the pieces are randomly placed, both non-Masters and Masters will get only about six pieces right.

As Neal Miller has pointed out, the human numerical span is about seven. The chess Masters probably analyse the twenty-five chessmen into some six or seven familiar groupings, which they remember as a whole. Such groupings Miller christened 'chunks'. Herbert Simon tested Miller's idea by trying to remember the following words after one reading: Lincoln, milky, criminal, differential, address, way, lawyer, calculus, Gettysburg. 'I had no success whatever,' he recalls. 'Then I rearranged the list a bit as follows:

Lincoln's Gettysburg Address
Milky Way
Criminal Lawyer
Differential Calculus

I had no difficulty at all. Obvious? It is only obvious if one accepts the chunk hypothesis, and if one knows that, in the culture in which I was raised, the four items in the list are, in fact, familiar chunks.' Simon found that four such chunks was usually the most he could retain, as if the length of the material in each chunk reduced the total number of chunks retainable.

In a now-famous experiment Sidney Smith, in 1954, found he could recall up to forty binary digits by recoding them as octals. Or, to take a simpler example, a Morse-code operator, when just beginning to learn the code, hears each dit and dah as a separate chunk. Soon he organises the sounds into letters and deals with the letters as chunks; later he organises letters as words, and eventually can hear whole phrases. We all do much the same in learning to read.

I seem to be discussing the cognitive process – as usual in such matters, one thing leads to another – but it is not a digression; the point I am seeking to make is that what we remember must also be chunked. Hence memory, like perception and other brain functions, must be hierarchic. As Bartlett said: 'The first notion to get rid of is that memory is primarily or literally reduplicative or reproductive.' And there are not only chunks but also chunks of chunks and chunks of chunks of chunks. Each level may have a different code.

Another curious aspect of memory, which exposes the inadequacy of many theories, is the fact that we remember best in the situation in which we learned. For example, divers who are being trained to perform some operation, such as welding under water, must be trained under water; and if a diver who has explored a wreck under water is debriefed under water he will recall more than he will on the surface. (This, I am sure, is one reason why languages taught in the classroom are much less well retained than languages learned in real-life situations; stronger motivation to communicate is another.) One can infer from this that memories are recorded in a context. When we register a face, we register where we saw it, and the name of the owner or what he said or did, together with many other details. Some of these we may soon forget, but in general the different components of memory lead to one another and we pursue elusive memories by exploring the associations which we do recall. ('It was when we went on the picnic, so who was there that day?') Memories are marvellously cross-indexed. From the idea of leaves I can get to gardening chores, to the leaves of a table, to lamellae in biology, to leafing through a book, or to trees, green objects, leaf insects and so on almost without limit.

One more phenomenon which reveals the poverty of current attempts to force memory into the strait-jacket of 'coding' is the occurrence of unusually vivid memories, technically known as hypermnesia. It seems usually to be at moments of great emotional involvement that memory is raised to this pitch. Thus a student whose father was brought home, without warning, seriously injured in a boiler explosion, recalled the scene, including a vivid recollection of the pattern of the hall rug. A girl, after being involved in a car accident, had vivid memories of what had happened before she went on the trip and that her mother's eyes had never looked so blue. G. M. Stratton at the University of California, who explored this topic back in 1919 – I doubt if anyone has looked at it since – found a girl whose father was killed in a car accident. She wrote out for him a list of hymns sung in church that day, a conversation she had had while drying the dishes, and described the face of a stranger, all of which had registered in her mind with unusual clarity.

Sometimes meeting an old acquaintance after many years will bring memories flooding back; sometimes a smell will do it; or, as in the instance made famous by Proust, a tiny incident such as dipping a cake in tea. But usually these hypermnesic records seemed to be formed during or just before an emotional stress. Details which one was not even aware of perceiving at the time come back.

Conversely, however, emotional stress may block recall – doctors have trouble extracting facts from frightened patients – or perhaps prevent registration altogether. Let us look at amnesia, therefore.

Total Black-outs

In 1935 a young man named Hulson Cason, who was living in Madison, Wisconsin, was skating with a friend when he fell heavily. The next thing he remembered was driving home in his car and being puzzled that it was already dark. 'I realised I did not remember leaving the ice, taking off my skates, putting on my shoes, or driving away in my car.' Very intelligently, he phoned his friend and got him to write an account of what had happened. Cason had lain on the ice for three or four minutes, unconscious, then had risen without help. His friend, observing that he did not seem entirely normal, tried to persuade him to go home, but he refused rather aggressively and went back to skating with more than his usual skill and daring. It was forty-eight minutes after his fall that his memory abruptly returned.

This is a good example of anterograde amnesia, i.e. memory failure which works forward from the time of shock. Commonly, there is retrograde amnesia too, i.e. loss of memories prior to the shock. Ritchie Russell, at Oxford, spends much of his time repairing young men who have landed on their heads when going too fast on their motor cycles, and is one of the world experts on the subject. Anterograde amnesia is mysterious enough: clearly Cason's fall did no structural damage to his brain. It was more as if a switch had snapped into the 'off' position and later snapped 'on' again. Current theories of memory scarcely allow for such a phenomenon: still less can they explain retrograde amnesia. Here memories for months or years before the shock are lost, but gradually return, in reverse order; that is, the remotest memories come back first. But there is usually no recovery for the period immediately before the accident.

The exception to this is that the patient may have one brilliant image: a wheel bearing down upon him was seen by one patient. The driver's hands wrestling with the wheel was seen by another; this vision was seen, quite suddenly, on six occasions, the first two weeks after the accident, the last about two months after. The patient said it was a 'half memory' not recalled in the ordinary way. Russell has no explanation to offer.

In these cases, of course, the patient is so severely concussed that he does not merely lose his memory, but comes to in hospital in a vague state, first groaning and responding to his name; later perhaps talkative but without awareness of what has happened or where he is. Then suddenly he says: 'Where am I?' Something like normality has returned. There is really no explanation for the abruptness of such recoveries: the soul re-entering the body fits the facts better than anything else!

It is not even understood why a severe concussion produces a longer disorder or forgetfulness for a longer time into the past. One would expect the recall mechanism to work fairly normally or not at all.

In contrast with amnesias caused by physical trauma are amnesias caused by mental stress. The repression of painful war memories is an obvious case in point. William Sargant has described how, in the early part of the war, he used drugs such as sodium amytal to recover such memories from soldiers in a state of shock at seeing their best friend sliced in half by a shell, or an airman who had been trapped in a burning plane. When the memory is recovered and the horrible facts are faced, the incident becomes less demoralising. Hypnosis can also be used to recover such repressed memories.

In the same general category of repressed memories come the fugues and multiple personalities, which have already been discussed. Neurologically, this must result from an inhibition of the recall mechanism, but just how this comes about is a fascinating and unstudied problem. Presumably some part of the brain detects the painful emotions associated and issues a countermand. But how does one countermand consciousness of a particular memory? If we knew, we would be on the way to knowing what and where consciousness is.

Perhaps similar and equally mysterious are the transient amnesias. There was sixty-year-old Matilda who had a 'black-out' for some six hours concerning all the facts in the previous six weeks. She had no recollection of watching at a friend's death-bed; shown her son's shirts, she recognised them but could not remember having ironed them. There was the thirty-five-year-old secretary who, coming from church on Christmas Eve, suddenly said to her friend, 'I don't know where to go. I don't think I can drive my car.' There was Mrs M. F., who, having twice thanked her hostess for lunch, said in a puzzled way: 'I have forgotten what to do.'

Transient amnesias sometimes affect motorists, who 'come to' in an unfamiliar part of the city, sitting in their car, and unaware of how they got there. This has been dubbed 'highway hypnosis' and perhaps links the topic to the questions I discussed when dealing with hypnosis. No explanation is available. Transient amnesias can be caused by oxygen shortage, certain drugs and by brain damage. Carbon monoxide causes spectacular irreversible amnesia. Memory is a function of the whole brain and all brain dysfunction implies memory dysfunction.

Finally, there is 'stage fright' or 'spotty forgetting'. Strong arousal, caused by fear or anxiety, swamps the cortex, in extreme cases knocking out the ability to respond rationally. Panic ensues; one runs or is rooted to the spot.

Total Recall

Possibly the most remarkable memory ever known, and certainly the most remarkable memory to be studied scientifically, has been described by Aleksandr Luria. He has handled many patients with head wounds and studied the effect on their behaviour, as I have already related.

In the twenties, when he was still a young man, into his office walked a newspaperman named Solomon Veniaminoff. At a conference his editor had noticed that he took no notes; but that when challenged, he was able immediately to recite the entire discussion. Veniaminoff had no idea that his memory was any different from usual. Luria read him lists of seventy numbers or letters. After one hearing, at a slow pace, he could recite the list forward or backward. Given any letter he would at once name the preceding one. Similarly for word lists. Shown a figure matrix such as this one:

6680
5432
1684
7935
4237
3891
1002
3451
2768
1926
2967
5520
x01x

he would study it for three minutes, then, putting the list away, call out all the numbers in order, vertically or horizontally, or read the diagonals (6485381466665x), and so on. Furthermore, he could recall the list – any list he had thus memorised – weeks, months or even years later.

Luria observes, 'As the experimenter I soon found myself in a state verging on utter confusion. I simply had to admit that the capacity of his memory had *no distinct limits*.'

Luria continued to study Veniaminoff for thirty years, during which time he gave up newspaper work and became a professional mnemonist or memory-man. Eventually he must have had hundreds of thousands of word-lists at his beck and call. He could even tell Luria what suit he was wearing when he had read him a list years before, and whether he was sitting down and how he introduced the subject.

He told Luria he converted the word or figures to writing on a blackboard and occasionally he would get a number wrong, such as an eight or a three, because it was badly written. His main problem was not to remember but to forget; and to get rid of a list he had visualised, he would mentally hang a cloth over it. Unlike us, he used to write down anything he wanted to forget.

On the other hand, he found faces hard to remember, because they were never the same. His imagery was so vivid that sometimes he confused it with reality. Thus he was late for school as a boy because he had visualised himself getting up and going to school while he actually remained in bed. And often he would visualise the hands of a clock so clearly as showing a particular time that he failed to see it was showing quite a different time.

Like the ancients, Veniaminoff used the technique of placing objects to be remembered along an imaginary street. He sometimes forgot an object because he had placed it in a shadow, and once he missed an egg because he had put it (mentally) in front of a white wall. When he became a professional, he worked out ways of avoiding such errors – for instance he would make the egg larger than life, or create a street-lamp to illuminate the object which was in the shadow.

Luria describes him as a timid, ponderous man, who had little grasp of the texts he memorised and no clear aim in life. Poetry defeated him: he was too literal-minded, and a metaphor confused him. 'Other people *think* as they read, but I *see* it all,' he explained. An expression like 'to weigh one's words' floored him. 'Now how can you weigh words?' he complained. His parents both had excellent but not extraordinary memories.

The technique of aiding memory by tying facts to a visualised scene is of great antiquity – Cicero recommends it for remembering the sequence of an oration. It suggests that visual memory is more reliable than memory for 'facts', and it must be older in evolutionary terms. Conjurors still use the method.

An instance of total recall which has become famous was noted by Myers, the nineteenth-century investigator of paranormal events. He found an uneducated girl, a servant in a Welsh parsonage, who appeared to have received the gift of tongues: she was spouting long passages in Aramaic and Hebrew. It turned out, later, that her master was in the habit of walking up and down in his study reading the Bible aloud in the original languages. She was reproducing this material like a tape-recorder. A few other instances are known. It seems therefore that the brain does have a method of making copies as well as a method of storing concepts. It has recently been suggested that recognition consists in matching an image with a copy, as distinct from recall, which is managed by looking for features which have been abstracted from the original; such, presumably, as those I have called 'impressions' or meta-feelings.

There is further evidence for the existence of 'copies' in the now rather well-known observations of Wilder Penfield, the Montreal neurosurgeon. When stimulating the exposed temporal cortex of conscious patients (during the course of an operation for epilepsy) a few of them suddenly recalled vivid memories. One such was a lady who heard a tune being played and thought it was coming from a radio. When Penfield stimulated again, the tune was repeated and she concluded that it must be a gramophone record. In the course of a TV programme which I devised, we brought this lady from New York to Penfield's laboratory; he showed her a photograph of her own brain, at which she looked with a mixture of curiosity and horror, and told her, 'When I stimulated this point you heard a tune. Do you remember?' 'Yes,' she said. 'Could you hum it?' and she hummed it for us.

Another patient recalled his mother telephoning. As Penfield tells it, these experiences were not like ordinary memories but more like re-experiencing the original event. However, the same method was later used by José Delgado, at Yale, on an Italian woman. He concluded that her recollections were memories, and that they were associated to whatever she had been thinking about just before the stimulation. He points out that many of Penfield's patients used words like 'dream' in describing their experience. It must be added that all those having this experience were epileptics and comprised only eight per cent of the patients who were stimulated in this way.

Very little attention has been given to the normal strategies of recall which could usefully be studied by introspection. Two American psychologists, R. Brown and D. McNeill, however, studied the 'tip of the tongue' phenomenon. They found that one ferrets around among ideas which are analogous to the idea sought, either because they sound similar or because they carry similar meanings.

I have myself made a number of studies of this kind and find the story a bit more complex; in fact what I have termed 'meta-feelings' play a basic part. Thus last night I thought of an English phrase for which I did not know the French equivalent; this promptly suggested to me a variant on the phrase, and then an expression which was comparable in meaning but differently structured in words. Now, some hours later, I am trying to recall what these three phrases were. The interesting point is that I do remember both that I had these thoughts and that they took the form described, although I am unable to remember the content at all. What has stayed with me are certain impressions of similarity and difference. I infer that recall is concerned with categories of this pragmatic kind rather than the conceptual categories of ordinary discourse. Or perhaps with both.

It seems to me that it would be worth trying to identify more of these categories, which must form the basis of cognitive thought as well as of memory.

Let me proceed further with my account of my attempts to recall the missing phrases. Intensive reflection yields the idea that the phrase I am seeking described a type of person – but I wonder whether I am now confusing two memories, since I remember that I had earlier wondered how to translate the expression 'a stick-in-the-mud fellow'. Furthermore, I find that I can remember something about the structure of the phrase: it had five or six words and hinged on a particle. The rhythm was --//-----. After reviewing several topics of which I might have been thinking, the phrase 'warm for the time of year' pops into my mind. This is wrong but structurally close. At once I think of 'old for his age'. Hooray, this was the second phrase I was seeking.

But I still cannot think of the analogous phrase which followed, and begin to wonder whether perhaps this idea – that there was a variant – is something I am importing from another similar problem. 'Horse' comes into my mind. 'The cart before the horse'? No, but this phrase seems to reflect the fact that I recalled the second of the two phrases first. At this point I am interrupted and abandon the search.

Note how 'warm for the time of year' led to 'old for his age', an association based entirely on rhythm, or perhaps on the notion of a conditional statement. It is clear that the search strategies we use are much fancier and more varied than most psychologists allow for.

The Seat of Memory

It seems to me that there are four things (if not more) which any worthwhile memory theory must incorporate, though not all do. Firstly, the fact that memory is distributed, as Lashley's butchery of rats made plain. And here the holographic parallel is the best clue we have. We can be pretty sure that memory is not recorded in a simple tape-recorder-like way, but consists of a vast tapestry or pattern in which smaller and smaller patterns are nested, in a way slightly reminiscent of some of Escher's unique etchings. (The hologram, of course, is only a parallel: more accurately, there is a Fourier transform.)

Secondly, and linked to the foregoing, memory has a hierarchic structure, based on coding and recording several times; or, if you prefer, on repeated transforms.

Thirdly, I feel sure memory has a common basis with cognition. What you think, you remember, and you do not remember what you have not thought (unconsciously perhaps as well as consciously). It would be prodigal if the brain contained two distinct systems and, miniaturised marvellously though it is, I doubt if evolution would have selected such a wasteful solution as this. There is, in fact, a strong correlation between a person's powers of memory and his intelligence.

Fourthly, we must allow for an hereditary component. We know that animals, notably birds and insects, inherit complex memories of the 'how to' kind. There is an ant which walls itself up in a cell it has dug, gives birth to young who have no contact with other ants, but which then go out and build elaborate nests. The cuckoo, brought up in the nest of its foster parent, has never seen a female cuckoo, but when it is able to fly, sets off in search of one of its own kind. This must have been the primal form of memory (unless we include reflexes) and points to information coded into the genes, or more probably the cytoplasm of the cell – since there is nothing to be gained from re-assorting the information, which is what genes are for. The subtler memories for images, ideas, words must either have developed from this primitive memory or, just possibly, have been superimposed on it. Whichever it was, the transmission mechanism must still be there or must have been remodelled, as often happens in evolution.

(Conversely, animal memories approximate the human: work with dolphins, for instance, has shown their recent memory span for sounds to be almost identical with that of humans.)

Finally, any theory of memory must explain how we recall things. It is comparatively easy to think of how information can be stored; locating it is far harder, as anyone with a filing system knows all too well. (And, as I have already said, both recall and recognition require to be explained.)

The generally held theory of memory is based on changes in the synapse – which, as you will remember, is the junction between the axon of one neurone and the cell-body or dendrites of another. When a pulse reaches a synapse, it is held, the threshold is shifted, so that on the next occasion, the pulse will produce a stronger effect. If such facilitation does not occur, the threshold drifts back to its original level. Thus the pattern of impulses in the brain is constantly shifting in response to experience. Behaviour which proves rewarding is repeated, and improved nervous transmission evokes that behaviour ever more smoothly and rapidly.

In this model, the electrical transmission corresponds to short-term memory – and it is assumed that some kind of reverberation continues for the fifteen or thirty seconds of short-term memory. The formation of long-term memory is thought to involve the manufacture of chemical substances, almost certainly members of the large group of substances called proteins. The Swedish scientist Holgar Hydén, in a series of beautifully precise experiments, has shown that chemical changes occur in the brain cells of educated rats.

Do these chemicals merely act as gatekeepers, regulating the synapses, or could they actually carry the stored information itself?

The idea of a chemical basis for memory receives some support from experiments such as that of D. J. Albert, who trained split-brain rats, removed the trained half of their brain, extracted the protein and injected it into the remaining half, and found that they learned more rapidly to do the same trick as before. The difficulty is to know what such experiments imply.

You can prove that a particular chemical substance is present in brains which have learned something, but how do you know whether it is a waste product of mental activity? Or it may have been a stimulant to mental activity. To prove it actually carries a memory record is another matter. There is only one set of experiments which supports the idea of a specific series of memory molecules in any mammalian species. Georges Ungar of Houston, Texas, trained rats to avoid the dark, which they normally prefer, by shocking them electrically every time they went into the darkened part of their cage. In two years he trained four thousand rats. He then killed them, minced up their brains and injected the liquor into the brains of other rats. Lo and behold! they avoided the dark corners. When given to mice, they avoided the dark too; ditto goldfish. By protracted chemical analyses, Ungar and his colleagues identified not a protein but a smaller molecule, known as a peptide, as the seat of this phenomenon and named it scotophobin. Earlier, James McConnell at Ann Arbor, Michigan, had got a similar effect with planarian worms, which he also trained to avoid light, McConnell even claimed that planarians which ate their mates could thus acquire their memories, at least about the undesirability of light.

However, Ungar's experiment only works if the rats are trained by giving them electric shocks, and even then it only works half the time and wears off in five days. In experiments where the animals could turn on a light if they wanted to, they failed to do so.

His pupil, Allan Jacobson, later made even more startling claims which no one could repeat; then the idea fell into disrepute until Ungar published his work. Various laboratories sought to jump on the bandwagon and got results which suggested something funny was happening, but they were so inconsistent that scepticism gradually regained ascendancy.

The inconsistency does not seem to me a strong reason for rejecting a chemical basis for memory, because such molecules, if they exist, may well be fragile and become damaged or inactivated during the process of extraction; or may fail to reach the proper site of action when injected into a new brain. What worries me more is that fear of the dark is such a very special kind of memory. It could be that 'scotophobin' merely carries the message: 'Nasty!' (Ungar originally called his work: 'The transfer of learned fear'.) That would be quite interesting in itself; but it is a long way from remembering how to ride a bicycle, let alone how to do quadratic equations, or what your mother looks like.

It does not account convincingly for the 'relived experience' sort of memory. S. E. Jelliffe, eminent as a neurologist and as a psychoanalyst, had a sleeping-sickness patient whose crisis hit just as he was catching a cricket ball: he had to be carried off the field, still entranced, with his right arm still outstretched and clutching the ball. 'Subsequently, whenever he had a crisis, it was ushered in by a total replay of this comic moment.

'He would suddenly feel it was 1919 once again, an unusually hot July afternoon, that the Saturday match was in progress again, that Trevelyan had just hit a probable "six", that the ball was approaching him, and that he had to catch it – RIGHT NOW.' Such phenomena, says Sacks, recounting the case, 'endorse the notion that our memories, or beings, are a "collection of moments". ' The phrase is Proust's; T. S. Eliot would also agree. 'History is a pattern of timeless moments,' he said. Somehow, that makes chemical theories of memory look a bit thin.

Prospect

If I have devoted a lot of space to memory it is because it occupies such a key position. If we could understand how it worked – how all the multifarious kinds of memory could possibly be registered, let alone recalled – many other aspects of mental function would become clearer.

When it was found that all the genetic information needed to build a complex living organism was coded into the minute structure of a single DNA molecule, many molecular biologists turned to the study of memory, thinking that this too must be molecularly coded, and that the solution was round the corner. I well remember the optimism of Francis Crick, to whom I talked at the time, on the prospect.

But in the quarter century which has passed, the problem has become more obscure and more complex. New facts keep being discovered which confuse the issue rather than clarify it. This is especially true of the electrical aspect of the picture. When I was at Cambridge, everyone knew that memory was an electrical pattern, created by the threshold levels at the synapses between neurones. This presumptive pattern was called the engram, or memory trace. But now it begins to look as if the impulse from one neurone changes the characteristics of the cell membrane (the cell wall) of the recipient neurone or alters its metabolism; perhaps it may alter the frequency and amplitude of the discharge it emits, instead of simply changing its threshold of sensitivity. Worse still, it has just been suggested that the axons may change in diameter for some good reason; it is known that such changes occur, but not why. Such changes might alter the speed of transmission, and this too might be a basis for memory. The most recent of these new subtleties suggests that it is the tiny spikes which everywhere stud the dendrites which are the seat of memory, and swell when stimulated. This would make sense of the fact, only recently uncovered, that some nerve connections are dendrite-to-dendrite (which I was once taught just didn't happen). Since there are many more spikes than neurones, by a factor of thousands, this would give memory a broader base. In contrast the Swedish scientist Holgar Hydén believes that a change takes place not in the atomic structure of the protein molecule but in its shape or conformation, when memory is registered, and believes he has demonstrated the existence of such a change in the brains of his rats. It is as plausible as any other theory. Then there is Lance Whyte's theory of the orienting of proteins within the cytoplasm and the creation of electrical circuits within the cytoplasmic mass, which also gives memory a broader basis. Finally, not to lengthen the list, there are the glia – the support cells which comprise two-thirds of the brain's mass. These two are known to change in some ill-defined way. I have long felt that the glia were too numerous and too elaborate just to provide a sort of manure in which neurones can grow. Wrapped round the axons as they are, they seem well placed to record what has been happening in them. At the same time, I believe we overemphasise the role of axons, and that electrotonic conduction and chemical diffusion between neighbouring cells must form part of the picture. In short, I think the basis of memory will prove extremely complex, with different mechanisms contributing to different aspects of this amazingly subtle capacity.

Nevertheless, many scientists seem rather optimistic about the possibility of a breakthrough in understanding memory.

The social effects of such a breakthrough might be even more startling than the scientific ones. If we understood the mechanism of memory we could perhaps improve it. We might be able to blot out unwanted memories, create new memories or even transfer memories or impressions from one person to another – conceivably even from animals to men and vice versa. Professor Holgar Hydén has observed that stimulating memory 'could change the whole structure of our society'.

However, there are other scientists who found the facts concerning memory so baffling and contradictory that they begin to doubt whether it will ever yield to manipulation in this kind of way. Indeed, some aspects of memory are so strange that we may be up against something more subtle than anyone realises. You can condition the small fruit fly called Drosophila to avoid ultra-violet light – but the strange thing is that only twenty per cent of any group of Drosophila respond to the conditioning and this response is randomly distributed. It doesn't make sense.

The psychologist J. A. Deutsch has warned: 'Many people now seem to believe that the race for discovering the physiological basis of memory is on and that in some sense attainment of this goal will be a feat similar to solving . . . the genetic code. But understanding the physiological or biochemical process will not even begin to help one to understand the main problems of memory – the organisation of stored memories so that when we see the face of a friend we can retrieve the appropriate information and recognise him within a few hundred milliseconds.'

There is one other theory of memory, which I have reserved until now, because it is quite different and because only one man really supports it: Heinz von Foerster, whom I went to see in Urbana, Illinois.

Essentially, von Foerster makes two points. The first is that it is often quicker to store data and calculate the result you want than to try to store all the results you might ever need. If, for example, you wanted to store the product of any number between one and ten billion multiplied by any other number from one to ten billion, you would require a book with pages eight and a half inches by eleven inches and about six billion miles thick. It would then take a librarian, travelling with the speed of light, half a day on the average, to look up any given result. It seems more practical, therefore, to have a small computer or large calculator and derive the figure you want when you want it. Of course what we remember is seldom figures, and I think that von Foerster is suggesting we should think of memory as broken down into elementary units and reassembled on demand, rather than as stored in the original form, or anything resembling it. Such units have been proposed before, and dubbed 'mnemons', but that's about as far as anyone has got.

Von Foerster's second suggestion is equally radical. He suggests that the problem is not remembering but forgetting. Remembering is, he suspects, a question of inhibition – of the suppression of unwanted responses – not of facilitation. This appeals to me, since, for reasons I have already advanced, I think the inhibitory aspect of brain action has been much under-emphasised. Such a theory would give some colour to the popular belief that 'we never forget anything'. Von Foerster goes on, with the aid of some rather advanced mathematics, to show how a system of superimposed networks could handle such a job in a computer-like manner.

The weakness of this theory is that, while we do have fairly frequent experience of people losing their memory, we do not have cases of people who begin to remember too much, unless perhaps this could be said of schizophrenics. The case of Veniaminoff, recounted earlier, seems unique. Jorge Luis Borges wrote a story concerning a man who could remember literally everything he had seen. 'He remembered the shapes of the clouds in the south at dawn on the 30th of April of 1882, and he could compare them in his recollection with the marbled grain in the design of a leather-bound book which he had seen only once, and with the lines in the spray which an oar raised in the Rio Negro on the eve of the battle of the Quebracho . . . A circumference on the blackboard, a rectangular triangle, a rhomb, are the forms which we can fully intuit; the same held true for [this man] for the tempestuous mane of a stallion, a herd of cattle in a pass, the everchanging flame of the innumerable ash, the many faces of a dead man during the course of a protracted wake . . .' This young man died early under the burden of such total recall, so perhaps it is well that we forget as efficiently as we do.

Of course, all these theories are limited in another respect. Even if they serve to explain how the brain produces patterns of behaviour which help us to survive, they fail entirely to explain how electric pulses and protein molecules are experienced, how

> Fond Memory brings the light
> Of other days around me
> The smiles, the tears,
> Of boyhood's years,
> The words of love then spoken
> The eyes that shone
> Now dimmed and gone
> The cheerful hearts now broken.

In these words, George Moore captures finely the emotional content of memory, an aspect on which neurologists are deafeningly silent.

Though I have far from exhausted this complex subject, I hope it is now clear that we are very far from understanding human memory.

16

Thinking About Thinking

HIGH Q KOREAN

It was reported from Korea some years ago that a child named Kim had mastered the differential calculus at the age of three. He had also started to write blank verse. Kim talked at three months, stood at five months and gave up wearing nappies at six months. At school he was put in the class for thirteen-year-olds. He had kept a diary full of pithy comments about life since he was two. His IQ is put at 210. (The scale is normally considered to stop at 200.) What has Kim got that a million other children have not got?

The brain of Albert Einstein, much of which resides in a jar kept in a cider box in New Jersey, turns out to be no larger than the brain of the average man.

Brighter Than a Thousand Sons

By any reasonable definition of intelligence the mathematician Karl Friedrich Gauss must have been one of the most intelligent men who ever lived. At the age of thirteen his teacher told him that he need not attend class any longer as there was nothing further he could teach him. When Gauss was six years old, attending the local school, the teacher, to keep the class busy, set them to adding up all the numbers from one to ten. Gauss at once raised his hand, crying, 'Ligget se', which means 'Here it is', and offered the answer: fifty-five. He explained that he had at once seen that one plus ten equalled eleven, that two plus nine, three plus eight and so on, must also come to eleven, and that there were five such pairs. By the same method one can, in a couple of seconds, provide the total of the digits from one to a hundred: five thousand and fifty. Indeed, one to a thousand is hardly more difficult.

Lightning calculators are not necessarily intelligent, as I shall relate in a moment, but insight into relationships is certainly part of intelligence. Intelligence sounds a straightforward idea. It is not. Genius is even more puzzling. Genius does not always manifest itself early in life. Einstein was late learning to talk and was later refused entry to a polytechnic. Paul Ehrlich, the founder of chemotherapy and pioneer of immunology, nearly failed to enter a university. The great surgeon John Hunter was 'a hopeless dunce'. Carl Jung was not good at mathematics; Zola got nought for literature; Picasso could not learn the alphabet. Tolstoy,

Darwin, Sheridan and Mendel were undistinguished in youth, among many others.

High intelligence is frequently associated with a prodigious memory. Volta, the pioneer of electricity, for example, memorised the contents of a twenty-volume encyclopaedia and could still recite whole pages from it fifty years later. Macaulay knew the position of every book in his library, and, given the page, could recite from memory the text of many of them. If intelligence is seeing interconnections, then evidently one's mind must be stocked with ideas with which the subject in view may be connected. Yet it has been shown that memory and intelligence are not indissolubly connected, since people who have lost their memory have not lost their intelligence.

However, the genius of a Goethe or a Shakespeare, a Sophocles or a Tolstoy, a Milton or a Racine, seems to be of a somewhat different kind. Here it is the imaginative projection which counts, the power to identify with the emotions of the others and to express them in words and simulated deeds. This demonstrates that thought is not solely a matter of intellect. There is a constant interplay between the coolly reasoning cortex and the impulsive, excitable mid-brain. And this is true not only of the works of geniuses but of the 'thinking' of everyday life. For the moment, however, it is the cool, cortical process on which I wish to concentrate.

Mozart said that he could hear a musical work as a single event, not successively, which I take to mean that he grasped all the temporal interrelationships of the music in a single pattern. Professor Aitken, a mathematician whom you will meet in a moment or two, said he could run through half an hour's music in half a minute. It is difficult to know what such assertions mean. It is unlikely that the brains of such people operate much faster in any simple, physiological sense. The speed of central nervous conduction does not vary widely from one human being to another. It is more likely that they could analyse music into temporal structures of greater scope and complexity than most of us. For this seems the essential feature of intellectual brilliance in general: the power to integrate isolated data into patterns, and then to integrate those patterns into still more general configurations.

When I was in my twenties I acquired a copy of a book which Einstein wrote in an attempt to explain his theory in non-mathematical terms. I read it with fierce attention, striving to hold in my mind each of the novel concepts he offered. At the end, for a few seconds, I managed to hold them all in my mind at once, so that their interrelationships became plain to me, and the whole marvellously integrated structure became clear. It was a moment of supreme experience, almost of rapture. Then the effort became too much and the vision faded. For a few seconds, nevertheless, I can honestly say that I believe that I in some profound sense 'understood' Einstein's general theory of relativity. What I can recall most vividly was my sense of awe that any man, unaided, could have arrived at such a beautiful, transcendent structure of concepts. What I had haltingly achieved, led by the hand by the simplest route, Einstein had worked out for himself and without even the assurance that there was a structure there, of that kind, to be apprehended. Even now, forty years later, I cannot find words to express the awe that I felt at his superb intellectual achievement.

Once the way was shown, later workers painstakingly evolved even more sophisticated intellectual schemes, but the supreme achievement was Einstein's. Between his insights and those of the young Gauss there is, however, an analogy. Both analysed the totality into new components and then brought the bits into a new synthesis. Analysis and synthesis lie at the core of intelligence.

If the brain of a Swiss customs official, no larger than average, is capable of such Promethean feats, one is forced to wonder how it differed from the norm. And also to wonder whether other brains, if suitably fostered, might not achieve a bit more than they do. The remarkable thing, I suspect, is not that man is intelligent but rather that, despite having a tool of extraordinary capacity, he manages to do so little with it. Every day we can see around us actions and statements which are plainly silly. If we could bring about a ten per cent rise in the national level of intelligence the efforts could be earth-shaking.

The first difficulty, and it is decisive, is that no one knows what intelligence is. After nearly a century of talking and testing – Galton's first studies were in the seventies and James Cattell started testing in the eighties – the subject has only recently shown a little progress. In fact the psychologist Thurstone despairingly remarked that intelligence was whatever intelligence tests measured. Today the view has hardened that the notion of intelligence as a single unitary trait is false. There are many kinds of intelligence, and different societies conceive it differently.

What is Intelligence?

In 1929 the psychologist Harold Lashley, whom we have already encountered, wrote, despairingly: 'The whole theory of learning and intelligence is in confusion. We know at present nothing of the organic basis of these functions . . . The concepts are so poorly defined that it has not been possible even to imagine a programme of physiological research which seemed likely to reveal more than superficial relationships.'

Since 1929 a great deal of research has been done and some minor advances have been made, but the physiological basis of intelligence remains very obscure. And while the physiology is puzzling, the structuring of thought remains totally baffling. 'Scientists studying brain function from the inside out simply haven't even approached a stage in which the investigation of complex thought processes is either reasonable or possible,' laments the neuroscientist Alan Fisher. We are not even sure whether thinking is a function of neurones; the eminent neuroscientist Robert Galambos has suggested it may be a function of the glia, the cells which enfold the neurones.

To start with intelligence, it is still debatable whether we are talking of one thing or many. In 1892 Sir Francis Galton made a first attempt to classify men 'according to their natural gifts'. Ten years later the great Charles Spearman, then at London University, undertook to determine intelligence objectively and, as if that weren't enough, to measure it. There was he said, a general factor (g) powering an array of special abilities (s). 'G' was, so to say, the horsepower of the motor: what you applied that energy to varied from case to case. 'G' was General Cognitive Ability. It is this which 'intelligence tests' seek to measure and express as an Intelligence Quotient.

I do not propose to weary you with the interminable debate which ensued as to whether any such entity as 'intelligence' exists – a debate which still drags on – but will simply contrast Spearman's view with an interesting alternative, namely that put forward soon after the Second World War by a Chicago psychologist named Ward C. Halstead. On the basis of observation of men suffering brain injuries in the war, he conceived a four-factor theory of intelligence which, though it makes a good deal of sense, has never commanded due attention.

Halstead called his four factors, A, C, D and P. The first of these, A, he defined as the power of Abstracting general propositions from particular cases – in other words, the power of comprehending similarities and differences – Halstead equated it with Spearman's 'g'.

The second factor he called the Central Integrative Factor: defined as the ability to integrate and to link material together. He noted that many brain-injured persons seemed unable to reorganise their existing responses so as to cope with a novel situation.

It seems to me that we can descry a neurological basis – in the light of what we know today – for these two factors. The first is, I suspect, connected with the vertical columns in the cortex, which, as Hubel and Wiesel have shown, are concerned with the formation of concepts. The integrative factor, on the other hand, seems to depend on the richness of cross connections in the cerebral cortex and threshold setting of such links. In psychological terms, these factors could be called Analytic and Synthetic – and that makes good sense, since it has often been noted that some people are preoccupied by differences – like the taxonomist who distinguishes three thousand varieties of beetle – while others find similarities between things which superficially are different. Recently the terms convergent and divergent thinking have become fashionable as a way of labelling this distinction.

Halstead's third factor, D, was the specific expression of responses – both motor skills and intellectual skills – and seems pretty much like Spearman's 's'. The D stood for Directional. Finally, the P stood for Power Factor, by which he implied curiosity and alertness or exploratory drive. Obviously it is not much good having analytic and synthetic ability if you do nothing with it. 'He has a good brain but he doesn't use it. He's lazy,' we say of such a one.

Certainly, motivation or drive is a major factor in intelligence; resistance to distraction, concentration upon the matter in hand, are keys. Newton said that he arrived at his discoveries 'by constantly thinking unto them'. Genius has always been marked by intense application. Haydn tells how he toiled over the composition of *The Creation* and the despair he felt when he could not find the right structure. Mozart said Haydn's string quartets involved incalculable labour, despite their spontaneous air. Mozart himself, though famed for rapid composition, wrote to his father that he was 'knee-deep in music', so to speak: 'that I busy myself with it all day long; that I like to speculate, study, ponder.' Stravinsky said much the same. It was Emerson who said that genius was fifty per cent inspiration and fifty per cent perspiration, a remark which Edison appropriated, changing the proportions to ten and ninety. So probably the most obvious thing we could do to raise the level of intelligence would be, like Avis, to try harder.

It is a curious fact that people low on P seem to need emotional props, such as an ideological belief, or a religious or political one. (That is not the same as saying that all people with strong beliefs are deficient in alertness. All cherries are fruit, but not all fruit are cherries.) Halstead thought that consciousness was probably linked in some way to 'C'. Looking around my friends and acquaintances, I find I can usually classify them fairly easily on these scales. There are high As with low C, low As with high C, and so on.

There have also been two-factor, three-factor and several multifactor theories, the ultimate being reached with J. P. Guilford's one hundred and twenty factor theory. Perhaps that is a little unfair: Guilford, who is a professor of psychology at the University of Southern California, considers that there are five intellectual operations and that they act on four types of content (images, symbols, meanings, behaviour) and at six levels (units, classes, relations, systems, transformations and implications). Four times five times six makes one hundred and twenty. There are various theoretical and practical objections to such a scheme. It does not allow for the hierarchic nature of intelligence and ignores the intercorrelations between its many units. It has been called by a rival theorist, the combative Professor Hans Eysenck, 'Hamlet without the Dane'. But I note that Guilford's five operations are not too remote from the kind of factors we have been discussing: two of them consist of convergent and divergent production. Guilford also stresses the role of memory, but the reason I bring him into the discussion is that he includes something the others have missed, which he calls Evaluation. The person incapable of self-criticism, who thinks all his ideas equally brilliant and equally practical is in some sense stupid, however original he may be.

There is an old story which has always appealed to me. It is visitors' day at the lunatic asylum (let us call a spade a spade) and one of the inmates has convinced a visitor that he has been wrongly incarcerated; he is perfectly sane. Convinced by his serious manner and logical arguments, the visitor promises to speak to the director of the institution. As he turns away he received a tremendous kick in the seat. 'That's just so you don't forget,' explains the lunatic. People who fail to assess how others will react to their behaviour, logical though it may be, are evidently lacking in some component of what we call intelligence.

The claim of traditional IQ tests to measure Spearman's 'g' has often been doubted for many reasons – but even if they do, it is pretty clear they are measuring only one component in intelligence in the common understanding of the word. A fact which has often puzzled psychologists is that removal of large parts of the cortex has so little effect on performance, especially in animal experiments. To meet this, Halstead suggested that there might be two kinds of intelligence. But human beings who have suffered cortical injuries do show defects of intelligence, and particularly when the frontal lobes are involved, so that we do not need to fall back on such desperate hypotheses. The problem – a behavioural one – of finding one's way through a maze is not in the same class as the intricate manipulation of symbolic systems involved in high intelligence.

Intelligence undoubtedly has a hereditary component, though how large it is and what factors it affects is hard to say, since it is far from clear what IQ tests measure. Such as they are, they show higher correlations between members of the family than between random pairs, higher still for non-identical twins, and are highest of all for identical ones. Experiments in which gravid rats were given hormones were conducted by Stephen Zamenhof of the Mental Retardation Center. The offspring proved brighter at learning tasks such as maze-running. When their brains were dissected, they proved no larger but they had much richer growth of dendritic connections. This may be the basis of intelligence and it is reasonable that it should be genetically influenced. It is equally true that experience after birth influences intellectual development. Malnutrition can stunt neuronal growth; a stimulating environment can boost it. Rats exposed to contrasting environments – some in solitary confinement, others with plenty to do – scored differently on tests. Dissected at fifteen weeks, the latter had a thicker cortex, more active enzyme systems, and more numerous glia, though the number of neurones was not increased, which supports Galambos' idea.

Parental influences also count, at least in the human case, and not only because parents provide stimulating or deadening environments. They can also provide motivation. Harvard's renowned psychologist Edwin Boring has cited the following figures for the average IQs of children from different family parental environments:

Children of demanding parents	124
Children of normal parents	110
Children of over-anxious parents	107
Children of concerned parents	97

According to Dr Mathew Besdine, a professor of clinical psychology at Adelphi University, New York, a necessary condition for the development of genius is a 'Jocasta mother'. (Jocasta, you recall, unwittingly married her son, Oedipus.) I doubt this: over-powering and seductive mothers frequently crush their sons, while plenty of geniuses can be found whose mothers were cold, or absent. While Besdine's view is too simple, it is surely true that early experiences can produce strong drives.

I am diffident about putting in my pennyworth, but I can't refrain from suggesting that, somewhere in the story, there must be a place for the power to organise ideas into groups (schemata) and these groups into higher-order things, or grasp things quickly. He does so because he has evolved for himself, by thought, schemata into which new data can be fitted or which provide analogies and models which simplify the absorption of novel material.

Clever Idiots

Somewhere into the account of intelligence we have to fit the curious phenomenon of the lightning calculator. Sometimes called 'mathematical prodigies' they have in fact little understanding of the art of mathematics; they just do conventional sums very fast. Jacques Inaudi, aged thirteen and still unable to read or write, was shown off in Paris in 1880. He calculated the cube-root of nine digit numbers and the fifth root of twelve digit numbers in his head. Asked by the psychologist Binet to factorise 13,411 he took about three minutes to conclude that it was comprised of 115^2 plus 13^2 plus 14^2 plus 1. A minute later he announced that it could also be factorised as 113^2 plus 25^2 plus 4^2 plus 1. Then he produced the squares of 113, 23, 8 and 7. For a more difficult number – 15,663 – he found two solutions in about twenty minutes. It is said that it would take an ordinary person fifteen days in his head.

Inaudi's gift seems to have been partly auditory: humming slowed him up. His only dreams, he said, were of numbers. Binet also examined Diamondi, whose gift was visual. Other calculators have specialised in working out what dates fell on what days. The American twins George and Charles, studied scientifically in 1963, could tell you after a few seconds' thought, that the fourth Monday in February 1993 will fall on the 22nd.

Bousfield and Barry studied one such calculator in the laboratory – he made it a condition that he be known as only S.F. They found that he could add a dozen two-digit numbers in a second, about twenty-five times as fast as most of us. His gift was highly visual. He could glance quickly at a long number such as 27875145387941732 and repeat it correctly, not only immediately afterwards but also twenty-four hours later. He could glance at a square composed of five rows of five digits for fifty seconds, then read the numbers off diagonally, vertically or how you like. Clearly he had eidetic imagery, but he also remembered numbers by associations. The one I have just quoted, he said, was comprised of the log of 1·9 followed by the date of the fall of Constantinople, a friend's telephone number and the square root of three.

Curiously enough, some of those who had this gift lost it as they grew older. Truman Safford was an all-round genius who became a Harvard professor at twenty. Asked to square 365,365,365,365,365,365, 'he flew round the room like a top, pulled his pantaloons over the top of his boots, bit his hand, rolled his eyes in their sockets, sometimes smiling and talking and then, seeming to be in an agony, in not more than one minute replied: 133,491,850,208,566,925,016,658,299,946,583,225.' (I trust you will check that for correctness, also in your head.) But his calculating ability lasted only six years.

Professor A. C. Aitken, a mathematics professor at Edinburgh University, was persuaded by Ian Hunter to comment on his methods of lightning calculation. They depended upon the combination of a powerful memory – he could recite 'π' to a thousand places, forwards or backwards – combined with an armoury of short-cuts. At first uninterested in calculation, he had been converted by a school master saying, after explaining that $(a+b)(a-b)$ equals a^2-b^2, 'and of course that can be used as a short cut in multiplication'. This remark, which would have passed over my head without registering, I fear, transformed Aitken's whole attitude, and he began to accumulate a repertoire of short-cuts and numerical relations. Given any number up to 1500 he can automatically say whether it is a prime number or, if not, what are its factors. When, in discussion, the year 1961 was mentioned, 'he immediately commented that this is 37 times 53, or alternatively 44 squared plus 5 squared, or alternatively 40 squared plus 19 squared'.

He also seems to have been able to check his calculations as he went along by making approximations, almost as if he were using one half of his brain to monitor the other. But these observations throw no light on the central mystery of why he should have felt so powerfully motivated to develop the faculty in the first place. Other schoolboys have been taught that $(a+b)(a-b)$ equals a^2-b^2 without it having this tremendous effect.

Almost equally puzzling are the infant prodigies – those who develop abnormally early in life. William Hamilton, probably the greatest man of science Ireland ever produced, could read when just turned three, spoke Latin, Hebrew and Greek at five, Italian and French at seven and at nine plunged into Sanskrit, Arabic, Chaldee and Syrian, followed by Hindustani, Malay, Mahratta, Bengali and others, topping off the list with Chinese. Even more astonishing was Christian Hernaker, who talked within a few hours of his birth, and at fourteen months knew the Bible by heart. At two and a half he was studying ancient history, geography, and anatomy, and could read German, Latin and French fluently. At three he could add, subtract and multiply. At four he knew two hundred and twenty songs, eighty psalms and one thousand five hundred lines of Latin verse. He died at four years and four months, presumably worn out.

Music has been a field where prodigies flourish. Mozart is a case too well known to discuss. More interesting perhaps is that of Blind Tom. He was the son of a slave owned by a Colonel George Bethune. One night the Colonel awoke, hearing music from his drawing-room. There, in the darkness, he found a small black boy playing perfectly a Mozart sonata which his daughter had been practising for weeks. Tom was then four. He proved able to play any piece of piano music after hearing it once. Recognising a good thing when he saw it, the Colonel undertook to have him taught music, and engaged a teacher from nearby Columbus, Ohio. It is said that the teacher, having heard Tom play, refused to take him as a pupil. Tom turned out to be mentally deficient, and never developed a vocabulary of more than a few hundred words, but when he attained the age of seven, the good Colonel put him on show and is said to have made $100,000 from exhibiting his powers in the first year alone. Being blind, Tom could only play what he had heard, but he built up a repertoire of five thousand pieces by all the principal classical composers, from Bach to Meyerbeer. Here again we find phenomenal memory of the auditory-eidetic kind. Tom could repeat a fifteen-minute discourse, of which he did not understand a word, after one hearing and sing songs (having once heard them) in French or German. His most extraordinary achievement was to play the second part of a duet, which he had never heard before, while the composer played the top part, thus improvising as the music developed. Then 'jumping up, he fairly shoved the man from his seat, and proceeded to play the treble with more brilliancy and power than its composer'.

One may guess that, owing to his inability to see and lacking any interesting verbal input, he had adapted a great part of his brain to the demands of music. But why did he far outstrip other blind children? No one knows. We are forced to recognise an innate ability. He seems to have had no creative musical powers, rather was he a sort of human tape-recorder. On the other hand, memory fails to account for the calendar calculations of Charles and George, since they could calculate in a range far beyond any available calendars, even of the so-called 'perpetual' kind. The most extensive of these extends to about AD 2400 but George could reach beyond AD 7000, making due allowance for leap years. The IQ of these twins was in the 40–50 range! Their minds were very concrete: they could subtract a number of apples but not of dollars. Asked how they managed their feats they said: 'It's in my head,' or, 'I just know.' As one of the investigators summed it up: 'The importance, then, of the Idiot Savant lies in our inability to explain him; he stands as a landmark of our own ignorance . . . and as a challenge to our capabilities.'

Le Style, C'est L'Homme

After nearly a century of trying to measure the quantity of intelligence, attention has been turned to examining its quality. It has been noticed that different people have, quite consistently, different modes of responding to and organising and using information. These 'cognitive styles' remain consistent across a wide range of tasks.

For instance, some people think more abstractly, others more concretely. The first lot tend to group objects by their class membership, the second by their appearance, or their purpose. There is a good story of a primitive tribesman asked by an anthropologist to sort into groups various fruits and vegetables mixed with plates, knives and household items. The tribesman placed the knife with the orange, explaining that it would be needed to peel it; he placed the vegetables with the plates, and so on. No, explained the anthropologist, that was not what he had in mind. 'But that is how a wise man would sort them,' said the native. 'Then how would a fool sort them?' asked the anthropologist in some irritation. 'Oh, he would put all the fruit together, and all the implements together,' was the reply. This is a true story: as it implies, abstract thinking is not inherently better than concrete thinking; it all depends what your purpose is. Children tend to think concretely, and we spend a lot of time encouraging them in abstract thought.

The idea of cognitive style arose when it was noted that some people were more 'field dependent' than others – that is, they trusted what they saw going on around them rather than what they felt. Placed in an experimental room which could tilt, and seated in a chair which could be tilted independently, some people declared they were upright when both they and the room were tilted by equal amounts – because things looked normal. Others trusted their bodily sensations more than their visual perceptions.

Francis Bacon, long ago, distinguished between the 'steady, acute' mind and the 'lofty, discursive' mind. In modern terms this has been called the 'narrow, deep' versus the 'broad, shallow' approach. It has also been called focusing as against scanning and articulated as against global. Jaensch called them J-type and S-type, identifying the former with conservatives and the latter with liberals. He approved the former as reliable, disapproved the latter as unstable. Being the broad and shallow type (actually, I prefer 'lofty, discursive') myself, I tend to side with those who criticise the former as rigid and admire the latter as flexible. My school reports often said: 'Has too many interests,' and I am quite conscious of my tendency to look at large subjects as a whole (*vide* this book) rather than snip manageable bits off them. Most scientists and other academics are concentrators who 'know more and more about less and less'. My preference for knowing less and less about more and more no doubt explains why I did not become a biologist.

This distinction corresponds to one I have already made between the analytic element in intelligence, and the synthetic element – in its proper sense of putting things together.

I have myself proposed in earlier books a closely related and still more radical dichotomy. Either you feel separate from your environment or you feel united with it. If the former, life seems divided into unrelated events. If the latter, everything seems part of a great whole. I called this thick-walled ego *vs* thin-walled, and I have touched on it in an earlier chapter of this book. There is a plain analogy between the person who draws firm boundaries between concepts and objects and one who draws boundaries between people – sees them as individuals – and draws boundaries between himself as an individual and the rest of the world.

People also differ in such factors as cognitive complexity, in preferring inductive or deductive reasoning, and in their rigidity or openness to new ideas.

Most of these dichotomies seem to me to be connected with the analysis/synthesis contrast which I mentioned first, and I am inclined to attach more importance to a distinction which the psychologists have largely ignored. To wit, spontaneous response *vs* inhibition and restraint. And perhaps akin to this is the disposition to agree with others *vs* a built-in tendency to doubt and challenge. (Conformity *vs* Rebellion; Faith *vs* Scepticism.) The subject needs a good deal more study. In the meantime we can watch ourselves for any tendency to proceed to extremes in any of these choices.

Psychologists are beginning to realise that distinctions of this kind are only a subsection of the whole question of personality differences. Impulsiveness *vs* Stolidity; Optimism *vs* Pessimism; Surgency *vs* Desurgency . . . It is a long story, and one which has always fascinated me, but it would take us too far from the theme I am trying to develop, and from the subject immediately in view, which is: what goes on inside the skull when we think.

Vive la Différence!

There are noticeable differences in cognitive style between the sexes. Thus women are more field-dependent and more concrete in their thinking. They also tend to prefer narrower categories. If you ask a number of people of both sexes a question like 'What is the average length of whales?' the women will produce a more restricted range of estimates than the men. It is also well established that boys excel in spatial judgment, whereas girls are superior to boys in verbal skill. (Such statements refer, of course, to averages: the most verbal boys will surpass the least verbal girls, and so on.) This difference persists throughout life.

It is a matter of hot dispute how far such differences are inherited and how far the result of different experience, arising from differences in the way boys and girls are raised and the different demands adults put upon them. Quite certainly both factors are at work and interact in subtle ways. For instance, D. B. Lynn has sought to show that the closeness of a child to one or other parent affects cognitive style. Thus, though boys in general are better problem-solvers and more field-independent than girls, the opposite is true of boys with distant fathers. Conversely, girls with distant mothers are better problem-solvers and more field-independent than girls with close mothers. So, if a boy is close to his father he is liable to be outshone in these respects by girls who are distant from their mothers.

There are certainly physiological differences between the sexes, many of which are present from birth, and they could eventually affect cognitive style. Girls are more sensitive to touch and taste and to loud sounds and more dexterous than men; they have better night vision. Men have faster reactions, are more stressed by cold, and more easily distracted by novelty than women. The girl's greater interest in sounds is noticeable soon after birth, so it is probably inherited. Indeed, differences can be found between the brain cells of male and female rats in the thirty-fifth day of uterine life. The fact that most such differences do not become more marked as age advances also speaks against an environmental origin. Some authorities think that male superiority in spatial judgment, problem-solving and reaction time evolved during the hunter-gatherer phase of human development, when these abilities would have had survival-value. But I am inclined to see an earlier origin, since there are marked differences in the behaviour of the two sexes in the animal world – as well as in their physique.

One clearly marked difference which has recently been added to the list is that women have a higher activation level: they become more aroused than men. This shows up clearly in EEG tracings and implies that women are more affected by alarming or stressful situations than men.

The recent interest in the functional differences between the two halves of the cerebral cortex has given rise to the idea that differences of lateralisation could account for some of the sex differences in behaviour, an idea first advanced by H. Lansdell in 1964. An experiment which lends colour to this idea has been performed by Mary Lou Reid of the University of Massachusetts. She found that those left-handed children who hold their pen straight up (some left-handed persons curl their hand round in a hook) have brains lateralised the opposite way to usual, i.e. with the speech centres on the right – and in this group, the girls were better than boys at spatial tasks and boys were better at verbal ones. Nevertheless, just as with right-handers, the right hemisphere of the boys developed more rapidly than the left, while with the girls the reverse was true.

However, the difference between the sexes – as far as lateralisation is concerned – is not so much in which hemisphere develops fastest as in how far the two hemispheres are specialised. The evidence suggests that men are more lateralised than women; hence men can run a machine and talk at the same time more readily than women, using a different hemisphere for each function. Women have the advantage in tasks which cannot be compartmentalised in this way, and co-ordinate speech and movement more smoothly than men. Perhaps this lack of hemispheric specialisation explains the odd fact that women are twice as likely as men to confuse their left and their right.

While lateralisation may explain some of the sex differences, it is beyond question that a major role is played by differences in hormonal output, more particularly the sex hormones. From the womb onward, women are producing hormones to a different pattern from men and this influences behaviour as well as physical development, including development of the brain. A clue as to how this might affect cognitive style is afforded by the fact that female hormones reduce the level of a group of substances known as monoamine oxidase inhibitors (MAOs) and it is known that MAOs are low in highly arousable people.

If I have written chiefly about the physiological origins of the differences between the sexes, it is because that is the aspect of such differences which is relevant to the theme of this book. There are, to be sure, numerous aspects of behaviour which are determined by the social environment or by interaction between environment and physique. For instance, Paula Johnson and Jacqueline Goodman found that women were much more likely than men to solve their problems by trading on their weakness and appealing for help. It hardly needed research to show this: the woman driver with a flat tyre who persuades a man to change the wheel for her is an instance known to everyone. But how far such a tactic is due to being physically weaker in face of the task and how far to a lifelong habit of solving problems by manipulating men as a *result* of being physically weaker than them is more difficult to establish.

But I have digressed from the subject of thinking and must now return to it.

Thinking, Knowing and Believing

Considering that thought is commonly regarded as a peculiarly human faculty – even as man's greatest achievement as he struggles up the evolutionary scale – it is curious that psychologists have made so little progress in understanding it. There has been little sustained research on the subject, which seems hard to get to grips with. 'Thinking is a concept which everyone understands but no one can explain,' say the authors of a recent book on the subject, before going on to demonstrate that they are no exceptions to their own rule. In part, it must be conceded, this sad state of affairs is due to the long reign of behaviourism, which studiously avoided asking what was going on inside the black box. That particular block has been dissolved and new schools of mentalist psychology are emerging. Problems which had been phrased, with some difficulty, in behaviourist terms are now being reformulated in a more productive way. The turnaround is often dated to 1967, when Ulric Neisser published a book, *Cognitive Psychology*, which offered many such reformulations and has become a milestone.

But the real trouble with thought is that it is not available to introspection. If I ask you what was your mother's maiden name, after a slight pause you would probably tell me – but what went on in the pause? You do not know. If I ask you to name an item of furniture beginning with C you might say Chair; but how did you arrive at that reply? It is possible that you visualised a room full of furniture and checked which began with C, but it is more likely the word just popped up.

It has been a subject of dispute whether thinking is dependent upon words or upon images.

The behaviourists have, in their single-minded attempt to obliterate the mind, asserted that thought, as such, does not occur. All that happens (they declare) is that we form words with our tongue, larynx and lip muscles, without actually producing speech. And it is true that, when thinking, we move these muscles. The Russians, especially Sokolov, have done extensive studies, measuring the electric currents in the muscles, and also trying to see if people can still think when their tongue is immobilised. They can, of course, and though there are currents in the muscles, they die away as the thought becomes more clearly established.

Since a thought can be expressed in various different verbal formulae, it seems unlikely on the face of it that thoughts should consist of silent speech. The mathematician Hadamard made a very original enquiry in 1927, writing to various distinguished people, including Einstein, to ask them how they thought. Einstein was quite clear that he thought in 'more or less clear images and certain signs'. His images were visual and motor. Hadamard himself insisted that when he was engaged in thought words were absent; on the other hand a lesser mathematician, George Polya, felt that the solution of mathematical problems was always verbal. As a writer, I know how hard it often is to find the words in which to express a thought, and am absolutely clear in my mind that some of my thinking, at least, is not verbal – it is, in fact, the kind of 'feeling' about which I wrote in an earlier section. It is also true, however, that when I am reluctant to think – tired or merely confused – I can force myself to do so by using words. And in two ways. As people often do, I apostrophise myself: 'Come on now, you can't just sit here staring at the typewriter,' I say to myself. And then I anchor the thoughts I have got by finding words for them.

You will recall Armande, the much put-upon daughter of Alfred Binet, who questioned the poor child incessantly about her thinking processes. When he asked her where her hat was, and then asked her how she had arrived at her reply, she said, 'The thinking is something I know at once without having sought it by means of words: it appears to me as some sort of feeling.' And on another occasion she explained a feeling of negation as, 'This quite vague feeling, but which I am sure of, is a thought without words.' Binet summarised this aspect of his studies thus: 'From these conversations it would seem to emerge that wordless thinking is experienced as "feeling" and above all one has awareness of it as an experience rather than knowledge of its nature. I surmise that the word gives precision to this "feeling" of thinking.' When in 1974 I read these words, I was overjoyed to find such strong confirmation of my own impressions. In fine, thought is neither words nor images, but feelings in the specific sense discussed in Chapter Nine of this book. Words and images can be employed to pin down these feelings, or to supplement them.

I have already suggested that such feelings are often, if not always, concerned with relations, and this is true in the context of directed thought. In old age the composer Ravel became aphasic; he could neither speak, write nor transcribe music. Nevertheless he could still sing, play and even compose. That suggests to me that in the absence of symbols (whether words or printed musical notation), he was still able to function on the basis of his awareness of relationships.

Binet also questioned leading chess-players and was so puzzled by their replies that he nearly abandoned his enquiries. One of them, questioned about whether he visualised the board, at first replied that he did, and then qualified this by saying that what he really saw was not so much the board but the position (i.e. the relationship between the pieces) adding, 'The squares on my imaginary board have neither distinct outline nor colour.' Tarrasch, a leading player, said that one must study with an empty board, until the properties of each square and the effect of any piece on it were unconsciously registered. This also sounds like the storing of relationships, not objects. Tarrasch added that he sometimes used verbal memory as a kind of check on progress. This recalls Armande's comment: 'I hardly notice that I'm thinking when I don't use words.'

Perhaps it is time to observe that the word thinking is very loosely used. 'I'm trying to think where I left it,' we say, meaning trying to remember. 'I think I shall go to London tomorrow,' means that a plan has been formulated but that the decision to implement it has not been taken. 'I've been thinking about my problems,' often means no more than an unproductive brooding has occurred. In the harsher world of the psychology lab., thinking is almost invariably taken to mean problem-solving and especially solving problems by logical steps. But actually logical thought is just what humans are bad at, though it is what computers do well. For human thinking is coloured at every stage by emotion, in the broad sense – by preferences, fears, and the weight of past experience. This emotive aspect is valuable when it contributes to creative work, harmful when it distorts rational conclusions.

Freud distinguished two kinds of thinking, which he called primary and secondary, and later workers have refined this distinction, speaking of paleological thinking as against logical thinking. In paleological thought all relationships are symmetrical: 'you are my son' is equivalent to 'I am your son'. Symbols are interchangeable with what they symbolise. (This is known as von Domarus' principle.) Something of this sort goes on in sleep and dreaming, and schizophrenics abandon logical for paleological thinking. This primitive, emotion-laden thinking may be a function of the mid-brain, rather than the cortex, though that is just a speculation. It proceeds without regard to past or future, predominantly at an unconscious level. Since 'I hate you' becomes 'You hate me', we begin to see how the Freudian process of 'projection' occurs, and how antagonism can arise between individuals, groups or nations. The control of paleological thought is something which matters to all of us. Unfortunately, psychologists confine themselves entirely to studying the logical kind, so untypical of most of our mental activity.

Thus it is that they concentrate on how concepts are formed and manipulated. 'All thinking is conceptual thinking,' declare the authors of *The Chemistry of Thinking* with a bland disregard of the facts. Or they study problem-solving, setting the luckless student some awful brain twister and then attempting to discover how he worked out the answer. Professor John Dewey was nearer the mark when he described thought as 'active uncertainty'. It is a casting about among alternatives and an assigning of probabilities to different outcomes which is the constitutive feature of thought.

Thought depends, of course, on knowledge and it is interesting to ask how knowledge differs from 'memories'. Knowledge seems to imply the organising of concepts into schemata, and the integration of these schemata into higher-order schemata.

Knowledge, in short, is structured into higher and higher units. The intelligent man is he whose structural schemata accommodate the maximum number of new facts as they are acquired, and whose schemata are themselves integrated into a unitary whole.

So, at the neural level, we are talking about a system of networks imposed on a system of networks imposed on another – how many times. There are six layers in the cortex, and even six such networks have fantastic discriminatory and integrative powers, as von Foerster has shown. But in each of the six layers are many cells ranged above one another. We should probably think, therefore, not of regular layers but of numerous folia dissolving into one another. And as the connections and thresholds shift, functional networks will appear, expand, contract, join up, separate and vanish within the structural network. That is a concept of the brain of such power, of such potentiality as to defeat the imagination. And when we elaborate it further with the ideas of anelectrotonic conduction and magnetic fields, which I mentioned in Chapter Four, we have an instrument which could well be capable of the intricate ballet which we call human thought.

Why Can't a Computer be More Like a Man?

The power of our muscles has long been outstripped by machinery. If computers are going to outstrip the power of thought, what is there left to be proud of? This nagging anxiety is little more than a Jack o' Lantern and it may add to the peace of mind of many to summarise why a computer is not and can never be like a man.

Computers can certainly carry out some of the logical operations which men painstakingly carry out and do it far faster and more reliably. The sort of problem a computer is good at, and a man poor at, is the following:

1. If a and b and c are selected, or if f, h, i or k together, then d and e together or b and d together must not be selected.
2. i should be selected if a, h, k together or b, f, l together.

As there are several thousand possible combinations to try, a human being would take days to find the answers; a computer could do it in a fraction of a second. Probably the most successful application of computing to intellectual activities is the evolution of computer chess programmes. Northwestern University's CHESS 4·5 has defeated a number of International Masters and two Grand Masters at 'blitz chess' and in 1977 won the Minnesota Open Championship. The Scottish International Master David Levy, who has been defeated by it, considers that it plays better chess than 99·5 per cent of the world's chess-players. But such programmes do not play chess like humans do. They systematically explore, very rapidly, millions of possible outcomes. They have no insight into the situation. Whereas a human player explores only sixty or so outcomes but has insight. In addition, a human player studies his opponent's psychology – can he be flurried? is he getting tired? What manoeuvres has he favoured in the past? and so on. Chess programmes can often be defeated by doing something which is, on the face of it, stupid, because such a manoeuvre is not in their book. However, computers can be programmed to profit from their mistakes, modifying their own programmes, while even faster computers will be able to explore even further ahead so that before long we can expect computers to beat the best human players almost all the time.

Though progress in this rather artificial, narrowly delimited field has been surprisingly rapid, progress towards 'artificial intelligence' in general has been far slower than computer theorists anticipated. In the mid-sixties people like Herbert Simon were prophesying that by the mid-seventies computers would recognise speech and faces, translate languages, write good music and poetry, solve intellectual problems and in general have man running to keep up. In the event, it has proved far more difficult to equip them to handle such matters than was expected. Speech, for instance, turns out to have a much more complex structure than had been realised; so does music, let alone poetry. We can take much comfort from this; it turns out that our brains/minds have been doing a far more sophisticated job than we usually gave them credit for.

Moreover, as the computer expert Joseph Weizenbaum has demonstrated, a computer can only work within a narrow context: it can be set up to play chess, or translate, or imitate psychoanalysis, or model human personality, or control a space-craft . . . but someone has to put the right programme for the job on to the tape. Man can do any of these things and can write himself new programmes for jobs never envisioned before.

But it is not only at the intellectual level that computers are in a different ball-park from man. Computers are not motivated, they have no curiosity, they only address a problem when instructed to do so. Computers have no moral sense, no conscience; they are incapable of generosity. Computers have no aesthetic feelings, no sense of wonder, and – worst of all – no sense of humour. Lastly, they have no emotions, hence no values, attitudes or preferences. The human cortex, as it reasons, constantly refers the data to the mid-brain, which assesses the desirability of each step. Computers do not, as man does, sleep on a problem while their unconscious explores imaginatively the emotional balance sheet of various possible outcomes of what is planned. Man has a memory stocked with a huge range of personal experience, as well as 'facts', and any provisional decision is liable to be checked against such experience, consciously or unconsciously.

Weizenbaum emphasises the danger of leaving decisions to computers, in view of these vast deficiencies. A military computer may devise a strategy which will maximise the chance of victory, within the definition of victory embodied in its programme, but this could be a victory which was at an unacceptable price in broad human terms. (Presumably two of 'us' left alive and none of 'them' would constitute victory. Of course, a computer would be instructed to reject certain solutions, such as those involving unacceptable loss of life, but programmers are most unlikely to foresee all the possibilities and provide for them.)

Computers now modify their own programmes in the light of their own calculations with the result that we can never know how they reach their conclusions. We are forced to trust them – that is, to trust to the wisdom, care and even the value systems of those who programmed them. It is an abdication of human responsibility which I, for one, regard as totally unacceptable, even mad.

Weizenbaum describes the extraordinary fascination which programming a computer has for those who do it – how they have Coke and sandwiches brought in, and even sleep by the machine, writing and re-writing their programmes. When the machines produce the results expected, they feel a thrill of power. The results themselves are not of interest, it is the fact that they have cozened the computer into doing what they want that gets them. And this is the computer's most dangerous feature – that it is all too easy to treat it as if it were human. Weizenbaum himself wrote a programme called ELIZA (in memory of Eliza Doolittle in Shaw's play) which was able to simulate Rogersian psychoanalysis. Rogers' method is largely to turn the patient's last statement into a question of some kind, and this leads the patients to talk further. Weizenbaum's object was to demonstrate the fact that computers have to be given a narrow context within which to operate. He was horrified when many people took up his programme with enthusiasm, and forecast the day when a single computer would be able to 'psychoanalyse' hundreds of patients at once. That anyone should really imagine that people can be given emotional help outside a human relationship is a ghastly commentary on how we educate our scientists and even our doctors. Plastic breakfast cereals are bad enough; plastic emotions are far more sinister.

Weizenbaum (in his excellent book *Human Reason and Computer Power*) tells how his secretary was communicating with Eliza and asked him to leave the room so that he should not overhear the confidences she was imparting to it. And when he proposed to analyse the data acquired by the computer in several such exchanges, he was told, in scandalised tones, that this would be highly unethical!

To take computers seriously, as if they had minds, could be the worst folly the human race has ever committed.

The Seat of Reason

Coming at last to the central problem, what can we say about the relationship between thinking and the brain? Where is the seat of reason?

From way back, almost all neurologists and psychiatrists have been emphatic that thought and brain function are opposed concepts – that the intellect cannot be reduced to brain function. Psychologists, spurning this dualistic position, tried for a long time to explain thinking in terms of the association of ideas, but, as critics often pointed out, this model totally fails to account for the purposive element which is such a characteristic feature of thinking. Thought involves analysing problems, making schemes, and evaluating results. In contrast, Russian psychologists – notably the great L. S. Vygotsky – argued that analysis and generalisation depended on the logical structure of speech, and tried to show that thought was only a kind of subvocal speech. The truth, surely, is just the reverse: the structure of language reflects the structure of thought – but that is an idea unwelcome to materialists.

While the ultimate nature of thought remains mysterious, two important steps towards understanding it have been taken in recent years. Firstly, it is now accepted that thinking involves half a dozen distinct processes. We only think when we have a problem to solve or a task to perform for which no appropriate habitual solution is available. So the first stage is recognition of the problem, followed by restraint of any impulse to act in a habitual manner and investigation of what is needed. Then various alternatives are examined and a plan is developed. Next operations must be chosen to carry out the plan.

One can see these processes at work fairly clearly when a person is given a simple task to perform, such as assembling coloured blocks to form a given pattern – the sort of test which psychologists frequently use to test ability. 'If I put two white blocks back to back,' the testee says to himself, 'that might make the diamond shape I need to fill the hole.'

It was long thought that the last stage in thinking was effecting the solution, but it is now realised that there is a further highly important stage, namely, evaluation of the results – and, I would personally add, storage of the successful routine for future use. Failure to evaluate the success of one's ploy, as I suggested earlier, is tantamount to insanity.

The second advance has been to realise that these several processes involve different parts of the brain, more or less simultaneously. Luria, for instance, has shown that an individual whose occipital-parietal area is damaged can easily visualise the problem he has been set – constructing a white diamond, let us say – but, having lost all spatial judgment, cannot see how to solve it. On the other hand, a person with frontal lobe damage cannot see the problem or work logically towards solving it, even when given hints, although his spatial sense is perfect. Nor can he judge whether or not the moves he makes have been successful. Luria, generalising from such instances, concludes that, in normal thought, many different brain processes are working harmoniously together. And all this is just as valid for verbal or mathematical problems as for simple constructional ones.

In short, the process of thinking takes place 'through a series of concertedly working brain zones', to borrow a phrase from Luria. Thinking involves the whole brain. Perhaps that explains why thinking is such hard work.

However, the psychologists in their pragmatic way allow no room, when they speak of thought, for rumination or the kind of thinking known as fantasy. Solving problems with wooden blocks is not, I submit, a completely adequate paradigm of human thought, which involves imagery, associations, emotional loadings, and even one's personal response to one's ideas after formulating them. And who chooses the problem? No one asked Einstein to brood on relativity. Much less can we account for a Milton, a Goethe or a Racine.

The American psychologist Alan Fisher makes no bones about it. 'Scientists studying brain function from the inside out simply haven't even approached the stage at which the investigation of complex thought processes is either reasonable or possible,' he says.

17

'It Depends How I Feel'

TELEPATHIC AWARENESS OF EMOTION.

Does telepathy really occur? Many attempts to establish the fact scientifically by guessing cards have been made over the past forty-five years, with results which have not convinced everybody. But if telepathy is an unconscious process, would it not be better to look for an unconscious not a conscious response? Douglas Dean, a British engineer working at the Newark College of Engineering in New Jersey, decided to test this idea. He fitted both the 'sender' and the 'receiver' subjects with a plethysmograph, a device which records changes in the blood flow in the fingers. Then the sender was shown cards bearing the names of people, some of whom were people emotionally involved with the receiver, while others had been picked at random from the telephone book. The plethysmograph recordings were noticeably different when the significant names were being exposed. The two subjects were in different rooms, in some cases 250 yards apart, so that communication by other means was ruled out. Dean is working on a means of transmitting information in this way.

Source: E. D. Dean, 'Plethysmograph Recordings as ESP Responses', *Int. J. Neuropsychiat.* (1966) *2*:439–46.

Fifty Emotions?

If there is one thing which distinguishes a human being from a machine, it is surely that human beings feel. The point is not as trivial as it sounds, for some philosophers have, tacitly or in so many words, confined the word 'mind' to cognitive processes, to thought. The Oxford philosopher Gilbert Ryle, you will remember, excluded animals and children under five from possession of a mind. You might think, therefore, that study of emotions and feelings occupied a large part of the researches of those scientists who claim that the mind *is* the brain. In reality, the subject hardly figures at all. Looking in the index of a recent work, I find 'fear' (several references), 'anxiety' and 'rage' (a few references), and that is about all. Nothing about love, nothing about hope or joy, nothing about indignation or gratitude, nothing about amazement, humiliation or pride.

The explanation is obvious enough, of course. It is relatively easy to induce anxiety or fear in laboratory animals – even in humans, for that matter. Rage can be identified by highly aggressive behaviour. And that's about the extent of it.

Yet such studies use the word 'emotion' cheerfully enough, as if observations on anxiety, fear and rage could be generalised over the whole field. Rats which have been frightened or disturbed defecate. This is part of the body's preparatory routine for fighting and flight. But down in the reports it goes as: 'The rats displayed heightened emotionality.' Perhaps the experimenters' own lives are so emotionally impoverished that they cannot really understand what the word means. (This suggestion is not entirely ironic.)

Let us face up to the problem the psychologists so often evade and ask what the word emotion, as commonly used, includes. How many emotions are there?

One of the few people who have tried to answer this question, obvious as it might seem, is Joel Davitz, of Teachers College, Columbia University. Finding himself in a muddle during the course of a survey of emotion, he collected all the words used to identify emotions and after eliminating overlaps ended up with fifty definitions. His list is rather an odd one, as a matter of fact. Thus it does not include despair – surely one of the most profound of emotions and the true opposite of 'hope', which he does include. On the other hand, he treats 'panic' as distinct from 'fear', and 'enjoyment' as separate from 'pleasure' and 'delight'. I would have thought them different only in degree. Furthermore, his list includes 'apathy' and 'excitement', which I should regard as indicating levels of arousal rather than as feelings in the normal sense.

There are other uncertainties. Should we class pleasure and displeasure as emotions? Since some emotions are themselves describable as pleasant or unpleasant it would seem that pleasure/unpleasure is a distinct system underlying the whole complex. Pain, too, is unpleasant and emotions can be painful, so it must be regarded as a distinct system. Then are we to class appetitive feelings like thirst, hunger and satiety as emotions? Hunger and thirst are controlled from the same brain area – the hypothalamus – as the emotions, so perhaps thirst and hunger, together with awareness of heat and cold, represent the earliest signs of the emergence of emotion in the long evolutionary story.

However, this is not the place to split hairs. It is enough to say that there are something like fifty distinct emotions or feeling states. It is not clear to me that they are all akin, but I shall refer to them all as emotions, since no better terms are readily available. The existence of such a large number of emotions is rather extraordinary. The brain has to generate, or act as a substrate for, not just 'feelings' but for a great many qualitatively very different feelings. It would be helpful if those who claim the brain 'is' the mind would indicate, even in broad terms, how they think the brain does this. There are certainly small brain areas which, when electrically stimulated, give rise to feelings of fear or rage, of pleasure or pain. Are there then dozens of other centres which give rise to pride, despair, hope and so forth? No one has, I believe, ever suggested such a thing. Or does the brain set up special circuits which have such properties? Or is the answer chemical? There are chemical substances which cause elation and depression: are there then also chemical bases for amazement, liquid hope or pride-juice?

The problem would appear a little simpler if we could classify all these emotions into groups or assign them to a few underlying factors, but this also has proved an intractable problem; none of the schemes which have been proposed has thrown any light on the situation.

Thus Davitz divides emotions into five groups:

excitation
pro and con feelings
comfort/discomfort
ego-feelings (e.g. pride, inadequacy)
tension (irritability)

It's a good try but does not, I feel, make the nature of emotion any clearer. The psychiatrist Silvano Arieti distinguishes three groups:

tension appetite fear rage satisfaction	elicited by attack or by change in internal homeostasis
anxiety (imaged fear) anger (image-determined rage) wishing (imaged appetite) security (imaged satisfaction)	concerned with inner states
depression, anguish hate love joy	depend upon language and concepts

This gets us a little further and brings out the fact that emotions are linked with concepts and memories as well as with external situations, but it does not allow room for many important emotions.

The language we use often provides subtle clues in matters like this, so let us consider how the English language treats emotions. There are about a dozen which are expressed by verbs and they come in pairs: I trust, I fear; I love, I hate; I rejoice, I grieve; I hope, I despair; I admire, I despise; I yearn, I abhor. These are all things which we *do*. But then there is a large number of states expressed by adjectives: confident, anxious, happy, sad, curious, proud, humble, grateful, nostalgic, tense and so on.

Finally, there are the past participles, suggesting that something has been done to one – such as startled, depressed, frustrated, enraged, elated, ashamed, disgusted, excited, etc. The second group might be called moods, rather than emotions, and the third group might be called reactions. Emotions, it seems, are several sorts, but all of them spring from some kind of discrepancy between our desires (using the word very broadly to include bodily needs) and the situation as it exists.

The Effects of Syproxin

A British psychologist, Kenneth Strongman, after reviewing no fewer than twenty theories of emotion, concluded regretfully, 'There appears to be no theory which successfully provides a description of experiential feelings, physiological change and emotional behaviour . . . Some are too narrow, others too broad; some move hardly at all from empirical data, others are too speculative.' In point of fact, few of the theories he discusses attempt to explain emotion as such. Many of them, emanating from behaviourists, simply try to analyse the behaviour resulting from emotion; they regard emotion, in consequence, simply as motivation, as if it were not possible to have – for example – emotional involvement in music as an experience in itself. The two words, of course, come from the same Latin root, *movere*, to move. And it is unquestionably true that some emotions provide motives, especially the unpleasant ones, and above all, fear. But I very much question whether the same is true of all emotions. I may feel proud if I am praised for writing a good book, but it certainly is not the reason I write. And how would you fit in serenity or surprise?

Yet Professor Robert Ward Leeper, of the University of Oregon at Eugene, says dogmatically: emotions and emotional processes *are* motives.

Dottiest of all are attempts to treat emotion as part of information theory. Thus a Russian psychologist, P. V. Siminov, produces the specious formula: $E = N (I_n - I_a)$, which is a pretentious way of saying that emotion equals needed information less available information. Not only is it pretentious, it is obviously untrue. Fact and feeling are as different as chalk and cheese.

One of the few people to have offered a theory to resolve the confusion is Stanley Schachter of the University of California, who carried out an experiment which has given rise to a whole school of thought. He claims that there is fundamentally only one emotional state, namely arousal, and that the quality we assign to it – pleasant, irritating, alarming, etc. – comes from the social circumstances in which we find ourselves. The experiment which supported this conclusion was one in which he told a number of students that he wished to test a new drug called 'Syproxin', as part of a study of the effect of vitamins on vision. No such drug exists, what he really gave them was epinephrine (widely known by its trade name Adrenalin), or the tranquilliser chlorpromazine (sold under many trade names, e.g. Librium). A third group received placebos (pills with no clinical effect). He found that the group aroused by epinephrine felt more euphoric in agreeable situations, more irritated in irritating ones. Later, in a variant on this manoeuvre, he showed the students a comic film; the aroused ones found it more amusing than the students given placebo (the control group); the tranquillised ones found it less amusing than did the controls.

This experiment is frequently cited in the scientific literature as if it solved the riddle of emotion once and for all. But, as some of his peers pointed out, it was a rather sloppy experiment. For instance, he only checked arousal by taking pulse-rates. Arousal is a subtler state than one might think. Show a student nude pictures and his pulse-rate goes *down*, though his palms begin to sweat; but give him a mental problem or alarm him by plunging his arm into icy water and keeping it there, and the reverse occurs. Furthermore, there is evidence that irritability is peculiarly linked with nor-epinephrine metabolism.

However, the real objection, as I see it, is that euphoria and irritation, not to mention amusement, are rather specialised states of mind and there is no evidence that what is true of them is true of other moods and reactions, still less of powerful emotions like grief. Given Adrenalin, a bereaved person might be more agitated, but will he or she be more grieved? Obviously, grief is caused by the circumstance of being bereaved; we don't need Schachter's experiment to prove that. All he showed was the effect of arousal and calming.

When Schachter has shown that the same experience can produce both joy and grief in the same person on successive occasions, perhaps I'll believe him.

To meet the objection that Schachter's results were limited to cases of extreme autonomic arousal, Stuart Valins, of the State University of New York at Stony Brook, devised a different version. He showed a number of young men ten pictures of nude women and asked them to choose which they liked best. On some involved excuse about monitoring their reactions, he played what was supposedly the sound of their heart-beats through a loudspeaker. Actually these were pre-recordings of heart-beats at various speeds. He found that the men tended to choose those pictures which were shown to them when their heart appeared to them to be beating unusually fast or slow. But when the deceit was revealed to them, they stuck by their choices. Valins felt this showed the validity of the test, but perhaps they simply felt that they would look foolish if they switched.

Since what the young men were displaying was sexual interest, which is an appetite rather than an emotion, the experiment does not seem to me to prove Schachter's hypothesis. Such experiments reveal, I fear, the indifferent quality of most of the research so far done on this important subject. Nevertheless 'attribution theory', as it is called, has a fervent following in the USA.

Of course, long before Schachter came on the scene there were other theories, but they have not stood the test of time.

Butterflies in the Stomach

I've already mentioned the famous question: do you run away because you are afraid, or are you afraid because you run away? For nearly a century this theory of emotion held the field, and was known as the James-Lange theory. Although today it is in eclipse, it is worth seeing where it went wrong.

The ordinary man is reasonably clear, I am sure, that emotions are causes not consequences of action. The paradoxical contrary seems to have been first stated by a Frenchman, namely Dufour, who in 1883 asserted that it was 'the disposition of the visceral system which transmits to the brain the excitement it has received'. The new ideas were picked up by an American, William James, who, the following year, wrote an essay which became famous, entitled: 'What is Emotion?' He said: 'My thesis on the contrary, is that *the bodily changes follow directly from the PERCEPTION of the exciting fact and that our feeling of the same changes as they occur is the emotion.*' (His italics.)

In this controversy, which raged for twenty years, we can see reflected the battle between materialism and dualism. To make their claim stand up, the materialists almost invariably cite the case of fear. When we are afraid, numerous bodily changes occur which prepare us to fight or flee. The blood vessels contract, making bleeding less likely. We breathe more deeply and our heart beats faster, carrying more oxygen to the muscles. In extreme cases, we may urinate or defecate, lightening the burden we have to carry if we run. Our stomach contracts, and so on. We are certainly aware of these changes in fear: we have 'butterflies in the stomach'. But it is much more difficult to make the argument stick for, say, confidence, and quite impossible for, say, love. I can feel proud of a genuine achievement lying in bed totally relaxed. As for love: do you love a girl because you kiss her or kiss her because you love her? I must confess that I have kissed girls whom I never got to love and, what is much sadder, loved girls I never got to kiss.

James asserted, 'If we imagine some strong emotion and try to abstract from our consciousness of it all the feeling of its bodily symptoms, we find we have nothing left behind . . .'. To which I can only reply that this may have been true for James but it is not true of my own introspections. If I am thinking of something funny, and abstract the idea of creasing my face muscles, it still seems like a joke. One wonders what, if anything, goes on in the limbic system of psychologists. Life must be a desert for them.

When it was shown that the viscera were not the cause of fear, the Jamesians said it was the proprioceptive system, which conveys information about limb position and muscle tension, which does the trick. Actually, the proprioceptive system is remarkable for conveying no feeling tone.

This may strike you as obvious, but it took the sacrifice of hundreds of animals to convince psychologists, and some are not converted yet. Sherrington cut through the brain-stem and the nerves which run to the stomach in dogs. Cannon went further and sectioned the entire ganglionic system. De Somer and Heymans (the year was 1912) studied dogs' and cats' heads which had been entirely separated from their bodies and were kept alive by cross circulation from other animals of the same species. In every case the faces of these unfortunate animals showed the whole range of emotions – fear, disgust, anger, etc. – when presented with appropriate stimuli. All the materialists could think of was to say that you couldn't be sure that animals were *really* feeling the emotions.

Nobody thought to reply that people who are paralysed from the neck down feel emotions, especially despair.

In fact, as James was eventually forced to admit, emotion increases when its physical expression is blocked.

Odder still is the fact that in some clinical conditions people display all the physical signs of emotion but say they feel nothing. Dr Oliver Sacks, in his remarkable book *Awakenings*, describes how one of his patients, a victim of sleeping sickness, suffered terrifying respiratory crises: a violent gasp, like a drowning man surfacing, would be followed by involuntary breath-holding for up to fifty seconds, while she became purple in the face. 'Finally the breath would be expelled with tremendous violence like the boom of a gun.' The body was rigid, the blood pressure rocketed. But despite an expression of terror on her face, she declared that she felt no special apprehension. Later, when the attacks grew worse and more frequent, she began to feel 'a special strange sort of fear', but it was 'not a normal fear'. It was unlike anything she had felt before. In a similar way, patients with spinal-cord injuries sometimes display the physical signs of feelings but say they feel nothing subjectively.

I do not go so far as to say that there is no feed-back from the physical to the psychological state. To adopt a confident pose when one is afraid may help. Mothers say to their children, crying from some small hurt, 'Come on, smile.' But James claimed more than the existence of a connection; he said that the awareness *was* the emotion.

As you will recall, Pasquarelli and Bull tried to explore this idea by testing hypnotised subjects. One told them that he would pronounce a word expressive of an emotion and that they were then to try to feel it and to simulate the appropriate bodily response. After they had practised this, he would say: 'Now hold that pose, but think of the opposite emotion.' Some of his subjects replied that they could not do so. Said one: 'I want to put my shoulders back, but I can't. No pride.' The weakness of this experiment, one feels, is that the emotions were only being simulated in any case. If the subjects had been presented with a genuine cause for feeling – let us suppose an earthquake made the building collapse when they were in the posture of confidence – perhaps they would have got a different result!

The whole question entered a new phase in the twenties when Walter Cannon, Harvard's top physiologist, claimed, in contradiction to James, that there *was* a brain centre responsible for emotion; namely, the thalamus. This, you recall, is a structure lying immediately under the roof brain – one in either hemisphere, to be exact. If, as Cannon showed, you remove the roof brain of a cat, it shows intense fury; if, as Bard showed, you remove the thalamus too, it doesn't. In humans, when cortical control is abolished by light anaesthesia, laughter, rage and other reactions indicative of emotion may occur. In some forms of facial paralysis, though grimacing or whistling is impossible, yet the face moves normally in laughter or crying, scowling or frowning. The reverse is also found in some tumours of the thalamus. A Russian neurologist reported a patient who could move his face normally when he wished, but if he laughed spontaneously or grimaced in pain the right side remained still. Damage to another part of the connections between thalamus and cortex may produce uncontrollable laughing or crying which continues for many hours. In other cases of thalamic damage, hypersensitivity results. Pin-pricks, heat or cold, pressure, on the corresponding side of the body, cause great distress; warmth may evoke intense pleasure. Music and other psychological stimuli are also more intensely experienced.

Later work showed that other centres deep in the brain – the limbic system of which I have already written – is even more closely concerned with emotion. Here in this older part of the brain was a second neural system, coarser, diffuser, more sluggish than the new; one which prompts vigilance, determines attention, reinforces learning, and integrates our endocrine and vegetative systems. It does not analyse or look ahead, and it is here where our inmost life is lived.

Thus materialist accounts of emotion as a kind of epiphenomenon do not hold water.

Alas, the James-Lange theory did not expire gracefully. As late as 1941 Elizabeth Duffy, a professor at the University of North Carolina, wrote an article which is still pressed on students, entitled 'An Explanation of "Emotional" Phenomena without the use of the concept "Emotion" '. In it she complained that her repeated advice to everyone to abandon the whole concept of emotion had been ignored. 'Psychologists remain convinced,' she lamented, 'that the term refers to a distinguishable category of response.' With a bland naïveté verging on the dotty, she continued, 'One reason for the well-nigh universal belief in "emotion" is that every man has experienced a vivid, unforgettable condition which is different from the ordinary condition in which he finds himself. It may be more pleasant or more unpleasant, but it appears to have a unique quality which differentiates it from the general run of experience.'

You have to read the *Journal of General Psychology* if you wish to pick up pearls of wisdom of this quality.

Another pearl in the same paper is: 'But *all* behaviour is motivated. Without motivation, there is *no* activity.' Obviously she has never heard of doodling, or even of St Vitus' dance. And then again: '*All* responses, not merely emotional responses, occur as adjustments to stimulating conditions.' But the word 'response' implies something to respond to, so the statement is tautologous. 'All responses occur at some particular energy level.' And this is her theme: we can forget about emotion and just discuss the energy level and direction of responses. And so we can. Likewise, we can discuss music in terms of sound vibrations or tone intervals. The scientific term for this sort of reductionism is 'throwing the baby out with the bath water'.

Physiological psychologists have done a lot of work on bodily responses to emotion, hoping to find distinctive patterns of chemical or electrical response for each emotion – but with absolutely no success. The variations in physiological state seem to be the result of the arousal involved, rather than of the emotion itself.

The Chemistry of Emotion

While the psychologists remain baffled by the nature and origins of the emotions, the biochemists and electrophysiologists seem to have got their feet in the door. The biochemists have found drugs which relieve depression or even induce euphoria, and others which relieve anxiety. The chemical breakthrough came in 1952–3, when chlorpromazine, the first of the tranquillisers, was found to induce relaxation. It had originally been created in the hope that it would cause hibernation. Soon after, reserpine was isolated from the root of Rauwolfia, long used in India as a sedative. Initially it was given for hypertension, but proved to be very effective for anxiety and obsessive behaviour.

Exploiting this breakthrough, a great array of drugs was synthesised and tested; some of them proved helpful in schizophrenia and other mental disturbances, but that lies outside the present discussion.

Here let me just refresh your memory a little.

The electrophysiologists found centres in the brain which, when stimulated electrically, induced rage or fear. Most of these centres lay in or near the hypothalamus, the structure (or rather group of structures) below the third ventricle which controls temperature regulation, visceral responses and other bodily functions, including sleep and arousal. Ernst Gellhorn, the eminent neurophysiologist who has spent his life exploring the functional bases of emotion, declares that the hypothalamus does not just control the motor expression of the emotions but causes the emotions themselves, sending volleys of impulses up to the cortex as well as downward. Damage to the hypothalamus can cause persistent sexual activity, disturbances of body temperature, and continuous consumption of food *despite* decreased hunger, which does not tally with Gellhorn's claim.

There are also drugs, such as benzyl dimethylthamca and medmain, which send dogs mad with rage for several days; the effects are so severe that no one has dared try them on human beings. Presumably they also act on the hypothalamus, or on the amygdala, damage to which may cause fear, or fearlessness, or placidity or rage. In cats repeated stimulation of the amygdala produces frenzy.

Useful as these researches have proved clinically, they do little to resolve the puzzle of emotion. Although physiologists have inserted their probes into every part of the brain, they have found no sign of centres concerned with the higher or more complex emotions. Only depression and elation, fear, anxiety and rage seem to mediate in this way. There seems, therefore, to be no prospect of drugs which will bestow a sense of pride, infuse a feeling of shame, or – like the apocryphal love philtres of the past – turn disdain to affection. I suspect that the five emotions named are in a different category from the rest. It seems more likely that the complex emotions arise from brain activity patterns as a whole: as we have seen, the brain prefers to distribute its functions whenever possible. Moreover, it is often found that a weak stimulation produces the opposite effect from a strong one, and that stimulation in one animal produces the opposite kind of behaviour to that produced by stimulating the same point in another animal. All this suggests the existence of a system in a state of balance; disturbance can tilt the system either way.

Most of our emotions depend on cognitive factors: on what we expect to happen or know has happened in the past. They must, therefore, involve the cortex as well as the older part of the brain where our most basic feelings – crude responses concerned with survival such as animals too must feel – are located. As the diagram on page 290 suggests, we are dealing with an elaborate interlocking pattern.

There are other mysteries associated with emotion besides the problem of where they arise. Why, for instance, do people vary in emotionality? There is some evidence that childhood stress increases emotionality, and some that it crushes it. There may well be an inherited component: do men differ from women as is often said, or is any difference due to differences in upbringing? And although we can now cure the persistent gloom known as endogenous depression, we are as far as ever from understanding the cause. It is established that childhood bereavement, such as the loss of a loved parent, can create a lifelong sense of depression. How does it come about that such an experience permanently alters brain chemistry?

Freud said: 'It is surely of the essence of an emotion that we should feel it, i.e. that it should enter consciousness.' Yet the fact is that emotion can persist at an unconscious level, as we know from those cases, mentioned earlier, when a painful experience is repressed from consciousness but comes pouring out after the administration of so-called 'truth drugs'. The traumatic experience is not just remembered, it is vividly *relived*. Two chapters earlier, when we discussed memory, I argued that we have a special memory system devoted to emotion. Such suppressed emotion could account for long-standing depression, or for long-standing elation, for that matter. But is it only primary emotion, like fear and horror, which thus persists? We do not know.

Oliver Sacks, in his book on sleeping sickness and Parkinsonism, emphasises the folly of trying to separate the emotional from the physical components in these diseases. Parkinsonism 'affects the very basis of action and perception'. The patient is unable to move because he feels unable to move. He is unable to initiate. He may not be able to speak unless he is first spoken to. Feelings, one may be sure, spring from the same neural patterns as those which initiate and organise behaviour.

But how and why this happens remains a total mystery, which the incantations of scientists and philosophers have done nothing at all to dispel.

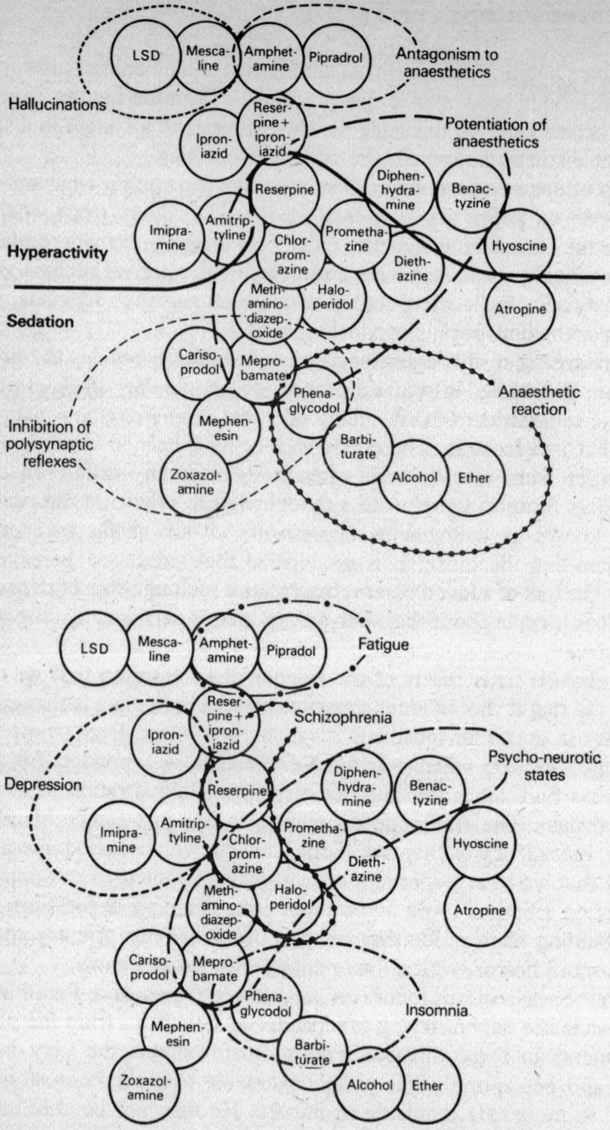

An idea of the complexity of brain chemistry is given by these diagrams, based on information available in 1959 and 1963, showing the interlocking and overlapping effects of various psychotropic drugs. Above, *the subjective effects: hallucination, etc.* Below, *the clinical applications, such as cure of depression.*

Conclusion

The common feature of all the theories I have mentioned – and most others, for that matter – is that they start from the assumption that emotions are epiphenomena, mere side effects. Emotions, it is assumed, arise from brain patterns but do not themselves bring about new brain patterns and hence are not causes of behaviour. This, of course, is precisely the opposite of our intuitive impression.

However, E. Jacobson, after very careful studies, has been unable to detect any time-lag between the electrical response to a stimulus and the experiencing of a subjective feeling. It is noticeable too that we tend to trust our feelings in preference to our cognitive knowledge. As the lady with the disturbed body image said: 'My eyes and my feelings don't agree and I have to trust my feelings.'

The materialists would like to show emotions as learned responses, but such evidence as there is suggests that they are inborn. For instance, the duckling separated from its mother utters cries of distress. This behaviour is certainly inherited genetically and, if any feeling accompanies it, then that must have been present from the start. Similarly, a baby recoils from the edge of a cliff with signs of alarm, even when it has never been placed on the edge of a cliff before.

It is also taken for granted that emotions are conscious in these discussions; but we do not always recognise our emotions immediately, while the casebooks of psychiatrists are full of accounts of emotions which have been repressed from consciousness. Finally, it is often overlooked that emotions manifest at several levels.

As I have tried to bring out, the brain functions by means of patterns: I would expect emotions to reflect overall patterns rather than to be produced by specific mechanisms, though it may be that the most basic emotions, such as rage and fear, established early in evolution, are produced by specific mechanisms and that only the higher emotions have an overall character. The failure of science to provide even a sketchy but convincing account of emotion suggests to me, very strongly, that some major factor in the story is still unidentified.

PART FIVE

Outcomes

18

Ghosts and Machines

LIMITED OUTLOOKS

Johannes Nielsen, a Scandinavian psychiatrist, describes a patient who could recognise animate objects, such as people, but not anything inanimate. He asked what cars were and what mountains were, but recognised a mule and a daffodil. He could see nothing in his left visual field and was found, when his brain was examined after his death, to have severe damage in Area 19. In contrast with this, another patient (a woman) could only see inanimate objects. She could see a hammer but not the doctor's finger, and did not perceive her own dentures on a tray! She insisted there were no teeth there. Shown a very realistic doll, she could only say, 'It's pink.'

Source: J. R. Nielsen, *Agnosia, Apraxia, Aphasia*, 1946.

Whatever Happened to the Soul?

The philosopher Bertrand Russell once told how his parents used to madden him by replying to his childish questions about mind with words: 'What is mind? Doesn't matter. What is matter? Never mind.' Doubtless it was the wish to prove to them that such questions do matter that impelled him to become a philosopher and spend a good part of his life debating such issues. Alas! what the philosophers have to say about mind has, for me at least, confused the issue, not clarified it.

As I briefly noted at the outset, ever since the days of the Greeks, there have been two main views about mind, and the conflict between them has never been resolved. We must now look more closely at this debate, since it concerns the very core of our subject. The classic view, known as dualism, sees mind as a mysterious insubstantial something acting on the brain but independent of it and capable of continued existence after the brain has turned to dust. Since this is compatible with the idea of the survival of the individual after death it appeals to many. (Some authorities distinguish mind from soul, some do not.) Though it originated in Greece, dualism is usually credited to Descartes, who certainly stated the position emphatically. The mind, Descartes said, is made of an immaterial substance (whatever that is), occupies no space and acts on the body through the pineal gland. Dualism is deeply embedded in our thinking and in our language, as when we speak of 'a healthy mind in a healthy body'.

The second position, known as monism, is materialist. It says that 'mind' is just a name for the activities of the brain and has no more existence on its own than, say, the 'performance' of a car. The philosopher D. M. Armstrong says the mind is 'that which has mental states. Less accurately but more epigrammatically, the mind is simply the brain.' In the past hundred years this view has gained more and more adherents. Most scientists are materialists and pour scorn on dualism as an attempt to rationalise our insecurity.

The vast defect of dualism is that you have to postulate the existence of a mysterious substance unknown to science and inconsistent with the normal laws of nature. What is a non-material substance which occupies no space? What reason have we to suppose anything of the sort exists? Scientists ask how a non-material substance can affect, or be affected by, the material substance of the brain, since in all other contexts, material substances are only causally affected by other material substances, or by the known forces such as gravity and electromagnetism. If the material can affect the immaterial, we should be able to manipulate it in some way. And where, asks the sceptic, does the mind exist? Is it situated within the skull or does it float loosely round its possessor like some kind of ectoplasm? Can minds affect other minds, and if so, how? Can they be fused together, diluted or otherwise tampered with? What kind of rules define their capacities? Do they continue to exist when the body dies, or do they need it as a sort of power-house, anchorage or sense-organ? To all such questions the dualists can return, at best, only speculative replies.

Further difficulties present themselves. If brain and mind are separate and distinct, can one affect the other? Three different answers are offered: (1) Brain can affect mind but not the reverse; (2) Brain and mind can affect each other or interact; (3) Brain and mind just happen to move in parallel. Few people now take the last view seriously. But the other two raise the problem of how a material thing can act on an immaterial thing. To create a physical effect you need energy. If the mind acts on the body, where does its physical energy come from; in the reverse case, where does it go to? The law of conservation of energy is at stake.

To postulate the existence of a substance of which we have no knowledge, which defies physical law and on which we cannot do any physical experiments, is to explain the obscure by the still more obscure. Few scientists feel able to take any stock in dualism.

The scientists' dislike of dualism goes deeper, however: it stems from the fact that dualism undermines the whole scientific attempt to provide a consistent rational explanation of the universe in terms of a few basic laws.

Less than a century ago many biologists, notably Hans Driesch, believed that life and living processes could never be explained by the laws of physics and chemistry. Driesch postulated a mysterious 'vital force' to account for the powers of living matter to form and repair itself. Today, however, biologists understand in some detail the physical and chemical processes involved and *élan vital* is seen to be unnecessary. This makes them all the more confident that 'mind' is likewise an unnecessary hypothesis. In the last fifty years the living cell has been revealed as a piece of complex machinery, microminiaturised in a manner which seemed inconceivable in the time of Driesch. (Even the origin of life no longer seems mysterious. To the biologists of the nineteenth century inheritance also seemed inexplicable: how could anything as small as the cell contain the necessary information to specify the whole organism, and how could egg and sperm, on fusing, recombine this information in the required manner? Today this is a well understood story.)

Thus materialism, in the philosophical sense, has been sweeping all before it. Scientists feel deeply uneasy at the suggestion that their system has some major weakness.

Science is popularly thought to be 'finding out how things work'. But scientists have a grander, almost religious aim. They like to believe that all phenomena are, in principle, explainable in terms of the basic physical laws. Biology can be reduced to chemistry, chemistry to physics. The behaviour of living organisms depends, in the last analysis, on the performance of a large number of chemical reactions. Chemical reactions depend on the physical properties of molecules and atoms. This belief is known as reductionism. To preserve this reductionist philosophy, it is necessary that psychology shall reduce to biology. Consequently, if to explain mental activity we have to introduce some new factor, unknown to physics, the whole position crumbles, and the prospect that everything is explainable becomes uncertain. It is for similar reasons that many scientists are so bitterly opposed to the notion of extra-sensory perception and to the idea of paranormal phenomena of any kind.

Thus, for many scientists, to treat the brain as a machine is essential to their peace of mind: and perhaps, to be fair, to their aesthetic sense, for the idea of the universe as a harmonious system of interactions has an aesthetic appeal. They scarcely consider the possibility that some additional hypothesis might have to be conjoined with what they already know, much as electro-magnetism has to be superimposed on to eighteenth-century physics, revealing a more complex harmony than had been envisaged.

In short, as Edinburgh's John Beloff has said, mind is 'the last important philosophical impediment to the unity of the sciences'.

Defects of Materialism

But if dualism is unsatisfactory, materialism is not much better. The dualists ask: 'how can a collection of nerve cells "be" mind?' The frequency of electric pulses in a nerve is not the same as smelling garlic. It is just this difference which is the source of the problem. Again, if the mind 'is' the brain, does this mean the whole mind is the whole brain? If so, why is it that one can cut out pieces of the brain with little or no perceptible effect on subjective experience, let alone on behaviour?

In their attempt to meet such objections, the monists try to explain away subjective phenomena such as mental images. Some even try to confine the term 'mind' to 'knowledge'. Thus James G. Taylor says: 'The essence of consciousness is simultaneity of knowing,' and, 'The simultaneous knowing of a large number of facts about the environment . . . is precisely what is meant by being conscious.' This seems to me pure nonsense! If knowing facts is a sufficient criterion of consciousness, then a computer is conscious. It totally fails to explain what I have called the Omega Effect.

The central idea of monism has been expressed in several forms, which I shall briefly examine, before making a different suggestion. I shall call them the Morning Star version, the gene/DNA version, and the screech-of-the-brakes version.

The first name I take from an analogy often used by philosophers. The Morning Star and the Evening Star, though we call them by different names, are identical. That is, they are the same object – namely, the planet Venus – viewed on different occasions and in different circumstances. So, too, the mind and the brain, they explain. However, I believe that the Morning and Evening Star are the same because they are the same kind of thing and because astronomers can explain convincingly how it is that one material object can suffice to explain the two observations. But the philosophers offer no such model to account for the alleged identity of brain and mind, which do not even look to be the same kind of thing. It is precisely this qualitative dissimilarity which constitutes the problem.

Philosophers have recently found a rather closer analogy in the relationship between the gene, in genetics, and the DNA molecule in biochemistry. The geneticist talks about inheritance in one language, they point out, the biochemist in another. The former is concerned with a process, the latter with the underlying mechanism. But is this really a valid analogy? Surely the high-level correlate for neurophysiological mechanisms is 'behaviour'? Both languages refer, in the last analysis, to the recombination of certain physical bits and pieces. Mind, precisely, does not.

Whether we talk of 'Identity Theory' or 'Double Aspect Theory', monism remains the assertion of a belief, not of an empirical fact.

Finally, there is the view that mind is an 'epiphenomenon' – an incidental effect of no more consequence than the screech of brakes when a car is slowed. But what does the word epiphenomenon really mean? All mechanisms produce effects (which may or may not be useful). Electrically pumped, a ruby surprises us by emitting a novel sort of light, coherent light. A computer calculates. Can we then show that if neurones are organised into a brain, subjective experience *necessarily* results? Once again, the point is that the screech of brakes is a physical phenomenon, explicable by the same laws which account for the deceleration of the car; whereas subjective experience is not to be accounted for by the laws of neurophysiology. One effect is predictable, the other not.

The screech-of-brakes theory carries the further implication that mind is secondary, something produced by the brain but not capable of influencing it. Hence it leads us into much the same position as does the upward-causation version of dualism; namely that we feel afraid incidentally to running away and do not run away because we are afraid. We are back at the Jamesian position.

In the course of their attempts to support monism, philosophers are often driven, unaware, into substantially dualist positions. For instance, they assert that we only know the contents of our own mind, we do not know about the world as it is. But the remarkable and significant fact is that we are *not* aware of our own neurophysiological processes. What we are aware of is the real world. Our impressions may not always be accurate, but at least we perceive it as having warmth, extension and so on. We do not perceive a train of pulses.

Note the implicit dualism of the notion of 'me' sitting within my brain observing. With what organs could I observe? We are back at Disney's little man with his television set, and an infinite regress. The truth is, the experience is co-present with the physiology. To the extent that dualism implies such a regress, it must be in error. So we have to face the fact that the co-presence of awareness with neurophysiology is a fact outside the present bounds of science, instead of trying to reduce it to mechanism.

The plain fact is that neither monism nor dualism offers satisfactory accounts of the facts. It is very noticeable, if one reads philosophical books on this question, that each side confines itself to pointing out the defects in the arguments of the other side and offers little or nothing in the way of positive support. But to dispute your opponent's cause does not prove your own. John Beloff has made the additional point that a strictly materialist view leaves paranormal phenomena, such as telepathy, without an explanation, whereas dualism at least provides some kind of basis for such phenomena.

And I can suggest a further reason for dissatisfaction. According to Paul Dirac and some other distinguished physicists, the best thing about a good theory is its elegance. On this basis, both monism and dualism fail. Faced with this impasse, scientists tend to react in different ways. Some just put the question on one side by referring to neurological mechanisms as 'the substrate of mind'. They appeal here to a biochemical analogy: substrates are materials on which enzymes act and which can also evoke appropriate enzymes. The phrase is meant to leave the issue for others to resolve.

Some of the leading figures, however, reject a mechanistic view. 'An explanation solely in terms of biochemistry is simply not possible.' These words are Roger Sperry's, but much the same thing has been said by Sir Charles Sherrington, in his day, and more recently by Sir John Eccles, Professor Seymour Kety and others.

Currently a number of eminent thinkers are moving towards the idea of 'emergent interactionism' as the most plausible assumption. The philosopher Karl Popper asserts this in his latest book (written in conjunction with Sir John Eccles) *The Self and its Brain*. Walter B. Weimer likewise concludes: 'Epistemologically, the only tenable mind-body position is an emergent interactionism.' On the biological side support comes from Roger Sperry, who says: 'Mind is an emergent property of cerebral excitation.' In the course of evolution, awareness developed into self-awareness, self-awareness into reflection. And Sperry is definite that mind can affect the brain as well as the reverse. However, the expression is dualist and Sperry does not really face up to the underlying question of *how* this comes about.

On Talking Nonsense

In 1949 a book appeared which enjoyed an immediate *succès d'estime*. It was called *The Concept of Mind* and was by the Wayneflete Professor of Metaphysical Philosophy at the University of Oxford, Gilbert Ryle, then forty-nine. It was a curious work, full of unsupported not to say unsupportable assertions ('There is no such thing as mental images') and logical confusions. It argued largely by analogy. It had no notes or bibliography and hardly, one might say, qualified as an academic work. It was written in what Ryle himself called a style of 'deliberate abusiveness' and set out the materialist position by attacking what he firmly called 'the Cartesian myth'. No doubt its success was due to the fact that an increasing number of people were looking for justification of a materialist (and incidentally Marxist) world-view. Consequently it was read far more widely than is usual with philosophical works and is still influential today. Yet it was all wrong.

Ryle opened his book with a vivid image. When the first locomotives crossed the American plains, the Indians could not understand how they were powered and assumed that there was a horse somewhere inside. In the same way, said Ryle, we – intelligent though we think ourselves – cannot understand how the brain functions and assume that hidden inside it is a ghost called the mind. This, said Ryle, is 'the dogma of the Ghost in the Machine', adding, 'I hope to prove that it is entirely false, and false not in detail but in principle.'

Ryle seemed to think of mind mainly as cognitive, intellectual activity and excluded from consideration animals and children as not having minds – a narrower definition than some of us would wish to make. He spends a lot of time denying the existence of mental images, since these are fatal to his position. Much of what he has to say is too involved to be of interest – it concerns the use of words more than the nature of the facts – but he does produce one argument which has won many converts and so deserves our attention. This is the claim that to talk about the mind is a 'category mistake'. I myself have met young philosophers who dismissed the whole subject as closed by citing this phrase, as if it were some kind of magic spell.

Language is such that we can, and often do, construct sentences which are syntactically satisfactory but logically absurd. Thus we might say: 'How do you spell the letter A?' The philosopher calls this a category mistake because he considers the word 'spell' to be in a different logical category from the letters of the alphabet. The example Ryle uses to illustrate his case about the mind is that of the foreign visitor to Oxford who, after being shown the colleges and other buildings, asks, 'Where is the University?' In Ryle's view, the word 'university' relates to the collegiate buildings much as 'spell' relates to collections of letters. Similarly, Ryle maintains, the word 'mind' refers to various brain activities, and to ask to see the mind is as vain as to ask to see the university.

But one can push this argument too far. There is a sense in which the university does exist and it can display behaviour, form plans and execute them in a way which the colleges themselves could not. So also the mind exists and displays unique behaviour, even if it cannot be distinguished from the brain in a physical sense.

Ryle uses a rather closer analogy when he imagines a foreigner watching a cricket match and asking, 'Where is the team spirit?' Notice that this is quite a different kind of instance from the previous one: the team spirit is not made up from the stumps, ball, umpires and players – it is not just a collective term. The collective term is 'team' or something of that kind. But 'team spirit' refers precisely to a mind-state of the kind we are worrying about. Thus *this* analogy actually defeats Ryle's purpose.

Philosophers are right to warn us against the pitfalls of language, to be sure, and we should not allow ourselves to be misled by the dualist nature of language into assuming a dualist view of the mind/brain problem. But of course the real problem is not whether it is permissible to employ certain words – this diversion of the problem on to *words* is typical of philosophers – but how to explain the Omega Effects. We can explain the performance of the car in terms of its structure. We cannot explain Omega Effects in terms of brain structure. There may not be a horse concealed in the locomotive, but if there isn't any steam there either, how does it run? Whether we drop the word 'mind' or not, this problem continues to plague us. Even if there were no such words as 'mind' and 'mental' in our vocabulary, the subjective phenomena which we all continuously experience would obstinately persist and demand some explanation. Using words carefully may help us to avoid erroneous conclusions, but linguistic precision does not itself solve factual problems.

As the philosopher Herbert Feigl declared, after a lengthy study of the question: 'I conclude that the mind-body problem is not a pseudo-problem.'

In the Beginning Was the Word

The fact of the matter is that philosophers are, in a profound sense, oriented towards words and not towards images. (As we saw in Chapter Sixteen, people tend to be oriented either to words or to images.) Thus they are preoccupied by statements about reality rather than models of it. John Beloff has wittily said that the object of philosophy is to prevent you talking nonsense. But he does not mean by this, 'making statements which do not conform with the real world' – as who should say: 'It looks like a fine day,' and receive the reply: 'What nonsense, it is snowing.' By nonsense he means (and it is the proper use of the word) sentences which don't make sense. As already noted, it is a property of language that we can construct sentences which are syntactically satisfactory but have no meaning, e.g. we can describe something as 'a square circle'. That is an obvious example, but other follies are not immediately obvious. It is this aspect of language which fascinates philosophers. For instance, in a book on *Dreaming* by Cornell University's Norman Malcolm, we do not find the expected discussion of sleep-patterns, dream content, etc. We start right off with the problem of what we should think if someone (who is not lying or joking) says to us: 'I am dreaming.' The practical man replies that in the nature of things such an event is unlikely but, if it did occur, it would be an interesting topic for research. (In point of fact, dreams which continue after waking are on record. Heavy doses of chlordiazepoxide [Librium] often have this effect, according to a report by D. S. Viscott. As one patient said: 'My dream wouldn't stop.')

One imagines at first that this question has been raised as a *jeu d'esprit* for the start of the book, then one is amazed to discover that the whole book is about it! This is really so odd and so typical, it calls for comment. Malcolm seems to see in it a paradox similar to the Cretan paradox beloved of philosophers. In case you do not know it, it goes like this. A Cretan says to you, 'All Cretans are liars.' If the statement is true, he has made it false by telling the truth. If it is false, he has made it true by telling a falsehood. The practical man will respond by asking whether it is being asserted that all Cretans lie on each and every occasion that they make a statement, or only some of the time. If it is replied that he is to assume they invariably lie, then he will respond by saying: 'In that case, the Cretan would not have made such a statement; he would have assured me that Cretans do not lie.' Alternatively, if he did make such a statement, the assertion would merely cease to be true as of that moment. But of course the philosopher is not concerned with the veracity or otherwise of actual Cretans. He is fascinated by the capacity of language to produce a logical paradox. (Bertrand Russell devised an even neater example: a card which bears on one side the words, 'The statement on the back of this card is true,' and on the other the words, 'The statement on the back of this card is false.')

Philosophers are very given to setting up an arbitrary distinction and then spending untold effort trying to fit the facts to it. It is rather as if they distinguished two kinds of cat: black and white, and then spent hours discussing in which category to put tabbies. Thus Ryle distinguishes specific senses (such as vision) from non-specific ones (such as the kinaesthetic sense which tells you about the position of your limbs) – but it is never demonstrated that this distinction has any functional significance.

Scholars much abler than I have analysed Ryle's errors in detail; for example, Professor C. W. K. Mundle. My object, however, is not simply to demolish Ryle, in case some reader has been misled by his casuistical arguments, but rather to demonstrate the emptiness of purely verbal analyses. The problem of mind will not go away just because of verbal reformulations. Philosophers, I fear, have little of value to tell us about the mind.

Rather disarmingly, Ryle, after castigating the psychologists for failing to provide an account of mind as comprehensive as Newton's account of physical law, adds that the philosophers are not much better. They promised us an account of 'the World as a Whole' but, 'in fact they have practised a highly proprietary brand of haggling'. I couldn't have put it better myself.

The distinctions made by philosophers generally confuse the issue because there is no unambiguous relationship between the verbal formulae in which they are made and the reality. The philosopher C. D. Broad has put this very well. When water was shown to consist of hydrogen plus oxygen, he asks, was this a Double Aspect theory? Or was it an instance of Epiphenomenalism – wateriness being an epiphenomenon of the chemical elements? Or was it perhaps Interactionism – since each produces the other? Or could it be called Parallelism – since when one appears the other disappears? As this analogy amusingly shows, the distinctions are ambiguous in themselves and, in any case, do not help us to understand the relationship between the two terms. Only physical chemistry does that.

Philosophers also confuse the issue by making category errors themselves. Does it make any sense (Broad asks) to speak of states of consciousness as being located anywhere? One does not speak of a car's performance as being 'located' in the car: to do so would be to reify the idea of 'performance'. Similarly, one does not speak of calculation as being 'located' in a computer.

As these examples suggest – and it would be easy to find many more – philosophers not only ask the wrong questions but encourage us to think in the wrong terms. The right question is: what processes are occurring? To infer these processes, we have to start from end-results. Just as the performance of a car leads us to infer things about the engine, steering, suspension, etc., so terms like 'thought', 'emotion', 'memory', 'attention', 'perception' lead us to study processes and to consider what structures underlie those processes.

Towards a New Synthesis

I have often noticed that when a controversy between two radically opposed theories drags on for a long time, it usually turns out that the dichotomy was a false one. The question had been wrongly posed. A classic instance is the fifty-year-long dispute between neurologists as to whether the conduction of nerve-impulses was electrical or chemical in nature. (The two factions were, as you recall, known as the 'spark' men and the 'soup' men.) It turned out that nerve conduction depended on both. The proponents hoped for a simple explanation, but it turned out that the answer was complex.

So I suspect that the controversy between monists and dualists may have the same character. The antithesis may be artificial. The choice the philosophers have presented to us, like the choice between black and white cats, is probably a needlessly restricted one. I would look for something which had both dualist and monist aspects, and I would expect it to resolve the apparent discrepancy between physical and mental at the same time.

The most obvious explanation would be that brain and mind are two aspects of something more fundamental – a 'tertium quid' as it has been called in philosophy. Though the idea has been mooted before (it was Bertrand Russell's view, among others), it has never found favour, perhaps because it seemed to complicate further a universe which was already complicated enough. However, modern physics has shown that the underlying structure of the universe is complicated to an incredible degree, so that *a priori* rejection of the idea no longer seems justifiable. We cannot exclude the possibility that the structures we perceive in three-dimensional space have extensions in a fourth dimension. In this case they must be endowed with properties manifesting mainly in hyper-space. What we detect in our space could be only a cross section of the totality, and its nature and cause would be as resistant to explanation as are some physical phenomena. As Professor J. B. S. Haldane remarked: 'The universe is not only queerer than we think but queerer than we *can* think.'

Be that as it may, we have to recognise that the phenomena we have been exploring demand a new postulate. William of Ockham warned us not to multiply assumptions unnecessarily; but, as biologists have repeatedly found, it often *is* necessary. As I said at the start, we may be rather in the position of primitive natural philosophers trying to explain thunder and lightning without the concept of electricity. The deity theory (Jove hurling thunderbolts) and the physical theory (clouds banging together) are equally unsatisfactory. A major new conceptual system, namely electro-magnetic theory, was needed. I suggest that the brain sciences are in a similar position.

The facts oblige us to recognise the *existence of a property not covered by existing theory* but (we may assume) not incompatible with it. The brain is an uniquely complex system and may well have unique properties. In short, the answer I foresee is that, while mind will be fitted into the scientific system, the system will have to be dramatically enlarged to accommodate it. Science will no longer be quite the same.

19

Who Holds the Reins?

HELP! HELP!

An acquaintance of mine, a youngish stockbroker, joined with some friends to spend a holiday hunting for sunken pirate gold in the West Indies. One day, his companions set off to explore a bay some distance away, but my friend, who was not feeling himself, stayed behind on their rented motor-vessel with the 'crew', a young West Indian. In the afternoon, feeling better, he donned his wet-suit and aqualung and, just to pass the time, began to explore the nearest reef. For a while he enjoyed looking at the seaweeds and brilliantly coloured fishes. Suddenly a wave swung him against the rock and his oxygen cylinder became wedged in a crack. He struggled to free himself but was unable to do so. At first there was ten minutes supply of oxygen left, then five, then three. He began to face the idea of death. Then suddenly he saw a black shape approaching. It was the deckhand, who succeeded in freeing him.

Later, when his friends returned, they reproached him for setting off under water unaccompanied. Then one of them was struck with a thought. Turning to the West Indian, he asked: 'But how did you know he was in trouble?'

'Man, I heard him calling,' he replied.

Does the Mind Have Undiscovered Powers?

As I move towards a conclusion, three curiously interrelated questions seem to demand an answer. The first is whether the mind has powers not recognised by orthodox science, such as the power of telepathy or of foreseeing the future. If it does, the case for supposing that science will have to be enlarged becomes much stronger; it becomes definite that science needs some new postulates. The second question is: are we machines? Is there any referent left for the word 'soul'? And, as a pendant to this, comes the much-argued question: do we have free will? The third question is foxiest of all. Does life have a purpose? For, according to some philosophers, including the great William James, 'Where you have purpose, there you have mind.'

Whole books have often been written on such matters, of course, and it may be an act of folly to compress them into a chapter. Nevertheless, although I cannot undertake to explore them in exhaustive detail, I shall try to show how they stand up in the light of what we have surveyed.

I start then with the question of what are usually called 'paranormal phenomena'. The implications of the term are not quite clear, but I take it to mean powers which, if they exist, are not explicable by the corpus of scientific knowledge as it exists, without any implication that science is defied. Rushton's dilemma states: 'The trouble with parapsychology is that it is nearly impossible to believe that it is true and nearly impossible to believe it is false.' That is also my impression. On the one hand, it is incredible that after a century of rather thorough investigation (the Society for Psychical Research was founded in 1882), there should be no generally accepted core of reliable data or any body of theory which has been experimentally tested.

In these circumstances I can only state a personal position. I feel confident of the existence of telepathy, and I am inclined to believe in the possibility of precognition. I know of no *a priori* reason why these phenomena should not be fitted into the scientific scheme of things sooner or later. I find it much harder to believe in the movement of solid objects by mental effort, known as psychokinesis, and still harder to believe in materialisation. I regard ghosts and apparitions as hallucinations probably triggered by association or suggestion.

My confidence in the existence of telepathy is based ultimately on personal experience, and I shall describe two rather clear-cut instances. Obviously for you who read they are second-hand information, but any other information would be third-hand, so it will have to do.

In 1933 I read a book by one C. W. Olliver called *The Extension of Consciousness* in which he described the kind of card-guessing experiments later made famous by J. B. Rhine. Rhine is usually given the credit, incorrectly, of having been the first to think of this approach. In 1933 I at once realised that making a large number of guesses on a simple choice offered advantages over trying to guess a few complex things, such as the subject of pictures, where it is difficult to score. I therefore made a number of experiments with friends and acquaintances, using blue and red plastic cards sealed in envelopes. Most of the results were insignificant or inconclusive, but I found one couple – a naval captain whose wife was also his first cousin – with whom the results were astonishing. The husband could transmit to the wife, but not vice versa. He was, in fact, a powerful visualiser, and the inventor of the navy's principal gunlaying system. As it was very soon obvious that telepathy was occurring, we dispensed with the time-consuming business of wrapping cards in envelopes, and simply had the two people in adjoining rooms, while I observed the operation from the hallway. It turned out that two conditions were necessary: first the recipient must not try to succeed. Results were best if she was engaged in some routine activity, such as sewing or washing up, and made her guess quite casually. Second, the faculty speedily tired (or the operators became bored). We therefore made guesses at intervals of several minutes or even more, at convenient moments, and we would not make more than ten guesses in an evening. In these conditions several runs of ninety per cent success were made. We also tried using ordinary playing cards; there were occasional confusions between hearts and diamonds, or clubs and spades (but none between red and black cards) while a nine might be mistaken for a ten, or a king for a knave. The captain went to Australia in the course of his duties and I was unable to find any other successful subjects; moreover I had to earn a living, so I was unable to pursue the subject. And when Rhine took it up it seemed unnecessary to do so.

The second anecdote concerns the playwright Wynyard Browne, who wrote *The Holly and the Ivy* and other plays. We had known each other at Cambridge, and in 1939 I found myself staying in Norwich with the producer Walter Nugent Monck, the director of the Maddermarket Theatre. Wynyard lived near Norwich and I spent an evening with him attending a séance (which we thought wholly unconvincing) as he wished to describe one in a novel he was writing. Afterwards we went to Monck's house in Ninham's Court and I introduced them to each other. After chatting on a number of subjects, Monck said that he had paranormal abilities. Challenged to demonstrate them, he described how two people, a man and a woman, were writing to Wynyard to ask him to come to stay with them. The man was seated, the woman – or possibly another man – was standing behind and they were laughing. Wynyard said he had two friends – a married couple, the wife being rather masculine in appearance, who might correspond, but that he had not received any such invitation. When he left, around midnight, Monck said: 'If you hear from those friends, you will let me know, won't you?' At breakfast next morning, my friend telephoned to say he had just received the invitation as foretold. As I knew both parties well, and continued to know them until their deaths, and in view of the time factors, I found it impossible not to be convinced.

Such experiences are not exactly rare. Ann Bridge, in her book, *Moments of Knowing*, has described several instances in her own life. Lawrence LeShan was chief of the Department of Psychology at Trafalgar Hospital and Institute of Applied Biology in New York for ten years. He once worked with a patient named Marla, an expert on modern art. Several years later another patient brought him a painting she had painted and asked for comments. He replied that he knew little about this type of art and asked if he might show it to a friend for an opinion. LeShan goes on: 'The patient replied, "Of course," then for a moment looked curiously blank. She then asked me: "Tell me, did anyone named Marla ever sit in this chair?" When I – quite startled – asked her why she had asked, she could only reply that she just felt she had to ask. She herself knew no one of that name, she said.'

Fundamentally, there are only two plausible theories of how telepathy could take place. The first is that it depends on some extension of our existing senses; it depends on a normal force. The question then arises: what is the sense organ involved? In view of the distances sometimes involved the force is unlikely to be magnetic and it is hard to know what other force would fill the bill. (There are only four forces known to physics.) The second theory proposes that all minds are in some way in touch, but that we normally ignore information reaching us in this way. The idea of a group mind or universal ground looks suspiciously like dualism, but could perhaps be accommodated by appealing to the fourth dimension.

Personally, I will go no further than to say that the existence of thought transference is enough to threaten our scientific complacency. If indeed there are capacities outside the scope of current physics, then we are – as I have already said – like physicists in the eighteenth century before electricity was understood. A whole new wing of science is perhaps waiting to be opened up. LeShan puts it more forcibly, 'To explain "damned facts" like this one, you need a new concept, a new definition of man and his relationship to the cosmos.'

The case he had in mind when he wrote that was a precognition by Mrs Verrall, one of the most carefully studied sensitives in psychic history. On 11 December 1911 she wrote in her diary: 'The cold was intense and a single candle gave poor light. He was lying on the sofa or a bed and was reading Marmontel by the light of a single candle . . . The book was lent to him, it did not belong to him.' On 17 December she continued the entry: 'The name Marmontel is correct . . . A French book, I think his memoirs. The name Passy may help him to remember. Passy or Fleury. The book was bound in two volumes, the binding was old and the book was lent to him. The name Marmontel is not on the cover.'

On 17 March the following year, nearly three months later, she was told by a friend named Marsh that he had been reading Marmontel's memoirs on a bitterly cold night in Paris on 20 and 21 February. Once he was in bed, at another time reclining on two chairs. There was only one candle. The book was borrowed – it was actually in three volumes. On 21 February he had read the chapter which describes the finding of a picture painted at Passy, the discovery being associated with a M. Fleury.

This extraordinary piece of precognition, more than two months before the event, is plainly too detailed to dismiss as coincidental. And if we have to admit precognition, then our physics and our world conception really are going to need rejigging.

What is needed, of course, is an experiment which can be frequently repeated, so that the conditions can be varied in the usual scientific manner. But telepathy, which seems to depend on strong motivation and a relaxed state of mind, fits with difficulty into the laboratory situation. However, Professor Hernández-Peón, a leading neurophysiologist, has done a number of experiments recording the EEG of a telepathic sender and a recipient. When the sender mentally called the name of the recipient, the latter's alpha rhythms desynchronised. On repeating, the effect declined and vanished. Such experiments suggest that the road-block is beginning to yield.

Let us turn now to the second question.

Are You a Machine?

Does the conclusion that consciousness is a property of complex neural systems imply that man is a machine? It depends on what you mean by a machine. To most people the word carries connotations of crudeness and inflexibility. The majority of machines with which we are familiar do not adapt themselves, much less make choices, and are capable of a very limited range of functions. Obviously this is not true of man, and we are certainly not machines in this interpretation of the word. Recently, of course, machines which adapt and make decisions have been invented, and as they become more complex, they begin to resemble man more closely. But, in the last analysis, machines do not display the Omega Effect. I see no prospect of inventing a machine which will fall in love. Man is therefore not a machine. But this does not mean that he never functions in a mechanical way. When we lift a weight we function (as far as our physical behaviour is concerned) very like a crane. That does not bother us. Nor should it bother us if our brain should function, in some respects, rather like a computer.

The question was put too crudely. Like the famous 'Have you left off beating your wife?' it is framed so as to exclude the possibility of an accurate reply. The point is worth making, because we are about to consider some more questions of this foxy kind.

Is our behaviour determined? Simple machines are, to be sure, deterministic. Put on a record of the *Blue Danube*, and the *Blue Danube* is what your record player emits and not some other music. Computers, however, make their own choices and the outcome of their deliberations is not implicit in their initial state, and therefore cannot be reliably predicted. Human unpredictability is no guarantee that we are not machines, therefore. Nevertheless, the processes by which a computer reaches its conclusion are deterministic; effects follow causes in a consistent and logically rigid manner. Are we, too, even if unpredictable, deterministic in some similar, even if more complex, manner?

Broadly, the answer must be yes. Cause and effect cannot be suspended for us. That is not to say that, knowing our past history and present state of mind, our future actions are settled for good and all. We are constantly affected by our environment, including other people. We may have to make a decision when we are tired or ill, and may consequently make a different choice from the one we would have made if we had been on the top of our form. We may be persuaded to change our mind by a friend or by the example of others. So knowledge of our internal state, however exhaustive, is a weak basis for predicting what we shall do in any given situation. The longer the time between prediction and realisation, the greater the uncertainty becomes, for we ourselves may change under the impact of experience. We do not make, at sixty, the decisions we would have made at twenty.

There is another consideration. Our brains, as we have seen, comprise two main systems: the mid-brain concerned with meeting our immediate needs and the cortex which looks ahead and considers the consequences of impulsive action, including its effect on other people and their possible reactions towards us. In short, as everyone knows, there is a continuous conflict between 'reason' and 'emotion'. Thus behavioural outcomes are dependent upon a conflict which can easily swing either way, and which is highly responsive to chance external influences.

Nevertheless, subject to all these qualifications about uncertainty, we must accept that, basically, we are determined. Does this mean we have no 'free will'? This is another foxy question. Once again, it depends what you mean. We do not feel we have lost our freedom of will when we are constrained by circumstances – if we have, for instance, to walk upstairs because the lift is out of order. Nor do we feel this when we subordinate our personal preference to some larger consideration. 'I did it of my own free will,' we say. It is only when some person or organisation compels us to a course we do not wish to follow by a physical or psychological threat that we say, 'I did not do it willingly.' Thus 'free will' is a term which refers to the behaviour of others towards us and not, as is often supposed, to our own mental mechanisms.

Or, if you prefer, we could say that 'free will' is a description of how we feel in a given situation – of whether we feel constrained or not. People do occasionally say, 'I did it in spite of myself,' or 'I felt I was under some compulsion.' The simplest examples are those of a mechanical kind, as when Penfield stimulated the motor cortex of his patient and his hand moved involuntarily. The compulsive behaviour of Oliver Sacks' sleeping sickness patients provides others. More to the point are obsessions, in which strong repressed needs overrule the conscious cortex: the man who exposes himself, the blaspheming nun of Loudun – but not, incidentally, the person carrying out a post-hypnotic suggestion. In short, it would be more accurate to say that we feel our will is free when our conscious ego is not constrained. To say we feel free is in no way incompatible with saying that our actions are determined. The term 'free will' is not the antonym of 'determined'.

What, I am pretty sure, bothers people about determinism is the feeling that it can so easily be used as an excuse, or rationalisation, for ignoring the recommendations of the cortex and abandoning ourselves to the more alluring suggestions of the mid-brain. And this is all too true. Many a delinquent, in these days of semi-education, is quick to excuse his anti-social behaviour by citing his unhappy childhood, as if this absolved him of all responsibility for his actions. (Pragmatically, therefore, it is desirable that people should believe themselves to be undetermined even if they are not!) It is also an error to assume that the fact of our actions being determined relieves us of responsibility. A drunk person is often described as 'not responsible for his actions', yet we hold a drunken driver responsible for the harm he causes. In short, whenever we weigh impulses against wider considerations, we have a moral duty to suppress impulses when we see the consequences to be harmful, subject to the further consideration that suppression of impulse can, if carried too far, itself be harmful. Often the decision is difficult to make – for we seldom can foresee the consequences of each choice – but the principle remains sound.

From failure to appreciate these considerations, moralists – and especially those with religious convictions – have often made heavy weather of the 'free will' issue and have assailed the whole idea of human beings as in any sense determined. A particularly curious argument was advanced in 1970 by Professor Donald MacKay and as it aroused considerable attention I shall say something about it, especially as it illustrates, in a negative sense, some of the points I have been trying to make.

MacKay argues that if you had complete knowledge of the state of a person's brain you could still not predict his actions because, the moment you told him your prediction, he would be free deliberately to do the opposite. The central error here is to assume that 'determined' and 'predictable' are interchangeable terms. To predict behaviour you have to know not only the internal state but the state of the situation the person is in, and that includes knowing whether anyone will say something to disturb the internally indicated outcome.

The course of a car is, in principle, determined by its driver – but it is also possible that it may skid or be run into by another car.

The compounding error is to overlook the fact that if you had *complete* knowledge of a person's brain state, you would know whether he was the sort of person who would react by doing the opposite or not. (MacKay says: the fact that we told him our prediction would be enough to change his brain state – but it does not follow that additional information will change behaviour: an anti-Semite will predictably object to his daughter marrying a Jew, even if we tell him that we expect this.) In short, predictability is not what people have in mind when they talk about 'free will'.

Even odder is Sir John Eccles' assertion that the existence of free will does not have to be proved, as it is a 'fact of experience'. In this book we have seen so many experienced 'facts' which proved to be false that I need spend no time on showing the feebleness of this argument. People who feel forced to fall back on such flimsy arguments are evidently desperate. They evidently have a strong subjective need to feel self-determining, and a more interesting question is why they should feel this.

I hope it will be obvious, nevertheless, that I am not arguing for a mechanical interpretation of man. There are solider reasons for supposing he is a mysterious being.

What is the Purpose?

While it is true that our behaviour is determined by events in the past, it is also true that we always have the future in view. We have aims and purposes and thus our behaviour is determined by the future too. This is possible because we can visualise future possibilities, so that our present contains, so to say, models of possible futures. When the Russian neurologist Beritoff saw one of Pavlov's dogs run downstairs and outside in search of a piece of meat which had just been thrown out of the window, he realised that even the behaviour of animals could not be wholly explained in terms of stimulus and response, and devised his theory of 'image-driven behaviour'. Though he took care to make it look as if it was in the Pavlovian tradition, it was in reality a major retreat from the behaviourist position. Animals, of course, cannot see very far ahead or imagine very complex situations, as we can, but nevertheless higher animals at least are purposive. Indeed, purposiveness is the characteristic mark of living things, and seems to be built into primitive instincts. The digger wasp stores food for its offspring while they are still pupae. The starfish knows enough to turn itself over when inverted. There are even little shells known as Arcella which attach themselves to air bubbles and thus transport themselves to the surface of the water though they have no brain at all. Biologists, while denying purpose in evolution, find great difficulty in talking about it without using purposive terms. 'The object of the immune system is to prevent us catching diseases.' 'We vomit in order to get rid of poisons.' 'The blood clots in order that we shall not bleed to death,' and so on. It is a strange fact that in evolution, organs seem to increase in size in advance of taking on a new function rather than as a result of doing so.

Thus there are, in any biological situation, two possible types of explanation: causal and purposive (or as Valentino Braitenberg would have it, contextual). When we are looking for purposive explanations, we get nowhere by examining the hardware. It follows that studying the behaviour of neurones, though it may tell us 'how' the brain works, will never tell us 'why' it works, or how it got to be the way it is.

Purposive explanations run back, in the last analysis, to human behaviour or to that of gods (who are imaginary people) or other animistically conceived beings – fairies, spirits, etc. Primitive man's mistake was to attempt to explain what seemed inexplicable by positing such personal agencies – thunder was caused by Vulcan's forge, lightning by Jove's thunderbolt, and bad crops by the displeasure of the gods. But as the psychoanalyst H. J. H. Home points out, today we are more likely to make the contrary mistake of explaining human purpose in mechanical terms. A massive example of this error was Marx's explanation of social behaviour in terms of historical 'forces' rather than of human motivations. To treat processes as 'things' is known as reification. To treat things as gods is deification. As Home neatly says, 'To reify is to deify.'

Prediction is a central function of the brain, and the brain constantly monitors discrepancies between intention and performance. Thus it is a cardinal error to regard it – as has so long been the case – as an input-output device.

The paradox of teleology is resolved when we realise that there are two levels of discourse which must not be confused. There is the physical plane of energy transfer, and the subtler plane of information transfer. The transfer of information, once coded, requires no energy addition. A radio carrier wave requires energy to generate, but the amount required is the same whether the carrier wave is modulated by a signal (such as speech) or not. The mind is an information system: it depends on the energy expended by brain neurones, just as the execution of a computer programme depends on the energy in its circuits, but the energy is not the programme. A computer uses just as much energy in calculating a recurring decimal as in performing some useful operation.

As the philosopher Michael Polanyi has pointed out, when dealing with hierarchies you cannot derive information about a higher level from studying a lower level. Knowledge about atoms cannot reveal the soapiness of soap. Thus we may never discover the nature of consciousness by studying the physiology of the brain. As the Swedish neuroscientist Ragnar Granit says: 'It is a futile task to hunt for structural parallelism or likenesses between the physical processes and conscious awareness when all we can do is to establish correlations.' The time has come to accept consciousness as an independent principle and to cease trying to treat it as something derived, as a mere 'epiphenomenon'. We are organisms and not things by virtue of an unforeseeable miracle, the emergence of consciousness, and this differentiates us decisively and permanently from machines.

20

The Great Adventure

MISERABLE MIRACLE

The French artist Henri Michaux has several times taken massive doses of hallucinogenic drugs, chiefly LSD-25, and has made a tremendous effort to record his experiences both in paintings and in prose. These experiences, he says, 'do not differ greatly from what goes on in many (unprovoked) mental illnesses'. But even people who pass as normal may experience them in a milder degree. Since they reveal some of the strangest Omega Effects, some of the furthest reaches of the mind, I here summarise, rather inadequately, what he reports in his remarkable book, The Major Ordeals of the Mind:

- *A diffuse interior excitation which can become many things: a distant murmur implying a threat, enigmatic voices, faint recriminations.*
- *An intrapsychic vibration: every object is charged, potential. Materials lose their dense, stable look. Everything is about to become animate.*
- *An impression of floating in one's body, which one no longer occupies satisfactorily. One is no longer protected; the body moves itself. Mistrust.*
- *The feeling one is no longer in command of all one's powers. One senses a risk of being reprimanded or punished by some powerful authority.*
- *One has the impression of being a free spirit, vibrating on another psychic level. A sense of other presences who invade one's territory. Guilt.*
- *A sensation of uncontrollable, seething expansion. You are extremely important – an emperor – God. You yield to violent impulses, betray secrets.*
- *Everything presses too closely, weighs heavily, penetrates. Ordinary sights are painful, alarming. Sensation rapidly becomes pain. One must be vigilant.*
- *Invasion by images and impressions from within oneself. Hallucinated sounds seem more real than actual sounds. Hallucinated visions too.*
- *Ordinary objects, people, even pictures, become charged with meaning, sometimes beneficent, more often sinister. Nothing is neutral.*
- *Ideas arise which cannot be got rid of. They dominate one's mind to the exclusion of all others.*
- *It becomes impossible to discriminate among one's thoughts. It becomes difficult to attribute to each person, each object, idea or action what is appropriate to it.*

Source: H. Michaux, *The Major Ordeals of the Mind*, Ch. 8, 1972.

The Crisis

As I look back over the areas we have surveyed, the thing which strikes me most forcibly is the almost total inability of scientists to explain the real nature of the phenomena which constitute the mind.

Scientists themselves admit their failure. 'Over all we are in a state of ignorance,' said Strongman, summing up his account of emotion. Scientists 'simply haven't reached the stage' at which the study of complex thought is possible, says Alan Fisher. It is 'not too sensational' to say that illusions are 'just as mysterious as they were in the nineteenth century', declares J. O. Robinson. 'It is very hard if not impossible' to explain psychosomatic phenomena, says Karl Schaefer; 'the machinery is unknown'. There is 'little agreement' about the nature of hypnosis, despite much research; 'the conditions necessary to produce [the phenomena] remain clouded in controversy' (Honorton). As to psychosomatic effects, 'there appears to be no theory which successfully provides a description of experiential feelings, physiological change and emotional behaviour' (Whitlock). Memory, pain, personal identity, the nature of consciousness are all conceded to be equally baffling. Consciousness 'is just as unclear as ever' (Luria). Rolling it all up into one, Seymour Kety laments 'our profound ignorance of processes underlying the nervous system and the mind'.

So it is quite surprising that some scientists express optimism about mopping up the subject in the lifetime of persons now living. For my part, I am left with the conviction that the attempt to explain subjective experience in mechanical terms has totally failed and shows no signs of doing anything else. We are not machines, and a completely different approach is called for.

That having been said, let us glance back and see if anything of significance *has* emerged – first about the brain, then about the mind.

The Brain

One salient fact is that the brain is a machine of a most unusual kind. Nevertheless, most scientists continue to look at it as if it were just a more complicated version of a man-made machine. In the first place, we have seen that it combines electrical and chemical features; yet it is constantly discussed as if it were primarily electrical, and even then little attention is paid to conduction other than by the classic route of nerve fibres. Secondly, it is distributive. Yet scientists continue to make local lesions and then assign functions to the damaged part. You might as well put out a man's right eye and then, finding that he had lost binocular vision, declare that the seat of binocular vision was in the right eye. Thirdly, the brain is primarily an inhibitory rather than a facilitatory device. Recall Sacks' patient who, from time to time, became unable to move, said: 'My essential symptom is that I cannot start and I cannot stop. Either I am held still or I am forced to accelerate. I no longer seem to have any in-between states.' Clearly the delicate balance of inhibition and facilitation was destroyed. Fourthly, the brain functions in an hierarchic manner. Just as vision is based on bringing together small fragments of information into wholes, and then organising these units into larger systems, so thinking itself is structured in systems and sub-systems. More than that, the total personality is seen to be compounded of sub-systems. And that brings us to the fifth and last point. The brain fights a constant battle against dissociation. If integration fails at the highest level, multiple personality may result. Failure to integrate the cognitive and emotional functions may be the central feature of schizophrenia. In fine, the brain is an integrating device.

Furthermore – and this is a point I have not made hitherto – the brain's integrative activity functions over different spans of time, so that in this sense too there are several levels. At the lowest level we bring together experiences which last for half a second or less: this is why the separate pictures of a cinema film fuse into continuous sequences of movement. Next, we integrate over a minute or two; this is the function supported by short-term memory. Arthur Blumenthal, who has made a close study of temporal integration, concludes that the ratio of the second to the first is about 7·5:1 – which may explain why we can only hold some seven items in the mind at one time. We also integrate our experience over longer periods and finally over our whole life, the total constituting our personality. According to Blumenthal, it is the transformation of *sequences* of events into *simultaneous* perceptions that 'generates consciousness'. Perhaps this is putting it too strongly, but it is certainly a major element in it. The integration itself occurs unconsciously.

Failure to make these larger integrations manifests itself in social pathology or mental disturbance. (One of the effects of marijuana is to impair such integration.)

To sum up, the brain is a mechanism which is constantly trying to extract patterns from the data it receives, and then patterns of patterns, until all is synthesised into the harmony of a single pattern. Only if and when it achieves this ultimate synthesis can we be said to be fully ourselves – and only then, I suspect, do we *feel* ourselves to be whole.

Now let us ask how this unusual machine is related to mind. What is it that the machinery has to subserve?

The Mind

We have established two facts about the mind and consciousness, both of great significance, yet seldom recognised. First, that we must make a real distinction between conscious awareness and unconscious awareness. It is time we conceded openly that the latter exists. Most of our analysis of situations and our appraisal of the environment goes on at the unconscious level. Often we see something but fail 'to take it in', as we say. We have hardly any awareness of perceptual processes (such as interpreting size constancy) or of memory processes (such as how we find a word which is on the tip of our tongue). And of course we have little direct conscious awareness of our autonomic responses. (Your finger swells when you hear a loud sound. Did you know?) Much information is held unconsciously, and it seems to be a function of consciousness to bring into conjunction things which the unconscious mind has failed to relate. Hence it seems that feeling and remembering are not in themselves manifestations of consciousness in the narrower sense. Most discussions of consciousness ignore such facts.

Odder still is the fact that we can, if we try, bring functions which are normally unconscious into consciousness. As Neal Miller of the Rockefeller University has shown (and as yogis have long known), autonomic functions like blood pressure can be brought under conscious control. One can even cause one hand to become hot and the other cold, as Zimbardo, in California, has demonstrated. And what is yet odder, as Russian experiments have proved, a person can be trained to respond to visceral stimuli of which he is not conscious. Dogs have even been conditioned to discriminate between signals from their right kidney and those from their left. Where do such discriminations take place? And why are they not available to consciousness? One thing at least is clear: brain action is not sufficient to cause consciousness. The truth is, the whole thing is a mystery. It is one of the key puzzles of neurology, why some neurophysiological processes appear in consciousness and some do not.

The second even more basic fact is that consciousness is not unitary. Time after time philosophers and scientists have treated it as a primary inner state, without structure or subdivision, which one could possess or not possess. I have sought by countless examples to establish the fact that consciousness has an elaborate structure. Damage to different parts of the brain impairs some elements in consciousness but not others. You recall the man who could not perceive colour because of damage to the prestriate cortex. Damage to the fore-brain impairs the ability to make plans and to evaluate, but leaves routine functions unimpaired. Damage to the mid-brain may affect thirst, or pain-sense, or have subtler effects, but it does not destroy consciousness. The man who does not know where he is or what day it is may still be able to write or perform arithmetical operations. If there is any part of the brain more closely implicated in consciousness than another, it is the brain-stem. The man with a damaged diencephalon does not know where he is, how long he has been there, who he is or what he has to do. But his cortex still functions.

Luria tells of a patient who, after a car accident, suffered severe haemorrhages into the brain-stem and diencephalon and who, for a long time, was in a very confused state. Yet he could converse with his physician in four languages, and never confused one with another; nor did he have any difficulty in switching. The undamaged part of his brain was working perfectly.

Thus we can lose parts of our consciousness and retain others; it is not an all-or-nothing affair, as is almost invariably assumed.

Now let us turn to the relationship between consciousness and the brain.

Consciousness and the Brain

The feature which strikes me here is the peculiar 'looseness of fit' between subjective experience and the stimuli which give rise to them. You will recall the experiments of Dr Land in the apprehension of colour; you will remember the paradoxes in the appreciation of pain. And Sacks' patient looked terrified but felt no terror.

A recent experiment by John McCann of the Polaroid Laboratory makes the point about colour-perception even more vividly. He illuminated a picture with light of two different wavelengths, chosen so that one would excite the cones in the retina of the eye (supposedly responsible for colour vision) while the other would only affect the rods (which convey shape and movement without colour). Nevertheless areas of the picture which appeared brown under one light appeared blue under the other!

The mystery of feelings (those I have called meta-feelings) deepens when we consider the illusion in which a straight rod is seen as curved, when distorting spectacles are worn, and is then *felt* as curved when the finger is rubbed along it. Our haptic sense is providing the brain with data which implies that the rod is straight – yet what we *feel* is dictated by what we see and not the reverse. OK, so vision overrules the haptic sense. But even if the converse had been true, we do not understand why 'consciousness of curvature' arises from one sense rather than the other. Why do we not get a mixture of the two?

There are also baffling quantitative aspects of consciousness. Drugs alter 'perceived brightness' – everything seems more vivid. And I have told how some forms of brain damage may have the reverse effect. But neither drugs nor damage is necessary. Experiment shows that it is possible to alter the 'perceived brightness' of a standard grey surface by manipulating the brightness of other features in the room. The psychologist will talk about constancies and suggest that, maybe, a neural coding mechanism will one day explain this. Does consciousness then depend on coding?

The mystery deepens when we consider the men, paralysed from the waist down, who thought they had moved their legs when they had not, and the men who thought they had fought to get free when immobilised by the chemical disconnection of their skeletal muscles. These men, it seems, were 'conscious' not of what happened but of what they intended to happen. That is, they were 'conscious' of something which went on in their brain but not in the external world. That is truly extraordinary.

Or, to take another aspect, why do visual illusions persist when we know that they are illusions? Measurement tells us, for instance, that two lines are of equal length, yet we continue to *feel* that they are not. So apparently consciousness of feelings and awareness of facts are not the same thing. No discussion of consciousness that I have seen has taken this startling fact into consideration.

From Alpha to Omega

The one solid fact to emerge from all the physiological experiments is that consciousness does not automatically arise from brain activity. There is a time-lag.

Between the quality of experience and brain function there seems to be no intelligible relationship. Why does stimulating one group of cells cause pleasure, stimulating another very similar group cause fear, yet another thirst, yet another memory recall, yet another euphoria? Are there differences in the structure of these cells, in their internal chemistry, or in their interconnections, which lie beyond our present powers of investigation? Nothing in the physiology of the brain tells us how Omega Effects are caused, or even looks as if one day it might. When scientists and philosophers attempt to address such questions they either confess their puzzlement (like Seymour Kety) or take refuge in empty tautologies. For example: 'Consciousness is strictly a property of brain currents specifically designed to produce the particular conscious effects obtained from different brain regions.' As Sir Kenelm Digby said three hundred years ago, in a slightly different context, such tautologies 'are the last refuge of ignorant men who, not knowing what to say, and yet presuming to say something, do often fall upon such expressions.' Could it be that we are asking the wrong question?

The multiform nature of consciousness explains why the prolonged attempt of neurologists to locate consciousness in some region of the brain was doomed to failure. It was the wrong question to ask. Obvious as it may seem, the point is critical. Sir John Eccles still believes that consciousness is located in the topmost layer of the cortex, at the summit of the Mountcastle columns. (Charles Fair put it in the cortex, but in the fourth layer.) In contrast, Wilder Penfield locates it in the brain-stem, in what he has called the 'centrencephalic system'. Beritoff assigns it to the interneurones. Roger Sperry sees it as a property of the brain circuitry as a whole. Others, like Donald MacKay, have abandoned this approach and seek to construct models of brain action which will exhibit the sort of behaviour which characterised brain action, thus by-passing the problem.

These approaches are based, in the last analysis, on the position taken by the Austrian physicist Ernst Mach (1838–1916). It was he who categorised consciousness as a unitary property. But consciousness is not like that. What we need to do, it is now becoming clear, is to examine not structures but consciousness itself. What I have attempted is a preliminary survey of the task.

With this realisation, progress becomes possible, and I am ready to believe that we shall see important, even startling, advances in the next twenty years or so. Specifically, I expect that brain chemistry will provide the major clues to elucidation of the basis of consciousness, rather than the electrophysiology which has been the main basis of research for nearly a century. I also expect to see interest turning to the neuroglia, those sheetlike cells which so curiously embrace the neurones, and which comprise five-sixths of the brain by weight. I cannot believe that nature was so prodigal simply to provide support. They may be the seat of memory and, as Galambos has suggested, of thinking too.

Finally, I take the view that consciousness is not an epiphenomenon or side effect. It is against the whole philosophy of evolution that capacities should evolve which have no function. Equally, if we take a teleological view, and recognise that everything in biology seems to work towards a purpose, we must concede that Omega Effects must have a purpose. We *do* run away because we feel fear, and not the reverse. Behaviourism is a dead duck.

Man is a wonderful machine, but he is not 'nothing but a machine'. He is a machine *plus*. The denigration of human status which has been in fashion for nearly a century is being revealed as wrong-headed. Shakespeare knew this: 'What a piece of work is a man! How noble in reason. how infinite in faculty! in form, in moving, how express and admirable! in action how like an angel! in apprehension how like a god! the beauty of the world! the paragon of animals!'

With the current renewal of interest in consciousness as such, real progress in understanding the mind becomes possible. The great adventure of exploring the most complex system we know of in the universe is at last under way.

ME

I think that I shall never see
A calculator made like me.
A me that likes Martinis dry
And on the rocks, a little rye.
A me that looks at girls and such,
But mostly girls, and very much,
A me that wears an overcoat
And likes a risky anecdote.
A me that taps a foot and grins
Whenever Dixieland begins.
They make computers for a fee,
But only moms can make a me.

Hilbert Schenk, jr.

Source Notes

1: Something Funny is Going On

laughter attacks:	Martin, J. P. (1950).
increased growth of breasts:	Willard (1977); Staib and Logan (1977); Erickson (1977).
'break-off':	Schaefer (ed.) (1962); contribution of Simons, D. G.
Lilly's experience:	Lilly (1973).
Slocum's apparition:	Slocum (1958), p. 94.
Smythe's companion:	Smythe in Everest (1933).
Noyce's out-of-the-body experience:	Noyce (1954), pp. 223, 224, 293.
Doppelgängers:	Dewhurst and Pearson (1955). The subject is discussed further in Chapter 6. For a clergyman who saw two of himself, Brierre de Boismont (1853).
Okinawan woman's story:	Bakker and Murphy (1969).

2: The Quiet Revolution

Tomkins cited:	Tomkins (ed.) (1962, 1963), Vol. 1, p. 5.
MacKay cited:	MacKay (1967), p. 43.
Taylor, John, cited:	Taylor, J. (1971).
the numinous:	Otto, R. (1925).
central state materialism:	see, for instance, Armstrong (1968). The subject of identity and of dualism is discussed further in Chapter 18, where further references are given.

3: Wond'rous Machine

For general background reading on the brain I recommend Wooldridge (1963); Luria (1973b); Rose, S. (1973). Granit (1977) is in a class of its own.

Rosenblueth's dictum:	Rosenblueth (1970).
Armstrong's dictum:	Armstrong (1968).
Gall and phrenology:	Young, R. M. (1970).
cerebellum:	Eccles, Ito and Szentagothai (1967); for a popular account see Snider (1958).
role of new brain:	Ewert (1974).
'hot' and 'cold' brains:	Olds, J., contribution to Ross Adey, *et al.* (1974), Chapter 12.
Koestler's argument:	Koestler (1978).
the triune brain:	MacLean (1962); MacLean (1973); contribution to Isaacson (ed.) (1974).
limbic system:	Papez (1937) reprinted in Isaacson (1964), Chapter 5; Isaacson (ed.) (1974); Richter (D.) (ed.), 1966.
hippocampus:	Smythies (1966); Black, A. H. (1978); Vinogradova's contribution to Pribram and Broadbent (1970).
spatial memory:	Olton (1977).
Russian observations:	described in Ross Adey, *et al.* (1974), by Olds, Chapter 3.
McLardy's view of the hippocampus:	McLardy (1959).
removal of temporal lobes:	Klüver and Bucy (1937) reprinted in Isaacson (1964), Chapter 4, but Bard and Mountcastle (1974) got different results.
amygdala:	Eleftheriou (1974).

hypothalamus: Haymaker, *et al.* (1969); Gellhorn and Loofbourrow (1963); Gellhorn (1954). Much else has been written, of course.
septum: Black, A. H. (1978).
work of Broca, Wernicke on speech: Geschwind (1972) gives a clear account of these classic studies.
role of the frontal lobes: Pribram and Luria (eds.) (1973); Nauta (1971).
specific brain lesions and behavioural deficit: Luria (1966a, 1966b). An enormous number of studies have been done on this subject.
number of neurones: Blinkov and Gleser (1968), Chapter 12. Only 2,600 m. in 1966. Each successive estimate tends to be lower. Gray, H. (1973).
number of neurones in the cerebellum: ibid., Chapter 8.
Kennedy's comment: Kennedy, D. (1967).
fibres in the corpus callosum: Gray (1973), p. 965; for a general account see Sperry (1964).
brain weights: Blinkov and Gleser (1968), Chapter 6.
A and B systems: Braitenberg (1977).
local circuit neurones: Rakič (1975).
Zamenhof's work: Zamenhof (1968); Zamenhof *et al.* (1971).
noticing order programmes: Pribram (1967b).
brain rhythms: Walter, W. G. (1953).
five types of coupling in brain: Braitenberg (1977), pp. 21–27.
electronic transmission in brain: Braitenberg (1977), p. 25; Schmitt (1976).
Whyte's theory of the basis of memory: Whyte (1954).
brain chemistry: on this large subject see perhaps Axelrod (1974); Warburton (1975); Featherstone and Simon (1959); Dunn and Bondy (1974); Russell, R. (ed.) (1966); Longo (1972).
endogeneous opioids: the original paper was Hughes, Smith and Kosterlitz (1975).
hypothalamic hormones: Schally (1978); Guillemin (1978); Guillemin and Burgus (1972).
hormones and sexual behaviour: Money and Ehrhardt (1973); contribution of Green to McGaugh (ed.) (1972), Chapter 2.

4: The Paradoxical Brain

Lashley's search for memory: The classic paper is Lashley (1950) but his publications started much earlier; see also Lashley (1964).
Kohler's inverting spectacles: Kohler (1962).
McCulloch's anecdote: in his contribution to Jeffress (1951).
kitten's visual environment: Blakemore and Cooper (1970).
brain's reliability: Gregory (1974), Chapter 49.
deLisle Burns cited: Burns (1968).
brain as an inhibitory system: for a general discussion see Florey (1961); Diamond (1963).
schizophrenics cannot disattend: McGhie (1965); McGhie and Chapman (1961).
sensory suppressor strips: Stanley Jones (1970), pp. 133ff.
Sechenov demonstrates inhibition: Diamond (1963) outlines the history of the topic.
satiety: Pribram's contribution to Brazier (1962).
reciprocal inhibition; flip-flops: Granit (1977); Warburton (1975), Chapter 2.
pleasure centres: Olds and Milner (1954); for a more popular account Olds (1956); Campbell (1973) has discussed the implications in detail but, in my view, greatly overstates his case.

hypothalamus and emotion: Gellhorn and Loofbourrow (1963).
paralysed man tries to raise his limb: Festinger (1967).
two kinds of thought: Pribram (1959).
magnetic fields and the brain: for a survey see Llaurado (1974); Barnothy (1964).
Hamer, Gavalas, *et al.*: cited by Ross Adey (ed.) (1974), Chapter 8, p. 390; Bawin, *et al.* (1953); see also Cohen (1968) for magnetic fields produced by brain rhythms.
admissions to mental hospitals: Becker, R. O., *et al.* (1965).
clocks in the brain: Richter, C. P. (1965), reviews.
pineal gland and light: Axelrod (1974).
soldier's response to musical note: Boernstein (1957).

5: On Knowing That You Know

For general reading one might suggest: Globus, *et al.* (1976); Eccles (ed.) (1966); Fair (1963); on subliminal perception, Dixon, N. F. (1971).

Humphrey's monkey: Humphrey and Weiskrantz (1967); Sanders (1974); Humphrey (1972) and (1974); Lewin, R. (1975); for two visual systems see Schneider (1969); Trevarthen, C. B. and Sperry R. W. (1973).
Place's paper: Place, U. T. (1956).
stellate neurones: Beritoff (1965).
anencephalic girl: Beritoff (1965).
Feldberg cited: Feldberg (1959).
consciousness of an auditory stimulus: Shagass and Schwartz (1961). But as a response occurs even in an anaesthetised patient, this does not equate with consciousness, as assumed by Eccles and others.
Libet cited: Libet (1967); his contribution to Eccles (ed.) (1966).
Geisler cited: Geisler (1958).
doctor prescribes while in amnesic state: Eccles (1965b), p. 32. Some epileptics continue to ride a bicycle during an attack.
Cairns cited: Cairns (1952).
Generalised reality orientation: Shor, R. (1959).
man sees room drained of colour: Stanley Jones (1970), p. 126.
ascending reticular system: the classic paper is Moruzzi and Magoun (1949).
Russian studies of alerting: Lynn, R. (1966).
sensitivity of ear rises: ibid.
pupil dilation: Hess, E. H. (1965).
cocktail party phenomenon: Treisman, A. (1960); Moray (1959).
sleep experiments: Oswald (1960).
subliminal perception: for an excellent review of the whole subject see Dixon, N. F. (1971), also the relevant section in Blake and Ramsey (1951).
Russian airpuff experiment: told me by the late W. Grey Walter.
'happy, sad' experiment: Somech and Wilding (1973).
Playboy's ploy: Key (1972), Chapter 7.
perceptual defence: much has been written on this subject. Dixon, N. F. (1971) summarises.
Gibson cited: Gibson, J. J. (1966).
Eriksen's criticism: Eriksen (1966).
McCleary and Lazarus: McCleary and Lazarus (1949).
Anoxic observer: Halstead (1947).
Razran's report: the main account is in Razran (1971), but see also Razran (1961).
autonomic control: Miller, N. and di Cara, L. V. (1967); di Cara (1970).

conditioning sleeping persons: Kratochvil, S. (1970); for American work see Cobb, *et al.* (1965), Evans, F. J. (1970).

awareness under anaesthesia: McKenna and Wilton (1973); Levinson, B. W. (1968); Mostert (1975); the first report was Winterbottom (1950); Cheek (1965).

17 per cent aware during Caesarean section: Wilson and Turner (1965).

hypnosis of terminal cancer patients: Crasilneck and Hall (1962).

highway hypnosis: Williams, G. W. (1963).

Rosenblueth's dictum: Rosenblueth (1970).

6: Unusual States of Consciousness

Tart (1969) – a collection of thirty-five papers – provides the best overview. Laski (1961) is an excellent survey of mystic states. Weitzenhoffer (1953) is the authoritative work on hypnotism, but see also Fromm and Shor (eds.) (1972) and Shor and Orne (1965). Also Kline (1962). On drug-induced states, Masters and Houston (1967).

Also recommended: Ornstein (1972); Ludwig (1966); Ludwig (1967); Belo (1960); Gowan (1975).

William James cited: James, W. (1882).

John Wesley cited: Wesley, J. (1909), ii. 479; for Patty Jenkins, iv. 314.

Cloud of Unknowing: Knowles (1961).

theta rhythm in meditation: Kasamatsu and Hirai (1966); Gastaut's contribution to Chertok (1969); for other physiological changes: Wallace and Benson (1972).

Suzuki cited: Suzuki (ed. Phillips) (1963).

Deikman's experiment: Deikman (1966a, 1966b).

Weir Mitchell cited: quoted without source in Masters and Houston (1973), p. 46.

a writer and painter cited: ibid., p. 63.

Pahnke's experiment: Pahnke and Richards (1966).

Naranjo: Naranjo (1975).

Mesmer's demonstrations: Ellenberger (1970) gives a vivid account.

trance can be self-induced: Kubie and Margolin (1944); but Gill and Brenman (1959) deny this. However, see Erickson, M. (1977).

hyperalert trance: Ludwig and Lyle (1964).

Y-state: Meares (1960).

induction of blisters: Paul (1963); Sarbin and Slagle in Fromm and Shor (eds.) (1972), Chapter 6.

allergic reaction induced: Ikemi and Nakagawa (1962).

warts removed: Obermeyer and Greenson (1970); Sulzberger and Wolf (1934).

warts removed in immunodeficient children: Tasini and Hackett (1977).

hypnotised WAAF: Black, S. (1969), p. 177.

recovery of memories: Kubie (1943); Orne's contribution to Biderman (ed.) (1961), by police: *Observer*, 27 August 1978; Dorcus (1960).

American boys quoted: White, R. W. (1941).

'experiment' mentioned: Fisher's contribution to Shor and Orne Pt. 2, Chapter 2 (1965).

'seal' mentioned: Orne's contribution to Chertok (1969).

physiological changes in hypnosis: Weitzenhoffer (1953), esp. pp. 91–4.

induction of blindness: Pattie (1935).

hypnotic analgesia: Barber and Hebb (1952); Barber (1959); Hilgard's contribution to Chertok (1969); much has been written on this subject, especially in connection with the use of hypnotic analgesia in dentistry, e.g. Marmet, M. J. (1959); Wall's contribution to Chertok (1969), Chapter 10; Weitzenhoffer (1953), pp. 120ff.

Estabrooks' subject: Estabrooks (1959).

simulation of hypnosis: Orne's contribution to Fromm and Shor (1972), Chapter 13; Shevkin's contribution to Fromm and Shor (1972), Chapter 18; see discussion in Weitzenhoffer (1953), pp. 300ff.

negative hallucinations: Orne's contribution to West, L. J. (ed.) (1962); Sidis (1906); Stewart, H. (1966); Orne (1959).

Tart's student: Tart, C. (1975).

hypnotic age regression: Weitzenhoffer (1953), pp. 184–192; Sarbin (1950); Kline (1951); Kupper (1945) claims that the EEG normalises when a subject is regressed to an earlier age than that at which trauma occurred. For criticism, Barber and Calverley (1964).

age-regression to womb: Kelsey, D. (1953).

hypnotic progression: Kline, M. V. (1958). See Best (1954) for a criticism. Rubinstein and Newman (1954).

similar effects with non-hypnotised subjects: Barber has written numerous papers on this theme; see, for instance, Barber (1958); his contribution to Fromm and Shor (1972), Chapter 5.

Bleuler's patient: White's contribution to Shor and Orne (1965) citing Bleuler, Chapter 4.

Cooper's ploys: Cooper and Tuthill (1952).

dream symbolism interpreted by hypnotised subjects: Kubie (1943).

Honorton and Krippner: Honorton and Krippner's contribution to White, R. H. (1976), Chapter 10; see also Honorton's contribution to Wolman (1977), Pt. V, Chapter 1.

Tart on subsystems of consciousness: Tart (1975), Chapter 8.

Blum's experiments: Blum, G. S. contribution to Fromm and Shor (1972), Chapter 11; Blum, G. S., *et al.* (1961).

MacLean's theory: his contribution to Boag and Campbell (1973); MacLean (1955); MacLean (1962); Brown, Jason (1977).

7: I Am Me

Though there are many books about the ego in the psychoanalytic sense, and also in relation to alienation, there is nothing which treats the subject in the manner followed here. The most comprehensive discussion of depersonalisation is Ackner, B. (1954); see also Dixon, J. C. (1963); Sedman. G. (1966). For ecstatic states, see Laski, M. (1961); for multiple personality Taylor and Martin (1944); Sidis and Goodhart (1968); for hemisphere disconnection (split-brain) work, Dimond (1972).

commando officer in depersonalised state: Ackner (1954), Case 5, p. 869.

students describe the condition: Roberts (1960); Dixon, J. C. (1963).

identity, sense of: Erikson, E., contribution to Stein, M. L., *et al.* (1960); Taylor, G. R. (1972), Chapter 7; Josephson, E. and M. (1962).

Hetherington cited: Hetherington (1975).

Berenson cited: Berenson (1950).

Paffard cited: Paffard (1973).

Coate cited: Coate (1964).

schizophrenics say they are too suggestible: Shakow (1962).

John Haime cited: Jackson (ed.) 1.272 (1865).

three faces of Eve: Thigpen and Cleckley (1954).

achieves a fusion . . .: but see Lancaster and Poling (1958) for some afterthoughts.

Gmelin cited: in Ellenberger (1970).

Mary Reynolds case: Taylor and Martin (1944).

Mrs G case: Stoller, R. (1973).
Violet X case: Muehl, A. (1922).
Jeanne des Anges: Huxley, A. (1952).
'possession' by many personalities: e.g. Ikin, A. (1924) and (1925); *Guardian* 2.9.78.
Sargant's comment: Sargant (1973).
Hélène Smith case: Oesterreich (1923), Chapter 1; Flournoy (n.d.).
Ikara case: Ellenberger (1970).
T.E. case: Stevenson (1974).
'Patience Worth': Prince, W. F. (1927).
aetiology of multiple personality: Horton and Miller (1972); Galdston (1947); Ackner (1954).
Sperry's work: numerous publications; for a popular account see Sperry, R. (1964).
Myers' contribution: Myers (1955).
independence of the hemispheres: see, for instance, Gazzaniga (1974); Gazzaniga (1975); Sperry (1968); the passage quoted is taken from Dimond (1972).
Eccles' comment: Eccles in: Popper and Eccles (1977) and Eccles (1965).
Mackay's comments: Mackay (1970); and see Mackay's contribution to Eccles (1965).
Ornstein's view of lateralisation: Lewin, R. (1974); Ornstein (1972).
Milner on musical lateralisation: Milner in Mountcastle (ed. (1962); but see Bever and Chiarello (1974) who show that the left hemisphere is dominant for analytic processing, the right hemisphere for holistic processing.
Galin on lateralisation: Galin, D. (1974).
EEG differences: Galin and Ornstein (1972).
cases of E.H., Z.I., H.G., and M.Q.: Ackner (1954), Cases 1, 3, 2 and 6 respectively.
Sedman's enquiry: Sedman (1966).
Schilder's comment: Schilder (1928).
a later writer: Shorvon (1946).
woman of thirty-nine: ibid., p. 847.
Miss W.D.'s comment: ibid., p. 846.
Brandes' comment: Brandes (1902).

8: It's All in the Mind

See Pierloot, R. A. (ed.) (1970); Wahl, C. W. (ed.) (1964); Whitlock, F. A. (1976). These authorities emphasise our ignorance of the mechanisms involved, and, in many cases, of the diseases themselves.

Origin of the word psychosomatic: Whyte (1960).
Ulcers and executives: Gellhorn and Loofbourrow (1963), Chapter 14.
'Some authorities claim . . . particular kinds of stress . . .': Alexander and French (1968).
Air traffic controllers: Rose, R. M., *et al.* (1978); Cobb and Rose (1973).
Blisters weep: Paul, G. L. (1963).
Arthritis linked to dominating parents: Groen, J., *et al.*, in Booij, J. (ed.) (1957).
Mind and psoriasis: Whitlock (1976), Chapter 12; Bethune and Kidd (1961).
Greying of hair: Whitlock (1976), p. 181. Also occurs in schizophrenics: Obermeyer (1955).
Rosacea and blushing: Whitlock (1976), Chapter 12.
Eczema and sex: Schur, M. (1955). And lack of caressing: Montagu (1971).
Mother-in-law allergy: Wahl (1964), Chapter 3.
Kissen emotion and TB: Kissen (1958); cancer: Kissen and LeShan (1964).

Rahe: Rahe, *et al.* (1967); and Toffler, A. (1970), pp. 291–4.
Dutch professor's cold: Groen, J. *et al.*, in Booij, J. (ed.) (1957).
Syndrome shift: ibid.
Freud cited: anxiety attack. Lowry says it was a typical case of hyperventilation: Lowry (1967).
Scared to death: Barker, J. C. (1968). See Dynes, J. for physical mechanisms involved (1969).
'Give-up-itis' and death from grief: Sacks (1973), esp. p. 218; also 160, 181, 224. Stewart, W. K. (1977): Beigler (1957).
Wavell: Wavell, Butt and Epton (1966).
Cannon: Cannon (1942) and (1957).
Animals given tranquillisers: cited by Barker, J. C. (1968).
premonition of death: Jones, J. C., *Brit. Med. J.* (1958), ii. 1041; Sacks (1976), p. 100: predilection to death, Weisman and Hackett (1961).
Richter's rats: Richter, C. P. (1957).
death after surgery: Barker, J. C. (1968); see also Morris and Zemchek (1946). Jacobson in Wahl (1964), Chapter 15.
give-up-itis: Seligman (1974); Beigler (1957); Murray Parkes (1972), Chapter 2.
stigmata: Thurston (1952) is the prime source.
San Francisco stigmatic: Early and Lifschutz (1974).
spontaneous bruising: Whitlock (1976); Gardner and Diamond (1955); Ratnoff and Agle (1968).
Moody's observations: Moody, R. L. (1946); Moody, R. L. (1948).
sadistic father: Moody, R. L. (1948).
muscle memory: Prof. Leonard Duhl, personal communication.
placebos, Osler cited: Byerly (1976) discusses; see Dinnerstein and Halm (1970).
phenmetrazine v. placebo: Penick and Hinkle (1964).
effect of colour: Blackwell *et al.* (1972), ii. 122.
Pihl and Altman's work: Pihl and Altman (1971).
Shapiro quoted: Shapiro, A. K. (1964).
blood composition affected by suggestion: Weitzenhoffer (1953), pp. 135–6; acidity and blood-sugar level are affected.
wart removal: Obermeyer (1970). Weitzenhoffer (1953), p. 145; and on blisters, p. 142–4. He says: 'No clear explanation of the reported phenomena has been given to date.'
ichthyosis cured: Mason, A. (1952).
Black's investigation: Black, S. (1969), pp. 192ff.
Dunbar cited: quoted by Melinsky (1968), p. 162.
Rose on faith-healing: Rose (1968).
posture and emotion: Pasquarelli and Bull (1951).
tactile stimulation and schizophrenia: Lowen, A. (1969).
Skinner's opinion: But Schaefer says: 'For such diseases we have neither models nor do we know their mechanisms . . . it is very hard if not impossible to explain local effects, such as blisters, eczema . . . the machinery is unknown.' (In Eccles 1965).

9: Traffic of the Mind

Many other instances of meta-feelings can be found; thus Colin Murray Parkes (1972) describes how bereaved persons often search for months for something they cannot name because of a quite distinct 'feeling' that something is missing. Renfrew and Melville (1960) in another context distinguish 'dermal touch feeling' from 'dermal space feeling'. See Reed, G. (1972) for further instances.

a feeling of 'if': James, W. (1890), i. 245.
on judging weight: Thomson (1968), p. 85.
Marguerite's feelings: Binet, cited by Reeves (1965).

Bartlett's student:	Bartlett (1932).
'meaning tone':	Cooper and Erickson (1952).
feelings of word meanings:	Werner (1965).
déjà vu: Efron's theory:	Efron (1963).
déjà vu induced by hypnosis:	Cole and Zangwill (1963).
'private codes':	Home (1966).
secret of the universe:	for James' experiences under nitrous oxide see James (1882).
Morag Coate's delusions:	Coate (1964).

10: Images of Reality

For accounts of body image disturbance, including the phantom limb phenomenon, see, above all, Critchley (1953), especially Chapter 8. Also relevant are Fisher, S. (1970); Werner and Wapner (1949) and (1952); Livingston (1976).

phantoms of breasts:	Simmel's contribution to Simmel (ed.) (1968).
eyes and feelings don't agree . . .:	Nielsen (1946), Chapter 8.
Gerstmann's patient:	Critchley (1953), Chapter 7.
patient shaves half face:	ibid., Chapter 8.
patient rolls in the snow:	Critchley (1953) citing Deney and Canues (1905), *Revue Neurol. 13*: 462.
supernumerary arm:	Fisher, S. (1970) citing Weinstein and Kahn.
woman's account of her sensations:	Wapner and Werner (1975).
nurse's arm:	Fisher, S. (1970).
erotic sensations from left side:	Critchley (1953), p. 235, citing Zingerli.
migraine sufferer: head unequal:	ibid.
head floating up to ceiling:	Lippmann (1953), pp. 748–9.
patient turns into a jelly:	Peto (1959).
Schilder on body image:	Schilder (1964).

11: The Puzzle of Pain

For an excellent semi-popular outline of the whole subject of pain, see Melzack, R., *The Puzzle of Pain* (1973). Other useful surveys are Sternbach, R. A. (1968) and Crue, B. L. (ed.) (1975).

Epigraph: Further to this: in two studies of patients suffering acute pain from surgery or chronic pain from cancer, 65–70 per cent obtained relief from 10 mg. of morphine, 35–40 per cent did so from placebo, but only 3 per cent obtained relief when pain was deliberately inflicted as part of an experiment.

Livingston cited:	Livingston, R. B. (1943, 1976).
hypersensitivity:	Stavakry, G. W. (1961); Marshall, J. (1951).
insensitivity to pain:	there is an extensive literature; see for instance Thrush, D. C. (1973); Sternbach, R. A. (1963); Schilder, P. and Stengel, C. (1931); Jewesbury, E. C. O. (1951) tells of a patient who let molten lead splash on his skin at 800° C without feeling anything, but who nevertheless had headaches and visceral pain when he had appendicitis.
Melzack cited:	for popular account see Melzack (1973).
Melzack and Torgerson on pain-words:	'On the Language of Pain' (1971), *34*: 50.
Pathways: types of fibre:	Bishop contribution to Grennell (ed.) (1962); Sternbach (1968), Chapter 3.
Melzack's gating theory:	Melzack and Wall, *Science* (1965), *150*: 971.
Dimond, E. G. on acupuncture:	*JAMA* (1971), *218*: 1558.
Central pain:	Cassinari and Pagni (1969); Melzack, Stotler and Livingston (1958); see also *New Sci.*, *73*: 12–13.
Sunderland and Kelly quoted:	Sunderland and Kelly (1948).

Skin stimulation blocks pain:	Melzack and Schechter (1965).
Change of size of receptive fields:	Melzack, Rose and McGinley (1972).
Japanese experiment:	Nakahama, *et al.* (1966).
The sensibility of Henry Head:	Head and Sherren, *Brain* (1905), *28*: 116–338. Melzack and Wall (1962) suggest that it is the *temporal* pattern of discharge which is relevant.
Neurones fire at different temperatures:	Zotterman's contribution to Field and Magoun (1959), p. 431.
Millodot cited:	*Nature* (1975), *255*: 151–2.
Hughes on endorphins:	Hughes, *et al.*, *Nature* (1975), *258*: 577–9.
Plumb and Posner:	Plumb and Posner (1972).
Beecher cited:	Beecher (1946, 1959).
Anxiety and pain:	Hill, *et al.* (1952).
Hearing the word pain:	Hall and Stride (1954).
Pam tries biofeedback:	Coger and Werbach: 'Biofeedback in Pain', in Crue, B. L. (ed.) (1975).
Wyke cited:	in Jayson, M. (ed.) (1976).
Memory for pain:	Melzack (1973), p. 117, 182. Hebb (1949).

12: Sensational News

For a thorough treatment of the senses, see Wyburn, *et al.* (1964), and for Gibson's special position, Gibson, J. J. (1966). For something more popular but restricted to animals, Droscher (1971).

tactile and haptic senses:	Gibson, J. J. (1966), Chapters 6 and 7.
many senses of animals:	Droscher (1975); interrelationships, Draeger and Hubel (1975).
electrical coding:	but even this is too simple. See Zotterman in Field (ed.) (1959).
local sign theory demolished:	Neff's contribution to Field, J. (ed.) (1959). See Melzack (1973), pp. 132ff. for a review of earlier studies.
taste receptors not specific:	Neff's contribution to Field, J. (ed.) (1959); Zotterman's contribution to Rosenblith (1961), Chapter 12.
taste of potassium bromide:	Burton (1973).
different end-organs may project to same neurone:	moreover one receptor may respond to thermal, tactile and noxious stimuli. See Melzack (1973), pp. 85–6.
cold receptor reports hot metal rod as cold:	see Zotterman's contribution to Field (ed.) (1959).
change in pleasantness of sugar:	Moskowitz, *et al.* (1974).
inability to smell jonquils as sweet:	letter from M. Ball, *New Sci.* (1977), *73*: 664.
Jim Phelan cited:	Burton (1973).
synaesthesia:	Langfield (1914); Richardson (1969); Simpson and McKellar (1955).
'looking without seeing':	Thomas, E. L. (1968).
discriminating musical notes:	Miller, G. A. (1964), pp. 154–6.
workers in press cutting agencies:	Neisser (1964).
nativism vs. empiricism:	see Taylor, J. G. (1962), for an account of these and other theories.
perception of unusual playing card:	Bruner, J. and Postman, L. (1949).
electric shock makes tone sound different:	Blake and Ramsey (1951), who give many other examples of perception altered by subjective factors.

'Honi effect':	Wittreich (1959).
defective perception of colour after brain lesions:	Meadows (1974).
Gregory on how we perceive:	Gregory (1968).
people hear the word they expect:	Warren and Warren (1975).
John Ross confirms this:	Ross, J. (1976).
how do we know a play is only a play?:	Leeper's contribution to Arnold, M. (ed.) (1968), Chapter 11.

13: Seeing and Believing

Davidoff (1975) surveys the subject in a readable way; Dodwell (1971) brings together many important papers at a more technical level. Teuber's contribution to Field's *Handbook* (1959) with its bibliography of 561 items is magisterial. Mundle (1971) is a clear account of the philosophical aspects.

Isherwood quoted:	cited by Richardson (1973), p. 144.
What the Frog's Eye tells the Frog's Brain:	Lettvin, *et al.* (1959); reprinted in Dodwell (1971).
work of Hartline:	Hartline (1942).
work of Barlow:	Barlow (1953).
how the visual cortex reconstructs the image:	Pollen (1971).
Hubel and Wiesel's classic paper:	Hubel and Wiesel (1959).
colour-responsive neurones:	Zeki (1973).
specialisation of rabbit and squirrel retinas:	Michael (1969), who gives fuller and more careful account of the Lettvin-Hartline-Hubel and Wiesel story.
kittens brought up in a world of verticals:	Blakemore and Cooper (1970); Shinkman and Bruce (1977) confirm by rotation of eyeballs.
animal's view of the world:	von Uexkull (1921).
sensitivity of tympanic organ of moths to bat sonar:	Contribution of Roeder and Treat to Rosenblith (ed.) (1961), Chapter 28.
vision after restoration of sight to a blinded man:	Gregory (1974), Chapter 3; von Senden (1960).
illusory triangle:	Kanisza (1955); see Gregory (1974), p. xxx, for discussion and development of the idea.
river illusion:	for this and other illusions see Gregory (1966).
Dallenbach's puzzle picture:	the original paper is Dallenbach (1951) but the version shown is from Davidoff (1975).
spatial constancy lost after brain damage:	Bender and Teuber (1947, 1948). Wyke (1960) discusses further cases and shows the disturbance must be in the brain itself.
cows taken for insects:	Turnbull (1974).
Mundle's two modes of looking:	Mundle (1971), pp. 17ff.
colour constancy:	Beck, J. (1975).
Kohler's spectacles:	Kohler, I. (1962); the English psychologist G. M. Stratton did the first experiments on these lines, however; see Gregory (1966), pp. 204ff.
Land's theory of colour:	Land (1959).
Land's demonstration at the Royal Institution:	Land (1962).
Rushton's comments on Land:	Rushton (1962).

luminosity and colour difference:	Padgham and Saunders (1975).
Craik described by Bartlett:	Sherwood (ed.) (1966), foreword.
Craik's self-experiment:	ibid., p. 98.
a vivid after-image:	Wood-Jones and Porteus (1929), p. 321.
after-images in general:	Brindley (1963); Gregory (1974), Chapter 22, etc. The subject is very little understood.

14: Just Imagine!

An excellent general survey of this long-neglected topic is Richardson (1969). See also Segal (1971); Sheehan (1972). For hallucination see West (ed.) (1962); Weinberger and Grant (1940).

Tesla's imagery:	O'Neill, J. J. (1945).
eidetic imagery:	Jaensch (1930); Haber and Haber (1964); in other cultures, Doob, L. W. (1966); images of taste and touch, Purdy, D. M. (1936); Klüver, H. in Murchison (ed.) (1931).
experiment with school children:	Haber, R. (1969).
Julesz' work:	Julesz (1965).
Harvard psychologists and Elizabeth:	Stromeyer and Psotka (1970); in view of the impossibility of verifying these reports, doubts have been cast on the reliability of the more extreme claims.
Ryle cited:	Ryle (1949).
abnormally clear imagery:	Hermann and Poetzl (1928).
Galton's estimate:	Galton (1907), p. 65.
Anne Roe's survey:	Roe (1952); (1956), p. 76.
Grey Walter on visualisers: and verbalisers:	Grey Walter (1953), pp. 148ff.; Bartlett (1932), the first to draw the distinction.
breathing differences:	Golla and Antonovich (1929), first reported; see Richardson, p. 72–3 for an outline of later work.
hypnopompic and hypnogogic imagery:	Foulkes, D. (1962); (1964); (1966a, 1966b).
REM and NREM sleep:	Freemon (1972), summarises the state of play.
Charcot's patient and Humphrey and Zangwill:	Humphrey and Zangwill (1951).
Walshe's patient:	Brain (1950).
vivid dreaming after cingulectomy:	Whitty and Lewin (1957).
dreams continue after waking on Librium:	Viscott (1968).
Perky's experiment:	Perky (1910).
Segal replicates it:	Segal, S. J. and Nathan, S. (1964).
difficulty in distinguishing phantasy and reality:	Whitty and Lewin (1957); for hallucination in general see Keup (1970); West, L. J. (1962).
hallucination in part of visual field only:	Russell and Dewar (1975), pp. 89ff.
truck drivers' hallucinations:	Heron, W., *et al* (1956).
Lilly's hallucination:	Lilly (1973).
hallucination evoked by conditioned stimulus:	Leuba (1940); Leuba and Dunlap (1951); Brady and Levett (1966); Ellson (1941); see also Seashore (1895) for experimentally induced hallucination.
taraxein:	Heath (1954); Heath's contribution to Sheehan (1972).
hallucination evoked by electrical stimulus:	Penfield (1952); however these were only auditory hallucinations in epileptic patients; Horowitz and Adams (1968).
schizophrenia as primitive thinking:	Arieti (1974).

autoscopy:	Lhermitte (1951); in migraine sufferers, Lippman, C. W. (1953).
out of the body experience:	Green, C. (1968b).
Tart's experiments:	contribution to White, J. (ed.) (1974), Chapter 15.
palinopsia:	Feldman and Bender in Keup (1970).
Lilliputian hallucinations:	Leroy (1922).
Blyton cited:	McKellar (1957).
Harding, examples of inspiration:	Harding, R. (1942).
Poincare's inspiration:	Hadamard (1954), p. 18.
lucid dreams:	Green, C. (1968a).
A.E. cited:	E., A. (1918).
Hilprecht's precognitive dream:	Romaine, W. (1896).
Gardner Murphy's comment:	Murphy, G. (1947), Chapter 17.
'Patience Worth':	Prince, W. F. (1927).
patient 'visits Mars':	Lindner, R. (1955).
Bridget Riley:	Bernstein, M. (1956).
Paivio's view:	Paivio (1971).
inability to perceive wholes:	Arieti (1974).
bookkeeper who could not see words:	Luria (1973b).

15: Thanks for the Memory

Here the problem, in recommending general surveys, is to select from a mass of material, most of it too specialised for the ordinary reader. Perhaps Ritchie Russell (1959) and Pribram and Broadbent (1970) with Bartlett's classic (1932) are the best bets. Talland's (1968) account of memory disorders is also to be recommended.

Jewish scholars:	Stratton (1917).
Huxley on Broad's theory:	Huxley (1954), pp. 22–4.
recognition ability:	Haber (1970).
verbal memory impaired by hemispherectomy:	Zaidel and Sperry (1974).
Blonsky's view:	Smirnov (1973), Chapter 3.
spatial memory:	Olton (1977).
Twenty-three types of memory:	Richter, D. (1966).
Korsakoff's syndrome:	Talland (1965); Talland (1968).
patient fails to recognise doctor:	Talland (1968), p. 123; Talland and Waugh (1969).
M. Bon's lack of imagery:	Barbizet (1970), Chapter 2; cf. Walshe's patient mentioned by Brain (1950).
goldfish experiments:	Agranoff (1965); Agranoff (1967); Agranoff's contribution to Carlson, F. D. (1968).
cooling and memory:	the evidence is by no means clear-cut; see Andjus, *et al.* (1956); Booth, D. A. (1967); Mrosovsky (1963).
type and thing memories:	Fair (1963).
Ebbinghaus and early work in this field:	O'Neil (1968); Thomson (1968), p. 75.
one of the stalwarts in this field:	Postman's contribution to Duncan *et al.* (1972); for an information processing approach to memory see Reitman (1965).
Bartlett:	Bartlett (1932).
chunk hypothesis:	Simon (1974).
state-determined learning:	Greenspoon and Raynard (1957); Godden and Baddeley (1975).
hypermnesia:	Stratton (1919).
amnesia after fall on the ice:	Cason (1935).
Ritchie Russell cited:	Russell (1959).
abreaction after amytal:	Sargant, W. (1973), Chapter 1.

Matilda's black out, etc.:	Barbizet (1970), pp. 107ff.
highway hypnosis:	Williams, G. W. (1963).
Veniaminoff:	Luria (1969).
Myer's story of maid speaking Hebrew:	this was taken from Coleridge's *Biographia Literaria*.
Penfield's experiment:	the original paper is: Penfield (1938), *40*: 417; see also Penfield (1952) and Penfield (1968); but there is a more readable and up-to-date account in Penfield (1975).
Delgado repeats this:	Mahl, G. F., *et al.* (1964).
tip-of-the-tongue phenomenon:	Brown, R. and McNeill, D. (1966).
holographic memory:	Pribram's contribution to Pribram (ed.) (1969a).
memory span of dolphins:	Thompson and Herman (1977).
memory and chemical changes in the brain:	for Hyden's work see, for instance, Quarton, *et al.* (1967), Chapter 48; or his contribution to Pribram and Broadbent (eds.) (1970); for a general review, Ungar (1970).
Albert's split-brain rats:	Albert (1966).
Ungar's work:	Ungar, *et al.* (1967); Ungar (1972); see also Bisping, *et al.* (1974) for a convincing replication of memory transfer experiments; see also Fjerdingstad (1968) for a review; Ungar (1970).
Jacobson:	Jacobson, A. (1965); Jacobson's work criticised by Luttges, *et al.* (1966).
Jelliffe's patient:	recalled in Sacks (1973), p. 37.
swelling of dendritic spikes:	Harreveld and Fifkova (1974); see also Purpura (1974) for association of defective spines with mental defect.
conformational changes:	Hyden (1972).
importance of glia:	Galambos (1961); Hyden (1962).
Drosophila, conditioning:	Quinn, Harris and Benzer (1974).
Oatley quoted:	Oatley, K. (1969).
von Foerster's idea:	his contribution to Kimble (ed.) (1967), pp. 388ff.
Borges quoted:	Borges (1975), pp. 91–2: Funes the Memorious.

16: Thinking About Thinking

For clear, general account see Radford and Burton (1974); I would also suggest Bruner and Goodnow (1956 and 1962), which advances a viewpoint that has greatly influenced recent thinking.

Gauss' precocity:	Stewart, I. (1978).
late maturers:	Illingworth, R. S. and C. M. (1966).
prodigious memories:	Barlow, F. (1951).
Prof. Aitken:	Hunter, I. M. (1962).
time-contraction and dilation:	Fischer, R. (1967); Cooper and Erickson (1952).
Lashley quoted:	cited by Reitan (1955).
Fisher quoted:	his contribution to Voss (1969), p. 73.
Halstead's theory of intelligence:	Halstead (1947, 1956); and his contribution to Jeffress (ed.) (1951); his work verified by Reitan (1955).
Mozart, Haydn:	Harding, R. (1942).
Guilford's theory:	Guilford (1967).
Zamenhof's work:	Zamenhof (1968); Zamenhof, *et al.* (1971).
figures cited by Boring:	in a book review by Boring in *Sci. Amer.* (July 1965), *213* (1): 113; but see Kent and Davis (1957).
Besdine's views:	*Sci. News* (1971), *99*: 40.
Inaudi, Diamondi:	Binet (1894).
Charles and George:	Horwitz, *et al.* (1965).
Bousfield and Barry:	Bousfield and Barry (1933).
Aitken:	Hunter, I. M. (1962).
William Hamilton, Hernacker, etc.:	Illingworth, ibid.
Blind Tom:	Brawley (1937); Goldenson (1973), pp. 126–33.

anthropologist's confusion: Goodnow's contribution to Resnick (1976), who notes many other examples. See Arnheim (1954) for a devastating criticism of our preoccupation with sets and numbers.

cognitive style: the most comprehensive discussions seem to be in Vinacke (1972, 1974), especially pp. 178ff and in Shouksmith (1970) especially Chapter 13. See also Ross, J. (1965); Hudson (1966).

sex differences: Maccoby and Jacklin (1975) is an exhaustive résumé of this topic. See Witkin, *et al.* (1954) and (1962) for field dependence.

intellectual differences: Hudson (ed.) (1970) especially Chapter 6. Dalton (1968) for effects of progesterone.

verbal and spatial: Maccoby and Jacklin (1975); true of chimpanzees and rats also, Dawson (1975).

effect of parental closeness: Lynn, D. B. (1969).

physiological differences: McGuinness (1976).

differences in activation level: Buchsbaum, M. cited by Goleman, D. (1978).

Mary Lou Read: ibid.

men more lateralised: Witelson, S. cited in ibid.

women confuse L. and R. more: Wolf, S. M. (1973).

hormonal differences: Friedman, *et al.* (1974); Money and Ehrhardt (1973).

behavioural differences at birth: Stoller (1968).

emotional differences: Gray, J. A. (1971); Gray and Buffery (1971).

influence of parents: Lynn, D. B. (1969); Bieri (1960).

women trade on weakness: *Sunday Times*, 17.10.76, citing *Psychology Today*.

differences in immature rats: Gregory, E. (1975).

broad and narrow attention: Wachtel (1967).

cognitive style: Shouksmith (1970); Vinacke (1970, 1974); Helson (1967).

thought as speech: Sokolov (1972).

Hadamard's enquiry: Hadamard (1949).

Armande's observations: Binet (1907) cited by Reeves (1965), Chapter 7.

feats of chessplayers: Binet (1894).

paleologic thinking: Arieti (1974), Chapter 16, ii; for van Domarus' principle see Matte Blanco's contribution to Kemali (ed.) (1975), Pt 11, Sec. 8; Kasanin (1944), pp. 104–14.

'all thinking is conceptual thinking': Humphrey and Coxon (1963); however, see Paivio (1971).

von Foerster on networks: his contribution to Kimble (1967).

chess-playing computers: Levy, D. (1978).

as Weizenbaum has demonstrated: Weizenbaum (1977).

Fisher quoted: contribution to Voss (1969), p. 73.

thinking in structures: Dienes and Jeeves (1965); Hayes-Roth (1977); Arieti (1962).

17: 'It Depends How I Feel'

Rather doubtfully, I suggest Arnold (1970) and Strongman (1973) for general reading. See Plutchik (1955) for a discussion of the problems.

'emotionality' of rats: Denenberg's contribution to Glass (1967), for example.

language of emotion: Davitz (1969), Chapter 2.

Arieti: his contribution to Arnold, M. (1970), Chapter 9.

no successful theory found by Strongman: Strongman (1973), p. 188, 'Overall we are in a state of ignorance . . .'

Leeper says emotions are motives: his contribution, with P. Madison, to Candland (1962), p. 44.

Pribram says emotions are not motives: Pribram (1967a).

Siminov's formula for emotion:	described in Strongman (1973), Chapter 2.
Schachter's experiment:	Schachter and Wheeler (1962).
Valins' experiment:	his contribution to P. Black (ed.) (1970), Chapter 11.
James-Lange theory of emotion:	James, W. (1884).
respiratory crises but no emotion:	Sacks (1976).
Cannon claims the thalamus the seat of emotion:	Cannon (1927).
Bard confirms:	Bard (1934).
Duffy abolishes emotion:	Duffy (1941).
role of hypothalamus:	Gellhorn (1963).
dimethylthamca and medmain:	Woolley (1957); Woolley (1962); his contribution to Glass (1967).
lithium for anxiety:	Gattozzi (1970).
neural basis of aggression:	Moyer's contribution to Singer, J. L. (ed.) (1971), Chapter 3; Moyer (1968).
Sacks cited:	Sacks (1976).
Jacobson and time-lag:	Jacobson, E. (1967).
baby recoils from edge of cliff:	Gibson and Walk (1960).

18: Ghosts and Machines

Much the clearest account of the mind-brain controversy that I have found is Beloff, J. (1962).

Armstrong cited:	Armstrong (1968), p. 73.
Hayek cited:	Hayek (1952), Sec. 13–18.
biochemical explanation out of the question:	Sperry (1969b).
nature of epiphenomena:	Popper and Eccles (1977), Chapter 3, Sec. 3; and pp. 72–5.
mind not a pseudo-problem:	Feigl's contribution to Scher (1962), p. 572.
Malcolm's problem:	Malcolm (1959).
'a brand of haggling':	Ryle (1949).
tertium quid:	Russell (1921), pp. 9ff; for a penetrating discussion, see Globus (1973).

19: Who Holds the Reins?

Much has been written about free will and determinism, most of it unhelpful. Landsberg and Evans (1970) put the materialist case; MacKay (1970 and elsewhere) has put the contrary view. See also Wald's contribution to Platt (ed.) (1965). Beloff (1974) gives a balanced account of the current state of parapsychology. See also Smythies (ed.) (1967) and Wheatley and Edge (eds.) (1976) for discussion of the philosophical problems underlying the subject. White, R. (ed.) (1976) also contains useful contributions.

mind implies purpose:	James (1890), p. 18ff.
Ann Bridge's experiences:	Bridge (1970).
LeShan's experience:	LeShan (1974), p. 10.
telepathy as an extension of existing powers:	Julian Huxley (1941), p. 30, suggests this, and Ehrenwald (1972) argues explicitly for it.
Mrs Verrall's precognitive vision:	cited by LeShan (1974), pp. 7–8.
Hernández-Peón's experiment:	see his contribution to Cavanna and Ullmann (1968), pp. 178–92; a similar experiment by Targ and Puthoff (1974) met with criticism.
free will not the same as acausality:	Feigl, H. (1959).
MacKay's views on free will:	MacKay (1970) and subsequent correspondence.

Sperry's theory of mind as an emergent property:	Sperry (1965), (1970), (1974), etc.
his dualist undertones:	see Bindra (1970) for a similar comment.
the notion of cause:	Toulmin (1962), especially pp. 124, 163–4.
purpose in biology:	Granit (1977), Chapter 1; see also Polanyi (1968); Taylor, C. (1970).
image-driven behaviour:	Beritoff (1965), Chapter 1.
Home's views on explanation:	Home (1966).
Polanyi on hierarchies:	Polanyi (1968).
Granit cited:	Granit (1977), Chapter 10.
free will a 'fact of experience':	Eccles (1965a), p. 16; contribution to Globus (1976), Chapter 4.

20: The Great Adventure

emotion baffling:	Strongman (1973), p. 188.
thinking baffling:	Fisher, A. in Voss (1969), p. 73.
illusions baffling:	Robinson, J. O. (1972), Epilogue.
psychosomatic phenomena baffling:	Schaefer, H. in Eccles (1965), pp. 522–35, likewise Whitlock (1976) says, 'we can do little more than make informed guesses at mechanisms whose workings require a great deal of research before they can be understood.'
hypnosis baffling:	Honorton, C. contribution to White, R. H. (1976), p. 230.
physiology of feeling baffling:	Whitlock (1976), p. 193.
consciousness baffling:	Luria (1969); (1973b) and elsewhere.
nervous system and mind baffling:	Kety, contribution to Featherstone and Simon (1959), p. 3.
integration over time:	Blumenthal (1977).
autonomic response to loud noise:	Horn, G. contribution to Lehrman, Hinde and Shaw (1965), Vol. 1.
autonomic functions consciously controlled:	di Cara (1970).
blood pressure controlled:	Benson, *et al.* (1971); Miller and di Cara (1967).
McCann's experiment:	McCann (1972).
location of consciousness:	Popper and Eccles (1977); Fair (1963), p. 184; Penfield (1975); Beritoff (1965), Chapter 14; Sperry (1969) (1970).

Bibliography

ABELES, N. and SCHILDER, P., 'Psychogenic loss of personal identity', *Neurol. Psychiat.* (1935), *34*: 587–604.
ACKNER, B. 'Depersonalisation', *J. ment. Sci.* (1954), *100*: 838–52 and 853–72.
ADEY, W. ROSS, *et al.*, *Brain Mechanisms and the Control of Behaviour*, Heinemann Educational Books, London (1974).
AGRANOFF, B., 'Memory fixation in the goldfish', *Proc. Nat. Acad. Sci.* (1965), *54*: 788.
——, 'Memory and protein synthesis', *Sci. Amer.* (1967), *216* (6): 115.
ALBERT, D. J., 'Memory in mammals', *Neuropsychologia* (1966), *4*: 79–92.
ALEXANDER, F. and FRENCH, T. M., *Psychosomatic Specificity*, University of Chicago Press, Chicago (1968).
ANDJUS, R. K., *et al.*, 'Some effects of severe hypothermia on learning and retention', *Quart. J. exptl. Psychol.* (1956), *8*: 15–23.
ARIETI, S., 'Microgeny of thought and perception', *Arch. Gen. Psychia.* (1962), *6*: 454–68.
——, *Interpretation of Schizophrenia*, Basic Books, New York (1974).
ARMSTRONG, D. M., *A Materialist Theory of the Mind*, Routledge & Kegan Paul, London (1968).
ARNHEIM, R., *Visual Thinking*, University of California Press, Los Angeles (1954).
ARNOLD, M. (ed.), *The Nature of Emotion*, Penguin Books, Harmondsworth (1968).
——, *Feelings and Emotions: the Loyola Symposium*, Academic Press, New York and London (1970).
AVANT, L., 'Vision in the Ganzfeld', *Psychol. Bull.* (1965), *64*: 246–58.
AXELROD, JULIUS, 'The pineal gland: a neurochemical transducer', *Science* (1974), *184*: 1341.
——, 'Neurotransmitters', *Sci. Amer.* (March 1974), *230* (6): 58.

BABICH, F. R., *et al.*, 'Cross-species transfer of learning', *Proc. Nat. Acad. Sci.* (1965), *54*: 1299.
BAKKER, C. B. and MURPHY, S. E., 'An unusual case of autoscopic hallucinations', *J. abn. & soc. Psychol.* (1969), *69* (6): 646–9.
BARBER, T. X., 'The concept of "hypnosis" ', *J. Psychol.* (1958), *45*: 115–31.
——, 'Towards a theory of pain', *Psychol. Bull.* (1959), *56*: 430–60.
BARBER, T. X. and HEBB, D., 'Physiological and subjective responses to pain producing stimulation under hypnosis', *J. abn. & soc. Psychol.* (1952), *65*: 411.
BARBER, T. and CALVERLEY, D., 'Towards a theory of "hypnotic" behaviour', *Arch. Gen. Psychia.* (1964), *10*: 209–16.
BARBIZET, J., *Human Memory and its Pathology*. Freeman, San Francisco (1970).
BARD, P., 'On emotional expression after decortication with some remarks on theoretical views', *Psychol. Rev.* (1934), *41*: 309–29; 424–49.
BARD, P. and MOUNTCASTLE, V. B., 'Some foreign mechanisms involved in expression of rage with special reference to suppression of angry behaviour', *Research Pubns. Assn. for Res. on Nervous & Mental Dis.* (1974), *27*: 363–404.
BARKER, J. C., *Scared to Death*, F. Muller, London (1968).
BARLOW, FRED, *Mathematical Prodigies: an enquiry*, Hutchinson, London (1951).
BARNOTHY, M. F. (ed.), *Biological Effects of Magnetic Fields*, Plenum Press, New York (1964).
BARTLETT, F., *Remembering, a study in experimental and social psychology*, Cambridge University Press (1932).
BAWIN, F. M., GAVALAS-MEDICI, R. and ADEY, W. R., 'Effect of modulated very high frequency fields on specific brain rhythm in cats', *Brain Research* (1953), *58*: 365.

BECK, J., 'The perception of surface colour', *Sci. Amer.* (1975), *233* (2): 62.
BECKER, R. O., BACHMAN, C. H. and FRIEDMAN, H., 'Psychiatric ward behaviour and geophysical parameters', *Nature* (1965), *205*: 1050.
BEECHER, H. K., *Measurement of Subjective Responses*, Oxford University Press, London (1959).
——, 'Pain in wounded men in battle', *Ann. of Surg.* (1946), *124*: 96.
BEIGLER, J. S., 'Anxiety as an aid in the prognostication of impending death', *Arch. Neurol. Psychia.* (1957), *77*: 171.
BELO, J., *Trance in Bali*, Columbia University Press, New York (1960).
BELOFF, J., *The Existence of Mind*, McGibbon & Kee, London (1962).
——, *New Directions in Parapsychology*, Elek, London (1974).
BENDER, M. B. and TEUBER, H. L., 'Spatial organisation of visual perception following injury to the brain', *Archiv. of Neurol & Psychiat.* (1947), *58*: 721–39; (1948) *59*: 39–62.
BENSON, Herbert, *et al.*, 'Decreased systolic blood pressure through operant conditioning techniques in patients with essential hypertension', *Science* (1971), *173*: 740–2.
BERENSON, B., *Aesthetics and History*, Constable, London (1950).
BERITOFF, J. S., *Neural Mechanisms of Higher Vertebrate Behaviour*, Little, Brown, Boston (1965), and A. Churchill, London (1965).
BERNSTEIN, MOREY, *The Search for Bridey Murphy*, Hutchinson, London (1965).
BESDINE, M., report in *Science News* (1971), *99*: 40.
BEST, H. K. 'Living out future experiences', *Science* (1954), *120*: 1077.
BETHUNE, H. C. and KIDD, C. B., 'Psychophysiological mechanisms in skin disease', *Lancet* (1961, ii), 1419–22.
BEVER, T. G. and CHIARELLO, R. J., 'Cerebral dominance in musicians and non-musicians', *Science* (1974), *185*: 537–9.
BIDERMAN, A. D. and ZIMMER, H. (eds.), *The Manipulation of Human Behaviour*, Wiley, London (1961).
BIERI, J., 'Parental identification and cognitive behaviour', *J. abn. & soc. Psychol.* (1960), *60*: 76–9.
BINDRA, D., 'The problem of subjective experience: puzzlement on reading R. W. Sperry's "A modified conception of consciousness" ', *Psychol. Rev.* (1970), *77*: 581–4.
BINET, A., *La psychologie des Grands Calculateurs et Joueurs d'Echecs*, Hachette, Paris (1894).
BISPING, R., *et al.*, 'Chemical transfer of learned colour discrimination in goldfish', *Nature* (1974), *249*: 771–3.
BLACK, A. H., 'Functions of the septo-hippocampal system', *Nature* (1978), *271*: 208–9.
BLACK, P., *Physiological Correlates of Emotion*, Academic Press, London and New York, (1970).
BLACK, S., *Mind and Body*, Kimber, London (1969).
BLACKWELL, B., *et al.*, 'Demonstration to medical students of placebo responses and non-drug factors', *Lancet* (1972), i. 1279.
BLAKE, R. R. and RAMSEY, G. (eds.), *Perception: an approach to personality*, Ronald Press, New York (1951).
BLAKEMORE, C. and COOPER, G. F., 'Development of the brain depends on the visual environment', *Nature* (1970), *228*: 477–8.
BLINKOV, S. M. and GLESER, I. I., *The Human Brain in Figures and Tables*, Plenum Press, Basic Books, New York (1968).
BLUM, G. S., *et al.*, *A Model of the Mind*, Wiley/University of Michigan, Ann Arbor (1961).
BLUMENTHAL, A. L., *The Process of Cognition*, Prentice-Hall, Homewood, N.J. (1977).
BOERNSTEIN, W. S., 'Visual images: induced hallucinations', *Trans. N.Y. Acad. Sci.* (1957), *20*: 72–4.
BOOIJ, J. (ed.), *Psychosomatics*, Elsevier, The Hague (1957).
BOOTH, D. A., 'Vertebrate brain RNAs and memory retention', *Psychol. Bull.* (1967), *68*: 149–73.
BORGES, J. L., *Labyrinths*, Penguin Books, Harmondsworth (1978).
BOUSFIELD, W. A. and BARRY, H. 'The visual imagery of a lightning calculator', *Amer. J. Psychol.* (1933), *45*: 353–8.
BRADY, J. P. and LEVETT, E. E., 'Hypnotically-induced visual hallucinations', *Psychosom. Med.* (1966), *28*: 351.
BRAIN, W. R., 'The cerebral basis of consciousness', *Brain* (1950), *73*: 465–79.
BRAITENBERG, V., *On the Texture of Brains*, Springer, New York; Heidelberg, Berlin (1977).

BRANDES, G., 'Main currents in nineteenth-century literature'; Vol. 2: *The Romantic School in Germany*, Heinemann, London (1902).
BRAWLEY, B. G., *The Negro Genius*, Dodd, Mead, New York (1937).
BRAZIER, M. A. B. (ed.), *Brain and Behavior*, Vol. 2, Amer. Inst. of Biol. Sciences, Washington (1962).
BRIDGE, A., *Moments of Knowing: some personal experiences*, Hodder and Stoughton, London (1970).
BRIERRE DE BOISMONT, A. J. P., *Hallucinations, or the rational history of apparitions, etc.*, Lindsay & Blakiston, Philadelphia (1853).
BRINDLEY, G. S., 'After images', *Sci. Amer.* (1963), *209* (4): 84.
BROAD, C. D., *The Mind and its Place in Nature*, Kegan Paul, Trench, Trubner, London (1937).
BROVERMAN, I. K., 'Sex differences in cognitive abilities', *Psychol. Rev.* (1968), *75*: 23–50.
BROWN, J., *Mind, Brain, Consciousness: the neuropsychology of cognition*, Academic Press, New York (1977).
BROWN, R. and MCNEILL, D., 'The tip-of-the-tongue phenomenon', *J. verb. Learn. & Verb. Behavior* (1966), 5: 325–37.
BROWN, S. C. (ed.), *The Philosophy of Psychology*, Macmillan, London (1974).
BRUNER, J. S., GOODNOW, J. J. and AUSTIN, G. A., *A Study of Thinking*, Wiley, New York (1956).
BUCHER, H. K., 'The powerful placebo', *J.A.M.A.* (1955), *159*: 1602.
BURNS, R. D., *The Uncertain Nervous System*, Arnold, London (1968).
BURTON, M., *The Sixth Sense of Animals*, Dent, London (1973).
BYERLY, H., 'Explaining and exploiting placebo effects', *Perspectives in Biol. and Med.* (1976), *19*: 423–36.
BYRD, R., *Alone*, Neville Spearman, London (1958).
BYRNE, W. L., *Molecular Approaches to Learning and Memory*, Academic Press, New York and London (1970).

CAIRNS, H., 'Disturbances of consciousness with lesions of the brain stem and diencephalon', *Brain* (1952), *75*: 109.
CAHAL, D. A., 'Effects of nalorphine on the behaviour of healthy human volunteers', *J. ment. Sci.* (1957), *103*: 850.
CAMPBELL, H. J., *The Pleasure Areas*, Eyre-Methuen, London (1973).
CANNON, W., 'Voodoo death', *Amer. Anthropol.* (1942), 44 (2); reprinted *Psychosom. Med.* (1957), *19*: 182.
CANDLAND, D. K. (ed.), *Emotion: Bodily Change*, van Nostrand, Princeton, N.J. (1962).
CARLSON, F. D. (ed.), *Physiological and Biochemical Aspects of Nervous Integration*, Prentice-Hall, Homewood, N.J. (1968).
CASON, H., 'A case of anterograde amnesia', *J. abn. Psychol.* (1935), *30*: 107.
CASSINARI, V. and PAGNI, C. A., *Central Pain: a neurological survey*, Harvard University Press, Boston, Mass. (1969).
CAVANNA, R. and ULLMANN, M., *Psi and altered states of Consciousness*, Parapsychology Foundation, New York (1969).
CHEEK, D. B., 'The meaning of continued hearing sense under anesthesia', *Amer. J. clin. Hypn.* (1965), *8*: 275.
CHERTOK, L. (ed.), *Psychophysiological Mechanisms of Hypnosis*, Springer, New York (1969).
COBB, J. C., *et al.*, 'Specific motor response during sleep to sleep-administered meaningful suggestion', *Percept. & Motor Skills* (1965), *20*: 629–36.
COBB, S. and ROSE, R. M., 'Hypertension, peptic ulcer and diabetes in air traffic controllers', *J.A.M.A.* (1973), *224*: 489–92.
COHEN, D., 'Magnetoencephalography: evidence of magnetic fields produced by alpha rhythm currents', *Science* (1968), *161*: 784.
COLE, M. and ZANGWILL, O., 'Déjà vu and temporal lobe epilepsy', *J. neurol. neurosurg. Psychol.* (1963), *26*: 37.
COOPER, L. F. and TUTHILL, C. E., 'Time distortion in hypnosis and motor learning', *J. Psychol.* (1952), *34*: 67–76.
COOPER, L. and ERICKSON, M., *Time Distortion in Hypnosis: an experimental and clinical investigation*, Williams & Wilkins, Baltimore (1952).
CRASILNECK, H. B. and HALL, J. A., 'The use of hypnosis with unconscious patients', *Int. J. clin. exptl. Hypn.* (1962), *10*: 141.
CRITCHLEY, M., *The Parietal Lobes*, Arnold, London (1953).

CRUE, B. L. (ed.), *Pain: research and treatment*, Academic Press, New York (1975).

DALLENBACH, K. M., 'A puzzle picture with a new principle of concealment', *Amer. J. Psychol.* (1951), *64*: 431.
DALTON, K., 'Antenatal progesterone and intelligence', *Brit. J. Psychiat.* (1968), *114*: 1377–81.
DAMASIO, E., *et al.*, 'Physiological effects during hypnotically requested emotions', *Psychosom. Med.* (1963), *25*: 334.
DAVIDOFF, J. B., *Differences in Visual Perception: the individual eye*, Crosby Lockwood Staples, London (1975).
DAVISON, K., 'Episodic depersonalisation', *Brit. J. Psychiat.* (1964), *110*: 505.
DAVITZ, JOEL, *The Language of Emotion*, Academic Press, New York and London (1969).
DAWSON, J. L. M., 'Cultural and physiological influences upon spatial and perceptual processes in West Africa', *Int. J. Psychol.* (1967), *2*: 115 and 171.
DEIKMAN, A. J., 'Implication of experimentally induced contemplative meditation', *J. nerv. ment. Dis.* (1966, a), *142*: 101–16.
——, 'Deautomatisation and the mystic experience', *Psychiatry* (1966, b), *29*: 324.
DEWHURST, K. and PEARSON, J., 'Visual hallucinations of the self in organic disease', *J. neurol. neurosurg. Psychiat.* (1955), *18*: 53.
DIAMOND, S., *et al.*, *Inhibition and Choice*, Harper and Row, New York (1963).
DI CARA, L. V., 'Learning in the autonomic system', *Sci. Amer.* (1970), *222* (1): 30.
DIENES, Z. P. and JEEVES, M. A., *Thinking in Structures*, Hutchinson, London (1965).
DIMOND, E. G., 'Acupuncture anesthesia', *J.A.M.A.* (1971), *218*: 1558.
DIMOND, S., *The Double Brain*, Churchill-Livingstone, Edinburgh and London (1972).
DINNERSTEIN, A. L. and HALM, J., 'Modification of the placebo effect by means of drugs', *J. abn. & soc. Psychol.* (1970), *75*: 308.
DIXON, J. C., 'Depersonalisation phenomena in a sample population of college students', *Brit. J. Psychiat.* (1963), *109*: 371.
DIXON, N. F., *Subliminal Perception*, McGraw-Hill, New York (1971).
DOCKRELL, W. B. (ed.), *On Intelligence*, Methuen, London (1970).
DODWELL, P. C. (ed.), *Perceptual Processing: stimulus equivalence and pattern recognition*, Appleton-Century-Crofts, New York (1971).
DOOB, L. W., 'Eidetic imagery: a cross-cultural will-o'-the-wisp?', *J. Psychol.* (1966), *63*: 13–34.
DORCUS, R. M., 'Recall under hypnosis of amnestic events', *Int. J. clin. exptl. Hypn.* (1960), *8*: 57.
DRAEGER, U. and HUBEL, T., 'Response to visual stimulation and the relationship between visual, auditory and somatosensory inputs in mouse superior colliculus', *J. neurophysiol.* (1975), *38*: 690–713.
DROSCHER, V. B., *The Magic of the Senses: new discoveries in animal perception*, Panther: Granada, London (1971).
DUFFY, E., 'An explanation of "emotional" phenomena without the use of the concept "emotion"', *J. gen. Psychol.* (1941), *25*: 283–93.
DUNCAN, C. P., *et al.* (eds.), *Human Memory*, Appleton-Century-Crofts, New York (1972).
DUNN, A. J. and BONDY, S. C., *Functional Chemistry of the Brain*, Spectrum, Flushing, New York (1974).
DYNES, J., 'Sudden Death', *Dis. nerv. Syst.* (1969), *30*: 24–8.

E., A. [i.e., G. W. Russell], *The Cradle of Vision*, Macmillan, London (1918).
EARLY, L. and LIFSCHUTZ, J. E., 'A case of stigmata', *Arch. gen. Psychiat.* (1974), *30*: 197.
ECCLES, J., *The Brain and the Person*, Australian Broadcasting Commn. (1965a).
——, *The Brain and the Unity of Conscious Experience*, Cambridge University Press, Cambridge (1965b).
——, (ed.) *The Brain and Conscious Experience*, Springer, New York (1966).
ECCLES, J. ITO, M. and SZENTAGOTHAI, J., *The Cerebellum as a neuronal machine*, Springer, Berlin, Heidelberg, New York (1967).
EFRON, R., 'Temporal perception, aphasia and déjà vu', *Brain* (1963), *86*: 403.
——, 'Biology without consciousness and its consequences', *Perspectives in Biol. and Med.* (1967), 11: 9–36.
EHRENWALD, J., 'A neurophysiological model of psi phenomena', *J. nerv. ment. Dis.* (1972), *154*: 406.
ELEFTHERIOU, B. E. (ed.), *Biology of the Amygdala*, Plenum Press, New York (1974).

ELLENBERGER, H. F., *The Discovery of the Unconscious*, Basic Books, New York (1970).
ELLSON, D., 'Hallucination produced by sensory conditioning', *J. exptl. Psychol.* (1941), *28*: 1–20.
ERICKSON, M. H., 'Control of physiological function by hypnosis', *Amer. J. clin. Hypn.* (1977), *20* (1): 8–19.
——, and ROSSI, E. L., 'Autohypnosis: experiments of M. Erickson', *Amer. J. clin. Hypn.* (1977), *19*: 113.
ERIKSEN, C. W., 'Discrimination and learning without awareness', *Psychol. Rev.* (1966), *67*: 279–300.
ERIKSON, E., *et al.* (eds.), *Identity and Anxiety*, The Free Press, New York (1960).
ESTABROOKS, G. H., *Hypnotism*, Dutton, New York (1957).
EVANS, F. J., 'Verbally-induced behavioural responses during sleep', *J. nerv. & ment. Dis.* (1970), *150*: 171.
EWERT, J-P., 'The neural basis of visually-guided behavior', *Sci. Amer.* (1974), *230* (3): 34.

FAIR, C. M., *The Physical Foundations of the Psyche*, Wesleyan Press, Middletown, Conn. (1963).
FEATHERSTONE, R. M. and SIMON, A. (eds.), *A Pharmacologic Approach to the Study of the Mind*, Thomas, Springfield, Mass. (1959).
FEHRER, E. and RAAB, D., 'Reaction time to stimuli masked by meta-contrast', *J. Exptl. Psychol.* (1962), *63*: 143.
FEIGL, H., 'Philosophical embarrassments of psychology', *Amer. Psychologist* (1959), *14*: 115–28.
FELDBERG, W., 'A physiological approach to the problem of general anaesthesia and loss of consciousness', *Brit. Med. J.* (1959), *2*: 771–82.
FERE, C. S., *The Pathology of Emotions*, University Press, London (1899).
FESTINGER, L., *et al.*, 'Efference and the *conscious* experience of perception', *J. exptl. Psychol.*, Monog. Whole No. 637 (1967), *74* (2): 1–36.
FIELD, J. and MAGOUN, H. (eds.), *Handbook of Physiology; Sec. 1: Neurophysiology*, Amer. Physiol. Soc., Washington (1959, 1960).
FISCHER, R., 'The biological fabric of time', *Ann. N.Y. Acad. Sci.* (1967), *138*: 440.
FISHER, S., *Body Experience in Fantasy and Behavior*, Appleton-Century-Crofts, New York (1970).
——, and CLEVELAND, S. E., *Body Image and Personality*, van Nostrand, Princeton, N.J. (1958).
FJERDINGSTAD, E. J., 'A historical review of memory transfer and some new evidence' (paper delivered to the Medical Sciences section of the AAAS 1968).
FLOREY, E. (ed.), *Nervous Inhibition*, Pergamon Press, Oxford (1961).
FLOURNOY, Th., *Des Indes à la Planète Mars*, Ed. Atar, Geneva, n.d.
FOULKES, D., 'Dream reports from different stages of sleep', *J. abn. & soc. Psychol.* (1962), *65*: 14–25.
——, 'Theories of dream formation and recent studies of sleep consciousness', *Psychol. Bull.* (1964), 62: 236–47.
——, *The Psychology of Sleep*, Charles Scribner's Sons, New York (1966a).
——, *et al.*., Individual differences in mental activity at sleep onset, *J. abn. Psychol.* (1966b), *71*: 280–6.
FREEMON, F. R., *Sleep Research: a critical review*, Thomas, Springfield, Ill. (1972).
FRIEDMAN, R. C., *et al.*, *Sex Differences in Behavior*, Wiley, New York and London (1974).
FROMM, E. and SHOR, R. E. (eds.), *Hypnosis: research developments and perspectives*, Aldine-Atherton, Chicago (1972); Elek, London (1973).

GALAMBOS, R., 'A glial and neuronal theory of brain function', *Proc. Nat. Acad. Sci.* (1961), *47* (1): 129–36.
GALDSTON, I., 'The etiology of depersonalisation', *J. nerv. ment. Dis.* (1947), *105*: 25–39.
GALIN, D. and ORNSTEIN, R. E., 'Lateral specialisation of cognitive mode: an EEG study', *Psychophysiol.* (1972), *9*: 412.
GALIN, D., 'Implications for psychiatry of left and right hemisphere specialisation', *Arch. Gen. Psychiat.* (1974), *31*: 572–82.
GALTON, F., *An Enquiry into Human Understanding*, Macmillan, London (1907).
GARDNER, F. H. and DIAMOND, L. K., 'Autoerythrocyte sensitization', *Blood* (1955), *10*: 675.

GATTOZZI, A. A., *Lithium in the Treatment of Mood Disorders*, US Dept. of Health, Education & Welfare (NIMH), Washington (1970).
GAZZANIGA, M. S., *The Bisected Brain*, Appleton-Century-Crofts, New York (1974).
——, *et al.*, 'Psychologic and neurologic consequences of partial and complete cerebral commissurotomy', *Neurology* (1975), *25*: 10–15.
GEISLER, C. D., *et al.*, 'Extracranial responses to acoustic clicks in man', *Science* (1958), *128*: 1210–11.
GELLHORN, E., 'Physiological processes related to consciousness and perception', *Brain* (1954), *77*: 401–15.
GELLHORN, E. and LOOFBOURROW, G. N., *Emotions and Emotional Disorders; a neurophysiological study*, Harper & Row, New York (1963).
GESCHWIND, N., 'Language and the brain', *Sci. Amer.* (1972), *226* (4): 76.
GIBSON, E. J. and WALK, R. D., 'The "Visual Cliff" ', *Sci. Amer.* (1960), *202* (4): 64.
GIBSON, James J., *The Senses Considered as a Perceptual System*, Houghton Mifflin, Boston (1966).
GILL, M. and BRENNAN, M., *Hypnosis and Related States*, Intl. University Press, New York (1958 and 1961).
GLASS, D. C. (ed.), *Neurophysiology in Emotion*, Rockefeller U.P., New York (1967).
GLOBUS, G. G., 'Unexpected symmetries in the "World Knot" ', *Science* (1973), *180*: 1129–36.
GLOBUS, G. G., MAXWELL, G. and SAVODNIK, L., *Consciousness and the Brain*, Plenum Press, New York and London (1976).
GODDEN, D. R. and BADDELEY, A. D., 'Context-dependent memory in two natural environments on land and under water', *Brit. J. Psychol.* (1975), *66* (3): 325–31.
GOLDENSON, R., *Mysteries of the Mind*, Doubleday, New York (1973).
GOLDSTEIN, K. M. and BLACKMAN, S., *Cognitive Style*, Wiley, New York (1978).
GOLLA, F. L. and ANTONOVICH, S., 'Relation of muscular tonus and patellar reflex to mental work', *J. ment. Sci.* (1929), *75*: 234–41.
GOWAN, J. C., *Trance and Creativity*, Creative Education Foundation, Buffalo (1975).
GRANIT, R., *The Purposive Brain*, M.I.T. Press, Cambridge, Mass. (1977).
GRAY, H., *Gray's Anatomy*, Longman's, London (1973).
GRAY, J. A., 'Sex differences in emotional behavior in mammals including man', *Acta Psychologica* (1971a), *35*: 29.
——, and BUFFERY, A. W. H., 'Sex differences in emotional and cognitive behavior in mammals including man: adaptive and neural bases', *Acta Psychologica* (1971b), *35*: 89.
GRAY, J. A., 'The mind-brain identity theory as a scientific hypothesis', *Philos. Qtly.* (1971c), *21*: 247–52.
GREEN, C. E., *Lucid Dreams*, Inst. of Psychophysical Research, Oxford (1968a).
——, 'Out of the body experiences: a symposium', ibid. (1968b).
GREENSPOON, J. and RAYNARD, R., 'Stimulus conditions and retroactive inhibition', *J. exptl. Psychol.* (1975), *53*: 55–9.
GREGORY, R. L., *Eye and Brain*, Weidenfeld & Nicolson, London (1966).
——, 'Visual Illusions', *Sci. Amer.* (1968), *219* (5): 66.
——, *Concepts and Mechanisms of Perception*, Duckworth, London (1974).
GREGORY, E., 'Comparison of post-natal CMS development between male and female rats', *Brain Research* (1975), *99*: 152.
GRENNELL, R. G. (ed.), *Progress in Neurobiology: (V) Neurophysiopathology*, Hoeber, New York (1962).
GUILFORD, J. P., *The Nature of Human Intelligence*, McGraw-Hill, New York (1967).
GUILLEMIN, R., 'Peptides in the brain: the new endocrinology of the neurone', *Science* (1978), *202* (4366): 390–402.
——, and BURGUS, R., 'The hormones of the hypothalamus', *Sci. Amer.* (1972), *227* (5): 24.

HABER, R. N., 'Eidetic images', *Sci. Amer.* (1969), *220* (4): 31.
——, 'How we remember what we see', *Sci. Amer.* (1970), *222* (5): 104.
——, and RUTH, B., 'Eidetic imagery: (I) Frequency', *Perceptual & Motor Skills* (1964), *19*: 131–8.
HADAMARD, J., *An Essay on the Psychology of Invention in the Mathematical Field*, Princeton U.P. (1949), Dover, New York (1954).
HALL, R. L. and STRIDE, E., 'The varying responses to pain in psychiatric disorders: a study in abnormal psychology', *Brit. J. med. Psychol.* (1954), *27*: 48.
HALSTEAD, W. C., *Brain and Intelligence*, University of Chicago Press, Chicago (1974).

HARDING, E. and ROSAMOND, E. M., *An Anatomy of Inspiration*, Heffer, Cambridge (1942).
HARREVELD, A. and FIFVOKA, E., 'Involvement of glutamate in memory formation', *Brain Res.* (1974), *81*: 455.
HARTLINE, H. K., *The neural Mechanisms of Vision*, The Harvey Lectures, 1941–2, series 37, pp. 39–68, London (1942).
HAYEK, F. A., *The Sensory Order: an enquiry into the foundations of theoretical psychology*, Routledge & Kegan Paul, London (1952).
HAYES-ROTH, B., 'Evolution of cognitive structures and processes', *Psychol. Rev.* (1977), *84*: 260–78.
HAYMAKER, W., *et al.* (eds.), *The Hypothalamus*, Thomas, Springfield (1969).
HEAD, H. and SHERREN, J., 'The consequences of injury to the peripheral nerves in man', *Brain* (1905), *28*: 116–338.
HEATH, R. G., *Studies in Schizophrenia: approaches to mind-brain relations*, Harvard University Press, Boston (1954).
——, 'Levels of Awareness', *Psychosom. Med.* (1955), *17*: 383–95.
HEBB, D. O., *A Textbook of Psychology*, Saunders, Philadelphia (1972).
——, *The Organisation of Behaviour*, Wiley, New York (1949).
HESS, E. H., 'Attitude and pupil size', *Sci. Amer.* (1965), *212* (4): 46.
HELSON, R., 'Sex differences in creative style', *J. person.* (1967), *35*: 214–33.
HERON, W., *et al.*, 'Visual disturbance after prolonged perceptual isolation', *Canad. J. Psychol.* (1956), *10* (1): 13–18.
HERRMANN, G. and POETZL, O., 'Die optische Allaesthesie', *Abhand. aus der Neurologie* (1928), *47*: 1–301.
HETHERINGTON, R., *The Sense of Glory: a psychological study of peak experiences*, Friends Home Service Committee, London (1975).
HILL, H. E., *et al.*, 'Studies of anxiety associated with anticipation of pain', *Arch. Neurol. Psychiat.* (1952), *67*: 612.
HOHMANN, G. W., 'Some effects of spinal cord lesions on experiencced emotional feelings', *Psychophysiol.* (1966), *3*: 143–56.
HOME, H. J. H., 'The concept of mind', *Int. J. Psychoanal.* (1966), *47*: 43–9.
HOROWITZ, M., *et al.*, 'Visual imagery in brain stimulation', *Arch. Gen. Psychiat.* (1968), *19*: 469–86.
HORTON, P. and MILLER, D., 'The etiology of multiple personality', *Comprehen. Psychiat.* (1972), *13*: 151–9.
HORWITZ, W., *et al.*, 'Identical twins, "Idiots Savants", calendar calculators', *Amer. J. Psychiat.* (1965), *121*: 1075–9.
HUBEL, D. H. and WIESEL, T. N., 'Receptive fields of single neurones in the cat's striate cortex', *J. physiol.* (1959), *148*: 574–91.
HUDSON, L., *Contrary Imaginations*, Methuen, London (1966).
——, (ed.) *The Ecology of Human Intelligence: Selected Readings*, Penguin Books, Harmondsworth (1970).
HUGHES, J., *et al.*, 'Identification of two related pentapeptides from the brain with potent opiate antagonist activity, *Nature* (1975), *258*: 577–9.
HUMPHREY, N., 'Vision in a monkey without striate cortex: a case study', *Perception* (1974), *3* (3): 241–55.
——, and WEISKRANTZ, L., 'Vision in monkeys after removal of the striate cortex', *Nature* (1967), *215*: 595–7.
——, 'Seeing and nothingness', *New Sci.* (1972), *53*: 682.
HUMPHREY, G. and COXON, R. V., *The Chemistry of Thinking*, Thomas, Springfield (1963).
——, and ZANGWILL, I., 'Cessation of dreaming after brain injury', *J. Neurol. Neurosurg. Psychiat.* (1951), *14*: 322.
HUNTER, I. M., 'An exceptional talent for calculative thinking', *Brit. J. Psychol.* (1962), *53*: 243–58.
HUXLEY, A., *The Devils of Loudun*, Chatto & Windus, London (1952).
——, *The Doors of Perception*, Chatto & Windus, London (1954).
HUXLEY, J., *The Uniqueness of Man*, Chatto & Windus, London (1941).
HYDÉN, H., 'The neuron and its glia', *Endeavour* (1962), *21*: 144–55.

IKEDA, M. and TAKEUCHI, T., 'The influence of foveal load on the functional visual field', *Percep. & Psychophys.* (1975), *18*: 255–60.
IKEMI, Y. and NAKAGAWA, S., 'A psychosomatic study of contagious dermatitis', *Kyushu J. Med. Sci.* (1962), *13*: 335–52.

IKIN, A., 'Vera: a study in dissociation of personality', *Brit. J. med. Psychol.* (1924), *4*: 179, and (1925), *4*: 273.
ILLINGWORTH, R. S. and C. M., *Lessons from Childhood*, Livingstone, Edinburgh and London (1966).
ISAACSON, R. (ed.), *Basic Readings in Neuropsychology*, Harper & Row, New York and Evanston (1964).
——, *The Limbic System*, Plenum, New York (1974).

JACOBSON, A., 'Transfer of a response to naïve rats by injection of RNA extracted from trained rats', *Science* (1965), *149*: 656.
JACOBSON, E., *Biology of Emotions*, Thomas, New York (1967).
JAENSCH, E. R., *Eidetic Imagery and typological methods of Investigation*, Kegan Paul, Trench, Trubner, London (1930).
JAMES, W., 'Subjective effects of nitrous oxide', *Mind* (1882), *7*: 186–208.
——, 'What is an emotion?', *Mind* (1884), *9*: 188–205.
——, *Principles of Psychology*, Holt, New York (1890).
——, *The Varieties of Religious Experience*, New American Library, New York (1958).
JAYSON, M. (ed.), *The Lumbar Spine and Back Pain*, Pitman Medical, Tunbridge Wells (1976).
JEFFRESS, L. A. (ed.), *Cerebral Mechanisms in Behavior*, Wiley, New York (1951).
JEWESBURY, E. C. O., 'Insensitivity to pain', *Brain* (1951), *74*: 336–53.
JONES, D. S. *Kybernetics of Mind and Brain*, Thomas, Springfield (1970).
JONES, J. C., 'Premonition of death', *Brit. Med. J.* (1959), ii. 1041.
JOSEPHSON, E. and M. (eds.), *Man Alone*, Dell, New York (1962).
JULESZ, B., 'Texture and visual perception', *Sci. Amer.* (1965), *212* (2): 38.

KANISZA, G., 'Margini quasi-percettivi in campi con stimolazione omogenea', *Revista di psicologia* (1955), *49*: 7.
——, 'Subjective contours', *Sci. Amer.* (1976), *234* (4): 48.
KASAMATSU, A. and HIRAI, T. 'An electroencephalographic study on the Zen meditation (Zazen)', *Foli Psychiat. & Neurol. Japan* (1966), *20*: 315–36.
KASANIN, J. S. (ed.), *Language and Thought in Schizophrenia: collected papers*, University of California Press, Los Angeles (1944).
KELSEY, D., 'Phantasies of birth and prenatal experiences recovered (under) hypnoanalysis', *J. ment. Sci.* (1953), *99*: 216–23.
KEMALI, D. *et al.* (eds.), *Schizophrenia To-day*, Pergamon, Oxford (1976).
KENNEDY, D., 'Small systems of nerve cells', *Sci. Amer.* (1967), *216* (5): 44.
KENT, NORMA and DAVIS, D. R., 'Discipline in the home and intellectual development', *Brit. J. med. Psychol.* (1957), *30*: 27.
KEUP, W. (ed.) *Origin and Mechanisms of Hallucination*, Plenum Press, New York and London (1970).
KEY, W. B., *Subliminal Seduction*, Signet, New American Library, New York (1972).
KIMBLE, D. P. (ed.), *The Anatomy of Memory*, Science & Behavior Books, Palo Alto (1967).
KISSEN, D. M., *Emotional Factors in Pulmonary Tuberculosis*, Tavistock, London (1958).
——, and LESHAN, L. (eds.), *Psychosomatic Aspects of Neoplastic Disease*, Lippincott, Philadelphia (1964).
KLINE, M. V., 'Hypnosis and age-regression: a case report', *J. genet. Psychol.* (1951), *78*: 195.
——, 'Living out "future" experiences under hypnosis', *Science* (1958), *120*: 1076–7.
KLINE, M. V. (ed.), *The Nature of Hypnosis*, Waverley Press, Baltimore (1962).
KLÜVER, H. and BUCY, P. C., '"Psychic blindness" and other symptoms following bilateral temporal lobectomy in rhesus monkeys', *Amer. J. Physiol.* (1937), *119*: 352–3.
KNOWLES, D., *The English Mystical Tradition*, Burns, Oates, London (1961).
KOESTLER, A., *Janus: a summing up*, Heinemann, London (1978).
KOHLER, I., 'Experiments with goggles', *Sci. Amer.* (1962), *206* (5): 62.
KRATOCHVIL, S., 'Sleep hypnosis and waking hypnosis', *Int. J. clin. exptl. Hypn.* (1970), *18*: 25–40.
KRNJEVIČ, K., *et al.*, 'Cortical inhibition', *Nature* (1964), *201*: 1294–6.
KUBIE, L. S., 'Use of induced hypnogogic memories in recovery of repressed amnesic data', *Bull. Menn. Clin.* (1943), *7*: 172.
——, and MARGOLIN, S., 'The process of hypnotism and the nature of the hypnotic state', *Amer. J. of Psychiat.* (1944), *100*: 611.

KUPPER, H. I., 'Psychic concomitants in wartime injuries', *Psychosom. Med.* (1945), *7*: 15–21.

LANCASTER, E. and POLING, J., *Strangers in my Body: the final face of Eve*, Secker & Warburg, London (1958).
LAND, E., 'Experiments in color vision', *Sci. Amer.* (1959), *200* (5): 84.
——, 'Colour in the natural image', *Proc. Roy. Inst. of Gt. Brit.* (1962), *39* (I), No 176: 1.
LANDSBERG, P. T. and EVANS, D. A., 'Free will in a mechanistic universe', *Brit. J. Philos. Sci.* (1970), *21*: 343.
LANGFIELD, H. S., 'Note on a case of chromaesthesia', *Psychol. Bull.* (1914), *11*: 113.
LANSDELL, H., 'Sex differences in hemispheric asymmetries of the human brain', *Nature* (1964), *203*: 550.
LASHLEY, K. S., 'In search of the engram', *Symp. Exp. Biol.* (1950), *4*: 454–82.
——, *Brain Mechanisms and Learning*, Hafner, New York and London (1964).
LASKI, M., *Ecstasy: a study of some secular and religious experiences*, Cresset Press, London (1961).
LEHRMAN, D. S., HINDE, R. A. and SHAW, E. (eds.), *Advances in the Study of Behavior*, Academic Press, New York (1965).
LEROY, R., 'The syndrome of lilliputian hallucinations', *J. nerv. & ment. Dis.* (1922), *56*: 325–33.
LESHAN, L., *The Medium, the Mystic and the Physicist*, Turnstone Books, London (1974).
LEUBA, C., 'Images as conditioned sensations', *J. exptl. Psychol.* (1940), *26*: 345–51.
—— and DUNLAP, R., 'Conditioning imagery', *J. exptl. Psychol.* (1951), *41*: 352.
LEVY, D., 'Computers are now chess masters', *New Sci.* (1978), *79*: 256.
LEVINSON, B. W., 'States of awareness during general anaesthesia', *Brit. J. Anaesth.* (1968), *37*: 544.
LEWIN, R., 'The brain's other half', *New Sci.* (1974), *62*: 606–8.
——, 'Seeing with a blind eye', *New Sci.* (1975), *66*: 696.
LHERMITTE, J., 'Visual hallucination of the self', *Brit. Med. J.* (1951), i. 431–4.
LIBET, B., *et al.*, 'Responses of human somatosensory cortex to stimuli below the threshold for conscious sensation', *Science* (1967), *158*: 1597–600.
LILLY, J., *The Centre of the Cyclone*, Calder & Boyars, London (1973).
LINDNER, R., *The Jet Propelled Couch and other Psychoanalytic Tales*, Secker & Warburg, London (1955).
LIPPMAN, C. W., 'Hallucinations of physical duality in migraine', *J. nerv. & ment. Dis.* (1953), *117*: 345–50.
LIVINGSTON, W. K., *Pain Mechanisms: a physiological interpretation of causalgia and its related states*, Plenum Press, New York (1976).
LLAURADO, J. G., *et al.*, *Biologic and Clinical Effects of L-F Magnetic and Electric Fields*, Thomas, Springfield, Ill. (1974).
LONGO, V. G., *Neuropharmacology and Behavior*, W. H. Freeman, San Francisco (1972).
LORD, J. A. H., *et al.*, 'Endogenous opioid peptides: multiple agonists and receptors', *Nature* (1977), *267*: 495–9.
LOWEN, A., *Betrayal of the Body*, Collier, New York (1969).
LOWRY, T. P. (ed.), *Hyperventilation and Hysteria*, C. C. Thomas, Philadelphia (1967).
LUDWIG, A., 'Altered states of consciousness', *Arch. Gen. Psychiat.* (1966), *15*: 225–34.
——, 'The trance', *Comprehens. Psychiat.* (1967), *8*: 7–15.
——, and LYLE, W. H., 'Tension induction and trance', *J. abn. & soc. Psychol.* (1964), *69*: 70.
LURIA, A. R., *Higher Cortical Functions in Man*, Tavistock, London (1966a).
——, *The Human Brain and Psychologic Processes*, Harper & Row, New York (1966b).
——, *The Mind of a Mnemonist*, Jonathan Cape, London (1969).
——, *The Man with a Shattered World: a history of a brain wound*, Jonathan Cape, London (1973a).
——, *The Working Brain: an introduction to neuropsychology*, Penguin, Harmondsworth (1973b).
LUTTGES, M., *et al.*, 'An examination of "transfer of learning" by nucleic acid', *Science* (1966), *151*: 834.
LYNN, D. B., 'Sex role and parent identification', *Child Dev.* (1962), *33*: 555–64.
LYNN, D. B., 'Cognitive function and distance of child from parent', *Psychol. Rev.* (1969), *76*: 236.
LYNN, R., *Attention, Arousal and the Orientation Reaction*, Pergamon, Oxford (1966).

McCann, J. J., 'Rod-cone interactions: different color sensations from identical stimuli', *Science* (1972), *176*: 1255–7.
MacCoby, E. and Jacklin, C., *The Psychology of Sex Differences*, Oxford University Press, London (1975).
McCleary, R. A. and Lazarus, R. S., 'Autonomic discrimination without awareness: an interim report', *J. person.* (1949), *18*: 171–9.
McGaugh, J. L. (ed.), *The Chemistry of Mood, Motivation and Memory*, Plenum, New York (1972).
McGhie, A., *The Pathology of Attention*, Penguin Books, Harmondsworth (1965).
——, and Chapman, J., 'Disorders of attention and perception in early schizophrenia', *Brit. J. med. Psychol.* (1961), *34*: 103–15.
McGuinness, D., 'Away from a unisex psychology: individual differences in visual, sensory and perceptual processes', *Perception* (1976), *5*: 279–94.
MacKay, D., 'The bankruptcy of determinism', *New Sci.* (1970), *47*: 24–6.
——, 'The human brain', *Science Journal* (May 1967), p. 43.
McKellar, P., *Imagination and Thinking*, Cohen and West, London (1957).
McKenna, T. and Wilton, T. N. P., 'Awareness during endotracheal intubation', *Anaesthesia.* (1973), *28*: 599–602.
McLardy, T., 'Hippocampal formation of brain as detector-coder of temporal patterns of information', *Perspectives in Biol. & Med.* (1959), *2*: 443–52.
MacLean, P., 'The limbic system ("Visceral Brain") in relation to central gray and the reticulum of the brain stem', *Psychosom. Med.* (1955), *17*: 355–66.
——, 'New findings relevant to the evolution of the psychosexual functions of brain', *J. nerv. ment. Dis.* (1962), *135*: 289–301.
——, *et al.* (ed. T. J. Boag and D. Campbell), *A triune concept of the Brain and Behaviour*, University of Toronto Press, Toronto (1973).

Mahl, G. F., *et al.*, 'Psychological responses in the human to intracerebral stimulation', *Psychosom. Med.* (1964), *26*: 337.
Malcolm, N. *Dreaming*, Routledge & Kegan Paul, London (1959).
Marmer, M. J., *Hypnosis in Anesthesiology*, Thomas, Springfield, Ill. (1959).
Marshall, J., 'Sensory disturbances in cortical wounds with reference to pain', *J. neurol. neurosurg. Psychiat.* (1951), *14*: 187.
Martin, J. P., 'Fits of laughter (sham mirth) in organic cerebral disease', *Brain* (1950), *73*: 453.
Maslach, C., Marshall, G. and Zimbardo, P., 'Hypnotic control of peripheral skin temperature', *Psychophysiol.* (1972), *9*: 600–605.
Mason, A. A., 'A case of congenital ichthyosiform erythrodermia of Brocq treated by hypnosis', *Brit. Med. J.* (1952), *2*: 442–3.
Masters, R. E. L. and Houston, J., *The Varieties of Psychedelic Experience*, Blond, London (1967), Turnstone (1973).
Meadows, J. C., 'Disturbed perception of colours associated with localised cerebral lesions', *Brain* (1974), *97*: 615–32.
Meares, A., 'The Y-State: an hypnotic variant', *Int. J. clin. and exptl. Hypn.* (1960) *8*: 237.
Melzack, R., *et al.*, 'Effects of discrete brainstem lesions in cats on perception of noxious stimulation', *J. Neurophysiol.* (1958), *21*: 353.
—— and Wall, P. D., 'On the nature of cutaneous sensory mechanisms', *Brain* (1962), *85*: 331.
——, *et al.*, 'Skin sensitivity to thermal stimuli', *Exper. Neurol.* (1962), *6*: 300.
—— and Schnechter, B., 'Itch and vibration', *Science* (1965a), *147*: 1047.
—— and Wall, P. D., 'Pain mechanisms: a new theory', *Science* (1965b), *150*: 971.
—— and Torgerson, W. S., 'On the language of pain', *Anesthesiology* (1971), *34*: 50.
——, *The Puzzle of Pain*, Penguin Books, Harmondsworth (1973).
Michael, C. R., 'Retinal processing of visual images', *Sci. Amer.* (1969), *220* (5): 104.
Michaux, H., *Misérable Miracle*, Gallimard, Paris (1972).
——, *The Major Ordeals of the Mind*, Secker & Warburg, London (1974).
Miller, G. A., *Psychology*, Hutchinson, London (1964).
Miller, N. and di Cara, L. V., 'Instrumental learning of heart rate changes in curarised rats', *J. comp. and physiol. Psychol.* (1967), *63* (1): 12–19.
Millodot, M., 'Do blue-eyed people have more sensitive corneas than brown-eyed people?', *Nature* (1975), *255*: 151–2.
Money, J. and Ehrhardt, A., *Man and Woman, Boy and Girl*, Johns Hopkins University Press, Baltimore (1973).

MOODY, R. L., 'Bodily changes during abreaction', *Lancet* (1946), *251* (ii): 934–5, and (1948), *254* (ii): 264.
MORAY, N., 'Attention in dichotic listening: affective cues and the influence of instructions', *Quart. J. exptl. Psychol.* (1959), *11*: 56–60.
MORITZ, A. R. and ZAMCHEK, N., 'Sudden unexpected death of young soldiers', *Arch. Pathol.* (1946), *42*: 459.
MORUZZI, G. and MAGOUN, H., 'Brain stem reticular formation and activation of the electroencephalogram', *Electroencephalography and clin. Neurophysiol.* (1949), *1*: 455–73.
MOSKOWITZ, H. R., *et al.*, 'Sugar sweetness and pleasantness: evidence for different psychological laws', *Science* (1974), *184*: 583.
MOSTERT, J. W., 'States of awareness during general anaesthesia', *Perspectives in Biol. and Med.* (1975), *19* (1): 68.
MOUNTCASTLE, V. B. (ed.), *Interhemispheric Relations and Cerebral Dominance*, Johns Hopkins Press, Baltimore (1962).
MOYER, K. E., 'Kinds of aggression and their physiological basis', *Communics. in Behav. Biol.* (1968), *2*: 65–87.
MROSOVSKY, N., 'Retention and reversal of conditioned avoidance following hypothermia', *J. comp. physiol. Psychol.* (1963), *56*: 811.
MUHL, A., 'Automatic writing as an indicator of the fundamental factors underlying the personality', *J. abn. & soc. Psychol.* (1922), *17*: 168.
MUNDLE, C. W. K., *Perception: facts and theories*, Oxford University Press, London (1971).
MURCHISON, C. (ed.), *Handbook of Child Psychology*, Clark University Press, Worcester, Mass. (1931).
MURPHY, G., *Personality*, Harper, New York and Evanston (1947).
MYERS, R. E., 'Interocular transfer of pattern discrimination in cats following section of crossed optic fibres', *J. comp. physiol. Psychol.* (1955), *48*: 470–3.

NAKAHAMA, H., *et al.*, 'Excitation and inhibition in ventrobasal thalamic neurons before and after cutaneous input deprivation', *Prog. Brain Res.* (1966), *21*: 180.
NARANJO, C., *The Healing Journey: a new approach to consciousness*, Hutchinson, London (1975).
NAUTA, W., 'The problem of the frontal lobe', *J. psychiat. Res.* (1971), *8*: 167–87.
NEISSER, U., *Cognitive Psychology*, Meredith (Appleton-Century-Crofts), New York (1967).
——, 'Visual search', *Sci. Amer.* (1964), *210* (6): 94.
NIELSEN, J. M., *Agnosia, Apraxia, Aphasia: their value in cerebral localisation*, Hoeber, New York and London (1946).
NOYCE, W., *South Col*, Heinemann, London (1954).

OATLEY, K., 'Brain research seeks an identity', *New Sci.* (1969), *43*: 277–8.
OBERMAYER, M. E., *Psychocutaneous Medicine*, Thomas, Springfield (1955).
—— and GREENSON, R. R., 'Treatment by suggestion of verrucae planae of the face', *Psychosom.* (1970), *11* (4): 163.
OESTERREICH, T. K., *Occultism and Medical Science*, Methuen, London (1923).
OLDS, J., 'Pleasure centers in the brain', *Sci. Amer.* (1956), *195* (4): 105.
—— and MILNER, P., 'Positive reinforcement produced by electrical stimulation of the septal area and other regions of rat', *J. comp. & physiol. Psychol.* (1954), *47*: 419–37.
OLLIVER, C. W., *The Extension of Consciousness: an introduction to the study of metapsychology*, Rider, London (1932).
OLTON, G., 'Spatial memory', *Sci. Amer.* (1977), *236* (6): 82.
O'NEILL, J. J., *Prodigal Genius: the life of Nikola Tesla*, Ives Washburn, New York (1945).
O'NEIL, W. M., *The Beginnings of Modern Psychology*, Penguin, Harmondsworth (1968).
ORNE, M. T., 'The nature of hypnosis', *J. abn. and soc. Psychol.* (1959), *58*: 227.
ORNSTEIN, R. E., *The Psychology of Consciousness*, Freeman, San Francisco (1972).
OSWALD, I., *et al.*, 'Discriminative responses to stimulation during human sleep', *Brain* (1960), *83*: 440.
OTTO, R., *The Idea of the Holy*, Milford, London (1925).

PADGHAM, A. and SAUNDERS, J. E., *The Perception of Light and Colour*, Academic Press, London and New York (1974).
PAFFARD, M. K., *Inglorious Wordsworths: a study of some transcendental experiences in childhood and adolescence*, Hodder & Stoughton, London (1973).

PAHNKE, W. N. and RICHARDS, W. A., 'Implications of LSD and experimental mysticism', *J. Relig. & Health* (1966), *5*: 175–208.
PAIVIO, A., *Imagery and Verbal Processes*, Holt, Rinehart, New York (1971).
PAPEZ, J. W., 'A proposed mechanism of emotion', *Arch. Neurol. Psychiat.* (1937), *38*: 725–43.
PARKES, C. M., *Bereavement*, Tavistock, London (1972).
PASQUARELLI, B. and BULL, N., 'Experimental investigations of the body-mind continuum in affective states', *J. nerv. ment. Dis.* (1951), *113*: 512–21.
PATTIE, F. A., 'Attempts to produce uniocular blindness', *Brit. J. med. Psychol.* (1935), *15*: 230–41.
PAUL, G. L., 'The production of blisters by hypnotic suggestion; another look', *Psychosom. Med.* (1963), *25*: 233–44.
PENFIELD, W., 'The cerebral cortex in man', *AMA Arch. Neurol. Psychiat.* (1938), *40*: 417–42.
——, 'Memory mechanisms', ibid (1952)., *67*: 178–98.
——, 'On memory', *Lancet* (20 April 1968), No 7547, p. 853.
——, *The Mystery of the Mind: a critical study of consciousness and the human brain*, Princeton University Press (1975).
PENICK, S. B. and HINKLE, L. E., jr., 'The effect of expectation on response to phenmetrazine', *Psychosom. Med.* (1964), *26*: 369.
PERKY, C. E., 'An experimental study of imagination', *Amer. J. Psychol.*, *21*: 422.
PETO, A., 'On so-called "depersonalisation" ', *Int. J. Psychoanal.* (1955), *36*: 379–86.
——, 'Body image and archaic thinking', *Int. J. Psychoanal.* (1959), *40*: 223–31.
PIERLOOT, R. A. (ed.), *Recent Researches in Psychosomatics*, Karger, Basel (1970).
PIHL, R. O. and ALTMAN, J., 'An experimental analysis of the placebo effect', *J. Clin. Pharm.* (1971), *11*: 91–5.
PLACE, U. T., 'Is consciousness a brain process?', *Brit. J. Psychol.* (1956), *47*: 44–56.
PLATT, J. R. (ed.), *New View of the Nature of Man*, University of Chicago Press (1965).
PLUMB, F. and POSNER, J. B., *The Diagnosis of Stupor and Coma*, Davis, Philadelphia (1972).
PLUTCHIK, R., 'Some problems for a theory of emotion', *Psychosom. Med.* (1955), *17*: 306.
POLANYI, M., 'Life's irreducible structure', *Science* (1968), *160*: 1308–12.
POLLEN, D., *et al.*, 'How does the striate cortex begin the reconstruction of the visual world?', *Science* (1971), *173*: 74–7.
POPPER, K. and ECCLES, J., *The Self and its Brain*, Springer International, Berlin (1977).
PREVOZNIK, S. J. and ECKERHOFF, J. E., 'Phantom Limb Sensations during Spinal Anaesthesia', *Anesthesiology* (1964), *25*: 767.
PRIBRAM, K. H., 'The neurology of thinking', *Behav. Sci.* (1959), *4*: 265–87.
——, 'The new neurology and the biology of emotion: a structural approach', *Amer. Psychologist* (1967a), *22*: 830–8.
—— (ed.), *The Biology of Learning*, Harcourt Brace and World, New York (1969).
—— and BROADBENT, D. (eds.), *Biology of Memory*, Academic Press, New York and London (1970).
—— and LURIA, A. R. (eds.), *Psychophysiology of the Frontal Lobes*, Academic Press, New York and London (1973).
—— and TUBBS, W. E., 'Short-term memory', *Science* (1967b), *156*: 1765–7.
PRINCE, W. F., *The Case of Patience Worth*, Soc. Psychol. Research, Boston (1927), and University Books, New Hyde Park, New York (1964).
PURDY, D. M., 'Eidetic imagery and plasticity in the nature of perception', *J. Gen. Psychol.* (1936), *15*: 437–53.
PURPURA, D. P., 'Dendritic spine "dysgenesis" and mental retardation', *Science* (1974), *186*: 1126.

QUARTON, G. C., *et al.*, *The Neurosciences: a study program*, Rockefeller University Press, New York (1967).
QUINN, W., *et al.*, 'Conditional behavior in drosophila melanogaster', *Proc. Nat. Acad. Sci., USA* (1974), *71*: 708.

RADFORD, J. and BURTON, A., *Thinking: its nature and development*, Wiley, London and New York (1974).
RAHE, R., *et al.*, 'A longer study of life change and illness patterns', *J. Psychosom. Res.* (1967), *10*: 355–60.

RAKIČ, P., 'Local circuit neurons', *Neurosci. Res. Prog. Bull.* (1975), *13*: 289.
RATNOFF, O. D. and AGLE, D. P., 'Psychogenic purpura: a re-evaluation of the syndrome of autoerythrocyte sensitization', *Medicine* (1968), *47*: 475–500.
RAZRAN, G., 'The observable unconscious and the inferable conscious in current Soviet psychology', *Psychol. Rev.* (1961), *68*: 81–147.
——, *Mind in Evolution: an east-west synthesis of learned behavior and cognition*, Houghton Mifflin, Boston (1971).
REED, G., *The Psychology of Anomalous Experience*, Hutchinson, London (1972).
REEVES, J., *Thinking about Thinking*, Secker & Warburg, London (1965).
REIFF, R. and SCHEERER, M., *Memory and Hypnotic Age Regression*, Internat. Univs. Press, New York (1959).
RESNICK, L. B. (ed.), *The Nature of Intelligence*, Erlsbaum Assocs., Hillsdale, N.J. (1976).
REITAN, R. M., 'Investigation of the validity of Halstead's measures of biological intelligence', *Arch. Neurol.* (1955), *73*: 28.
RENFREW, S. and MELVILLE, I. D., 'The somatic sense of space (choraesthesia) and its threshold', *Brain* (1960), *80*: 93.
REYHER, J., 'Brain mechanisms, intrapsychic processes and behavior: a theory of hypnosis and psychopathology', *Amer. J. clin. Hypn.* (1964), *7*: 167–9.
RICHARDSON, A., *Mental Imagery*, Routledge & Kegan Paul, London (1969).
RICHTER, C. P., 'On the phenomenon of sudden death in animals and men', *Psychosom. Med.* (1957), *19*: 191.
——, *Biological Clocks in Medicine and Psychiatry*, Thomas, Springfield (1965).
RICHTER, D. (ed.), *Aspects of Learning and Memory*, Heinemann Medical Books, London (1966).
ROBERTS, W., 'Normal and abnormal depersonalisation', *J. ment. Sci.* (1960), *106*: 478–93.
ROE, A., *The Psychology of Occupations*, Wiley, Chapman and Hall, New York/London (1956).
ROMAINE, W., 'Subconscious reasoning', *Proc. S.P.R.* (1896), *12*: 11–20.
ROSE, L. (ed. B. Morgan), *Faith Healing*, Gollancz, London (1968).
ROSE, R. M., *et al.*, 'Health change in air traffic controllers', *Psychosom. Med.* (1978), *40*: 143.
ROSE, S., *The Conscious Brain*, Weidenfeld & Nicholson, London (1973).
ROSENBLITH, W. (ed.), *Sensory Communication*, MIT and Wiley, Boston/New York (1961).
ROSENBLUETH, A., *Mind and Brain: a philosophy of science*, MIT Press, Cambridge, Mass. (1970).
ROSS, J., 'Three cognitive dimensions', *Psychol. Reports* (1965), *17*: 291–300.
——, 'Resources of binocular perception', *Sci. Amer.* (1976), *234* (3): 80.
RUBINSTEIN, R. and NEWMAN, R., 'Living out of "future" experiences under hypnosis', *Science* (1954), *119*: 472.
RUSHTON, W. A. H., 'Visual pigments in man', *Sci. Amer.* (1962), *207* (5): 120.
RUSSELL, B., *The Analysis of Mind*, Allen & Unwin, London (1921).
RUSSELL, R. W. (ed.), *Physiological Psychology*, Academic Press, London and New York (1966).
RUSSELL, W. R., *Brain, Memory, Learning: a neurologist's view*, Clarendon Press, Oxford (1959).
——, with A. J. DEWAR, *Explaining the Brain*, Oxford University Press, London (1975).
RYLE, G., *The Concept of Mind*, Hutchinson University Library, London (1949).

SACKS, P., *Awakenings*, Penguin Books, Harmondsworth (1976) (revised edn).
SANDERS, M. D., *et al.*, '"Blindsight": vision in a field defect', *Lancet* (1974), i: 707.
SARBIN, T. R., 'Contributions to role-taking theory; 1. hypnotic behaviour', *Psychol. Rev.* (1950), *5*: 255–70.
SARGANT, W., *The Mind Possessed: a physiology of possession, mysticism and faith-healing*, Heinemann, London (1973).
SCHACHTER, S. and WHEELER, L., 'Epinephrine, chlorpromazine and amusement', *J.abn. & soc. Psychol.* (1962), *65*: 121.
—— and SINGER, J. E., 'Cognitive, social and physiological determinants of emotional state', *Psychol. Rev.* (1962), *69*: 379–99.
SCHAEFER, K. (ed.), *Environmental Effects on Consciousness*, Macmillan, New York (1962).
SCHALLY, A. V., 'Aspects of hypothalamic regulation of the pituitary gland', *Science* (1978), *202*: 18.

SCHER, J. M. (ed.), *Theories of the Mind*, Free Press of Glencoe (Macmillan), New York (1962).
SCHILDER, P., 'Depersonalisation', *Nerv. ment. Dis. Monogs.* (1928), Series 50.
—— and STENGEL, C., 'Asymbolia for pain', *Arch. neurol. Psychiat.* (1931), *25*: 598–600.
——, *The Image and Appearance of the Human Body*, Wiley, New York (1964).
SCHMITT, F. O., *et al.*, 'Electrotonic processing of information by brain cells', *Science* (1976), *193*: 114.
SCHNECHTER, M. D., 'Visual agnosias for animate objects', *J. nerv. ment. Dis.* (1953), *117*: 341.
SCHNEIDER, G., 'Two visual systems', *Science* (1969), *163*: 895–902.
SCHUR, M., 'Comments on the metapsychology of somatisation', *Psychoanal. Study of the Child* (1955), *10* (1): 119/64.
SCHWARTZ, M. and SHAGASS, C., 'Physiological limits for subliminal perception', *Science* (1961), *133*: 1017.
SEASHORE, C. E., 'Measurements of illusions and hallucinations in normal life', *Stud. Yale Psychol. Lab.* (1895), *2*: 167.
SEDMAN, G., 'Depersonalisation in a small group of normal subjects', *Brit. J. Psychiat.* (1966), *112*: 907.
——, 'Theories of depersonalisation: a re-appraisal', ibid. (1970), *117*: 1–14.
SEGAL, S. J. and NATHAN, S., 'The Perky Effect: incorporation of an external stimulus into an imaginary experience, etc.', *Percept. & Motor Skills* (1964), *18*: 385.
——, *Imagery: current cognitive approaches*, Academic Press, London and New York (1971).
SELIGMAN, M., *Helplessness*, Freeman, San Francisco (1975).
SHAGASS, C. and SCHWARTZ, M., 'Evoked cortical potentials and sensation in man', *J. neuropsychiat.* (1961), *2*: 262.
SHAW, R. and BRANSFORD, J., *Perceiving, Acting and Knowing*, Erlbaum Assocs., Hillsdale, N.J. (1977).
SHAKOW, D., 'Segmental Set', *Arch. gen. Psychiat.* (1962), *6*: 1–17.
SHAPIRO, A. K., 'Etiological factors in placebo effect', *J.A.M.A.* (1964), *187*: 712 and 762.
SHEEHAN, P. W. (ed.), *The Function and Nature of Imagery*, Academic Press, New York and London (1972).
SHERWOOD, S. L. (ed.), *The Nature of Psychology: writings by K. Craik*, Cambridge University Press (1966).
SHINKMAN, P. G. and BRUCE, C. J., 'Binocular differences in cortical receptive fields of kittens after rotationally disparate binocular experience', *Science* (1977), *197*: 285.
SHOR, R. E. and ORNE, M. T. (eds.), *The Nature of Hypnosis*, Holt, Rinehart, Winston, New York (1965).
——, 'Hypnosis and the concept of the generalised reality orientation', *Amer. J. Psychother.* (1959), *13*: 582–602.
SHORVON, H. J., 'The depersonalisation syndrome', *Proc. Roy. Soc. Med.* (1946), *39*: 779.
SHOUKSMITH, G., *Intelligence, Creativity and Cognitive Style*, Batsford, London (1970).
SIDIS, B. and GOODHART, S. P., *Multiple Personality*, Greenwood Press, New York (1968).
SIIPOLA, E. and HAYDEN, S., 'Exploring eidetic imagery among the retarded', *Percept. and Motor Skills* (1965), *21*: 275.
SIMMEL, M. (ed.), *The Reach of Mind: essays in honor of Kurt Goldstein*, Springer, New York (1968).
SIMON, H. A., 'How big is a chunk?', *Science* (1974), *183*: 482.
SIMPSON, L. and MCKELLAR, P., 'Types of synaesthesia', *J. ment. Sci.* (1955), *100*: 141–7.
SINGER, J. L. (ed.), *The Control of Aggression and Violence*, Academic Press, New York and London (1971).
SLOCUM, J., *Sailing around the World*, Collier, New York (1958).
SMIRNOFF, A. A., *Problems of the Psychology of Memory*, Plenum Press, New York and London (1973).
SMYTHE, F., *Everest, 1933*, Hodder & Stoughton, London (1934).
SMYTHIES, J. R., *The Neurological Foundations of Psychiatry*, Blackwell, Oxford and Edinburgh (1966).
—— (ed.), *Science and ESP*, Routledge & Kegan Paul, London (1967).
SNIDER, R. S., 'The cerebellum', *Sci. Amer.* (1958), *199* (2): 84.
SOKOLOV, A. N., *Inner Speech and Thought*, Plenum Press, London and New York (1972).

SOMECH, D. E. and WILDING, J. M., 'Perception without awareness in a dichoptic viewing situation, *Brit. J. Psychol.* (1973), *64*: 339.
SPERRY, R. W., 'The great cerebral commissure', *Sci. Amer.* (1964), *210* (1): 42.
——, 'Hemisphere deconnection and unity in conscious awareness', *Amer. Psychologist* (1968), *23*: 723–33.
——, 'A modified concept of consciousness', *Psychol. Rev.* (1969a), *76*: 532–6.
——, 'Towards a theory of mind', *Proc. Nat. Acad. Sci.* (1969b), *63*: 230–1.
STAIB, A. and LOGAN, D. N., 'Hypnotic stimulation of breast growth', *Amer. J. clin. Hypn.* (1977), *19* (4): 201.
STAVAKRY, G. W., *Supersensitivity: an aspect of the relativity of nervous integration*, University of Toronto Press, Toronto (1961).
STERNBACH, R. A., 'Congenital insensitivity to pain: a critique', *Psychol. Bull.* (1963), *60*: 252.
——, *Pain: a psychophysiological analysis*, Academic Press, New York and London (1968).
STEVENSON, I., *Xenoglossy: a review and a report of a case*, Wright, Bristol (1974).
STEWART, H., 'On consciousness, negative hallucinations and the hypnotic state', *Int. J. Psychoanal.* (1966), *47*: 50.
STEWART, I., 'Gauss', *Sci. Amer.* (1978), *237* (1): 122.
STEWART, W. K., 'Hopelessness following illness in middle age', *Psychosom.* (1977), *18* (2): 29.
STOLLER, R. J., *Sex and Gender* Vol. 1, Hogarth Press, London (1968).
——, *Splitting: a case of female masculinity*, Quadrangle Books, New York (1973).
STRATTON, G. M., 'The mnemonic feat of the "Shass Pollack" ', *Psychol. Rev.* (1917), *24*: 244.
——, 'Retroactive hypermnesia and other emotional effects on memory', *Psychol. Rev.* (1919), *26*: 474–86.
STROMEYER, III, C. F. and PSOTKA, J., 'The detailed structure of eidetic images', *Nature* (1970), *225*: 346.
STRONGMAN, K., *The Psychology of Emotion*, Wiley, New York (1973).
SUNDERLAND, S. and KELLY, M., 'The painful sequelae to injuries to peripheral nerves', *Aust. N.Z. J. Surg.* (1948), *18*: 75.
SUZUKI, D. T. (ed. Phillips, B.), *Essentials of Zen Buddhism*, Rider, London (1963).

TALLAND, G. A., *Deranged Memory*, Academic Press, New York and London (1965).
——, *Disorders of Memory and Learning*, Penguin Books, Harmondsworth, (1968).
—— and WAUGH, N. C. (eds.), *The Pathology of Memory*, Academic Press, New York and London (1969).
TARG, R. and PUTHOFF, H., 'Information transmission under conditions of sensory shielding', *Nature* (1974), *210*: 602–7.
TART, C. T. (ed.), *Altered States of Consciousness: a book of readings*, Wiley, New York (1969).
——, *States of Consciousness*, Dutton, New York (1975).
TASINI, M. F. and HACKETT, T. P., 'Hypnosis in the treatment of warts in immunodeficient children', *Amer. J. clin. Hypn.* (1977), *19*: (3): 152.
TAYLOR, C., *The Explanation of Purposive Behaviour*, Cambridge University Press (1970).
TAYLOR, G. R., *Rethink: a paraprimitive solution*, Secker & Warburg, London (1972).
TAYLOR, J. G., *The Behavioral Basis of Perception*, Yale University Press, New Haven (1962).
TAYLOR, J., 'The shadow of the mind', *New Sci.* (1971), *51*: 735–7.
—— and MARTIN, M. F., 'Multiple personality', *J. abn. & soc. Psychol.* (1944), *39*: 281–300.
THIGPEN, C. H. and CLECKLEY, H. M., *The Three Faces of Eve*, Secker & Warburg, London (1957).
THOMAS, E. L., 'Movements of the Eye', *Sci. Amer.* (1964), *219* (2): 88.
THOMPSON, R. K. R. and HERMAN, L. M., 'Memory for lists of sounds by the bottle-nosed dolphin', *Science* (1977), *195*: 501–3.
THOMSON, R., *The Pelican History of Psychology*, Penguin, Harmondsworth (1968).
THRUSH, D. C., 'Congenital insensitivity to pain', *Brain* (1973), *96*: 369 and 591.
THURSTON, H., *The Physical Phenomena of Mysticism*, Burns Oates, London (1952).
TOFFLER, A., *Future Shock*, Random House, New York (1970).
TOMKINS, S. S. (ed.), *Affect, Imagery, Consciousness Vols 1, 2 & 3*, Springer, New York (1962, 1963).

TREVARTHEN, C. B. and SPERRY, R. W., 'Perceptual unity of the ambient visual field in human commissurotomy patients', *Brain* (1973), *96*: 547–70.
TURNBULL, C. M., *The Forest People*, Jonathan Cape, London (1974).

UNGAR, G. and IRWIN, L. N., 'Transfer of acquired information by brain extracts', *Nature* (1967), *214*: 453.
UNGAR, G. (ed.), *Molecular Mechanisms in Memory and Learning*, Plenum Press, New York (1970).
——, *et al.*, 'Isolation, identification and synthesis of a specific-behaviour-inducing brain peptide', *Nature* (1972), *238*: 198–202.

VINACKE, W. E., *The Psychology of Thinking*, McGraw-Hill, New York (1952, 1972 and 1974).
VISCOTT, D. S., 'Chlordiazepoxide and hallucinations: report of cases', *Arch. Gen. Psychia.* (1968), *19*: 370–6.
VON BÉKÉSY, G., *Sensory Inhibition*, Princeton University Press, Princeton, New Jersey (1967).
VON BONIN, G., *Essay on the Cerebral Cortex*, Thomas, Springfield, Mass. (1950).
VON SENDEN, M., *Space and Sight: the perception of space and shape in congenitally blind patients before and after operation*, Methuen, London (1960).
VON UEXKULL, S., *Umwelt und Innenwelt der Tiere*, Springer, Berlin (1921).
VOSS, J. F. (ed.), *Approaches to Thought*, Merrill, Columbus, Ohio (1969).

WACHTEL, P. L., 'Conceptions of broad and narrow attention', *Psychol. Bull.* (1967), *68*: 413.
WAHL, C. W. (ed.), *New Dimensions in Psychosomatic Medicine*, J. & A. Churchill, London (1964).
WALLACE, R. K. and BENSON, H., 'The physiology of meditation', *Sci. Amer.* (1972), *226* (2): 84–90.
WALLACH, H., 'The perception of neutral colors', *Sci. Amer.* (1963), *208* (1): 107.
WAPNER, S. and WERNER, H. (eds.), *The Body Percept*, Random House, New York (1965).
WALTER, W. GREY, *The Living Brain*, Duckworth, London (1953).
WARBURTON, D. M. *Brain, Behaviour and Drugs*, Wiley, New York and London (1975).
WAVELL, S., *et al.*, *Trances*, Allen & Unwin, London (1966).
WEINBERGER, L. M. and GRANT, F. C., 'Visual hallucinations and their neuro-optical correlates', *Arch. Ophthalmol.* (1940), *23*: 116.
WEISMAN, A. D. and HACKETT, T. P., 'Predilection to death', *Psychosom. Med.* (1961), *23*: 232–55.
WEITZENHOFFER, A. M., *Hypnotism: an objective study in suggestibility*, Science Edns. Wiley, New York (1953).
WEIZENBAUM, J., *Computer Power & Human Reason*, W. H. Freeman, San Francisco (1977).
WERNER, H., 'Microgenesis and aphasia', *J. abn. & soc. Psychol.* (1956), *52*: 347–53.
—— and WAPNER, G., 'Sensory-tonic field theory of perception', *J. person.* (1949), *18*: 88–107.
WESLEY, JOHN, *Journal*, Epworth (1909).
WEST, L. J. (ed.), *Hallucinations*, Grune & Stratton, New York (1962).
WHEATLEY, J. M. O. and EDGE, H. L. (eds.), *Philosophical Dimensions of Parapsychology*, Thomas, Springfield, Ill. (1976).
WHITE, J. (ed.), *Psychic Exploration*, Putnam's Sons, New York (1974).
WHITE, R. H. (ed.), *Surveys in Parapsychology: a review of the literature*, Scarecrow Press, Metuchen, N.J. (1976).
WHITE, R. W., 'Preface to a theory of hypnotism', *J. abn. & soc. Psychol.* (1941), *36*: 477.
WHITLOCK, F. A., *Psychophysiological Aspects of Skin Diseases*, W. B. Saunders, Philadelphia (1976).
WHITTY, C. W. M. and LEWIN, W., 'Vivid day-dreaming after cingulectomy', *Brain* (1957), *80*: 72–6.
WHYTE, L. L., 'A hypothesis regarding the brain modifications underlying memory', *Brain* (1954), *77*: 158–65.
——, *The Unconscious before Freud*, Basic Books, New York (1960).
WIGAN, A. L. *The Duality of the Mind*, Longman, London (1844).
WILLARD, R. D., 'Breast enlargement through visual imagery and hypnosis', *Amer. J. clin. Hypn.* (1977), *19* (4): 195.

WILLIAMS, G. W., 'Highway hypnosis: an hypothesis', *Int. J. clin. & exptl. Hypn.* (1963), *11*: 143–51.
WILSON, J. and TURNER, D., 'Awareness during caesarean section under general anaesthesia', *Brit. Med. J.* (1965), i. 281–3.
WINTERBOTTOM, E. H., 'Insufficient anaesthesia', *Brit. Med. J.* (1950), *i*: 247.
WITKIN, H. A., *et al.*, *Personality through Perception*, Harper, New York (1954).
——, *Psychological Differentiation: studies of development*, Wiley, New York (1962).
WITTREICH, W. J., 'Visual perception and personality', *Sci. Amer.* (1959), *200* (4): 56.
WOLMAN, B. B. (ed.), *Handbook of Parapsychology*, van Nostrand, Reinhold, New York (1977).
WOOD JONES, F. W. and PORTEUS, S. D., *The Matrix of the Mind*, Arnold, London (1929).
WOOLDRIDGE, D. E., *The Machinery of the Brain*, McGraw Hill, New York (1963).
WOOLLEY, D. W. and SHAW, E. W., 'Evidence for the participation of serotonin in mental processes', *Ann. N.Y. Acad. Sci.* (1957), *66* (3): 649–65.
——, *Biochemical Bases of Psychoses*, Wiley, New York (1962).
WYBURN, G. McC., *et al.*, *Human Senses and Perception*, Oliver & Boyd, London (1964).
WOLF, S. M., 'Difficulties in right-left discrimination in a normal population', *Arch. Neurology* (1973), *29*: 128.

YOUNG, R. M., *Mind, Brain and Adaptation in the Nineteenth Century, etc.*, Clarendon Press, Oxford (1970).
YOUNG, W. C., *et al.*, 'Hormones and sexual behaviour', *Science* (1964), *143*: 212.

ZAIDEL, D. and SPERRY, R. W., 'Memory impairment after commissurotomy in man', *Brain* (1974), *97*: 263.
ZAMENHOF, S., 'DNA (cell number) and protein in neonatal brain: alteration by maternal dietary protein restriction', *Science* (1968), *160*: 322.
——, *et al.*, 'Prenatal cerebral development: effect of restricted diet, reversal by growth hormone', *Science* (1971), *174*: 954.
ZEKI, S. M., 'Colour coding in rhesus monkey prestriate cortex for cells sensitive only to particular colours and shapes', *Brain Res.* (1973), *53*: 422–7.
ZUBIN, J. and FREYHAN, F. A., *Disorders of Mood*, Johns Hopkins Press, Baltimore (1972).

Index